Critical Essays on
JAMES JOYCE'S
A Portrait of the Artist as a Young Man

CRITICAL ESSAYS
ON
BRITISH LITERATURE

Zack Bowen, General Editor
University of Miami

Critical Essays on
JAMES JOYCE'S
A Portrait of the Artist as a Young Man

edited by

PHILIP BRADY AND JAMES F. CARENS

G. K. Hall & Co.
An Imprint of Simon & Schuster Macmillan
New York

Prentice Hall International
London • Mexico City • New Delhi • Singapore • Sydney • Toronto

G. K. Hall & Co.
An Imprint of Simon & Schuster Macmillan
1633 Broadway
New York, NY 10019

Library of Congress Cataloging-in-Publication Data

Critical essays on James Joyce's A portrait of the artist as a young
    man / edited by Philip Brady and James F. Carens.
        p.   cm. — (Critical essays on British literature)
    Includes bibliographical references and index.
    ISBN 0-7838-0035-5 (alk. paper)
    1. Joyce, James, 1882–1941. Portrait of the artist as a young
man. 2. Dublin (Ireland)—In literature. 3. Young men in
literature. I. Brady, Philip, 1955–   . II. Carens, James F.
(James Francis), 1927–   . III. Series.
PR6019.09P64413 1998
823'.912—dc21   98-18912
                                                                      CIP

This paper meets the requirements of ANSI/NISO Z3948–1992 (Permanence of Paper).

10 9 8 7 6 5 4 3 2 1

Printed in the United States of America

Contents

General Editor's Note

♦

The Critical Essays on British Literature series provides a variety of approaches to both classical and contemporary writers of Britain and Ireland. The formats of the volumes in the series vary with the thematic designs of individual editors and with the amount and nature of existing reviews and criticism, augmented, where appropriate, by original essays by recognized authorities. It is hoped that each volume will be unique in developing a new overall perspective on its particular subject.

In their introduction Brady and Carens first trace the composition and publication of James Joyce's *A Portrait of the Artist as a Young Man* from its inception as a short story, through its iteration as a long manuscript, *Stephen Hero,* to its final form in 1916 as a full book. They then offer a perceptive analysis of Joyce's place in modern letters and conclude by detailing their overall selection of essays.

The selections themselves cover the last 30 years of criticism from three perspectives. The first, "Critical Cruxes," deals with interpretation of such important issues and events in the book as the epiphany concept, the diary entries, the villanelle, and the aesthetic theory. The second section contains source studies and their relation to structure and design, while the third demonstrates a variety of theoretical approaches to the book.

ZACK BOWEN
University of Miami

Publisher's Note

◆

Producing a volume that contains both newly commissioned and reprinted material presents the publisher with the challenge of balancing the desire to achieve stylistic consistency with the need to preserve the integrity of works first published elsewhere. In the Critical Essays series, essays commissioned especially for a particular volume are edited to be consistent with G. K. Hall's house style; reprinted essays appear in the style in which they were first published, with only typographical errors corrected. Consequently, shifts in style from one essay to another are the result of our efforts to be faithful to each text as it was originally published.

Introduction

PHILIP BRADY AND JAMES F. CARENS

I

James Joyce's first manuscript to be accepted for publication appeared in print early in the first year of the twentieth century. That publication was a review of Henrik Ibsen's *When We Dead Awaken* and it appeared in the *Fortnightly Review,* a London periodical. Joyce was then 18 years old and in the second year of study at University College in Dublin.[1] According to Stanislaus Joyce, almost a year before the publication of his brother's review of the Ibsen play, James had remarked to his parents of a play they had attended together, "The subject of the play is genius breaking out in the home and against the home. . . . It's going to happen in your own house."[2] Such a declaration might be regarded as either the ironic jest or the arrogant boast of a precocious youth. Nevertheless, James Joyce's *Fortnightly* article—a wonderment to his fellow students—and another Ibsenist paper he had delivered before the college Literary and Historical Society some weeks earlier—a direct assault on the conventional literary assumptions of his fellows and masters (Ellmann, 70–74)—were surely evidence of something more intense than youthful braggadocio and more compelling than precocity. This Irish youth already knew that there was genius in him, and he was determined that he would express it.

In the paper "Drama and Life," in the *Fortnightly* essay on *When We Dead Awaken,* and in the 1901 letter composed in the Dano-Norwegian he taught himself in order to write the aging dramatist in celebration of his 73rd birthday, Joyce, although he denied that he was a hero-worshiper, expressed his admiration for a culture hero who defined for him the essential role of the modern European artist. In Ibsen, Joyce admired not merely the masterly dramaturgy, nor even just the verisimilitude of the plays, but the energy with which Ibsen seized upon the issues of his time, the courage that enabled him to stand alone against hypocrisy and convention. The paper "Drama and Life" pays tribute to Ibsen's understanding that "even the most commonplace, the deadest among the living, may play a part in the great drama."[3] Above all, as he indicated when he wrote him in 1901, Joyce admired Ibsen's "impersonal power" and "wilful resolution to wrest the secret from life."[4] (Joyce's language reveals how important the symbolic element in Ibsen was to him.)

1

During the summer of 1900, Joyce devoted himself to his first substantial creative effort, the lost or destroyed drama *A Brilliant Career,* a work apparently influenced by Ibsen's *An Enemy of the People* (Ellmann, 78–80). A decade and a half later, Joyce would publish *Exiles,* a play in the tradition of Ibsen but intensely original in the way it dramatizes Joyce's own psychic torments. Yet it cannot be said that *Exiles* is comparable in interest or inventiveness to Joyce's major works. The stage was not really Joyce's medium; it was in the rich detail, evocative imagery, and stylistic boldness of his narratives that he found the way to explore the social and psychological realities of the commonplace and to depict the world as he knew it: ironically, comically, and unencumbered by outmoded notions of heroic ideality.

Over the months when Joyce was reading and celebrating Ibsen, he was also reading widely among the recent works of other Scandinavian writers and of Russian, French, German, and Italian authors (Ellmann, 75–77 and passim). In these same months Dublin itself was pulsing with new literary energies. What came to be known as the Irish Literary Renaissance was budding and about to burst into flower. With the support of Lady Gregory, W. B. Yeats was bent upon creating an Irish theatre entirely unlike the commercial theatre of London. George Moore, who after years in France had introduced French Symbolism and the Naturalism of Zola to England, had returned to Ireland and remained in Dublin for a decade. And J. M. Synge, who returned from Paris at the urging of Yeats, discovered a rich language and the material of his plays among the folk of western Ireland and the Aran Isles. (It has even been suggested that Joyce originally intended *A Brilliant Career* for production by the Irish Literary Theatre, for which it would not have been suited.) In October of 1901 Joyce published, at his own expense, "The Day of the Rabblement," having been denied publication in a new college magazine (*CW,* 68). The essay was a fierce attack on the direction the theatre was taking, as well as on Yeats and Moore. Not a youth to suffer easily what he disdained, this undergraduate utterly rejected the influence of more established artists in Dublin. Although Joyce granted that Yeats's *The Wind among the Reeds* (1899) was a collection of poems "of the highest order," he more grudgingly described "some" of Moore's best novel, *Esther Waters,* as "fine original work." Yeats he denounced for surrendering the original impulse of the Irish Literary Theatre to the "popular will" of the Irish rabble. Moore he assailed as a dated writer "struggling in the backwash of the tide which has advanced from Flaubert through Jakobsen to D'Annunzio," the Italian writer Joyce then most esteemed. At the heart of Joyce's argument was his insistence that the artist must "isolate himself from the crowd." The true artist must free "himself from the mean influences about him" (*CW,* 69–72).

From the commitment Joyce made in this essay of 1901 to the necessary apartness of the artist was but a short distance to the decision he made in 1904 to exile himself and his companion, Nora Barnacle, from Dublin and Ireland. The journeys he made and the residences he established with Nora in

Pola, and thereafter in Trieste and following that in Rome and then again in Trieste were extremely stressful. But during the years of penury and stress, mostly as a teacher of English, Joyce produced among other things "The Dead," his first masterpiece, and *A Portrait of the Artist as a Young Man,* the supreme novel in our language of the education and growth of a potential artist. Though usually identified as in the tradition of the *Bildungsroman,* Joyce's *Portrait* belongs to a special class within that genre: it is an account of the maturation of a creative spirit, a *Künstlerroman.*

II

Critical attention has often been called to Joyce's careful placing and dating of *A Portrait of the Artist as a Young Man* on the very last page by "Dublin 1904/Trieste 1914." Thus Joyce drew attention to his fulfillment of a pledge made in his youth to finish a novel within 10 years (Ellmann, 354), to his rejection of Ireland's insularity, and to the exile that had enabled him to become a mature artist. But there are yet more important considerations than these in Joyce's choice of 1904 as the initiating date of *Portrait.* In his biography of Joyce (still the authoritative work, however much one might question minor details) Richard Ellmann accepts the account of Stanislaus Joyce that on January 7, 1904, his brother James, having learned that *Dana,* a new Dublin journal, was to appear, in a single day produced a work to which he gave the title "A Portrait of the Artist" and submitted it to *Dana.* Ellmann describes this first "Portrait" as "an autobiographical story" and also as an "essay or story" and as an "essay narrative" (Ellmann, 144–47). Actually, neither the term "story" nor "essay" is adequate to define the quality of the "Portrait" of 1904, for its young author, indifferent to the purity of literary genres, mixes these two with a lacing of the prose poem. (In tone, Joyce shifts from apostrophic to ironic, from self-encomiastic to self-deflating, from misanthropic to humanistic.) The 1904 "Portrait" was, Ellmann indicates, following Stanislaus, the basis for *Stephen Hero,* a long but unfinished autobiographical work, and also for *A Portrait of the Artist as a Young Man.* In a more recent biographical work on Joyce's early years, Peter Costello follows the same line as Ellmann, though classifying "Portrait" as a "long essay." Costello describes how Joyce, following the rejection of his essay, "sat down at the kitchen table," and "embarked on . . . the scheme of a long satirical novel" (and "lying autobiography," according to Stanislaus): that is, *Stephen Hero.*[5] Not surprisingly, given these later descriptions of the 1904 "Portrait," *Dana's* John Eglinton (W. K. Magee), who later in the year did publish one of Joyce's delicate lyrics, explained to Joyce that he could not "print what I can't understand" (Ellmann, 147).

It was not until Hans Walter Gabler's critically edited text of *Portrait* (1993) that a crucial piece of evidence was introduced to question the authority of Stanislaus Joyce and the notion that the 1904 "Portrait" was linked to *Stephen Hero*. Observing that "We have all persistently overlooked" a letter of September 1916 from May, sister of James and Stanislaus, in which she describes how she had listened as Joyce read sections from his "autobiographical novel" to their mother some months before her death, Gabler argued the plausible view that Joyce had begun *Stephen Hero* nearly a year before he had hitherto been assumed to have done so and that the brief first "Portrait" represents Joyce's attempt to liberate himself from the style of *Stephen Hero* and to approach a new kind of treatment.[6]

Stylistically, the 1904 "Portrait" is dense, hyperbole-laden, and elusive. In method, it resembles not at all the discursive, rather conventional, almost plodding narrative mode of the surviving portion of *Stephen Hero*. Often bombastic, strained, and "poetical," this "Portrait" is the work of a Joyce who has not yet found the brilliant techniques he would master for rendering fictional point of view and who has very little of the assured control of a dense metaphoric and mythic structure that would be his. And yet there is excitement in the reading of the first "Portrait" because of the uncertainties it provokes as we read it; and there are powerful moments, particularly when we recognize language we know to have been carried over to *Portrait*.

Throughout a reading of the rather extraordinary confession, a Joyce is revealed to us who gropes toward the central concerns we find in the later account of a youth growing into an artist. Opening with the suggestion that autobiography must not be produced as an "iron memorial" but must render life as "a fluid succession of presents," this brief, intense work implies a portrait to be "the curve of an emotion": almost a prophecy of the rendering of consciousness Joyce would later achieve. The heroic figure of the young artist limned in 1904 disdains male competition and rivalry, but he refuses to submit to the conventional male compromise with mediocrity and thus flashes his antlers staglike in defiance. The heroic artist, hitherto devout and reverential, is described as he rebels against the falsehoods and repressions of religion; his "leaving" the Church and flirting with the esoteric—a Dublin enthusiasm not developed in *Portrait* but used to comic effect in *Ulysses*—are treated, the first with sympathy, the second with irony. Feminists may despise a long, entirely sexist passage. In this there are wading girls on the strand, a succubus figure who tempts the sleeping hero, another murky figure who drives him to masturbation, groups of whores, a particular whore, a "witch" who releases our hero from the "agony of the self-devourer" but who is also "an envoy from the courts of life" (a phrase more wonderful in *Portrait*). This "witch" is "sacramental"; her kiss, an ecstasy. In every sense of the word, this passage is climactic. But the natural imagery of a litany to the sacramental whore suggests that the Virgin has not yet been discarded. In an apocalyptic conclusion State and Church, "Their Intensities and their Bullockships," are scorned and the rebirth of man, competition and aristocracies defeated, is envisioned.[7] By the time he finished *Portrait,* Joyce knew better than to close on such a universal fantasy. By the time he wrote *Ulysses,* he knew how to convert such fantasy to joyous comedy, painful irony, and pathetic hope.

III

John Eglinton and others involved in *Dana* were of course perfectly able to comprehend the sexual implications of "A Portrait of the Artist"; that element alone would have been enough to alarm them to the point of rejection. Indeed, the rejections of publishers and eventually even the hostility of printers were to vex Joyce for most of a decade. Though W. B. Yeats could not but resent Joyce's unfriendly words about the literary movement and his purported surrender to the rabble, he recognized Joyce's talent and intervened at certain moments to support the younger man. In London Yeats introduced Joyce to his friend Arthur Symons; it was the latter who subsequently made the connection resulting in the publication of Joyce's poems, *Chamber Music,* in 1907 (Ellmann, 111, 232). But the excruciating publication histories of *Dubliners* and *A Portrait of the Artist as a Young Man* are distressing to follow. When the collection of Dublin stories, accepted early in 1906 by the English firm of Grant Richards, upset his printers, Richards demanded numerous censorious revisions and finally refused to honor the contract. A second negotiation was even more devastating for Joyce. Rejected by numerous publishers, Joyce finally responded to a request from Joseph Hone that he submit *Dubliners* to Maunsel and Company of Dublin, in which Hone had investments. Unfortunately, Joyce had to deal with George Roberts, the managing editor of the firm and a cad as shabby in his business practices as he was narrow in his views of life and letters. After months of delay and demands for revisions and cuts, Roberts finally offered Joyce the printed sheets, which Joyce intended to publish himself, only to be told that the printer had destroyed the very printed sheets Roberts had offered (Ellmann, 219–335 passim).

In December 1913, however, Joyce received a letter from Ezra Pound, hitherto unknown to him. This American expatriate had already established himself in the London literary world, determined to reform the language of contemporary poetry and prose. Pound was closely enough associated with Yeats to assist as the latter "remade" his poetry, and it was at the suggestion of Yeats that Pound contacted Joyce. A second letter from Pound soon followed the first, for Yeats had located Joyce's "I hear an army," and Pound, delighted, requested permission to include it in his forthcoming anthology, *Des Imagistes.* When Joyce responded to his encouragement, sending him the opening chapter of *Portrait* and the complete *Dubliners,* Pound arranged for the serial publication of *Portrait* in the avant-garde magazine *The Egoist* in 1914–1915. Given this evidence of Joyce's recognized talent, Grant Richards summoned enough courage to publish *Dubliners* in 1914. Both braver and shrewder, B. W. Huebsch published the American edition of *Dubliners* and the first edition of *Portrait* as a book in 1916; the Egoist Press edition followed the next year (Ellmann, 349–406 passim).

The reader's report to Duckworth, one of the firms that considered but rejected *Portrait,* anticipated some of the attitudes of the reviews that greeted Joyce's novel on its publication. Duckworth's reader (probably, though not certainly, Edward Garnett throughout the complete report) complained that *Portrait* seemed " 'a little sordid' " and "too 'unconventional' "; he also complained that "ugly things, ugly words are too prominent." The squeamishness of this line of thought has to be understood in terms of the lingering repressiveness and evasiveness of late Victorian culture weighing upon the new century but is nevertheless startling in a reader who did recognize the talent he confronted. Joyce, he argued, should be encouraged to rewrite the novel, now "too discursive, formless, unrestrained." Stephen's diary, at the conclusion of *Portrait,* particularly distressed this reader, for whom it was "a complete falling to bits . . . the thoughts all in pieces."[8] Another possibility, of course, is that the publisher's reader simply failed to recognize the craft by which Joyce's compression and selectiveness had produced a new kind of novel for a new century.

When *A Portrait of the Artist as a Young Man* was published, scarcely any of the reviewers questioned the author's talent. But the review for the *Irish Booklover* insisted that no "clean-minded person" should allow the book within reach of any family member. (He did not explain how these pure beings could either understand or be depraved by what they read.) Even H. G. Wells, who had stronger praise than most for the realism of the book and the "reality" of Stephen, and who also felt that the technical innovations worked, prissily complained of words both "coarse and unfamiliar." Almost alone among the English reviewers, the reviewer for the *Times Literary Supplement* was clever enough to defend the language of *Portrait* as an aspect of the realism he found in Joyce. And in the United States, John Quinn, always a supporter of Irish art and letters, sprang to Joyce's defense. In *Vanity Fair,* he contrasted the "soft, false, and dangerous" *Ann Veronica* by H. G. Wells to Joyce's "bracing and hard and clean" novel.

All these reviewers, Irish, English, and American, saw Joyce as working in the tradition of literary realism, or naturalism. Even Ezra Pound, when he wrote his note for *The Egoist* on the occasion of the Egoist Press edition, failed to explore other aspects of the novel. Claiming that this book "written by an Irishman in Trieste and first published in New York City" would "remain a permanent part of English literature," he praised the author as writing "the nearest thing to Flaubertian prose that we now have in English," a mere hint at the precision and suggestiveness of Joyce's language. But Pound, poet and translator, ignored such matters as design, structure, and patterns of imagery.[9]

So persistent was the view of Joyce's *Portrait* as starkly realistic or naturalistic that when Harry Levin published the first critical introduction to Joyce's oeuvre—something of a classic in the history of Joyce scholarship—both in the first edition (1941) and its revision 20 years later he defined *Portrait* as "fitting squarely into the naturalist tradition" by contrast to *Finnegans Wake,* a "symbolist experiment." Yet Levin, citing Joyce's own aesthetic, classifies *Portrait* as lyric and grants that the "germs of symbolism" are in the book. Nothing in his analysis implies Joyce's "naturalism" to be of a kind influenced by biological or sociological theory; rather he seems to imply a naturalism more frankly carnal and physical in its depiction of experience and fearless in depicting aspects of human experience that a facile realism would avoid.[10] Joyce himself, as early as the brief 1904 "Portrait of the Artist," expressed disdain for the master of naturalism, Emile Zola, describing him as "a dull French novelist." By 1950, moreover, it was possible for William York Tindall, who produced a series of books on Joyce, to observe even of the *Dubliner* stories, "These stories of trivial events are not naturalistic. The naturalistic details that appear in them are in the service of symbolism."[11] By the middle of the decade, the Joycean oeuvre was widely seen as shaped by the convergence of symbolism and realism/naturalism, although important voices protested the "symbol hunting." Nevertheless, Joyce himself published his first three stories, later to find their places among *Dubliners,* under the pseudonym Stephen Daedalus and then attached the flagrantly non-Irish patronymic Dedalus to the hero of *A Portrait of the Artist as a Young Man,* more than drawing his reader's attention to symbol and myth.

IV

In the preface to his 1992 biographical study of Joyce's early years, Peter Costello makes the following observation: "Born in 1882 and dead for over half a century, James Joyce has long ceased to be modern" (4). The assertion emerges from Costello's perspective on his subject, but our concern here is with the term *modern,* which like a related one, *modernism,* has meant many different things. *Modern history,* for instance, may signify European history from the Middle Ages to the present; *modern literature* may imply, among other things, the literature in English from the last decade of the nineteenth century to the present, or only English literature of the twentieth century. *Modernism* has been used to describe certain religious tendencies of the late nineteenth century and early twentieth century, but it also refers to a phase of imaginative experiment and exploration among writers in English, particularly in the second and third decade of the twentieth century. It has proven useful to distinguish *contemporary* literature—perhaps post–World War II to the present, perhaps only the past two or three decades—from *early modern literature.*

Startling in this context is the argument of Weldon Thornton that *Portrait* is "antimodernist." Thornton defines the intellectual tradition rejected by Joyce in terms of dualistic and rationalistic assumptions descending from the seventeenth and eighteenth centuries. A thoughtful book, Thornton's has much to tell us about the history of ideas and Joyce's rejection of empiricism, but it leaves us with a struggle over literary terminology.[12] There are, moreover, the terms *postmodern* and *postmodernist,* used to describe writers and writing that differ from the "modernists" of the earlier decades of the century. (Some would apply the terms to the Joyce of *Finnegans Wake* and even to the Joyce of *Ulysses.*) Insufficiently prescient to determine what literary tags may seem appropriate around the middle of the twenty-first century for another past and another present or how James Joyce will be regarded then, it seems entirely appropriate to define him in literary terminology as a modern and modernist, even if he was an early modern who was one of the "high modernists," and, in philosophical terms, "antimodernist." These terms and tags we use to place our writers are neither rational nor sufficient.

After decades of Joyce studies, the body of biographical, bibliographical, textual, and critical writing that has accumulated is vast. As Bernard Benstock observed in an earlier volume on Joyce in this series, the "explosion in Joyce studies was a phenomenon of the 1960s." Certainly the founding of the *James Joyce Quarterly* in 1963, the establishment of a Joyce Foundation with an international perspective, and the development of International Joyce Symposia all encouraged the phenomenon.[13] But these developments themselves were consequences of the sense, particularly prevalent in the American academic world, that Joyce was of central importance in the literature of the age. Nor does there seem to be any sign of a diminution of interest in Joyce such as certain of his contemporaries suffered. In the case of *Portrait,* a computer search early in the preparation of this volume provided the information that between 1986 and 1996 240 items, mostly journal articles, chapters in books, and essays in collections, were published—a substantial rise over the preceding decade, probably registering the impact of another "explosion" in Joyce studies due to theoretical approaches. While computer searches are not definitive, given some slight distortions in the process of classification, they surely provide substantial evidence of the level of interest in a particular period, as this one did.

In selecting the critical essays for this volume, the editors made certain fundamental choices. Given the numerous available collections of critical essays on *Portrait* or with essays on *Portrait,* both those of a retrospective and historical nature and those reflecting recent critical approaches, it seemed appropriate to select essays mostly dating from the 1960s to the present and ones not immediately available in other collections. We have, moreover, sought challenging criticism, whether expressing a traditional critical method or committed to one of the more theoretical approaches. We did not seek only articles confirming our own assumptions and commitments. (Indeed, there are instances where one or both of us may disagree with particular lines of argument.) We sought what was informed and informative, stimulating and exacting. We also sought criticism unburdened by jargon and cliché, rejecting elaborate conceptual structures concealing an inner emptiness. In some very few instances, we have reprinted sections from published books and collections, because what these had to offer seemed of particular import; and in certain instances we were especially grateful for the willingness of authors to rework published texts, editing their work so as to make it available to a new audience.

The first group of essays in this collection deals with major issues that have been raised—and sometimes fiercely argued—throughout the decades in which *Portrait* has been read and analyzed. The second group of essays is as paradoxical as Joyce would appreciate, for not only is it concentrated on what unifies his design but it probes the complexity brought to the work by allusion, figurative language, symbol, and myth. The third and final group of essays is, as the heading implies, most focused on theoretical approaches. In this group we have not sought essays representing every major theoretical stand but rather essays in which the theoretical commitment of the author may lead to a variety of new responses on the part of the reader.

V

Over the course of Joyce studies, there have been sharp differences about particular aspects of and elements in *A Portrait of the Artist as a Young Man*. Among these are the concept of the epiphany and its relation to the aesthetic theory of Stephen Dedalus and that of the mature James Joyce, the quality of the poem Stephen composes in the last chapter of the novel, and the degree to which Stephen's diary at the novel's end succeeds in bringing closure. The first group of essays in this collection, entitled "Critical Cruxes," deals with these and related matters.

Theodore Spencer was not entirely fortunate to be the first to struggle with the surviving fragment of *Stephen Hero* and its confusing history. Although Spencer gave a succinct account of the differences between *Stephen Hero* and *Portrait* and took the first steps in attempting to date the fragment, much of what he reported about the composition of the fragment had to be corrected later. The most influential aspect of Spencer's prefatory remarks was his analysis of the development of Stephen's aesthetic theory. In particular what Spencer asserted about the term *epiphany* and its relation to Joyce's major works was to have a lasting and contentious influence. Citing Stephen's definition of epiphany, Spencer then applied the term to *Dubliners*—"a series of epiphanies"—and also to *Portrait, Ulysses,* and *Finnegans Wake.*

By 1964 Robert Scholes had concluded that a general and careless use of the term *epiphany* had developed. Even today one cannot help but enjoy the gusto with which Scholes took on the Joyce establishment, specifically Hugh Kenner and others who argued that the absence of any allusion to epiphany in *Portrait* revealed Joyce's disdain for the character of Stephen. Robert Scholes's essay also advanced a tough-minded demonstration of how Joyce reveals the limits of the aesthetic theory and then explored the various uses to which Joyce put his early collection of epiphanies. Several years later, in *Epiphany in the Modern Novel* and elsewhere, Morris Beja defended, against the Scholes argument, his own position that the Joycean epiphany is a uniquely modernist fictional technique, distinct from intense moments in earlier fiction. Throughout this collection the term *epiphany* is frequently used to refer not only to Joyce's early vignettes but also to intense climactic and revelatory moments in the works of other writers. Still, Scholes's argument that the term should be used exclusively for Joyce's early brief efforts continues to provoke and challenge. At present the term used so precisely by the "heroic" Stephen for aesthetic analysis, now altogether detached from a Joycean or literary context, may appear in a modish but subliterary context to imply anything or nothing.

In Chapter V of *Portrait* Stephen Dedalus performs two creative acts: he develops an aesthetic theory—one not burdened with the notion of epiphany—and he composes a poem, a villanelle. The theory and the poem have been subjects of debate among Joyce's interpreters, as Cordell Yee's essay on the influence of Aquinas and Robert Adams Day's essay on the "Villanelle of the Temptress" manifest. Were Yee's tone not so ironical, one might describe this essay of his as polemical! It is Yee's aim to refute the notion that the aesthetic of Stephen dilutes Aquinas with late Romantic notions and to confront those he regards as detractors of Stephen's creativity. He insists that the form and design of Stephen's aesthetic is itself an artistic creation and the triumph of a hero. The late Robert Adams Day's treatment of the "Villanelle Perplex" would have its place in such a collection as this if for no other reason than that, with civility and wit, it embodies a phase of modern American literary study. Day toys with our "post-deconstructionist" age and merges the old New Criticism and certain of its enemies—biography and the intentional fallacy. He urbanely refutes those who have praised the art of Stephen's villanelle but then paradoxically praises the art of Joyce, who saw that his own early and very minor poem fit perfectly Stephen's age, culture, and talent.

Michael Levenson's essay on Stephen's diary opens with the observation that "remarkably little attention has been paid to the ending" of Joyce's *Portrait,* which is not to say that hostile judgments have not been delivered against the novel's conclusion. Indeed, from the inept report by Duckworth's reader to Hugh Kenner's complaint that the novel closes on "a suspended chord" and Wayne Booth's protest against the openness of the ending, little progress was made in critical understanding of the function of the diary. (Levenson responds to both of these critics, as does Robert Day in his essay on Stephen's villanelle.) In an authoritative argument, Levenson defines the diary as belonging to a unique narrative genre that demands seriality and resists closure, thus leading to paradox, ambiguity, and irony. His critical approach is one that explores the diary and all that precedes it, recognizing that words, images, and details of the diary are intricately related to phrases, details, and situations found throughout the earlier parts of the novel. This definitive explication dispels any notion that the final passage of *Portrait* is random or that the novel's ambiguities are either evasive or inconclusive.

Last among the first group of essays is Hans Walter Gabler's recent merging of two important essays in the history of Joyce textual scholarship. In combining the substance of his "The Christmas Dinner Scene, Parnell's Death, and the Genesis of *A Portrait of the Artist as a Young Man*" (1975) with "The Seven Lost Years of *A Portrait of the Artist as a Young Man*" (1976) in "The Genesis of *A Portrait of the Artist as a Young Man*," Gabler has, through the manuscript history, contributed to our appreciation of Joyce's genius as he struggled with and fused the complex elements of the work. The portmanteau version of the two essays is exciting as an instance of literary detection and essential to our understanding of how Joyce, by abandoning a traditional narrative, wrought a new kind of formal structure—both diverse and unified—in the arrangement of the parts of his chapters and the intricate balance of patterns and rhythms within them. The cooperative nature of literary scholarship is well illustrated also in that Gabler's demonstration of the chiastic arrangement of the parts within *Portrait* prepared the way for Levenson to demonstrate that matching elements within the coda to *Portrait* reverse the overture, thus returning us from the last words of the diary to the first words of the book.

The second group of essays in this volume, under the general title "Structure, Image, Symbol, Myth," opens with an essay by David Hayman. Although it has been possible for many decades to recognize *Portrait* as belonging in the tradition of the *Bildungroman* (or *Künstlerroman,* if you wish), it has not been possible to associate it with other works in the genre among English works of fiction except in the most general terms. The reprinting among these essays of Hayman's analysis of structural affinities between Gustave Flaubert's *L'Education Sentimentale* and *Portrait,* published first in a European journal, at last makes another of many scholarly contributions by Hayman as available as it should be. Given that Hayman establishes Joyce's significant indebtedness to Flaubert, Jakobsen, and D'Annunzio, one can understand why attempts to link Joyce's work to the English tradition have been unrewarding. The principle concern of Hayman's essay is to demonstrate Flaubert's profound impact on Joyce and to establish ways in which the technical and stylistic experiments of Flaubert stimulated Joyce's experiments in point of view and structure. Comparative and formalist in approach, Hayman links the two writers by close analysis of parallel scenes and structures, making the case that Joyce's techniques of epiphany and anti-epiphany (Hayman's coinage) originate in Flaubertian techniques, then given a conceptual significance by Joycean theory. In view of Robert Scholes's condemnation of the critical use of the term *epiphany* and the debasement of the term in recent popular usage, it is important to draw attention to the scrupulous and informed treatment that Hayman gives to Stephen's aesthetic theory. One must attend as well to the conclusion Hayman draws that the ironic "Joyce has used the epiphany with more daring and greater subtlety" than the satiric and comic Flaubert.

In 1923 T. S. Eliot published an important review of *Ulysses* in which he observed that Joyce had "written one novel—the *Portrait*" and famously claimed that the triumph of *Ulysses* (for which Eliot seemed to find the term *novel* inadequate) was the "manipulation of a continuous parallel between contemporaneity and antiquity."[14] It took decades of critical reading before *Portrait,* like *Ulysses,* could be seen as a fusion of naturalist novel and symbolic romance in which densely woven patterns of symbol and myth are pervasive. Several essays in this second group affirm, no less than Eliot on *Ulysses,* the deep structure that underlies *Portrait.* These essays range in subject from Aristotle to Neoplatonism to Cretan and Irish myth and even to significant Biblical prototypes.

Sidney Feshbach's "A Slow and Dark Birth: A Study of the Organization" proffers one thread that will surely guide us through the labyrinth. Grounding his argument in Joyce's use of Aristotelian and Thomistic thought as well as in Neoplatonist symbolic concepts, Feshbach relates these elements to the five-chapter structure that embodies the stages of Stephen's spiritual development. Feshbach's critical method is a nice balance of the history of ideas and formalist concern with parallel incidents, verbal clusters, patterns of imagery, and fundamental rhythms of each chapter. Both Feshbach's essay and Diane Fortuna's exhaustive treatment of Joyce's use of Cretan myth and pagan mystery rituals represent complementary stages in critical comprehension of the spiritual implications and mythic structure of Joyce's book. Fortuna's revised version of her original essay is commanding and intense from the moment that she points to the elaboration of detail in Joyce's design, noting that the first name of Stephen's father, Simon, is an anagram of Minos, for whom the labyrinth was created. Opening with an account of archaeological discoveries made by Sir Arthur Evans and the myth analyses of such anthropologists as Sir James Frazer and Jane Harrison with which the Dublin intelligentsia and James Joyce were made familiar in the first decade of the century, Fortuna moves on to the central elements of the Cretan mysteries: the labyrinth (which she relates to the *Inferno* of Dante), lustration, epiphany, Minotaur, ritual sacrifice, descent into the underworld, rebirth, and ritual dance.

Strange as it may seem that these mysteries should be of interest to a gifted Dubliner seeking fame as a writer in the first decade of the twentieth century, it is worth reflecting that the pagan labyrinth had such appeal as a symbol of quest, death, and rebirth that it was used as a design in some of the major cathedrals of Europe. The young writer who named his hero after Stephen, the first Christian martyr, and the great artificer Daedalus knew exactly what he was doing and what universal myth he was exploiting. The weight of Fortuna's evidence and the sweep of her argument are nothing short of gripping, as she relates the myth to the structure, details, imagery, and episodes of Joyce's poetic triumph in prose.

In another ancient culture, Nehama Aschkenasy has discovered more evidence of James Joyce's love of correspondences. Sceptics should note that Joyce himself declared his love of the *Bible* (Ellmann 228). Aschkenasy's unique grounding in both Judaic studies and Joyce is manifest in her treatment of the Davin-Stephen passage in the fifth chapter of *Portrait*. Selecting the single episode for analysis, this writer is entirely persuasive in her argument that the story of Jael and Sisera (in *Judges* chapter 4) together with passages from *Proverbs* depicting the "eternal woman" and "prototypical seductress" are behind the passage in *Portrait*. Beyond her interest in proving the formative impact of the Biblical story and the archetypal temptress figure on the Davin-Stephen episode, Aschkenasy explores the various ways in which Stephen converts Davin's story and the female archetype to his own perceptions and predicament. This essay taps the strengths of the comparative approach, archetypal analysis, and contemporary feminism. Even prototypical chauvinists should appreciate the restraint with which Aschkenasy notes Stephen's transposition of the values found in the Biblical text: there is "a certain amount of gynophobia" in Stephen. F. L. Radford also focuses on a particular episode in Joyce's novel/romance, and he also startles us with a thesis that reveals Joyce's voracious eclecticism. Radford argues that Joyce, scorner of the Celtic Twilight and Irish Revival, was in his early study of Celtic materials—whatever his initial motive—far more engrossed than he has usually been taken to be. Throughout *Portrait*, Radford argues, the Irish "otherworld" is evoked, and at the climactic moment of the girl on the beach, images, allusions, and details from Celtic myth suffuse the atmosphere, amounting to no less than a subtext that Joyce fully intended, even though Stephen may not have. Radford's essay is the product of an impressive scholarship and of the ability to explicate multiplicity; the subtext that he brings to light was the product of Joyce's imaginative power, as early as *Portrait*, to synthesize and sustain multiple levels of implication and suggestion. Once read, the Aschkenasy and Radford essays should enrich any subsequent reader's response to the art of Joyce. None of those represented in this particular group of critical essays argues for a reductive correlation between a single source and *Portrait*. Individually, the essays explore in detail layers within a rich, dense, complex, and organic structure. Taken together, they reveal the analogical sensibility of a writer fascinated by correspondences, metaphors, motifs, and myths and able to make something quite new of them. Indeed, these essays reveal the genius of this Irish writer who transcended any simply chronological and univocal form and produced a work of prose with the density of a great poem.

Among the essays in this second group, Maurice Beebe's treatment of *Portrait* in relation to Impressionism is unique: Beebe deals not with a particular structural rhythm or figurative pattern in the novel but with the influence of a style, both pictorial and literary, upon Joyce. Richard Ellmann has asserted that Joyce, though once expressing an interest in portraiture, tended to disparage painting (Ellmann, 491); Peter Costello has maintained that Joyce had little interest in visual art but did keep, during the college years, "a well-marked copy of the catalogue of the National Gallery" (Costello, 162). Moreover, despite Joyce's poor vision, *Portrait* is as emphatically visual as it is auditory. Beebe's essay is richly and persuasively detailed, beginning with its account of Joyce's own translation of an essay on *Portrait* by the Italian Diego Angeli, which Joyce then placed in *The Egoist*. Angeli's essay identifies Joyce with the naturalism of the late Impressionists; and, in a subtle, scrupulous analysis of Joyce's prose, Beebe links *Portrait* to the literary impressionism of Flaubert, George Moore, Walter Pater, and Henry James as well as to the *vistazo* effect sought by the Impressionist painters.

In the first of the essays in the final group, which reveals the impact of theory on critical analysis, James Sosnoski urges his readers to imagine a conference at which 300 successive papers on Joyce's *Portrait* are read. Having evoked this grotesque vision, comic or tragic, Sosnoski then captures us by promising a rational discourse on the "controversy about 'aesthetic distance' in *A Portrait*": that is to say on the nature of Joycean irony. Thereafter, in rigorous analysis and argument, Sosnoski explores various "warrants" that have been advanced to support claims about the text, specifically as to how it should be read. Of the arguments that flourished in the 1950s and thereafter as various new critical methods emerged, Sosnoski asserts that, despite apparently irreconcilable conflicts, the major critical readers actually made "reconcilable claims." It is to a reader-oriented theory that Sosnoski turns in hope that a critical community may develop. Like other influential theories, reader response analysis originated in Europe, but in the American Jonathan Culler's *Structural Poetics* Sosnoski notes a comprehensive sense of the response of experienced readers to writer, text, and context.

R. B. Kershner's "The Artist as Text: Dialogism and Incremental Repetition in *Portrait*" turns to the Russian critic M. M. Bakhtin, who managed to fuse the influence of Russian Formalism with sufficient political orthodoxy to survive, for a provocative concept of the relation of the artist to the language. In Bakhtin's *The Dialogic Imagination* (a posthumous translation of which appeared in the United States in 1981) Kershner finds a complex of ideas that help to reveal how words create Stephen's world and certain characteristic

techniques of Joyce as well, including the relation between narrator and protagonist. Kershner writes persuasively of Bakhtin's concept of the stratification of language, which helps to explain how, as Stephen matures, words still
make his world, words derived from the multiple strata of language that have
shaped his consciousness. The Stephen Dedalus who has sought individuality
and a unique imaginative independence never realizes how little he is his own
creator, how much the creature of the language he has absorbed: surely as
ironic a reading of *Portrait* as any.

The final three essays in this group, all products of the 1990s, represent
the triumph of various theoretical approaches. What is particularly interesting about the three essays seen in relation to one another is the variety of
means they employ in scrutinizing Joyce's *Portrait.* Thomas Singer writes of
Portrait in relation to the *Tractatus Logico-Philosophicus* of Ludwig Wittgenstein. In a tour de force, Singer shows how the careers of the Dubliner and the
Viennese briefly intersected, how words created the world of each, how each
disdained the ideal and the absolute, regarding the ordinary as extraordinary,
how the aesthetic of each complemented that of the other, and how each conceived of the appropriate uses of silence. Furthermore, Singer uses Wittgenstein to cast light on Joyce and Joyce to illuminate how the philosopher transformed the positivist tradition. Few individual essays have had as much to
tell us about the modernity of Joyce. By contrast to Singer's running parallel
of two sensibilities, Michael McDonald examines the dialectic of harmony
and dissonance throughout *Portrait,* influenced by the aesthetic theory of
Theodore Adorno. (McDonald's readers are urged to attend to the dense foot-
notes supporting his analysis and ranging far beyond the concepts of
Adorno.) McDonald argues that both Joyce and Stephen to some degree
responded to a longing among early writers of the Irish literary revival for
transcendence of discord. Stephen sought harmony in an idealized aesthetic,
failing to realize that life cannot be transformed by art without the necessary
clash between dissonance and harmony, whereas Joyce recognized that pure
harmony is not attainable and that art must accept the dialectic of the clash.

It seems more than appropriate that this collection of essays on *Portrait*
should close with the redaction Vicki Mahaffey has prepared from a segment
of *Reauthorizing Joyce.* In "Framing, Being Framed, and the Janus Faces of
Authority" Mahaffey gives us a reading of the five chapters of *Portrait* that is
informed by a wide-ranging familiarity with the theoretical criticism that has
altered the landscape of critical thinking about literature in the past two
decades. The multiple puns of Mahaffey's title—evoking cinema, portraiture,
the influence of culture on character, and even modern slang—prepare
Mahaffey's readers for the fearless exploration of paradox in the text. Semiotics, deconstruction, reader response theory, mainline feminism, Derrida,
Lacan: these are all here, handled freshly and independently. In Vicki Mahaffey's criticism, the author of a work has not entirely disappeared, though not
to the diminution of reader, character, and social context. In *Portrait,* she

writes, language "acts as a complex frame of reference for the perception of author, character and reader." If Mahaffey thinks that Stephen Dedalus, both as a Christ figure and Satanic heretic, remains a slave to the vision of transcendence that has "framed" him, unlike critics who have seemed utterly to condemn Joyce's protagonist, she does not assume that Joyce handled his irony as if it were a meat cleaver.

Notes

1. Richard Ellmann, *James Joyce,* rev. ed. (New York: Oxford University Press, 1982; paperback with corrections, 1983), 73–74; hereafter cited in the text.

2. Stanislaus Joyce, *My Brother's Keeper: James Joyce's Early Years* (New York: Viking Press, 1958; reprint, New York and Toronto: McGraw-Hill, 1964), 87.

3. James Joyce, "Drama and Life," in *The Critical Writings of James Joyce,* ed. Ellsworth Mason and Richard Ellmann (1959; reprint, New York: Viking Press, 1964), 45; hereafter cited in the text as *CW.*

4. James Joyce, *Letters of James Joyce,* ed. Stuart Gilbert (New York: Viking Press, 1957), 1:52.

5. Peter Costello, *James Joyce: The Years of Growth, 1882–1915* (New York: Pantheon Books, 1992), 219; hereafter cited in the text.

6. Hans Walter Gabler, introduction to *A Portrait of the Artist as a Young Man,* by James Joyce (New York: Garland, 1993), 1–2.

7. James Joyce, "A Portrait of the Artist," in *The Workshop of Daedalus: James Joyce and the Raw Materials of A Portrait of the Artist as a Young Man,* ed. Robert Scholes and Richard M. Kain (Evanston, Ill.: Northwestern University Press, 1965), 60–68.

8. See Chester G. Anderson's note and the text of the report in James Joyce, *A Portrait of the Artist as a Young Man: Text, Criticism, and Notes* (New York: Viking Press, 1968), 319–20.

9. For a fuller account of critical responses, see James F. Carens, "A Portrait of the Artist as a Young Man," in *A Companion to Joyce Studies,* ed. Zack Bowen and James F. Carens (Westport, Conn.: Greenwood Press, 1984), 260–62.

10. Harry Levin, *James Joyce: A Critical Introduction,* revised, augmented ed. (Norfolk, Conn.: New Directions, 1960), 19; hereafter cited in the text.

11. W. Y. Tindall, *James Joyce: His Way of Interpreting the Modern World* (New York: Charles Scribner's Sons, 1950), 120–21.

12. Weldon Thornton, *The Antimodernism of Joyce's "Portrait of the Artist as a Young Man"* (Syracuse, N.Y.: Syracuse University Press, 1994).

13. Bernard Benstock, *Critical Essays on James Joyce* (Boston: G. K. Hall, 1985), 10.

14. T. S. Eliot, "Myth and Literary Classicism," in *The Modern Tradition: Backgrounds of Modern Literature,* ed. Richard Ellmann and Charles Feidelson (New York: Oxford University Press), 681.

CRITICAL CRUXES

◆

Introduction to *Stephen Hero*

THEODORE SPENCER

In 1935, Miss Sylvia Beach, the first publisher of *Ulysses,* issued a catalogue from her bookshop, Shakespeare and Company, 12 Rue de l'Odéon, Paris, in which she offered for sale, among other things, certain manuscripts of James Joyce. One of these consisted of pp. 519–902 of an early version of *A Portrait of the Artist as a Young Man,* in Joyce's handwriting. These pages were bought by the Harvard College Library in the autumn of 1938, and are here, with the permission of Joyce's executors, and of the Harvard College Library, printed for the first time.

There is some confusion about the date of this manuscript. In her catalogue Miss Beach, to whom Joyce originally gave it, says that it dates from 1903, and adds the following sentence: "When the manuscript came back to its author, after the twentieth publisher had rejected it, he threw it in the fire, from which Mrs. Joyce, at the risk of burning her hands, rescued these pages." This story is to some extent supported by Mr. Herbert Gorman, who says in his life of Joyce, writing of the year 1908: "Joyce burned a portion of *Stephen Hero* [as the book was then called] in a fit of momentary despair and then started the novel anew in a more compressed form."[1]

No surviving page of the manuscript shows any signs of burning.

Joyce himself was not very communicative on the subject. When the present writer wrote to him about the manuscript at the end of 1938, he received a reply from Joyce's secretary which said: "Apparently the very large MS of about 1000 pages of the first draft of *A Portrait of the Artist as a Young Man,* which he calls a schoolboy's production written when he was 19 or 20, has been sold in lots to different institutions in America. He feels that he can do nothing in the matter except to state this fact which he certainly can scarcely be blamed for not having foreseen at the moment of the presentation he made of it [*sic*]."

Since Joyce was born in 1882, the ages here mentioned suggest that the manuscript was written in 1901–1902, instead of 1903, as Miss Beach's catalogue says. Both dates, however, are apparently too early. Mr. Gorman, whose book was checked by Joyce, tells us that when Joyce left Ireland in 1904, he took with him a first chapter and notes for *Stephen Hero,* and he prints

Reprinted from *Stephen Hero,* ed. Theodore Spencer (New York: New Directions, 1944), 7–18.

[p. 148] a letter from Joyce to Grant Richards written on March 13, 1906, which speaks of the book as half finished:

> You suggest I should write a novel in some sense autobiographical. I have already written a thousand pages of such a novel, as I think I told you, 914 pages to be accurate. I calculate that these twenty-five chapters, about half the book, run into 150,000 words. But it is quite impossible for me in present circumstances to think the rest of the book much less to write it.

From this account it seems clear that *Stephen Hero* was written between 1904 and 1906.

The discrepancy between the different dates may be reconciled, I believe, by remembering that when Joyce left Ireland he took with him "notes" for his book. Mr. Gorman prints some of them [pp. 135 ff.]. It seems highly probable that there were also fuller notes than these, consisting of transcripts of conversations, etc., which were incorporated without much change into the manuscript: the reader of the following pages will undoubtedly agree that much of the talk sounds as if it had been taken down immediately after it had been spoken. If this is so, then we can think of the manuscript as representing the work of the years 1901 to 1906. It is a very clean copy, with only a few corrections, and Joyce's handwriting is remarkably legible.

The first 518 pages have apparently disappeared for good; I doubt very much if they have been "sold in lots to different institutions in America."[2] Probably the story of their having been burnt is correct—although there is no evidence in Mr. Gorman's book to indicate that the manuscript was ever sent to twenty publishers. Yet though the loss of the early pages is greatly to be regretted, the 383 pages that remain have a kind of unity in themselves. As Joyce planned it, *Stephen Hero* was to be "an autobiographical book, a personal history, as it were, of the growth of a mind, his own mind, and his own intensive absorption in himself and what he had been and how he had grown out of the Jesuitical garden of his youth. He endeavoured to see himself objectively, to assume a godlike poise of watchfulness over the small boy and youth he called Stephen and who was really himself." [Gorman, p. 133.] The Harvard manuscript describes about two years of Stephen's life; it begins shortly after he enters the National University, and it breaks off just as Stephen's emancipation from all that the University implies reaches a kind of climax. It does not give us a picture of the "small boy," but it gives us a very vivid and coherent picture of the "youth" who is called Stephen Daedalus, but who, in his appearance, his actions and his thought, is so evidently James Joyce.

It can be seen at a glance that this early version is very different from the version eventually published as *A Portrait of the Artist as a Young Man*. The period covered by the 383 pages of the manuscript occupies only the last 93 pages of the published version [Modern Library Edition]—the manuscript account of Stephen's two years at the University is at least as long as the whole history of his development in its final form. It portrays many characters and incidents which the published version leaves out, and it describes the growth of Stephen's mind in a far more direct and less elliptical form than that with which we are familiar. Consequently, though Joyce rejected it, and in his later year scorned it—from the reader's point of view, unjustifiably—as a "schoolboy's production," the interest of the manuscript to admirers of Joyce is great. It not only gives us a wonderfully convincing transcript of life, it throws light on Joyce's whole development as an artist by showing us more clearly than we have been able to see before what the beginning of that development was like.

II

Every reader of the present text will want to make his own comparisons between its picture of Stephen Daedalus and the picture given by the final version; I do not want to forestall any such critical pleasure by making exhaustive comparisons myself. Nevertheless there are certain characteristics of the manuscript which are of such special interest that they may, I hope not too obtrusively, be briefly pointed out in advance.[3]

The most obvious of these characteristics is the wealth of detail with which incidents and people are described. For example the Daedalus family is much more clearly seen than in the final form of the book; the family gives a richly sordid background to the arrogant growth of Stephen's mental independence through his University years: in the final version, the members of the family have virtually disappeared from the scene by the time Stephen has gone to the University. In the *Portrait* we have nothing like the description of Mr. Wilkinson's house [pp. 159 f.]; we hear nothing of Stephen's intimacy with his brother Maurice; the pathetic and shocking account of the illness and death of Stephen's sister Isabel [pp. 164 ff.] is entirely omitted; nothing is said of Stephen's attempt to convert his family to an admiration of Ibsen [pp. 84 ff.]. Even when the same incidents are mentioned, the present text usually treats them in a different manner—a more direct and dramatic manner— than that used in the *Portrait*. A typical illustration of this is the handling of Stephen's refusal to perform his Easter duty. In the present text [p. 131 ff.] the argument between Stephen and his mother is given as a dialogue—no doubt as it actually occurred—and it is a very effective piece of writing. But in the *Portrait* [Modern Library Edition, p. 281] the scene, which is a crucial one in Stephen's history, is merely referred to in a conversation with Cranly.

We can easily understand, of course, what Joyce was aiming at when he discarded his first draft and re-wrote the material. He was aiming at economy, and he was trying to place his center of action as much as possible inside the consciousness of his hero. To do this he evidently decided to sacrifice the method—which is, after all, the method of *Dubliners* rather than that of the *Portrait*—of objectively presenting one episode or character after another. As a result the *Portrait* has more intensity and concentration, a more controlled focus, than the earlier version. In the *Portrait,* as Mr. Levin observes, "drama has retired before soliloquy." The diffuseness of real life is controlled and ordered by being presented from a single point of view. Furthermore the method used in the *Portrait* of merely hinting at an episode or conversation instead of describing it in full (compare the way Giordano Bruno is introduced in the *Portrait* [p. 294] with the way he is introduced in the present version [p. 170])—this method makes Stephen's thoughts and actions more suggestive than they are as Joyce describes them here. In the *Portrait* we are looking at a room through a keyhole instead of through an open door; the vague shapes which we can with difficulty see in the dark corners add portentousness to what our framed and limited vision can perceive. In the present version the door is open, and everything is made as visible as possible. To change the image: we here see things in daylight, instead of under a spotlight; here there is less emphasis, less selection, less art.

But the increased pressure of concentration to be found in the *Portrait,* however desirable or admirable it may be, is gained at a loss. For example: in the *Portrait* we are introduced to Stephen's friends—Cranly, Lynch and the rest—as items, so to speak, in Stephen's mind. They are not pictured for us; Joyce expects us to take them for granted, as features in Stephen's landscape which need no further identification beyond their names and their way of speaking. But in the present text these friends are much more clearly identified; Joyce introduces us to them by describing their appearance and their points of view; they have an independent reality of their own, like the people in *Dubliners;* they are not merely sounding boxes or slot-machines, as they are in the *Portrait,* for the ideas of the all-important Stephen.

This is particularly true of the girl to whom Stephen is physically (though not otherwise) attracted. In the *Portrait* she had only initials E——— C———, and Stephen's reveries center round a virtually anonymous young girl. But in the present text the girl is named Emma Clery, and she has a living personality which is lacking in her merely initialed successor. There are several scenes in the present text [particularly that on pp. 66 ff.] where we see Emma very clearly indeed, and as a result Stephen's relations with her become, like his relations with other people, more dramatic than they are in the final version.[4]

The most striking differences which the reader will notice between the two versions is in the way Stephen himself is described. In the present text he is emotionally and intellectually a cruder and more youthful figure than in his creator's eyes he was later to become; he is more like the average undergraduate and, in spite or because of the fact that he is portrayed more diffusely, he is on the whole a more sympathetic person, proud and arrogant as he may be.

He has more weaknesses and does more foolish things (such as his pursuit of Emma) than are entirely consistent with the self-possession of his later portrait. He has a hero-worship for Ibsen, which is scarcely mentioned later, and his reaction from his Jesuit training makes him rage in a more sophomoric fury against what he calls the "plague of Catholicism." He is more dependent on his family for approval and support.

In the development of Stephen Daedalus, as presented in both the earlier and later versions, there are five main themes, all closely related to the central theme of Stephen himself. The themes are these: Stephen's family; his friends, male and female; the life of Dublin; Catholicism; Art. Stephen's development as an individual may be described as a process which sloughs off the first four in order that the fifth may stand clear. When this happens, and art is defined, the artist may then return to the first four for his subject matter. In fact he *has* to return to them if his function as an artist is to be fulfilled.

But before he can do this he has to determine what sort of man the artist is and also what art is: the two, for autobiographical purposes, are in many respects the same. It is not only Stephen Hero who matters—Joyce mentions "that old English ballad *Turpin Hero,* which begins in the first person and ends in the third person" [*Portrait,* p. 252];—it is the portrait of the *artist* as well. Stephen as hero is an adolescent; Stephen as artist is an adult. That is, perhaps, the major difference between the two versions of his career.

Yet the aesthetic theory with which we are familiar in the *Portrait* is already fully outlined in *Stephen Hero,* and no doubt one of the chief interests of the present text for most readers will consist in discovering how differently it is presented here from the way it is presented in the *Portrait.* In the *Portrait* Stephen outlines his aesthetic program in a conversation with Lynch, and the intellectual integrity and hardness of Stephen's ideas are contrasted with the coarse ejaculations and comments of his companion. This is an effective way of sustaining interest in an abstract exposition, and by setting Stephen's seriousness against Lynch's humor, what might be heavy or monotonous becomes lively and entertaining. The theory is presented objectively and with a comic background. But in the *Portrait* Stephen merely expounds his views; we are made to feel that he is so convinced of their truth that it doesn't in the least matter to him whether anybody else agrees with him or not. Cold fish that he is, he is above approval or disapproval; he is already prepared for "silence, exile and cunning."

Not so the younger Stephen of the present text. To him the setting forth of his ideas is a matter of great personal importance, and he delivers them, not in the casual form of a conversation with a friend, but in the form of a public paper to a literary society; it is a public event, an event for which Stephen prepares with great care. Furthermore his ideas are not contrasted merely with one other man's semi-humorous comments: they are contrasted with the conventionality of Catholicism, and the passage [pp. 90 ff.] which describes Stephen's conversation on the subject with the President of the University is one of the best in the book. Stephen's ideas are also contrasted, in the present text, with the intellectual paralysis of Dublin. For when he delivers his paper, which, word for word, he had so carefully planned, it gets only an indifferent and misunderstanding response; the philistines cannot be conquered on their own ground, and Stephen falls back more than ever on his own resources.[5]

The advantages of presenting the theory in such a fashion are obvious. We follow Stephen as he develops it through his conversations with his brother Maurice, the situation comes to a crisis in the delivery of the paper, and we are interested, as we are interested in a drama, as we wait to hear how the audience will react. We share Stephen's disappointment and disillusionment. Yet the method has its disadvantages as well: the development of Stephen's theory is spread out over a long period, it is intercepted by other episodes (the five main themes are interwoven throughout), and its exposition does not occupy, as in the *Portrait,* a crucial place in Stephen's career. In the *Portrait* the statement of Stephen's theory is an immediate prologue to his abandonment of Ireland, and hence is a climax to the whole book; in the present version, however dramatically it may be described, it is only one episode among many.

In fact the way the theory is finally presented in the *Portrait* is an illustration of the theory itself. One of Stephen's central ideas is that only improper art is "kinetic"; it moves us to do something, which true art should not do; on the contrary, the true "esthetic emotion" is static, and the true art is essentially impersonal: "The artist, like the God of the creation, remains within or behind or beyond or above his handiwork, invisible, refined out of existence, indifferent, paring his fingernails" [*Portrait,* p. 252]. It is in this impersonal, static, non-kinetic fashion that Stephen expounds his theory to Lynch. But in the present text it is expounded kinetically. Stephen is personally interested in the success of his paper, his intellectual fortunes seem to depend on it, and we are moved, not necessarily to do something, but to sympathy and concern for the outcome. The later text is, as usual, more mature, and shows Joyce, as the earlier version does not, illustrating his theory by his practice.[6]

III

There is one aspect of Stephen's aesthetic theory which appears in the manuscript alone, and is left out of the *Portrait* entirely. In my opinion the passage describing it is the most interesting and revealing in the entire text. It is the passage on pp. 210 ff. beginning with the words, "He was passing through Eccles Street," which explains Joyce's theory of epiphanies.[7]

I ask the reader to turn to this passage, and read it. [See Scholes, "Joyce and the Epiphany," 27–35]

This theory seems to me central to an understanding of Joyce as an artist, and we might describe his successive works as illustrations, intensifications and enlargements of it. *Dubliners,* we may say, is a series of epiphanies describing apparently trivial but actually crucial and revealing moments in the lives of different characters. The *Portrait* may be seen as a kind of epiphany—a showing forth—of Joyce himself as a young man; *Ulysses,* by taking one day in the life of the average man, describes that man, according to Joyce's intention, more fully than any human being had ever been described before; it is the epiphany of Leopold Bloom, just as, years earlier, the trivial conversation overheard on a misty evening in Eccles Street (where, incidentally, Mr. Bloom lived) was the epiphany of those two people's lives, shown forth in a moment. And *Finnegans Wake* may be seen as a vast enlargement, of course unconceived by Joyce as a young man, of the same view. Here it is not any one individual that is "epiphanized"; it is all of human history, symbolized in certain types the representatives of which combine with one another as the words describing them combine various meanings, so that H. C. Earwicker and his family, his acquaintances, the city of Dublin where he lives, his morality and religion, become symbols of an epiphanic view of human life as a whole, and the final end of the artist is achieved.

And if we keep this theory in mind, as a further aspect of the static theory of art developed throughout the present text, it helps us to understand what kind of writer Joyce is. A theory like this is not of much use to a dramatist, as Joyce seems to have realized when he first conceived it. It is a theory which implies a lyrical rather than a dramatic view of life. It emphasizes the radiance, the effulgence, of the thing itself revealed in a special moment, an unmoving moment, of time. The moment, as in the macrocosmic lyric of *Finnegans Wake,* may involve all other moments, but it still remains essentially static, and though it may have all time for its subject matter it is essentially timeless.

IV

But this fragment of *Stephen Hero* does not have to be considered in relation to Joyce's later writing to be thought worth preserving. It can stand on its own merits as a remarkable piece of work. Though it is not as carefully planned and concentrated as the *Portrait,* it has a freshness and directness, an accuracy of observation and an economy and sharpness of style that make it, in spite of its occasional immaturities, something to be enjoyed and admired for its own sake. It is one of the best descriptions of a growing mind that has ever been written.

Notes

1. Herbert Gorman: *James Joyce,* Farrar & Rinehart, New York, 1940, p. 196.

2. Mr. Gorman agrees with me on this point. I quote a letter from him dated January 21, 1941: "I . . . believe that what you have is all that Miss Beach possessed. Neither do I believe that any other portion of the draft exists. When Mr. Joyce's secretary (I presume you mean M. Paul Léon) wrote you that 'lots' had been sold to 'different institutions in America' I think his informant (presumably Mr. Joyce) had mixed up in his mind other material that Miss Beach was selling."

3. Mr. Harry Levin has already used the manuscript to excellent critical effect in his *James Joyce, a Critical Introduction,* New Directions, 1941.

4. In the present text, Stephen meets Emma at the house of a Mr. Daniel, where he sometimes goes on Sunday evenings. Nothing is said about Mr. Daniel and his household in the *Portrait,* but Joyce transfers, in a shortened form, his description of Mr. Daniel's living room to describe "her" house [*Portrait,* p. 257]. The change is a typical example of Joyce's economy and concentration in the published work.

5. In the manuscript Stephen does, to be sure, discuss his aesthetic theory with a friend [see pp. 212 ff.]. But it is interesting to note that the friend is Cranly, not Lynch, that the conversation comes long after the main theory is expounded in the public essay, and that Stephen is personally disappointed in Cranly's failure to be interested in the argument.

6. There are traces of Stephen's paper on aesthetics left in the *Portrait.* On page 217 the dean of studies asks Stephen: "When may we expect to have something from you on the esthetic question?" And on p. 247 Donovan says to Stephen: "I hear you are writing some essay about esthetics." These remarks, like several others in the *Portrait* (for example the references to "that certain young lady" [Emma] and Father Moran, p. 236) take on richer connotations—and sometimes can only be fully understood—if we read them with a knowledge of the present text in mind.

7. This theory is mentioned once in *Ulysses* [Random House edition, p. 41]. Stephen is meditating: "Remember your epiphanies on green oval leaves, deeply deep, copies to be sent if you died to all the great libraries of the world, including Alexandria?" Dr. Gogarty also refers to it in his autobiography, *As I {Was Going} down Sackville Street* [American edition, p. 295]. Gogarty is spending the evening with Joyce and others; Joyce says "Excuse me," and leaves the room. "I don't mind being reported," Gogarty writes, "but to be an unwilling contributor to one of his Epiphanies is irritating.

"Probably Fr. Darlington had taught him, as an aside in his Latin class—for Joyce knew no Greek—that 'Epiphany' meant 'a showing forth.' So he recorded under 'Epiphany' any showing forth of the mind by which he considered one gave oneself away.

"Which of us had endowed him with an 'Epiphany' and sent him to the lavatory to take it down?"

Joyce and the Epiphany:
The Key to the Labyrinth?

ROBERT SCHOLES

Ever since the manuscript of *Stephen Hero* turned up in the Harvard library, the term "epiphany" has been an important concept in the criticism of Joyce's works. In 1941, Harry Levin, working with the manuscript, came upon Stephen Daedalus' theory of the epiphany and, doing the natural thing, he applied the theory to Joyce's work as a whole.[1] Since then countless students and critics have turned their attention to this aspect of Joyce. Theodore Spencer, in the preface to his edition of *Stephen Hero;* Irene Hendry, in a well-known essay, reprinted in *Two Decades of Joyce Criticism;* Hugh Kenner; William York Tindall; and S. L. Goldberg are only the most obvious names in this group. Since Levin's discovery of the concept, forty of Joyce's own Epiphanies have been found, and twenty-two of them have been published by Oscar Silverman; the rest are in manuscript at Cornell.[2] Every discussion of the epiphany which I have seen is derived from Harry Levin's original discussion of the term. Later critics have elaborated on the term, refined it, located and categorized numerous passages in Joyce which they call epiphanies. But they have essentially treated the term in the same way—as a key to the labyrinth of Joyce's work. Where Mr. Levin says that *Dubliners* is a collection of epiphanies, Mr. Tindall says that each story "may be thought of as a great epiphany, and the container of little epiphanies, an epiphany of epiphanies."[3]

It may be suggested that this does not help very much in the understanding of Joyce's work, but it may be argued in defense that it does not hurt much either. Epiphany-hunting is a harmless pastime and ought probably to be condoned, like symbol-hunting, archetype-hunting, Scrabble, and other intellectual recreations. But recently two formidable critics have raised the question of the epiphany in Joyce to a higher sphere. I refer to Hugh Kenner and S. L. Goldberg, who make the epiphany crucial to our whole view of *A Portrait of the Artist as a Young Man,* and especially to our view of the character of Stephen Dedalus in that work and in *Ulysses.*[4] The argument turns on the presence of the theory of the epiphany in the esthetic of Stephen Daedalus in

First published in the *Sewanee Review,* vol. 72, no. 1, Winter 1964, 65–77. Copyright 1964, 1993 by the University of the South. Reprinted with the permission of the editor.

Stephen Hero but not in that of his descendant Stephen Dedalus in *Portrait*. Assuming that the theory of the epiphany is crucial to Joyce's own esthetic, these critics find in its absence from Stephen's esthetic in *Portrait* a clue to Joyce's attitude toward Stephen in that work and, consequently, to the attitude we as readers should take toward Stephen. Mr. Kenner finds Stephen's esthetic in *Portrait* deliberately weakened by Joyce so as to expose Stephen as a sham artist: "the crucial principle of epiphanization has been withdrawn." Mr. Goldberg finds Stephen's esthetic in *Portrait* deliberately weakened by Joyce so as to expose Stephen as a shallow human being. For Mr. Goldberg the epiphany has a "moral" quality because it links art to life; thus, Stephen's failure to include it in his esthetic theory in *Portrait* indicates that Joyce has limited Stephen's "understanding of art just as he limits his understanding of life." Mr. Goldberg further complicates his case by insisting that in *Ulysses* Stephen "seems to revert to the more satisfactory, though still vaguely formulated, insight expressed in *Stephen Hero*. To understand what the notion of epiphany properly means—a meaning that Stephen now, but only now, tacitly assumes—we must turn to the remaining aspects of the Thomist theory of knowledge." Mr. Goldberg suggests that the notion of the epiphany has been withdrawn from Stephen in *Portrait* and "tacitly" returned in *Ulysses*. Which means, I am afraid, that he can find no mention of the theory in either *Portrait* or *Ulysses* but chooses, in order to implement his own interpretation of the works, to smuggle the notion back into one but not the other. He complains about critics who want to "save" Stephen's esthetic in *Portrait* "by interpreting it in the light of—or rather, by conflating it with—ideas from outside the *Portrait*. Some want to add the notion of 'epiphany' from *Stephen Hero* to give a moral content to claritas. . . ." But Mr. Goldberg finds it necessary to "save" Stephen in *Ulysses* by the same kind of ingenious conflation.

In this essay, I wish to raise the question of whether the concept is worth all the importance attached to it by Joyce's critics; whether it is indeed a key, and if so, a key to what. In the process of dealing with these questions I hope to clarify to some extent what Joyce himself understood by the term: what it means in *Stephen Hero,* and what the forty extant samples of Joyce's own Epiphanies indicate that it must have meant for Joyce. These questions are all, obviously, interrelated. The only specific definition of epiphany in Joyce's writings, including those unpublished manuscripts which are available for inspection, is that given in *Stephen Hero*. It is there that we must begin.

Most students of literature will be familiar with this definition, but I must quote it again here in the interests of exactness. In *Stephen Hero* Joyce uses two narrative devices to acquaint the reader with Stephen's theory. First the narrator presents Stephen's thoughts on the subject in the context in which he first conceived the notion of epiphany:

> He was passing through Eccles' St. one evening, one misty evening, with all these thoughts dancing the dance of unrest in his brain when a trivial incident

set him composing some ardent verses which he entitled a "Vilanelle of the Temptress." A young lady was standing on the steps of one of those brown brick houses which seem the very incarnation of Irish paralysis. A young gentleman was leaning on the rusty railings of the area. Stephen as he passed on his quest heard the following fragment of colloquy out of which he received an impression keen enough to afflict his sensitiveness very severely.

The Young Lady—(drawling discreetly) . . . O, yes . . . I was . . . at the . . . cha . . . pel . . .

The Young Gentleman—(inaudibly) . . . I . . . (again inaudibly) . . . I . . .

The Young Lady—(softly) . . . O . . . but you're . . . ve . . . ry . . . wick . . . ed

This triviality made him think of collecting many such moments together in a book of epiphanies. By an epiphany he meant a sudden spiritual manifestation, whether in the vulgarity of speech or of gesture or in a memorable phase of the mind itself. He believed that it was for the man of letters to record these epiphanies with extreme care, seeing that they themselves are the most delicate and evanescent of moments.[5]

Following this we see Stephen explain the concept to Cranly, relating it to the three stages in esthetic apprehension which he has derived from Aquinas. The epiphany is associated with the third and final phase of esthetic apprehension. After the wholeness and symmetry of the object are apprehended, its radiance is apprehended:

—Now for the third quality. For a long time I couldn't make out what Aquinas meant. He uses a figurative word (a very unusual thing for him) but I have solved it. *Claritas* is *quidditas*. After the analysis which discovers the second quality the mind makes the only logically possible synthesis and discovers the third quality. This is the moment which I call epiphany. First we recognise that the object is *one* integral thing, then we recognise that it is an organised composite structure, a *thing* in fact: finally, when the relation of the parts is exquisite, when the parts are adjusted to the special point, we recognise that it is *that* thing which it is. Its soul, its whatness, leaps to us from the vestment of its appearance. The soul of the commonest object, the structure of which is so adjusted, seems to us radiant. The object achieves its epiphany.[6]

The heart of this definition, in both its contexts, I take to be the notion that an epiphany is a *spiritual* manifestation. Joyce was certainly aware of the use of the term in Christian tradition for the showing forth of Christ to the Magi and for other spiritual manifestations, and was probably aware of its use to designate that climactic moment in Greek drama when a god makes his appearance to resolve the action. The *spiritual* nature of the phenomenon is emphasized in the second context in *Stephen Hero* as well as in the first. "Its soul, its whatness, leaps to us from the vestment of its appearance. The soul of the commonest object, the structure of which is so adjusted, seems to us radiant."

In the discussion with Lynch which replaces the discussion with Cranly as the vehicle for the presentation of esthetic theory in *Portrait,* we arrive ultimately at a moment analogous to the moment in *Stephen Hero* when *claritas,* or radiance, was explained as the achievement of epiphany:

> —The connotation of the word—Stephen said—is rather vague. Aquinas uses a term which seems to be inexact. It baffled me for a long time. It would lead you to believe that he had in mind symbolism or idealism, the supreme quality of beauty being a light from some other world, the idea of which the matter was but the shadow, the reality of which it was but the symbol. I thought he might mean that *claritas* was the artistic discovery and representation of the divine purpose in anything or a force of generalization which would make the esthetic image a universal one, make it outshine its proper conditions. But that is literary talk. I understand it so. When you have apprehended that basket as one thing and have then analysed it according to its form and apprehended it as a thing you make the only synthesis which is logically and esthetically permissible. You see that it is that thing which it is and no other thing. The radiance of which he speaks is the scholastic *quidditas,* the *whatness* of a thing.[7]

Here the notion of the actual thing being merely a symbol of some ideal thing is specifically rejected by Stephen. He indicates that, though he once held that view, he no longer does. The concept of the epiphany, the spiritual manifestation, is not beyond Stephen; he is beyond it. The thing in itself is now enough for him. He has worked himself free of Platonic idealism, in theory at least. Joyce must have gone through the same process. But when we try to move from Stephen's esthetic to Joyce's we are on very shaky ground. Nearly all of Joyce's own statements on esthetics antedate the final writing of *Portrait* by many years. In fact, almost all the extant writings on this subject antedate *Stephen Hero* as well. Probably Joyce lost interest in it. A rejection of idealism leads ultimately to a rejection of esthetics itself, which deals not with things but with ideas.

We can be certain, however, that Stephen is more of an idealist in *Stephen Hero* and more of a realist in *Portrait.* Which position is superior, I must leave to the estheticians. Still, certain other aspects of the theory of the epiphany in *Stephen Hero* should be examined. The sample epiphany we are given should not be ignored, nor should the specific terms of the definition. We are given a snatch of overheard dialogue as a sample, and two forms of epiphany are specifically designated. Both the sample and the forms may be related to Joyce's own practice in writing his Epiphanies.

We are told that the epiphany may take either of two forms: (a) vulgarity of speech or gesture, and (b) a memorable phase of the mind itself. We will find, on examination, that Joyce's own Epiphanies readily fall into one or the other of these two categories, but before turning to Joyce's practice we should examine the theory more closely. The assumptions which underlie the dual formula of epiphanization are interesting. Form (a) involves observation of phenomena external to the observer. Form (b) involves observation of phenomena within the observer's mind. The observer assumes that the external phenomena will be "vulgar" and that the internal phenomena will be "memorable." The assumption that the observer (the "man of letters," as he is termed) is superior to his environment is built into the concept itself. Stephen in *Stephen Hero* is not only much closer to the symbolist movement in his neo-Platonic insistence on spiritual manifestations; he is also much closer to *fin de siècle* estheticism than Stephen in *Portrait*. In a word, the earlier Stephen is much more a man of the nineteenth century than the later Stephen.

If the separation of the observer and the world is clear in the theory of the epiphany, other aspects of the theory are far from clear. The achievement of epiphany seems to depend on the eye of the observer, but the *object* achieves *its* epiphany. One aspect Stephen does not consider is the reaction of the observer to an epiphany. Does it work any change in him? Is he wiser because of it? We do not know. Nor do we know the relationship of the epiphany to art, and this is a great question. Any object—a person, a clock, a mind—can achieve epiphany. The phenomenon is in no way related to the creative process. Even the recording of the phenomenon can be done by a "man of letters." No artist is required. In *Portrait* Stephen carefully distinguishes the process of esthetic apprehension from artistic creation. And he says, with a certain amount of humility, "When we come to the phenomena of artistic conception, artistic gestation, and artistic reproduction, I require a new terminology and a new personal experience."[8] The intention here seems to be to project three stages of creation parallel to the three stages of apprehension. But Stephen does not feel competent enough yet as a creative artist to deal with these stages. He needs "a new personal experience." He suggests, however, in his discussion of the final phase of apprehension, that this last phase may be in the mind of an artist the first phase of creation: "This supreme quality [*quidditas,* the *whatness* of a thing] is felt by the artist when the esthetic image is first conceived in his imagination."

By making Stephen aware of his limitations, Joyce has, in effect, strengthened Stephen's hand. Moreover, the esthetic theory in *Portrait* is in fact much clearer than that in *Stephen Hero*. This is so partly because of the clarification of the relationship between creation and apprehension and partly because of the elimination of the troublesome and confusing theory of the epiphany. For Joyce's critics, however, the very sketchiness of the theory has been an asset. They have been able to make whatever they wanted of it. They have even been able to consider it what it never was in Stephen's theory, and certainly not in Joyce's mind, a principle of structure in fiction. One may sympathize with them in this attempt. But when devotion to the theory goes so far that its absence from *Portrait* is held against Stephen, it is time to call for a return to sanity. If Joyce himself took the theory seriously after 1904 we would almost certainly have some mention of it in his letters or notebooks or conversations. Certainly, as his behavior over *Ulysses* and *Finnegans Wake* shows, he was not backward about giving clues to sympathetic readers for the understanding of his works. But the epiphany seems never to have been in his recorded thoughts except in *Stephen Hero,* a manuscript with which he was dissatisified and which he never meant to publish. The term, it is true, appears once in *Ulysses,* in a passage which ought to embarrass epiphanizing critics more than it has in the past. On Sandymount strand Stephen recalls his early literary pretensions, among which were his Epiphanies:

> Reading two pages a piece of seven books every night, eh' I was young. You bowed to yourself in the mirror, stepping forward to applause earnestly, strik- ing face. Hurray for the God-damned idiot! Hray! No-one saw: tell no-one. Books you were going to write with letters for titles. Have you read his F? O yes, but I prefer Q. Yes, but W is wonderful. O yes, W. Remember your epiphanies, on green oval leaves, deeply deep, copies to be sent if you died to all the great libraries of the world, including Alexandria? Someone was to read them there after a few thousand years, a mahamanvantara. Pico della Miran- dola like. Ay, very like a whale. When one reads these strange pages of one long gone one feels that one is at one with one who once. . . .[9]

The Epiphanies themselves for the most part bear out Stephen's con- demnation of them. They are trivial and supercilious or florid and lugubrious, in the main. Their chief significance is in the use Joyce often made of them in his later works. Twenty-two of them which are in manuscript at the Univer- sity of Buffalo have already been published. Twenty-five are in manuscript at Cornell and have not been published, except for seven which are the same as those at Buffalo. These forty Epiphanies fall readily into the two categories which Joyce outlined in *Stephen Hero:* vulgarities of speech or gesture, and memorable phases of the mind itself. I cannot examine all the Epiphanies in detail here, but I will make one or two assertions about their use and attempt to illustrate these assertions. First, more of the known Epiphanies are used by Joyce in *Stephen Hero* than in *Portrait,* and more in *Portrait* than in *Ulysses.*[10] Second, Joyce's use of the Epiphanies became freer and more creative progres- sively. I believe I can illustrate this tendency by examining Joyce's subsequent use of two Epiphanies. The first, number XIV in the Buffalo volume pub- lished by Oscar Silverman, is used in both *Stephen Hero* and *Ulysses.* The three versions are as follows:

1. Epiphany
   Two mourners push on through the crowd. The girl, one hand catching the woman's skirt, runs in advance. The girl's face is the face of a fish, discoloured and oblique-eyed; the woman's face is small and square, the face of a bargainer. The girl, her mouth distorted, looks up at the woman to see if it is time to cry; the woman, settling a flat bonnet, hurries on towards the mortuary chapel.
2. *Stephen Hero*
   Two of them who were late pushed their way viciously through the crowd. /A girl, one hand catching the woman's skirt, ran a pace in advance. The girl's face was the face of a fish, discoloured and oblique-eyed; the woman's face was square and

punched, the face of a bargainer. The girl, her mouth distorted, looked up at the woman to see if it was time to cry:/ the woman, settling a flat bonnet, hurried on towards the mortuary chapel.[11]

3. *Ulysses*

Mourners came out through the gates: woman and a girl. Leanjawed harpy, hard woman at a bargain, her bonnet awry. Girl's face stained with dirt and tears, holding the woman's arm looking up at her for a sign to cry. Fish's face, bloodless and livid.[12]

The changes in the *Stephen Hero* version are the minimum necessary to accommodate the present-tense Epiphany to the past-tense narrative. In the *Ulysses* version, however, the scene has to be accommodated not merely to narrative prose but to the mental processes of Leopold Bloom. Thus, "leanjawed harpy, hard woman at a bargain" is not merely description but Bloom's shrewd appraisal of character. The incident itself has been subordinated to Bloom's view of it, the prose pared down to the essential minimum required to indicate Bloom's apprehension. The manuscript of *Stephen Hero* bears Joyce's selecting crayon marks through the part of the passage he borrowed for re-use. The original "spiritual manifestation" through vulgarity of gesture has become a very tiny building block in a very large edifice. An essentially artless recording of actuality has been given a place in a work of art by the shaping imagination of its creator. It has become more meaningful in relation to Bloom than it ever was in its own right. But it is no longer an "epiphany"; it has become an incident. We can observe a similar process at work in Joyce's use of the following Epiphany in *Portrait:*

1. Epiphany

Faintly, under the heavy summer night, through the silence of the town which has turned from dreams to dreamless sleep as a weary lover whom no carresses move, the sound of hoofs upon the Dublin road. Not so faintly now as they come near the bridge: and in a moment as they pass the dark windows the silence is cloven by alarm as by an arrow. They are heard now far away—hoofs that shine amid the heavy night as diamonds, hurrying beyond the grey, still marshes to what journey's end—what heart—bearing what tidings?[13]

2. *Portrait*

April 10. Faintly, under the heavy night, through the silence of the city which has turned from dreams to dreamless sleep as a weary lover whom no caresses move, the sound of hoofs upon the road. Not so faintly now as they come near the bridge: and in a moment as they pass the darkened windows the silence is cloven by alarm as by an arrow. They are heard now far away, hoofs that shine amid the heavy night as gems, hurrying beyond the sleeping fields to what journey's end—what heart?—bearing what tidings?[14]

Here, though there are changes, they are insignificant. The former Epiphany has become the entry for April 10 in Stephen's diary. But the significant difference lies in the context. It was the essence of epiphany in Joyce's youthful theory and practice that it had no context. Each was a little independent gem of vulgarity or "a memorable phase of the mind itself." The sample we have here is of the latter kind. But it is now in a context. It is followed immediately by another diary entry:

> *April* 11. Read what I wrote last night. Vague words for a vague emotion. Would she like it? I think so. Then I should have to like it also.

Stephen here is given by Joyce the advantage of some of his own ten or more years of maturity since the Epiphany was first recorded. Stephen is critical of it himself but prepared to accept it if "she" (presumably E. C.) likes it. The Epiphany here is no longer a "spiritual manifestation" but a piece of prose, subject to criticism like any other. And it is functioning dramatically in an artistic context, revealing character, attitude, and emotion. Another fragment, recorded by young James Joyce in his "man of letters" phase, has been rescued from the "green oval leaves, deeply deep," and been put to work by an older James Joyce, a literary artist. From that last phase of apprehension which makes the object radiant and coincides with artistic conception, this object has passed through ten years of gestation to its final reproduction in *A Portrait of the Artist as a Young Man.*

What then, finally, is to be the use of this term epiphany in Joyce criticism? I would suggest a very limited use. The phrase should designate those little bits of prose which Joyce himself gave the name to, as we find them in their raw and inartistic state. As a term to be used in the criticism of Joyce's art itself, I would like to see it abandoned entirely. To those who first discovered the term in *Stephen Hero* it must have seemed indeed to be the key to the labyrinth of Daedalus. But the way to the labyrinth, like the descent to Avernus, is an easy journey. It is only the return which presents difficulties. In André Gide's *Theseus* the fabulous artificer tells the aspiring hero that the most dangerous aspect of the labyrinth is not the difficulty of the passage nor the Minotaur himself, but the headiness of the vapours of the place, which make its tenants reluctant to return. Icarus himself, in Gide's story, has succumbed to these vapours and, though rescued physically, he is a dead thing, his mind wandering in mazes of metaphysics. I should like to suggest that both Joyce and Stephen entered this Platonic darkness at one time via the key of the epiphany, and that they both emerged, tempered by their trials. It is the critics who love those heady vapours so much that they refuse to emerge. To them, I can say only, "Come up, come up, you fearful Jesuits."

Notes

1.   Harry Levin, *James Joyce,* New York (New Directions), 1960, especially pages 28–31.

2.   Silverman's volume was published by the University of Buffalo Press. The Cornell items are listed in my catalogue of the Cornell Joyce Collection, published by the Cornell Press, items 15, 17, and 18.

3.   William York Tindall, *A Reader's Guide to James Joyce,* New York (Farrar, Straus and Cudahy), 1951, p. 11.

4.   See Hugh Kenner, *Dublin's Joyce,* Bloomington (University of Indiana Press), 1956, Chapter 9, "The School of Old Aquinas," *passim;* and S. L. Goldberg, *The Classical Temper,* New York (Barnes and Noble), 1961, Chapters 2 and 3, especially pp. 63, 71.

5.   James Joyce, *Stephen Hero,* New York (New Directions), 1955, pp. 210–211.

6.   *Ibid.,* p. 213.

7.   James Joyce, *A Portrait of the Artist as a Young Man,* New York (Modern Library), pp. 249–250.

8.   *Ibid.,* pp. 245–246.

9.   James Joyce, *Ulysses,* New York (Modern Library, unrevised edition), p. 41.

10.   In a study still in progress Mr. Henry Taylor has located thirteen passages in *Stephen Hero* based on Epiphanies, nine in *Portrait,* and five in *Ulysses.* Though others may turn up, the proportions will probably be preserved.

11.   *Stephen Hero,* p. 167. I have used slantlines here to indicate that part of the passage subsequently crossed out by Joyce with crayon, as indicated in this edition.

12.   *Ulysses,* p. 100.

13.   In manuscript at Cornell, item 17d in my catalogue. The misspelling "carresses" may be the fault of Stanislaus Joyce, whose copy this is taken from.

14.   *Portrait,* p. 297.

[Stephen's Diary: The Shape of Life]

MICHAEL LEVENSON

Despite the unflagging controversy over the character of Stephen Dedalus, remarkably little attention has been paid to the ending of *A Portrait of the Artist as a Young Man,* where one might have supposed that the problem would become acute. The diary that concludes the novel has had the rare distinction of being a virtually unannotated specimen within the Joycean *oeuvre,*[1] and while it is tempting to keep it free from the endless profusion of inky scholia, it raises issues too important to leave unremarked. One of the most intricate mechanisms in an intricate novel, its workings bear directly on the problem of interpreting Stephen's development. Questions of characterization join with questions of genre, and the relationship between individual agency and impersonal form becomes vivid. In elaborate, though submerged, patterns the diary reinterprets the narrative that it will soon conclude and offers some trenchant answers to a question that governs the novel as it governs this essay: What is the shape of a life?

Those who have not neglected the conclusion of *A Portrait of the Artist* have typically mentioned it only to express their dismay. Edward Garnett, reporting on the manuscript for Duckworth, spoke of the ending as "a complete falling to bits; the pieces of writing and the thoughts are all in pieces and they fall like damp, ineffective rockets." More recently Kenneth Grose has called it a "flat ending" which contains "many trivialities and unexplained references." The few attempts to interpret this puzzling conclusion have usually tried to understand it by assimilating it—either to Stephen's own theory of genre or to the larger design of Joyce's career. Susan Lanser, for instance, holds that the diary is Stephen's lyric but Joyce's drama, while Anthony Burgess, addressing the problem biographically, writes that the diary entries "anticipate, in their clipped lyricism and impatient ellipsis, the interior monologue of *Ulysses.*" Both approaches have their merits, but in each case the novel's ending tends to disappear, lost in the configurations brought forth to explain it.[2] The method of proceeding here will be to acknowledge the diary as an independent genre with its own norms and ambiguities, and then to pay close attention to its particular manifestation in Joyce's novel, where it

Reprinted from *English Literary History* 52:4 (Winter 1985), 1017–1035. © The Johns Hopkins University Press.

reveals technical virtuosity in the service of larger fictional concerns. Consequently, this essay will move from considerations of genre to textual niceties, since it is between genre and text that the character of Stephen Dedalus hangs suspended.

According to Robert Martin Adams, "the final pages [of *A Portrait of the Artist*] splinter into isolated and laconic entries in a diary, which is anticlimactic unless one estimates its purpose as the detachment of Stephen Dedalus from what has, after all, been the world of his past, and the preparation of his mind for a launch into the future."[3] Adams alludes here to what one might, without being invidious, call the sentimental view of the novel's ending, which regards the final pages as a decisive expression of revolt. The shift to the first person then appears as an assertion of individuality and a repudiation of public norms. Thus Marilyn French writes that "having searched among many kinds of linguistic structurings of experience, Stephen creates his own—his diary." In Lanser's terms, the "public self" finally gives way to the private self; narrative detachment yields to personal expression: Stephen begins to compose his life in his own language.[4] Moreover, within a novel that has only vaguely indicated the movement of time, the diary allows Stephen to engage with time, to measure his development in a precise way and so to complete the pattern of the *Bildungsroman* which culminates in that break with the past and preparation for the future to which Adams refers. In this sense the diary is a new mode of writing for a new mode of living. The question, of course, is whether it is something else besides.

I

Sir Arthur Ponsonby, that indefatigable collector of English diaries, offered a useful working definition of the form as "the daily or periodic record of personal experience and impressions"—a characterization that succinctly identifies two leading features of the genre: intimacy and periodicity.[5] For if a first convention of the diary demands fidelity to the experience of its author, a second requires this fidelity to be sustained over time, and sustained in some regular way. But as we former diarists all know, personal experience and periodic accounting do not always consort well together, and the commitment to regularity can quickly become a burden and even a source of shame The pages of diary-keepers are full of self-recriminations and hopeful new resolves. "Hold fast to the diary from today on!" enjoins Kafka, "Write regularly! Don't surrender!" Fanny Burney regrets that she "let this month creep along unrecorded," because she "could not muster courage for a journal," and promises "to avoid any future long arrears." Burney's economic image is telling; it indicates the element of compulsion built into a form in which the writer incurs a new debt every day. "I have so long accustomed myself to write a Diary," says Boswell, "that when I omit it the day seems to be lost." At the extreme, which Boswell wittily anticipates, the diary ceases merely to reflect one's life and begins to govern it: "Sometimes it has occurred to me that a man should not live longer than he can record, as a farmer should not have a larger crop than he can gather in."[6]

The rhythm of the form has a further and disquieting consequence: it makes ending difficult. Once begun, the diary silently imposes the obligation to continue; this is the tyranny of the genre; it makes no provision for an end. Indeed, in important respects it is incompatible with an aesthetically or morally satisfying culmination. One of the most rending aspects of the diary of Alice James is that after she has delivered a courageous moral summation she lives longer than she had expected and her diary continues past her eloquent valediction to become a record of confusion, regret and pain. By its governing convention the diary must unfold as life unfolds, and any attempt to bring it to conclusion will always invite the question, Why stop here? Behind that question looms another: How can one be sure that one *has* stopped?

These questions have a direct bearing on *A Portrait of the Artist as a Young Man*. A novel on the point of reaching its end suddenly alters to a form that only uneasily accommodates an end. In careless paraphrases it is sometimes said that the novel concludes with Stephen's exile from Ireland; in fact, of course, it does no such thing. In the last scene before the diary begins, Stephen tells Cranly of his decision to leave, but a month later he is still in Dublin, writing in his journal. The entry of 16 April begins "Away! Away!" and Stephen describes himself as "making ready to go."[7] However, ten days of silence pass before he announces a new resolve, "to forge in the smithy of my soul the uncreated conscience of my race" (253). This surely has the ring of finality, but Stephen lingers at least one more day, making his appeal to "Old father, old artificer" (253), and here the diary and the novel cease, before the exile-to-be has taken his first step.

Stephen's intention to break with the past is evident, but that intention, restated from day to day, acquires a past of its own; his romantic revolt threatens to become a tradition. Even as one grants Stephen's sincerity on each occasion, the repetitions create a cadence that risks turning the promised culmination into an ongoing sequence of culminations, with each trumping the one before until the spirit of revolt begins to languish. As the novel ends, the diary patiently awaits the next entry, and even the reader who shares the ardor of 27 April must begin to suspect that 28 April will bring not exile, only more ardor.

This is not just a difficulty for the reader, nor does it appear for the first time at the conclusion of the novel. Stephen himself has consistently worried over endings, from his early concern that "he did not know where the universe ended" (17) to his moment of anxiety during a late conversation with Cranly: "Stephen, struck by [Cranly's] tone of closure, reopened the discussion at once" (243). The refusal of closure represents a powerful motive for

Stephen; his succession of rebellions can be seen as attempts to avoid closed forms, to "reopen discussion." The proud cry of the aspiring artist, "On and on and on and on!" (172) is a demand for a perpetual crossing of limits, a resolute march to the end of the universe. Yet, as Hugh Kenner has noticed, "on and on and on and on" carries an ominous undertone.[8] There is perhaps one "on" too many. The cry of romantic freedom begins to resemble the plaint of Sisyphus. When at the end of the novel Stephen makes his stirring vow "to encounter for the millionth time the reality of experience" (253), the magnitude of the number implies a deed equally grand, but it must not blind us to an unnerving implication. Either Stephen has *already* encountered experience many times or many others have encountered it before him. In either case, his defiant act of individuality is only the latest instance, the millionth instance, of a persistently repeated gesture.

Thus a leading pattern in the novel is the *series,* which depends not on movement toward an end but on the recurrence of identities and similarities. Examples of serial form include several structural devices that have figured prominently in discussions of *A Portrait of the Artist*—for example the repetition of motifs and Stephen's oscillation between achievement and decline—as well as such diverse manifestations as the villanelle, the many lists, and the frequent verbal alternations (e.g., "First came the vacation and then the next term and then vacation again and then again another term and then again the vacation" [17]). The novel, in other words, relies heavily on a formal principle that challenges finality with repetition and that encourages a view of Stephen as bound within a perpetually unfolding series—as the sort of character, that is, who having done a thing once, would as soon do it a million times. Though not aimed at Stephen, a question in the hell-fire sermon hits him squarely: "Why did you not, even after you had fallen the first or the second or the third or the fourth or the hundredth time, repent of your evil ways and turn to God . . . ?" (123). The threat is that obsessive repetition will turn the individual into something abstract and mechanical, and it should be clear that Joyce means to contemplate just such a threat.

After the ecstatic vision that leads to the writing of the villanelle, Stephen raises a pertinent question: "Was it an instant of enchantment only or long hours and days and years and ages?" (217). As in many other places, Stephen imagines the epiphanic moment stretching endlessly outward, unfolding into eternity, but this visionary prospect coincides in disturbing ways with the image of damnation as "an evil of boundless extension, of limitless duration" (130). Indeed, one of the most forbidding implications in the plotting of Stephen's character is precisely the suggestion that the revelatory moment may prolong itself through "hours and days and years and ages," and so prevent not only a satisfying culmination but even the consolations of catastrophe. The enchanted instant that lasts forever has its mirror image in the prospect of Stephen "falling, falling but not yet fallen, still unfallen but about to fall"(162).

It should be evident that the conventions of the *Bildungsroman* cannot be assimilated to the pattern of serial repetition. The *Bildungsroman* presupposes some principle of development, which in turn presupposes some concept of an end. To the extent that Joyce's novel depends on these conventions, the image of the exiled artist serves as its end, as the point against which development can be measured.[9] To our question, What is the shape of a life? the upward curve of *bildung* suggests one answer, the unswerving line of repetitions another. A first approach to the question of character in *A Portrait of the Artist* must acknowledge both formal principles and acknowledge, too that they compete.

It is at the novel's conclusion that they compete most directly, and this is an initial reason for paying attention to Stephen's diary, part of whose force is that it confirms both patterns. The ambiguity between novelty and similarity inheres in the genre: on the one hand, the precisely dated entries ensure an advance through time; on the other hand, the unit of form is methodically reiterated. A harmless manifestation of this ambiguity can be found in Pepys where the sometimes harsh notes of change are muted by the gentle drumming of that "Up" which begins so many of his daily accounts. In *A Portrait of the Artist* the conflict is sharper and aligns with our earlier distinction between personality and periodicity. The diary places intimate conviction, certain that it has at last identified its purpose, in the context of an ongoing series of intimacies. It provides a record of development through the mode of repetition, creating the disturbingly ambiguous image of a young man finally becoming an artist for the millionth time.

Even this image, however, is too simple, and it does not yet lead to an interpretation of Stephen's character that departs significantly from certain prevailing views. But it establishes terms for the argument to follow, where it will be possible to bring forward some new evidence and to suggest some new conclusions. Here the analysis will become unavoidably more detailed, since it will be necessary to pursue Joyce to that level of composition where his secrets are better kept and their exposure is more satisfying.

II

A source for Stephen's diary was undoubtedly Turgenev's *The Diary of a Superfluous Man*. Joyce had read it by 1904 at the urging of Stanislaus, who records in *his* diary his elder brother's unilluminating opinion: "I asked him what he thought about it. He said he thought the man very like me. This was my idea too."[10] In a letter of 1905, Joyce wrote dismissively of Turgenev, whom he compared unfavorably to Lermontov;[11] on the other hand, we learn in *Stephen Hero* that young Dedalus "had read and admired certain translations of Turgeniéff's novels and stories." Joyce himself was sufficiently interested to acquire eleven volumes of the edition that Heinemann began to publish in 1910,[12] and whatever his final judgment of Turgenev, he did not hesitate to borrow from him.

Tchulkaturin, the protagonist of *The Diary of a Superfluous Man,* writes his diary in the last weeks of his life, beginning on 20 March. Stephen composes his diary in the final weeks of his Dublin life; he too begins on 20 March. This is the sort of superfine ligature that we have come to expect from Joyce, a scarcely perceptible stitch whose only contribution is to remind us that there is one more thread to follow. If we trace it back to Turgenev's novel, we discover first of all a number of rather slight anticipations of *A Portrait of the Artist.* It seems probable, for instance, that Tchulkaturin's maladroit appeal to his beloved Liza suggested an image for Stephen's final meeting with E—— C——, and that the "Farewell, life!" of the superfluous man gave (by inversion) Stephen's roseate "Welcome, O Life!" (253). After a particularly bathetic piece of exposition, Tchulkaturin writes that "I have read over what I wrote yesterday, and was all but tearing up the whole manuscript. I think my story's too spun out and too sentimental."[13] In Stephen's leaner prose (leaner, that is, than the prose of Constance Garnett) this becomes, "Read what I wrote last night. Vague words for a vague emotion" (251).

This last example begins to raise a more substantial concern. As opposed to the memoir or the autobiography, which typically are written from a fixed standpoint, the diary must continually change its perspective. Its retrospective view is daily rendered obsolete as life outstrips the diary; each entry brings a new retrospect, inviting a restless process of self-correction and self-revision. In this aspect of the genre it is *reversal* not repetition that challenges the prospect of uninterrupted individual development. "Could his mind then not trust itself?" (233). Stephen had wondered, and the diary reveals a mind increasingly suspicious of its own habits. The entry of 30 March concludes with a fanciful *mot*—"Then into Nilemud with it!"—and the next day's account consists only of the observation, "Disapprove of this last phrase" (250). When Cranly had pressed him to admit that he was happy in his early religious conviction, Stephen had responded, "I was someone else then" (240), and one of the effects of the diary is to make this self-obsolescence more rapid, opening the possibility that Stephen will reverse himself from sentence to sentence. He risks becoming "someone else" at every new utterance, as in the account of his final meeting with E—— C——, where he contemplates a "new feeling": "Then, in that case, all the rest, all that I thought I thought and all that I felt I felt, all the rest before now, in fact . . . O, give it up, old chap! Sleep it off!" (252).

This problem becomes still more severe when the diary is situated in relation to the third-person narrative that precedes it. For perhaps the most telling idea that Joyce derived from *The Diary of a Superfluous Man* was that an intimate account of the present could become an involuntary record of the past, and that the self could never know how much of its life history it might inadvertently disclose. As Tchulkaturin nears the end of his life, an old romantic misadventure comes to dominate his thoughts, and even as his death approaches he adverts to his old failure rather than to his impending fate. Joyce, too, turns Stephen's present reflections into a commentary on the past, but his methods are characteristically more athletic. The diary's "events and conversations which baffle us by their incongruity and seeming unimportance"[14] possess an active underlife where they are neither incongruous nor unimportant.

The record of 25 March recalls a "troubled night of dreams," the first of which Stephen describes in this way:

> A long curving gallery. From the floor ascend pillars of dark vapours. It is peopled by the images of fabulous kings, set in stone. Their hands are folded upon their knees, in token of weariness and their eyes are darkened for the errors of men go up before them for ever as dark vapours. (249–50)

The dream receives no commentary; it is placed in no context, but it constructs its own context through a cipher that we must learn to read. The "errors of men" had been at issue before in the novel, in the third chapter during the period of Stephen's crippling guilt, relieved at last when he confesses his sins. At that culminating moment he feels that "his prayers *ascended* to heaven from his purified heart like perfume streaming upwards from a heart of white rose" (145, my emphasis); in his dream there "ascended pillars of dark vapours."[15] If the verbal parallel stopped here, one could dismiss it as incidental. But the word "vapours" immediately secures another connection, appearing twice in the diary and twice during the scene at the church where the sound of a penitent floats "in vaporous cloudlets out of the box," a "soft whispering vapour" (142). Furthermore and decisively, the "token of weariness" in Stephen's dream recalls the "token of forgiveness" that he had received from the priest (145). The dream, that is, glances back to the confession through a set of masked references which, however, invoke the earlier event only to recast its implications. In place of the joyous ascent of prayers (from "a heart of white rose") Stephen envisions the ascent of dark vapours; the token of forgiveness becomes a token of weariness; and the priest with hand "raised above" Stephen gives way to those dark-eyed kings with hands "folded upon their knees," heedless of the "errors of men." Through a series of linguistic transpositions the triumph of the confession is overturned, and we are left with the bleak dreamscape where human sins ("the errors of men") win no remission but pass before dark eyes in stony faces.

Stephen himself betrays no awareness of the connection between the dream and the earlier incident, but the startling method of the diary is to look past conscious recognitions in favor of subterranean relations established among words themselves. Stephen had regarded language, together with nationality and religion, as a collective form that inhibited the freedom of the artist, and as will become clear, the final movement of the novel plays out a drama between the individual speaker and the speech of the tribe. His language knows what Stephen may not. Here is the entry of 5 April:

> Wild spring. Scudding clouds. O life! Dark stream of swirling bogwater on which appletrees have cast down their delicate flowers. Eyes of girls among leaves. Girls demure and romping. All fair or auburn: no dark ones. They blush better. Houp-la! (250–51)

The word "wild" should itself be enough to send us back to the epiphany on Dublin bay, to a sequence such as this: "He was unheeded, happy and near to the *wild* heart of life. He was alone and young and wilful and *wild*hearted, alone amid a waste of *wild* air and brackish waters . . ." (171, my emphasis). The word and its variants appear a dozen times in the few pages of the scene. The second phrase from the diary, "scudding clouds," calls to mind the phrase that arouses Stephen's artistic piety: "A day of dappled seaborne clouds" (166). "O life!" returns us to his euphoric pledge: "To live, to err, to fall, to triumph, to recreate life out of life" (172). The "swirling bogwater" had been anticipated in "shallow swirling water" (166), "appletrees" in "apple orchards" (166). At this point the diary, like the epiphany that it recalls, turns to Stephen's contemplation of young girls, but in keeping with the altered mood, the later vision displays none of the romantic reverence of the earlier scene. The girl Stephen had admired on the bay had "long fair hair" and thighs "softhued as ivory" (171), while in the later description he offers a jaunty appraisal of not one fair girl but several: "All fair or auburn: no dark ones," and his Paterian metaphor—"a faint flame trembled on her cheek" (171)—now becomes rudely literal: "They blush better." The sacred aura of the epiphany yields to the levity of the diary, a transformation well emphasized in the final link between the scenes. In the last lines of chapter four, Stephen compares the rim of the moon to "the rim of a silver hoop" (173). And how does that entry of 5 April conclude?[16] Look for yourself.

The diary abounds with such echoes of earlier passages, repetitions of key words, puns, verbal substitutions. Long sequences from the earlier narrative reappear in a form of symbolic notation that allows Joyce to compress events and implications. Beneath the casual surface of Stephen's personal record, there is an extraordinary linguistic density, and here, as elsewhere in Joyce, one might speak of a linguistic unconscious which carries meanings that do not depend on the intentions of the speaker. It scarcely needs saying that this cunning technique violates one of the most familiar assumptions about the diary form: that it aspires to be a perfect transparency, that it is indeed the sincere literary form *par excellence*. Sincere Stephen may be, but it is plain that his diary is a mocking and duplicitous thing. Quite apart from Stephen's own perceptions, his language itself establishes connections, sees resemblances, marks differences. A space opens between the self and its form of representation. Stephen has high romantic intentions, but his language has intentions of its own.

Kenner has pointed out that the first two pages of *A Portrait of the Artist* "enact the entire action in microcosm";[17] as will become increasingly clear, the diary serves as an epilogue that does not merely conclude the action of the novel but recapitulates it through an elaborate set of veiled references.

> 22 *March:* In company with Lynch followed a sizable hospital nurse. Lynch's idea. Dislike it. Two lean hungry greyhounds walking after a heifer. (248)

It was with Lynch that Stephen had pursued the theory of aesthetics, offering his definition of art, drawing distinctions between static and kinetic emotions, characterizing pity and terror, describing the rhythm of beauty, until Lynch impatiently interrupts, "But what is beauty?" "Let us take woman," suggests Stephen. "Let us take her!" says Lynch "fervently" (208). The diary, that is, exploits the link between aesthetics and erotics; the pursuit of beauty becomes the pursuit of a "sizable hospital nurse" (during their conversation Lynch and Stephen had walked past "the corner of sir Patrick Dun's hospital" [209]). The rarefied principles of Aquinas fall heavily to earth and Stephen, who had venerated that "static" emotion in which the "mind is arrested and raised above desire and loathing," succumbs to the "kinetic" emotion that "urges us to possess, to go to something." "We are all animals," Stephen had confessed, "I also am an animal." "You are," agrees Lynch (205–6). Within the diary, accordingly, both young men metamorphose into greyhounds, and beauty, having been a hospital nurse, becomes a *heifer.* Please recall that during the earlier conversation Lynch admits to having eaten "pieces of dried cow-dung" (205); that Stephen poses the question, *"If a man hacking in fury at a block of wood . . . make there an image of a cow, is that image a work of art?"* (214);[18] and that when he defines *integritas* Lynch responds, "Bull's eye!" (212).

In each of these examples, as telling as the submerged references to a past scene is the rhetorical inflection that the new context provides. The exultation of the confession becomes the troubled dream, much as the romantic euphoria on the bay passes into an almost jaded sensualism, and the rather ponderous disquisition on art transforms into a sexual prowl. In looking for a way to characterize these changes, we might consider the second of the dreams that Stephen records on the morning of 25 March:

> Strange figures advance from a cave. They are not as tall as men. One does not seem to stand quite apart from another. Their faces are phosphorescent, with darker streaks. They peer at me and their eyes seem to ask me something. They do not speak. (250)

Once the general pattern has been recognized, this reference can be quickly identified. It points back to Stephen's horrific vision after the hell-fire sermon, when he returns to his room, terror-stricken, too shaken at first to pass through the door: "He waited still at the threshold as at the entrance to some dark cave. Faces were there; eyes: they waited and watched" (136). In another page these become "goatish creatures" "lightly bearded," lit by "marsh-light" (137); in the dream they are "not as tall as men," with "darker streaks" on their "phosphorescent" faces.

At present, more significant than this connection is a suggestion that might be drawn from it. It should be clear, first of all, that the "lecherous goatish fiends" with their "human faces," who move "hither and thither trailing their long tails behind them" (137–38), are *satyrs* who appear during Stephen's crisis to taunt him for his fall into sensuality. Their reappearance in his dream suggests a way to regard the series of reversals at the novel's conclusion. For in one of its aspects Stephen's diary follows the precedent of the Greek satyr play, which concluded a tetralogy by replacing tragic gravity with comedy and parody. Much like a satyr play, the diary recalls motifs that had been treated seriously and casts them in a comic light, tweaking the solemnity that precedes it. Through the set of concealed references that we have been considering, decisive moments in the main narrative are invoked— the vision of hell, the confession, the affirmation of art, the meditation on beauty—but the tone has thoroughly changed, with the result that events which Stephen had regarded with grave earnestness now appear within a deft parody, almost a burlesque. Without disturbing the thematic surface which dutifully records Stephen's emotions and aspirations, Joyce dexterously suggests competing modes of interpretation. In the first implication pursued in this essay, the diary enforced a principle of serial repetition that challenged Stephen's confident advance, but here the challenge has become both more fundamental and better disguised. The quietly shifting mode intimates that while Stephen strikes heroic poses, his language plays a comedy.

III

This diary, which had seemed a harmless fizzle, an elusive whimsy, or an ill-motivated contrivance, discloses itself as a precise instrument of many and ingenious purposes. Its methods will ultimately need to be weighed against other methods in the novel, but already it seems fair to say that the provocations of the diary, coming as they do at such a sensitive moment, have a special privilege and oblige us to take them into account in any interpretation of the whole.

To this point, the considerations offered here would seem to lend more weight to that already weighty body of opinion that regards *A Portrait of the Artist* as preeminently an ironic novel. Certainly, the submerged references to the past and the recasting of momentous incidents in a parodic mode make it

impossible to take Stephen's concluding pronouncements at their own valua-
tion He emits a tone of intrepid temerity, but other less heroic tones sound in
muffled counterpoint. He marches into the future, surrounded by jeering
echoes of the past, and when he makes his impetuous promise "to forge in the
smithy of my soul the uncreated conscience of my race" (253), one must suspect that his own conscience has already been forged. He has vowed to "fly by
those nets" of nationality, language and religion (203), but at least one of
those nets, the fine mesh of language, continues to trammel the artist who
would be free. And yet, before drawing an ironic conclusion from these disturbing facts, we ought to consider one last flourish of Joycean virtuosity.

A Portrait of the Artist concludes with the apostrophe of 27 April—"old
father, old artificer, stand me now and ever in good stead" (253)—and it is
common to say that Stephen is speaking here not of his biographical father
but of his mythical parent, the "hawklike man," "the fabulous artificer"
whose name is "a symbol of the artist" (169). Certainly, the mythical reference is pertinent. But it is worth recalling that Simon Dedalus makes his first
appearance precisely as an artificer who recounts the story of the "moocow"
and "baby tuckoo." The novel, that is, begins with the father as storyteller
and ends by invoking him as "old artificer."

The *second* person in the novel to tend Stephen is also the *second to last,* his
mother, whose tasks have only nominally changed. When young Stephen wet
the bed, "his mother put on the oilsheet" (7), and when an older Stephen prepares to leave Ireland, he describes her as "putting my new secondhand
clothes in order" (252). Between an oilsheet and new secondhand clothes
there is perhaps less to choose than an ambitious young artist would hope.

The preceding entry, 16 April, is a slightly revised version of one of
Joyce's early epiphanies which had also appeared in *Stephen Hero* and which
contains the following passage:

> The spell of arms and voices: the white arms of roads, their promise of close
> embraces and the black arms of tall ships that stand against the moon, their
> tale of distant nations. They are held out to say: We are alone. Come. And the
> voices say with them: We are your kinsmen. (252)

The original version of the epiphany had "people" where we now find "kinsmen," and that change, together with the placement, connects this *third to
last* passage with the *third* sequence in the prologue, in which Charles and
Dante, Stephen's "kinsmen," make their first appearance as the ones who clap
during the singing and dancing. In the diary this becomes the "spell of arms
and voices."

The next event in the prologue involves Stephen's early fantasy of marrying Eileen Vance, while the *previous* entry in the diary, 15 April, describes
the awkward final meeting with his current romantic avatar, E—— C——.
In the childhood incident, the idea of marrying Eileen, a Protestant, provokes

a threat of punishment. In Joyce's original epiphany the threat had been attributed to Mr. Vance, but in *A Portrait of the Artist* it is assigned to "Aunt" Dante, a decision that prepares for another cunning link between prologue and epilogue. For when Stephen feels "sorry and mean" over his treatment of E—— C—— he checks himself by suddenly invoking "the spiritual-heroic refrigerating apparatus, invented and patented in all countries by *Dante* Alighieri" (252, my emphasis).

Finally, the specific threat that concludes the prologue should be re-called: if Stephen does not apologize, "the eagles will come and pull out his eyes" (8). In the mysterious entry of 14 April Stephen records a description of an old man from the west of Ireland, as it has been reported to him by John Alphonsus Mulrennan. Mulrennan quotes the old man as saying, "Ah, there must be terrible queer creatures at the latter end of the world." "I fear him," writes Stephen of the old man, "It is with him I must struggle all through this night till day come, till he or I lie dead . . ." (252). In itself this response to a man he has never met appears thoroughly mysterious, but in light of the broader pattern, there is reason to believe—is there not?—that "the terrible queer creatures" revive a memory of those eagles bringing retribution, as does the old man himself, who in his "mountain cabin" (his airie?), with his "short pipe" (beak?), his "redrimmed horny eyes" and "his sinewy throat" seems more bird than man.

Allow me, then to register an implication that may already be evident. The novel begins with the sequence: father telling a story, mother putting on the oilsheet, Charles and Dante, the fantasy of marrying Eileen, Dante's threat, the eagles. It concludes with "terrible queer creatures," E—— C—— and Dante Alighieri, the "kinsmen," mother putting his clothes in order, old father, old artificer. With unfailing verbal dexterity Joyce concludes the novel by alluding to its beginning and, what is more, by inverting the initial order of events. In an elegantly disguised chiasmus, *A Portrait of the Artist* ends by reversing its opening.[19] It retraces its own steps and concludes where it began.

This last thrust not only wounds an aspiring artist; it constitutes a final assault upon the diary as a genre, and by extension upon time itself. On its surface the diary lays claim to an unambiguous temporal progression, a res-olute march into the future, duly measured and duly chronicled. It therefore encourages that sentimental view of the conclusion that regards Stephen as advancing steadily toward his new life. Within this view the distant past has ceased to matter; the artist ministers to the present in service of the future. Or, as Stephen himself puts it on 6 April, "The past is consumed in the pres-ent and the present is living only because it brings forth the future" (251). When Cranly had asked about his early life, Stephen had responded that he was not then "myself as I am now, as I had to become" (240), and he later wonders whether he "was ever a child" (251). He wilfully orients himself toward an unformed future, dismissing the importunity of the past: "Michael

Robartes remembers forgotten beauty and, when his arms wrap her round, he presses in his arms the loveliness which has long faded from the world. Not this. Not at all. I desire to press in my arms the loveliness which has not yet come into the world" (251).

The burden of this essay, of course, has been that the past is most important in this novel when it is least respected and that the diary, committed to the sentiments of the present as they prepare the future, is haunted with echoes of early life which recur with a mocking persistence. Indeed, as the most recent example shows, the past does not merely echo in the present; it threatens to govern the future. The submerged pattern of events suggests that Stephen's bright promise is no more than "new secondhand clothes."

At the end of the third chapter Stephen had watched as the "equation on the page of his scribbler began to spread out a widening tail" and then "began slowly to fold itself together again." He imagines the equation as "his own soul going forth to experience, unfolding itself sin by sin, spreading abroad the balefire of its burning stars and folding back upon itself, fading slowly, quenching its own lights and fires" (103). The phrase "going forth to experience" anticipates the climactic promise to "encounter for the millionth time the reality of experience," but the further notion of a soul "folding back upon itself" gives us another way to regard that promise. It provides a compelling image for the chiastic inversions of the novel's close and suggests the darkest of answers to our question, What is the shape of life? Moreover, it broadens the import of Joyce's allusions to Turgenev, for in terms of this conceit Stephen appears as just that "superfluous man" whose life folds back upon itself in a long retrogression. Just as he means to begin the future, the form suggests that he is receding into his past, that he is boldly advancing—toward his origins.

The individual artist who seeks "to discover the mode of life or of art whereby [his] spirit could express itself in unfettered freedom" (246) participates, in spite of himself, in a meticulously contrived form that silently contests this possibility. The novel, at the last, establishes a severe and unsettling disjunction between what Stephen means and what he says, between freedom and form.

The question of irony thus returns with a sharp force. If Stephen—who means to soar into the future—is last seen descending into the past, if the verbal echoes suggest that he is confined to the history he has disowned, and if the pattern of events intimates that what he takes to be progress may only be movement around a circle, then it is impossible to read the conclusion in the terms that Stephen himself offers. It would seem, on the contrary, that we must disregard the literal surface and, as in so many recent readings of the novel, assume an ironic standpoint putatively congruent with Joyce's own. Seen in such terms the diary would represent the severe conclusion of Joyce's spurning of his own protagonist, in which the arrangement of words and events opens a widening distance between what Stephen intends and what Joyce intends for him.

However, the provocation offered at the novel's conclusion is so great that it not only disturbs the literal surface; it stirs the ironic depths. In one of its implications, as I began by noting, the diary seems to herald a sequence of endless repetitions in which Stephen, always on the point of freedom and therefore never free, will ceaselessly reenact past events and reexperience past emotions. At the same time, it suggests a series of reversals in which incidents and emotions recur in debased form, the serious rendered comic, the grave made playful. Finally, the last paragraphs of the novel subtly intimate that Stephen will revert to his original condition and that what he takes as exile will be a return.

All of these possibilities, it is true, challenge a simple pattern of artistic maturity, but it is worth stressing that they constitute not one but many assaults. Much like sentimentality, irony has its variants, and before settling upon an ironic reading one must surely ask: which irony? As with the historical and mythological parallels that link Stephen to Parnell, Christ, Daedalus, Icarus, and James Joyce (among others), the several ironies do not coincide, and we must avoid assuming that all departures from the literal surface arrive at the same figural destination. Indeed, in an important sense, the multiple ironies restore the integrity of a literal reading, because they prevent the simplicity of a yea or nay.[20] Repetition and reversal certainly challenge the ideal of undisturbed personal development, but they also challenge one another. At the end of the novel, we confront at least four forms of the individual life: a pattern of *bildung* (Stephen will become the artist he has aspired to be); a pattern of repetition (he will remain where he has arrived); a pattern of reversal (he will rehearse serious events in a comic mode); and a pattern of regression (he will return to where he began). To those who would object that these diverse alternatives discourage judgment of Stephen's character, the question might be put: What judgment is more appropriate for youth than to connect its ambition to all its possible issues?[21]

In another context John Gross has bluntly formulated the question that has dominated interpretation of Stephen's character: "How exactly are we to take all this?"[22] But in a sense the critical locution is itself a source of the problem. The reader does not need to "take" Stephen—to wrench him from the dense web that surrounds him, to appropriate him to a single mode, to assimilate him to a controlling myth—but to *place* him, to situate him within a set of concurrent possibilities and to embed him in several modes. The persistent contention over the novel's irony threatens to obscure its workings. Joyce is less concerned to submit sentiment to the astringencies of irony than to conjoin all pertinent implications and to disclose the copresence of incongruous designs. Stronger than the attraction of irony is the allure of the pun, which depends not upon a collision but a union of meanings and which functions at every level of Joyce's work. Stephen's diary represents an elaborate narrative pun in which one sequence of events yields several lines of development; and Stephen himself exists as both romantic personality and modern *paronomasia.* He is more than his qualities; he is all those forms in which his life inheres, the myths which enclose him in the past which begot him, the prospects which await him. This is the heavy burden that Joycean character must bear; it must be all that it has been and all that it might become.

Notes

1. Exceptions include Zack R. Bowen, "Epiphanies, Stephen's Diary, and the Narrative Perspective of *A Portrait of the Artist as a Young Man,*" *James Joyce Quarterly* 16 (Summer 1979): 485–88; Susan Sniader Lanser, "Stephen's Diary: The Hero Unveiled," *James Joyce Quarterly* 16 (Summer 1979): 417–24; John Paul Riquelme, *Teller and Tale* (Baltimore: The Johns Hopkins Univ. Press, 1983).

2. Edward Garnett, quoted in Richard Ellmann, *James Joyce* (New York: Oxford Univ. Press, 1959), 417. Kenneth Grose, *James Joyce* (London: Evans Brothers, 1975), 39; Lanser, 418–19; Anthony Burgess, *Re Joyce* (New York: W. W. Norton, 1965), 68.

3. Robert Martin Adams, *Afterjoyce* (New York: Oxford Univ. Press, 1977), 21.

4. Marilyn French, "Joyce and Language," *James Joyce Quarterly* 19 (Spring 1982): 250; Lanser, 420.

5. Arthur Ponsonby, *English Diaries* (London: Methuen, 1923), 1.

6. Franz Kafka, *Diaries 1900–1913,* trans. Joseph Kresh, ed. Max Brod (New York: Schocken, 1965), 233; Fanny Burney, *The Diary and Letters,* vol. 2, rev. and ed. Sarah Chauncey Woolsey (Boston: Little, Brown, 1902), 172; James Boswell, "The Hypochondriack," no. 66 (March 1783), in *The Hypochondriack,* ed. Margery Bailey (Stanford Univ. Press, 1928), 266, 259.

7. James Joyce, *A Portrait of the Artist as a Young Man* (Harmondsworth: Penguin, 1976), 252. Subsequent references to this edition will be cited by page parenthetically within the text.

8. Hugh Kenner, *Dublin's Joyce* (Boston: Beacon Press, 1962), 132.

9. It is worth observing that the end toward which the *Bildungsroman* points need not appear within the fiction itself. It can exist as the implied *telos* that organizes the whole. Jerome Hamilton Buckley has offered the firmest argument for the pertinence of these conventions: "the *Portrait* is developed within the recognizable general framework of the Bildungsroman. It is an autobiographical novel of 'education,' tracing the growth of the hero from infancy to young manhood, describing his slowly decreased dependence on father and mother, his schooldays, his adolescent fantasies, his choice of a career, and his ultimate approach to his maturity or at least to his legal majority" (*Season of Youth* [Cambridge: Harvard Univ. Press, 1971], 230).

10. Stanislaus Joyce, *The Complete Dublin Diary of Stanislaus Joyce* (Ithaca: Cornell Univ. Press, 1971), 62. In his reminiscences written years later Stanislaus still had Turgenev's novella on his mind "The conclusion of the *Diary,* with the man's face drawn on the blank space at the foot of the last page, and the aimless scribbling by someone who had found and read the diary after the unfortunate Tchulkaturin's death, seemed to me a masterstroke in the expression of futility. Jim was interested; he said he would read it again" (Stanislaus Joyce, *My Brother's Keeper,* ed. Richard Ellmann [New York: Viking, 1958], 167–68). No doubt he did. Joyce was never one to defer to the masterstroke of a predecessor.

11. Letter to Stanislaus Joyce in *Letters of James Joyce,* vol. 2, ed. Richard Ellmann (New York, Viking, 1966), 111.

12. James Joyce, *Stephen Hero,* ed. Theodore Spencer, rev. ed. John J. Slocum and Herbert Cahoon (London: Jonathan Cape, 1969), 47. On Joyce's acquisition of Turgenev's works

see the list of books Joyce left behind in Trieste, in Richard Ellmann, *The Consciousness of Joyce* (London: Faber & Faber, 1977), 131.

13. Ivan Turgenev, *The Diary of a Superfluous Man,* trans. Constance Garnett (London: William Heinemann, 1906), 95, 36. For the similarity of the romantic confrontations compare, for instance, the two disruptive physical gestures. Tchulkaturin: "suddenly, without awaiting her reply, I gave my features an extraordinarily cheerful and free-and-easy expression, with a set grin, passed my hand above my head in the the direction of the ceiling . . . Liza failed absolutely to understand me; she looked in my face with amazement, gave a hasty smile, as though she wanted to get rid of me as quickly as possible." Stephen: "In the midst of it unluckily I made a sudden gesture of a revolutionary nature. I must have looked like a fellow throwing a handful of peas into the air . . . She shook hands a moment after and, in going away, said she hoped I would do what I said" (252).

14. Bowen, 487.

15. In the original version of the epiphany Joyce wrote "arise" rather than "ascend" (*The Workshop of Dedalus,* collected and edited by Robert Scholes and Richard M. Kain [Evanston: Northwestern Univ. Press, 1963], 29). It should become clear as we proceed that in drawing on his store of epiphanies Joyce adjusted them to the text (and the text to them) in order to secure connections between the first-person diary and the third-person narrative.

16. In "Circe," which stands to *Ulysses* much as the diary stands to *A Portrait of the Artist,* and which frequently recalls the earlier novel even as it recalls its own beginning, the English "hoop" and the Frenchified "houp-la" meet in Lynch's "Hoopla" (James Joyce, *Ulysses* [New York: Random House, 1961], 557).

17. Kenner, *Dublin's Joyce,* 114.

18. I have James Soderholm to thank for calling my attention to this sculptor hacking in fury.

19. Hans Walter Gabler has astutely identified another chiastic relation between the novel's opening and its close: "In its four-part structure, the fifth chapter of *A Portrait of the Artist* is the exact symmetrical counterpart of the first. The childhood overture and the two Clongowes episodes, separated by the Christmas dinner scene, are the mirror image of the two movements of Stephens's wanderings through Dublin, separated by the villanelle episode, and the diary finale. In both chapters, bibliographical and textual evidence reveals that the final organization of their parts was established by intercalation of a contrasting episode into a homogenous stretch of narrative" ("The Seven Lost Years of *A Portrait of the Artist as a Young Man,*" in *Approaches to Joyce's Portrait,* ed. Thomas F. Staley and Bernard Benstock [Univ. of Pittsburgh Press, 1976], 50).

20. Hugh Kenner has justly observed that "the sharpest exegetical instrument we can bring to the work of Joyce is Aristotle's great conception of potency and act . . . [In] the mind of Joyce there hung a radiant field of multiple possibilities" ("The Cubist Portrait," in *Approaches to Joyce's Portrait,* ed. Thomas F. Staley and Bernard Benstock [Univ. of Pittsburgh Press, 1976], 179).

21. Wayne Booth has posed the problem of judgment forcefully in *The Rhetoric of Fiction* (Chicago: The Univ. of Chicago Press, 1961), 323–26.

22. John Gross, *James Joyce* (New York: The Viking Press, 1970), 34.

The Villanelle Perplex: Reading Joyce

ROBERT ADAMS DAY

No humanist academic is astonished, on consulting an up-to-date bibliography, to discover how much has been published on such a major lyric as Marvell's "To His Coy Mistress," for example; but the non-specialist or even the Joycean who contemplates the amount of criticism and comment that has been generated by a certain nineteen-line poem, only ten lines of which are not repeated, and which, rather than being by a canonical author, is only by a character in a novel—an artifact within an artifact—is apt to be slightly shaken. We have in Stephen Dedalus' villanelle what we like to call a crux. Our fundamental attitudes toward cruxes are two and depend ultimately on our innate or pre-logical attitudes toward validity in interpretation and hermeneutic puzzles: we either happily reflect that here is something we can keep on arguing about forever, or we feel a deep if vague conviction that the crux can be solved (also forever) if someone will only use the right method. Much can be said on both sides, and the following investigation will begin with a proposal that should gratify adherents of both: it is time for yet another consideration of Stephen's villanelle.

Critical opinion on this particular Joycean crux has tended to coalesce around two notable exchanges of views: the first, in which Hugh Kenner, Wayne Booth, and Robert Scholes marked out the area of debate, and the second, in the mid-seventies, centering on articles in the *James Joyce Quarterly*. But more recently the villanelle has been ably examined in several important books dealing with larger aspects of Joyce's work; new facts have been brought to light; and the Joyce Conference at Provincetown in 1980 devoted a panel to considering at least thirteen ways of looking at a villanelle.[1]

A report on the state of the art is surely justified, but stock-taking becomes imperative if one is persuaded that a most important source of opinion on the villanelle has yet to be heard from—James Joyce. Most of those who have seriously considered *A Portrait* 217–24 in print seem to have been so intimidated by thunderings from Sinai on the biographical, intentional, and affective fallacies, so nervously inclined to fear that the New Criticism is old hat, and lately so timorous about maintaining that there really is such a

This essay was originally published in the *James Joyce Quarterly,* Vol. 25.1 (Fall 1987), 69–85, and is reprinted with permission.

thing as a stable text, that, however subtle and sinuous their chains of argument, they have shied away from the text itself. They have also tended to forget that Joyce, however great his genius, was a human author with a human audience in mind, and that though he shaped *A Portrait* with consummate care for a highly intelligent and observant reader with ideally cultivated taste, he could hardly have envisaged at the same time readers who would professionally employ the critical microscope, or telescope, or both at once, rather than using their own sharp eyes. Joyce's deliberate insertion of puzzles for the professors came later, with *Ulysses*.

I do not maintain that villanelle criticism has invariably been engrossed in subtleties only, or that no one has carefully read Joyce's text, but theoretical considerations and a dislike of unfashionable or old-fashioned methods have apparently functioned unduly as critical blinders. I take the three quotations that follow as illustrative of what I mean and as points of departure:

John Paul Riquelme in a stimulating book says of the villanelle, "The important value is not in the poem as something signified, as part of the narrative, but in the poem's place as a signifier, as part of the style of narration"[2] Surely to say this is no more than to make the familiar point that the reader is not to apprehend the poem as he or she might if it were in an anthology of lyric verse, but rather as if it were a symbolic goldfinch held by the infant Jesus in another kind of portrait in a different medium; or that bits of a modernist novel comment on the other bits; or, specifically, that the function of the poem is to show that Stephen is the kind of person who wrote this kind of poem at that point in his artistic development. The point at issue about Riquelme's observation is not that it is wrong, but that he felt the necessity of making it.[3]

Secondly (and thirdly), Bernard Benstock, referring to Hugh Kenner's bombshell in villanelle criticism, said in 1976:

> Anyone who can read the opening paragraph of the villanelle section and fail to realize that Stephen has awakened before dawn because of a nocturnal emission might just as well skip the entire section and go on to the next. Kenner did not present his "wet dream" observation as a revelation but a statement of the obvious. How much dewy wetness over limbs does a reader need to see the source of the inspiration?

and in the same essay:

> An evaluation of the poetic merits of the villanelle would probably do little to augment comprehension of *A Portrait of the Artist,* even if it could tell us something about Stephen's level of attainment as an artist. Whether it is intrinsically a good poem depends upon one's predilection for the kind of verbiage employed, and it would take a die-hard New Critic to examine the poem out of context. Actually, the villanelle has no intrinsic existence because it has no direct creator; it is an actual villanelle written by a fictional poet.[4]

The discussion that follows will try to show that both of these statements are wrong—the first as a reading and the second as a dictum on appropriate methods of reading. I will take as my motto the following decidedly old-fashioned credo:

> We must strive to understand clearly the connection between the artist's inner mental process and the realization of his ideas in his work. Unless we can show this mental process, demonstrate it, so to speak, *ad oculos,* then all insight into art remains obscure and it is left to each individual to interpret the process this way or that according to the refinement of his senses. Finding that most theories of Art exhibit a useless quantity of reasoning and a dearth of practical experience, I have attempted to avoid this in my work by giving prominence, not to theoretical considerations, but to the actual process of creating a work of art.[5]

And in method I will be eclectic or post-deconstructionist, using biographical information, the intentional fallacy, the affective fallacy, and New Criticism, if by this last term we mean the careful examination of what is on the page, not of what might be.

To begin with facts: James Joyce himself wrote the villanelle, around 1900. We may assume that the late adolescent Joyce wrote it mainly with the idea of writing as good a poem as he could, not with the intention of embedding it in a novel as "the product of Stephen's genius."[6] Not surprisingly, considering its writer's age, its form, tone, and diction echo the English (and perhaps French) Decadents rather than striking out in new directions, as he would begin to do very soon. Nevertheless he evidently thought well of the verses for some time after they were composed since we have Stanislaus' word that the villanelle and a translation of Verlaine's "Les Sanglots longs" were the only early poems that he preserved ([Ellmann, *James Joyce,* 1983], 76n). We now know that the episode of the poem's composition was the very last segment of *A Portrait* to be included, inserted in 1914 after the remainder of the manuscript was in fair copy, and indeed that it may not have been written until about that time. Moreover, it may be based on material which, though found in the "Trieste Notebook," was written during Joyce's Dublin visit of 1909, when he was combining inspiration with onanism in his famous erotic letters to his love-goddess Nora.[7] Lastly, "bibliographical and textual evidence reveals that the final organization of [the parts of Chapters I and V] was established by the intercalation of a contrasting episode into a homogeneous narrative," so that the villanelle scene is the climactic and central section of V, echoing the structure of I with its Christmas dinner scene.[8]

Further facts of a different nature have been recently brought to bear on the episode. About 1912, when he was beginning his radical revisions of the manuscript, Joyce bought in Trieste a facsimile of the heavily adorned pre-Raphaelite edition of Dante's *Vita Nuova* with decorations by Dante Gabriel Rossetti; and Mary Reynolds has convincingly demonstrated, with abundant

illustrations and persuasively close parallel passages, that in the prose seg-
ments of the villanelle section Joyce was consciously alluding to the Dantean
poet figure of the *Vita Nuova* in the awakening Stephen with very close
echoes, in his half-dreaming images, of Dante's description of his persona's
heavenly inspiration to write of Beatrice. But Joyce was also closely echoing a
chapter from D'Annunzio's novel *The Child of Pleasure* in which the hero
writes a cycle of sonnets, and we see examples of them, though both poems
and poet are vastly altered in Joyce. Thus the "Gabriel" who enters the virgin's chamber (*P* 217) is Dante Gabriel Rossetti and Gabriele D'Annunzio as
well as "the seraph."[9] Unless we belong to that school of criticism which
holds that the nature of acknowledged source material has nothing to do with
the texture of the finished work, we cannot neglect these Dantes and Gabriels
in accounting for the villanelle episode and trying to find out what it means.

So much for the facts of the scene's composition, with some not very far-
fetched conjectures on their significance; these we shall revert to from time to
time. We must now proceed to some practical but general considerations.
Much modern fiction is autobiographical; many novels therefore deal with
the lives of artists, but few directly show the artist practicing his art, and
fewer give samples of it. The reason is obvious: you, the author, must yourself
create or describe your hero's poem or sonata or painting, and your aesthetic
judgment of your/his work must be impeccable. The artifact must create
upon the audience precisely the effect that you want, or you will look like a
fool. (Thus in the film *The Light that Failed* the viewer is tactfully given only
the most fleeting glimpses of Dick Heldar's "masterpiece," not really enough
to form a judgment, whereas Kipling could say at length in the purely verbal
medium of the novel that the painting was a masterpiece and reasonably
expect full credence.) The problem is easier if you wish to show, say, that the
hero considers a mediocre poem of his to be superb; but even in this case the
author must be sure that an adequately wide segment of his audience will
agree that the poem is really mediocre, or the desired effect will be spoiled.
Another sort of solution to such a dilemma is found in Nabokov's *Pale Fire*
where we are treated to John Shade's entire poem of that title. But since
Nabokov carefully shows us that his narrator Kinbote is an obsessed pedant
and in some degree mad to boot, we are justified in concluding that his aesthetic criteria are as shaky as the rest of his mental apparatus and are thus left
free to judge the poem in any way we like. (The same kind of problem arises
in operas in which the plot requires a character to sing ineptly or off key, and
so on.)[10]

How did Joyce tackle this artistic problem? Without pretending to read
the mind of a deceased genius we can nevertheless draw certain firm conclusions. Whatever his opinion of his villanelle may have been when he wrote it,
we can say on the basis of *Dubliners* and the transformation of *Stephen Hero*
into *A Portrait* that by mid-1914 he was at the height of his critical and creative powers, or close to it; therefore that he was fully conscious of the diffi-

culties outlined above, and that he must have dealt with them to his own satisfaction. In such an artistic situation the writer has two choices: he can write the artifact for his hero then and there, hoping that he will be able to strike just the qualities of content and tone that he wants, or he can use what we call an *objet trouvé,* as in collage, if he can find one that will create precisely the desired effect at a particular place in the narrative. Joyce in 1914 elected to use a poem which another Joyce had written years before with another end in view, and to imbed it in a scene of composition using materials probably written by yet another Joyce only a few years earlier and for a very different purpose. Unless we despise the abilities of the pre-*Ulysses* Joyce, we must admit that he had made the right choice, indeed an admirable one, and that *A Portrait* 217–24, in that it transcribes a poem written by the Joyce of 1900 as being written by a youth whose emotions are equivalent to those of the jealous and agonized young lover and father of 1909 is, in many passages at least, a self-portrait, but of the *young* man as the writer of thirty-two judged him to have been ("I haven't let this young man off very lightly, have I?").[11]

At this point we should be satisfied that Joyce had done all he could and was eminently right; but reader response theory slyly whispers that we can never be sure that what we feel was what Joyce wanted us to feel, or that we all feel or should feel the same thing. Again, however, Joyce may be summoned up to testify that if we have not had the correct response it is our fault for being inattentive—this time to what the artist says by his disposition of materials, large and small. (By "large" I intend to refer to scenes or episodes and to their general content, style, and tone; by "small" to individual words and phrases, and to both as they are placed realties to one another.)

We have seen that *A Portrait* 217–24 was a last-minute insertion and must therefore see the importance of comparing Chapter V without the episode to the same chapter with it. The old Chapter V might be described as follows: a series of short takes, in which Stephen reacts characteristically to sights, sounds, and memories, converses with the dean of studies, attends a lecture, talks with various acquaintances and at greater length with his more intimate friends Lynch and Cranly, concluding with a group of diary entries in which the effect is ultimately the same: Stephen's reactions to and comments upon his daily life, his developing personality as man, critic, and artist, and his erotic feelings about the vague "she" into whom the Emma Clery of *Stephen Hero* has been attenuated. The result is certainly very different from and far more innovative than the go-ahead plot of *Stephen Hero;* but one might wonder whether Joyce's intention in revising had amounted to anything more than the conversion of his material into a modernist—or pointillist—but static rendering of vignettes: "Here are the significant bits of data about Stephen that I choose to give you; make what you like of them." Whether the bits are going anywhere is a permanently ambiguous question; the effect is cinematic, but does it add up to more than "this *is* how Stephen is"? The insertion of the villanelle episode, located where it is and not elsewhere, instantly resolves the apparent dissonance. It creates a chiastic structure—antithetical subjects in identical order—and by its placement it underlines and thus brings out an existing pattern that had hardly been visible before.

The new Chapter V is structured thus: first the data of external experience (sights, sounds, smells, emotions, talk) are perceived, but always through the filter of Stephen's word-hoard. They are disgustedly contrasted with beautiful or vivid words or phrases treasured in memory, transformed into verbal art, seen as raw material; in short, Stephen is subordinating life to art. A climax arrives with the elaborate presentation to Lynch of Stephen's theory of art, followed by a short coda, the sight of "her." The stream of vignettes is then punctuated by the villanelle episode. After it the order of scenes is partly reversed: "she" appears early rather than late in the string of vignettes, but the subject matter too is reversed. Now it seems to be life (or at least the artist's life) rather than art; the living present seeks to master Stephen, but in renouncing the peace petition, mother love, and other lures Stephen struggles to release himself from the trammels of life, and at last a second climax is reached with the declaration to Cranly of his credo and his plans for living as an artist. The diary entries follow and end the book.

The insertion of the villanelle scene clarifies other structural details, less apparent but no less important. In addition to mechanically underscoring the contrasting art-life split in the presentation of Stephen's works and days, the insertion sections time. The art-section vignettes are arranged in a steady and close temporal succession on a certain day, but the writing of the villanelle, though at dawn, is deliberately unmarked by date or place.[12] Another time-break is followed by the connected episodes of the life-section; another break, and the diary entries appear without introduction. And if we doubt that time-breaks, jumps, or shifts are intended, Joyce emphasizes them in each case with asterisks (P 216, 224, 247). Other chiastic devices structure the chapter. Stephen, after all, is not an aspiring orator, but he talks, with increasing length and intensity, then is seen writing; talks, again with climactic arrangement, then writes (or has written). The oral-written, oral-written alternation is surely no accident, though if it had not been for the villanelle episode and its placement we might be forgiven for wondering whether Joyce, like many lesser artists, in despair of finding a fitting end to his modernist non-story, had not cut the Gordian knot by simply stopping short and appending a sizable chunk of radically different material as a sort of outsize period.[13] Lastly (a point to be considered later) our two samples of Stephen's writing are spontaneous. He changes no word in the villanelle; and if he had been so finicky as to alter the wording of his diary effusions, we are not allowed to see him do it. One further point, now passing from evidence to deduction: are we not expected to infer a theory-practice, cause-effect, or process-product relationship—that the speeches on art produce the villanelle and those on life the diary entries? (So far as we know, Stephen has not kept a

diary before.) If we are to suppose such an implied relationship, its own further implications are highly significant, as we shall see.

Joyce has spoken to us, and very clearly, by elucidating the final structure of Chapter V, but what did he mean to mean? And especially, what did
he mean by the villanelle episode? Turning to a careful examination of that
passage in and of itself before drawing back for a final estimate of its meaning
for the novel, I propose to invoke a critical approach that should offend few
readers, Hugh Kenner's celebrated "Uncle Charles Principle."[14] This, simply
put, maintains that Joyce, who could make words do anything he wanted and
therefore had no style whatever as such, caused the style of narration to
swerve briefly, like a Lucretian *clinamen* or Einsteinian bending of light by a
massive body, to accommodate itself to the mind of whoever was being
described, or rather, to pursue the narration in a style which the character
might use. So Stephen's Uncle Charles shabby-genteelly and with stilted elegance "repaired" to the outhouse and "creased and brushed scrupulously his
back hair" (*P* 60) because that is how he himself might have described those
actions. To be sure, the Uncle Charles effect requires a reader whose literary
sensitivity and taste are sufficiently developed to enable him or her instantly
and effortlessly to take the tone of the passage, almost subliminally, and register its effect while reading for the narrative content; but if any author has a
right to expect such readers, Joyce does.

With our literary palates cleared by a dish of asterisks, like the sherbet
course at old-fashioned banquets, of the taste of Stephen's musings on the
library steps, we may now turn to the villanelle episode.

> Towards dawn he awoke. O what sweet music! His soul was all dewy wet. Over
> his limbs in sleep pale cool waves of light had passed. He lay still, as if his soul
> lay amid cool water, conscious of fine sweet music. His mind was waking
> slowly to a tremulous morning knowledge, a morning inspiration. A spirit
> filled him, pure as the purest water, sweet as dew, moving as music. But how
> faintly it was inbreathed, how passionlessly, as if the seraphim themselves were
> breathing upon him! His soul was waking slowly, fearing to awake wholly. It
> was that windless hour of dawn when madness wakes and strange plants open
> to the light and the moth flies forth silently. (*P* 217)

These sentences, Kenner and Benstock have assured us, when decoded mean
"wet dream"; but let us scrutinize them. After the first neutral sentence we
have "O what sweet music! His soul was all dewy wet." The girlishly insipid
"O," "sweet," and the w-alliteration and floppy falling intonation of "dewy
wet" are the closest approach to the "namby-pamby jammy marmalady
drawersy" style of "Nausicaa" (*Letters I* 135) that we can find in *A Portrait*.
And if Stephen has had a wet dream, his preconscious mind or his "spiritual-
heroic refrigerating apparatus" (*P* 252) has gone to remarkable lengths to
conceal that phenomenon, with "pale," "cool," "light," "soul," "spirit,"
"pure," "dew," and "passionlessly" reinforcing one another. His limbs have

been washed (*lavabis me, Domine, et mundabor*) in "pale cool waves of light"; the dewy wetness that Benstock berates us for not seeing is not visible because it is some distance away, on his soul. If Mary Reynolds is right (and she has argued very persuasively), it is the ultimately erotic but highly spiritualized poet of Dante's *Vita Nuova* who in Stephen's associated images is being purified with dew, or perhaps even the Dante of *Purgatorio* I, who at dawn has his face washed with dew by Virgil to clarify his sight, cleanse his visage of the tear stains of Hell, and prepare him for God-bound pilgrimage.[15] But in any case, in these first sentences the emphasis is all, and perhaps too reiteratively, on purity, clarity, passionlessness, the spiritual. The excessive harping on lack of passion is essential if the prose of the episode is arranged in an ironical order of climax, progressing unfalteringly downward in tone and atmosphere from a heavenly Beatrice to pornography and masturbation. But the final sentences of the paragraph, with their sappy homoioteleuton of "waking slowly . . . awake wholly" and their sick stage props of madness, plants, and moth are evidence of another voice; the effete preciousness of Walter Pater is ventriloquizing through Stephen, or perhaps it is D'Annunzian tutti-frutti; at any rate, it is the Uncle Charles Principle in action.[16]

The overripe prose continues in the next paragraph, with the point of light that is the Dantean God, an echo of the rose light of the wading girl episode (*P* 172), and the Annunciation. (This last is a favorite Joycean image for artistic inspiration of a certain kind, and it is repeated three times in *Ulysses* and at least six times in *Finnegans Wake*.) But in the slightly incoherent syntax of the prose ("her strange wilful heart, strange that no man had known or would know"—*P* 217) of Stephen's stream of thought, the Virgin in whom the Word was made flesh has evidently become the demon-temptress Lilith, favorite of the Pre-Raphaelites and of Swinburne because she has existed "before the beginning of the world" (*P* 217) and the seraphim are falling from heaven because of her. It is at this point that Stephen's spirituality begins to go awry. A Jesuit-trained youth knows very well that the Virgin is the second Eve; but the second Lilith she is not, though the temptress may have been incarnate in descendants of the first Eve, as when the sons of God lay with the daughters of men (Genesis 6:4). Now the first tercet materializes, and Stephen feels "the rhythmic movement of a villanelle pass through [his lips]" (*P* 217–18) as the rays from the heart of the temptress produce, by rhyming association, a series of possible nouns—raise, blaze, praise.

This blunt statement by the narrator demands analysis. Dryden said that the requirement of finding a rhyme in making heroic couplets had often helped him to a thought; but Stephen is a late romantic, not a neoclassicist. Too many formal requirements at once are apt to be a straitjacket on poetic thought (especially for embryonic poets, and except for such technical prodigies as Auden), and a villanelle requires that the first and third lines of the first tercet must rhyme, and must also make perfect sense, three times each and in different contexts, throughout the rest of the poem; in addition, only one other rhyme is permitted. Moreover, though Stephen is not quite so arrogant as to say to himself, "I think I'll write a villanelle this morning," he virtually says so, and this fact shows that he is thinking in clichés, for the villanelle, though an ancient and beautiful French form, had had a great vogue among the precious poetasters of the naughty nineties in England, and by the time *A Portrait* appeared had already become as wearily conventional and thoroughly exhausted as the Petrarchan sonnet had become by the death of Queen Elizabeth.

Another tercet, and then smoke begins to arise in Stephen's mental picture, becoming more precisely conceived as incense. Stephen may be thinking of Milton's dawn scene in *Paradise Lost,* Adam and Eve yet uncorrupted, the whole earth breathing incense up to God (IX. 192–97), but the earth as a ball becomes an ellipsoidal ball, reminding the alert reader of Gilbert and Sullivan, the physics lecture, and balls as testicles (*P* 192). The temptress' lures are becoming sexier by the minute, but at this point the poem gets stuck, and Stephen writes what there is of it on a cigarette packet. Paralleling his mood, the prose flattens out as well, with only an occasional rhetorical swelling— "Fearing to lose all" (*P* 218), "the untenanted sideboard," "to her who leaned beside the mantelpiece," "her hand . . . a soft merchandise" (*P* 219), " a lithe web of sophistry" (*P* 220)—mirroring the occasional pomposity of Stephen's self-image as he recalls scenes with "her." But presently, as his own ego begins to overshadow "her," the rhetoric thickens; and with himself as priest of art the image of "eucharist" (*P* 221), rather grotesquely metamorphosed from a Jacob's biscuit, swings Stephen back from sex to religiosity, and two more tercets emerge.

Though the villanelle is unfinished (and will not receive the smallest revision), Stephen seems to be satisfied with his efforts; repeating its line turns his mind to "quiet indulgence" (*P* 221—surely an authorial nudge to the reader), and he begins to reflect on the sordidness of his surroundings and by implication on his own refinement and superiority. He has already copied the first verses "wearily," and now the narrator asserts, too loudly, "Weary! Weary! He too was weary of ardent ways" (*P* 222). "Weary" is a favorite adjective of the Decadents who were fond of posing as delicate souls, eternally weary of the sordid world around them; but a young man of eighteen or so who has just enjoyed a good night's sleep is not weary; and if he thinks he is, it is a case of life trying to imitate art without much success, for the word has come from the poem, not from his own feelings ("He too was weary," he insists).[17] But he cannot be conscious of this posturing for he has all along been thinking of the poem not as art but as a possible offering to "her," a verbal box of chocolates. He pictures the scene if he should send her the poem: the precious thing will be violated by profane hands. The narrator's rhetoric has become overblown again, to the point where the inattentive reader may overlook the fact that Stephen's Beatrice, with "the strange humiliation of her nature," and the "dark shame of womanhood" (*P* 222–23), has become all too womanly; she has been menstruating.[18] Perhaps fired by a picture of the locus of menstruation, Stephen reflects in lofty language about a spiritual communion, with the girl "conscious of his homage. . . . While his soul had passed from ecstasy to languor" (*P* 223); does one go too far to translate this into plain English and suspect that Stephen may be wondering if "she," presumably also in bed at this hour, has also wakened in the dawn and is thinking erotically of him as he is of her? If so, remote-control sex is possible. With lust conquering anger, Stephen imagines that her "nakedness yielded to him, radiant, warm, odorous and lavishlimbed . . . enfolded him like water with a liquid life: and . . . like waters circumfluent in space the liquid letters of speech, symbols of the element of mystery, flowed forth over his brain" (*P* 223). We have here as clear a description of self-induced orgasm and liquids pouring forth as Stephen's fancy language and the 1914 obscenity laws will permit; he is now violating his own precious thing with profane hands.[19] (If the reader is willing to admit this supposition, another argument against the "wet dream" interpretation suggests itself. While a youth of Stephen's age is perfectly capable of having two orgasms in fairly quick succession, the satiety induced by a nocturnal emission makes a second one, or even the highly charged erotic imagery of the end of the passage, less likely.) And we should remember that the letters to Nora of 1909, which seem to have been involved in the imagery of the prose sections of this passage, abound in references to masturbation while writing or reading the words of love—again, remote-control sex ([*Selected Letters of James Joyce,* ed. Ellmann], 184–86, 190–91). Further, the first member of the sequence wet dream-pure spirituality-borrowed literary refinement-steadily increasing but honest self-absorption-masturbation spoils the climactic order of Joyce's carefully modulated prose style and counters the whole atmospheric progression of the episode.

Finally, as the completion of Stephen's erotic reverie, after the flowing forth of liquids, the villanelle stands isolated in its complete form, without further comment.

Before considering the implications of the work as a whole of this scene of onanistic composition, we must introduce a note of contrast from another scene. Benstock maintains that it would take "a die-hard New Critic" to examine the poem out of context, but perhaps Joyce says otherwise: that we should examine it out of context in order to examine it adequately *in* context. If Joyce did not intend the villanelle to stand out like a sore artifact, why repeat it when we have most of it already? Why locate it (in its entirety, rather than merely giving the missing lines) at the very end of the episode, with no comment or narration to follow and distract our attention, and with the poem's isolation further emphasized by asterisks, so that the beginning of the next scene cannot be rushed into by the reader's eye? Inattention to the quality of the verse fragments embedded in Stephen's reverie is not only pardonable but in order; Joyce's placement of them says so. But his placement of the completed poem should be trusted equally. To echo Northrop Frye's useful distinction, the author's emphasis has turned from the process of composition to its product.

Product of what? I suggested earlier that we are entitled to ask whether Joyce did not intend to evoke a theory-practice, cause-effect relationship between Stephen's utterances on art and his writing, between his credo on life and his diary reflections. To the extent that *A Portrait* is a self-portrait it reflects the young Joyce; and the pre-exilic Joyce was a person who had attracted some notice in Dublin with his critical work (the essays on Ibsen, the reviews), but except for a few unremarkable lyric poems and a deceptively ordinary short story or two, he had done nothing as an artist. The question of the villanelle's significance and aesthetic merit, if we take it in connection with Stephen's literary theory or criticism, can be restated as the question of whether the early Joyce, long on theory, short on practice, has been accurately but artistically portrayed or has been artistically transformed.

The lecture to Lynch on true art that constitutes Stephen's notes toward a supreme fiction is a remarkable (and a remarkably mature) pronouncement for any critic, old or young. He claims to base his theory firmly on Aquinas, and thus on Aristotle, hardly feeble supports for a theory; and though commentators have argued at great length about what it means, none have brushed it aside. It contains three great pronouncements: 1) supreme or classic art is static, arousing neither desire nor aversion but merely a wish to contemplate; inferior art tends toward the pornographic or the didactic; 2) three things are required for beauty: *integritas, consonantia, claritas,* or wholeness, harmony, and radiance. The beautiful thing must be separated from everything else; all its parts must belong together; we must be able to apprehend its essence in a single instant, a single image; 3) the personality of the artist must be refined or purified out of the work of art. It must stand by itself, independent of its creator.

This is a very ambitious and exigent program for art and the artist. It requires the very highest of standards, and the mind that could form such ideals is clearly a superior mind and much to be admired. We must suppose that Stephen has spent long hours in developing these thoughts, and that he has partially memorized them. They are a finished product, a discourse on aesthetics, and Joyce allows Stephen to speak them gracefully, eloquently, clearly, with very few interruptions, only enough to remind us that we are supposed to be listening to a latter-day Platonic dialogue—two real young men talking seriously in a real place. More important, Stephen does not allow these distractions to break the train of his thought, interrupt the flow of his eloquence, or damage the logic of his presentation. To the extent that criticism can be an art, Stephen has followed his own requirements in making and presenting a whole, harmonious, radiant piece of critical theory.

This is presently followed by the scene in which Stephen composes the villanelle, and as before we have the work in pieces, with interruptions. But there are two important differences. At the end of the episode we have the work again in its final form, as though inviting us to judge it; and we have been present as witnesses at the process of its making, whereas the critical essay had been finished before we were allowed to hear it. If the criticism may comment on the poem, and vice versa, one is tempted to echo Scripture and say, "Out of thine own mouth have I condemned thee" (Luke 19:22), for it would seem that Stephen the youthful poet systematically violates every rule and requirement of Stephen the precocious critic.

When, having followed the villanelle through its composition as Joyce has obliged us to do, we judge it by its author's three criteria, we can be left in no doubt. Far from Stephen's personality having been refined out of the poem, that personality has obliterated any consideration of the poem as art (to say nothing of polishing and improvement) in favor of contemplating images of its own inspiration, most of which do not get into the poem; then by contemplating the poet's own refinement and his sordid surroundings; then by picturing the poem's reception by crass worldlings; and lastly by a sexual fantasy about the real girl, rather than the idealized image of her which had started the whole process. Whatever the villanelle, with its progression from seraphim to lavish limb, might do for the detached reader, we have seen it veering wildly between the sacred and the sexy; and if Stephen's previous rejection of religion has been genuine the poem's religious elements have become merely didactic and therefore repellent to him, while static contemplation has been replaced by the word acting on the flesh in a very literal sense.[20]

As to wholeness, harmony, and radiance, a post-deconstructionist old New Critic might venture a summary opinion. The poem as a whole seems to be addressed to a Rossettian-Swinburnian-Wildean temptress-figure, eternal (since she has managed to tempt the seraphim, once fallen, or to have caused their fall), who is being asked, as a rhetorical question, if she has not had enough of ruining men; she is besought to end her seductive sales talk (or else to cease reminiscing of her conquests; line 3 is ambiguous). "You have had your will of him": this phrase is a cliché, but it is usually found in Victorian descriptions of what rakes have done to innocent girls; the sexual reversal conjures up Swinburne's Lady With the Whip. Sacrifices are being offered all over the globe to the Belle Dame Sans Merci; thus she is a goddess. The "broken cries" (presumably of broken victims) and "mournful lays" (presumably with nothing in the poet's mind except a rhyme, since "lay" had long been archaic) suddenly take on a Christian tinge with "eucharistic hymn," inevitably suggesting thanksgiving or the Host to Stephen or his audience; but if the Christian veneer is a regrettable accident, are the victims thanking the goddess for tempting them? A similar problem arises with the next tercet: if the "chalice" is a pagan version of the Christian chalice all is well enough, but a Christian priest who raises a "chalice flowing to the brim" is likely to spill the blood of Christ on the altar or floor and commit sacrilege (one thinks of the lucky chance that the chalice broken by the priest in "The

Sisters" was empty). And is the goddess being asked to be satisfied with homage or to withdraw (*retro me, Satana*) from a Christian ceremony? Finally the goddess, to whom flames, smoke, praise, and chalices have been rising, makes a sudden stoop to conquer, since she is able to tempt with "lavish limb" (corpulent or wantonly disposed?). In short, however melodious the sounds may be, and however vivid the individual images, the villanelle, from the point of view of a seeker after wholeness, harmony, and radiance, is a hodgepodge of cliché and a farrago of nonsense.

This analysis is perhaps cruel, but Stephen ought to approve of it even if he had not just enunciated his rigorous program for true art, for he too has been something of a New Critic, requiring consistency of imagery on the literal level. In *Stephen Hero*, having been shown, under the seal of secrecy, some verses by one of his teachers,

> Art thou real, my Ideal?
> Wilt thou ever come to me
> In the soft and gentle twilight
> With your baby on your knee?
> (*SH* 83)

he reacts silently but with vigor:

> the [combined] effect of this apparition on Stephen was a long staining blush of anger. The tawdry lines, the futile change of number, the ludicrous waddling approach of Hughes's "Ideal" weighed down by an inexplicable infant combined to cause him a sharp agony in the sensitive region. Again he handed back the verse without saying a word of praise or of blame but he decided that attendance in Mr. Hughes's class was no longer possible for him. (*SH* 83).

The single trait most characteristic of adolescence is its funny yet touching alternation between the mature and the childish, as with a boy whose voice is changing; we are tempted to laugh, yet we sympathize. It is just this trait that Joyce has dramatized with the villanelle scene; and an analysis of what Joyce has set before us as art enables us to solve any critical problem that the poem poses. Lest we miss the point, he has shown us not only the text, but the ideas, memories, and associations that have made it what it is and not otherwise: a highly imperfect work of art, alternately didactic and pornographic. But we are not to condemn Stephen, nor did Joyce. Talent is there, but Cupid gets in the way. Stephen's ability to discipline his artistic impulses has not yet equaled his ability to tell others how to discipline theirs. Just as Uncle Charles, with false elegance that he could not tell was false, repaired to the outhouse, Stephen thinks of himself in the luscious prose of Pater and Wilde rather than finding his own terms, and pours his sexual and religious emotions into the mold of someone like Ernest Dowson, but without the control of Dowson's best poems.

Joyce knew as well as Wordsworth that poetry is emotion recollected in tranquillity; but his Cubist portrait of Stephen includes bits of snapshots as well as the finished lines of the painter. The last of Stephen that we find in *A Portrait* is a series of diary entries that fluctuate in style just as wildly as the villanelle and the episode of its composition. To my mind the only reason that critics have been puzzled by the villanelle is that they have not analyzed it by Joyce's own principles. He did not call his book simply *A Portrait of an Artist.* Joyce sympathetically understood that whatever his talent, Stephen had not yet fully absorbed the truth that Joyce himself had learned, and that T. S. Eliot once stated so memorably: "One is prepared for art when one has ceased to be interested in one's own emotions and experiences except as material."[21]

Notes

1. Because the present essay largely passes over theoretical considerations relating to reader orientation and the continuing controversy over the problem of aesthetic distance in Joyce's *A Portrait,* the reader is referred to the excellent article of James J. Sosnoski, "Reading Acts and Reading Warrants: Some Implications for Readers Responding to Joyce's Portrait of Stephen," *JJQ* [*James Joyce Quarterly*], 16 (Fall 1978/Winter 1979), 43–63, and to the valuable bibliography appended to it. An exhaustive list of extended discussions of the villanelle in articles and books would be prohibitively lengthy. Booth may be said to have commenced the evaluative criticism by vigorously proposing, according to his idea of the "unreliable narrator," that the villanelle passage was irrevocably ambiguous; Kenner and Scholes were convinced that it was not, though their readings differed radically; and the views of all three achieved wide circulation by being reprinted in the manner of a debate in the Viking Critical Edition of *A Portrait,* edited by Chester G. Anderson (1968), pp. 416–39, 446–80. Bernard Benstock, in "The Temptation of St. Stephen: A View of the Villanelle," *JJQ,* 14 (Fall 1976), 31–38, developed ideas presented in an article by Charles Rossman, "Stephen Dedalus' Villanelle," *JJQ,* 12 (Spring 1975), 281–93. Most of the later discussions are cited in the notes that follow. The Provincetown panel had as its chairman Zack Bowen, who also has published "Stephen's Villanelle: Antecedents, Manifestations, and Aftermath," *MBL* [*Modern British Literature*], 5 (1980), 63–67.

2. John Paul Riquelme, *Teller and Tale in Joyce's Fiction: Oscillating Perspectives* (Baltimore and London: Johns Hopkins Univ. Press, 1983), p. 76.

3. And yet if we brood on the slippery linguistic status of the terms in this sentence, it turns out to have several possible and distinct meanings. The villanelle *is* something signified because we are induced or persuaded to think of it as a real poem; it *is* part of the narrative, being in it; and can a "signifier" be part of the style of narration or of anything else, except insofar as the selection of words or phrases is one of the elements of style?

4. Benstock, "The Temptation," pp. 34, 37. The poem, however, as I shall argue, is both an actual villanelle written by an actual poet (Joyce) and a fictional villanelle written by a fictional poet (Stephen), and we are obliged to take its double ontological status into account if we want to understand it properly. In *The Undiscover'd Country* (New York: Barnes and Noble, 1977) Benstock somewhat modifies his position. The poem's "primary value is extrinsic: what it reveals about Stephen at an important phase of his development" (with which I would

entirely agree), but it is still "an enigma, especially if the reader approaches it critically and expects to determine whether it is a 'sound' piece of poetic art" (from which I would dissent). Benstock continues to maintain that Stephen has an emission and later (as I also argue) that he masturbates at the end of the section (pp. 150–54).

5. The sculptor Adolf Hildebrand, in *The Problem of Form* (1893), trans. Max Meyer (1907), quoted by Marshall McLuhan, "Joyce, Aquinas, and the Poetic Process," in *Joyce's "Portrait": Criticisms and Critiques,* ed. Thomas E. Connolly (New York: Appleton-Century Crofts, 1962), p. 262.

6. Benstock, "The Temptation," p. 37.

7. Hans Walter Gabler, "The Seven Lost Years of *A Portrait of the Artist as a Young Man,*" in *Approaches to Joyce's "Portrait": Ten Essays,* ed. Thomas Staley and Bernard Benstock (Pittsburgh: Univ. of Pittsburgh Press, 1976), pp. 44–45, 49, 52–53.

8. Gabler, p. 50. I feel, however (see below), that the structure of V is importantly modified by the insertion in several other ways as well.

9. Mary Reynolds, *Joyce and Dante* (Princeton: Princeton Univ. Press, 1981), pp. 178–83, 194–99, 262.

10. An instructive example of a failure in this respect occurs in a novel called *Quatrefoil* by James Barr (New York: Greenberg, 1950). We are told that the hero, an amateur pianist of almost professional caliber and unerring taste, considers Chopin's waltzes to be the quintessence of the art. Readers who favor Beethoven's late sonatas will be inclined to sneer.

11. Frank Budgen, *James Joyce and the Making of "Ulysses"* (London: Oxford Univ. Press, 1972), p. 52.

12. See Gabler, p. 48.

13. We might consider "Penelope" as a similar (but not despairing) solution to a similar narrative problem in *Ulysses: "Penelope* is the clou of the book" (*Letters I* 170). The crucial importance and the pervasive presence of chiastic structures in Joyce's presentation of Stephen's creativity is brought out in an illuminating study by Elliott B. Gose, Jr., "Destruction and Creation in *A Portrait of the Artist as a Young Man,*" *JJQ,* 22 (Spring 1985), 259–70.

14. Described and illustrated in *Joyce's Voices* (Berkeley: Univ. of California Press, 1978), pp. 15–38. A qualification that makes Kenner's idea both more precise and applicable to a wider range of Joyce's work, however, is introduced by Bernard and Shari Benstock in "The Benstock Principle," in *The Seventh of Joyce,* ed. Bernard Benstock (Bloomington: Indiana Univ. Press, 1982), pp. 18–19, and should be considered in the present context.

15. Reynolds, pp. 119–20.

16. The passage is a touching-up of a fragment from the "Trieste Notebook," where it reads, much more prosaically: "There is a morning inspiration as there is a morning knowledge about the windless hour when the moth escapes from the chrysalis, and certain plants bloom and the fever-fit of madness comes on the insane" (Robert Scholes and Richard M. Kain, eds., *The Workshop of Daedalus: James Joyce and the Materials for "A Portrait of the Artist as a Young Man"* [Evanston: Northwestern Univ. Press, 1965], p. 96).

17. Thus Ronald Firbank's *Odette* was subtitled "A Fairy Tale for Weary People" (London: Grant Richards, 1916); and thus in "Swinburne as Poet," in *Selected Essays* (London: Faber, 1932), p. 313, T. S. Eliot wrote: "Language in a healthy state presents the object, is so close to the object that the two are identified. They are identical in the verse of Swinburne solely because the object has ceased to exist, because the meaning is merely the hallucination of meaning. . . . In Swinburne, for example, we see the word 'weary' flourishing in this way independent of the particular and actual weariness of flesh or spirit. The bad poet dwells partly in a world of objects and partly in a world of words, and he never can get them to fit."

18. Benstock seems to have been the first reader to recognize this nuance clearly, or at least to mention it in print; he takes Rossman to task for being puzzled by it ("Temptation," p. 37).

19. Anthony Storr, in *The Dynamics of Creation* (New York: Athenaeum, 1972), pp. 180–200, provides extra-literary but very relevant comment both on the timing of Stephen's inspiration and on his masturbation as he completes the poem: "creative inspiration more usually makes its appearance during a state of reverie, intermediate between sleep and waking. . . . But the fact that [elaborate but ultimately onanistic fantasies] cause direct physical excitement which is discharged in masturbation means that they never undergo the process of transformation and integration which might transmute them into works of art."

20. Robert Boyle, S. J., "The Priesthoods of Stephen and Buck," *in Approaches to "Ulysses": Ten Essays,* ed. Thomas F. Staley and Bernard Benstock (Pittsburgh: Univ. of Pittsburgh Press, 1970), pp. 29–41, gives a complex and impressive analysis of the imagery of the villanelle and of Stephen's thoughts, but the result is to demonstrate yet again the muddle and inconsistency of the sources of Stephen's imagery.

21. T. S. Eliot, "A Brief Introduction to the Method of Paul Valéry," *Le Serpent* (London: Criterion, 1924), p. 12.

[The Aesthetics of Stephen's Aesthetic]

CORDELL D. K. YEE

According to a large body of criticism, the Stephen Dedalus of *A Portrait of the Artist as a Young Man* has been suffering from a number of character problems. In an attempt to put *A Portrait* in perspective, Hugh Kenner described him as "indigestibly Byronic."[1] Subsequent critical work has not changed this portrait much. There seems to be little positive to say about Stephen by the end of *A Portrait*. By most accounts, Stephen's story does not end with a rise but with a fall. The book is thus an example of anti-*Bildungsroman* or, more specifically, anti-*Künstlerroman*. It is structured according to a pattern of epiphany and anti-epiphany. Moments of illumination, of progress, turn out to be illusory, followed by episodes of disillusionment. For Stephen, no education really takes place, and it is not clear that he has made much progress toward becoming an artist.

Much of the critical and scholarly literature on Stephen's aesthetic theory has corroborated this view of Stephen's progress. His failings as a theorist are as great as, if not greater than, his failings as an artist: "That Stephen's rapturous discovery of his artistic calling and his scholastic theory of art in *Portrait* are subjected to a complicated array of ironic qualifications and sentimental investments . . . has been understood for some time."[2] The placement of his theory before the composition of his villanelle and the appearance of his diary is crucial. His theoretical shortcomings prefigure his practical failings. If the theory is deficient, the practice must be, too. A sound artistic practice, after all, should be grounded in a sound understanding of art. Stephen's lack of this understanding shows that by the end of *A Portrait* he is not an artist in a fundamental way. He is immature: the would-be artist is also a would-be theorist.

Under this view, Stephen's shortcomings as aesthetic theoretician show up most clearly in his choice of source material. Thomas Aquinas, Stephen's authority on beauty, did not develop an aesthetic theory, or a theory of fine art. From his own reading of Scholastic writings, Joyce himself was aware of

Revised for this volume from "St. Thomas Aquinas as Figura of James Joyce: A Medieval View of Literary Influence," *James Joyce Quarterly* 22, no. 1 (1984): 25–38; and, in part, from *The Word according to James Joyce: Reconstructing Representation* (Lewisburg: Bucknell University Press, 1997), ch. 1, with the permission of the author.

this. He knew better than his character, deliberately making him misapply Aquinas. To undercut Stephen's intellectual pretensions even further, Joyce makes Stephen falter in other ways. His theory is "long-winded and contrived, and even he must be aware that talking about art is not art."[3] Stephen's theory also does not even fulfill his aim of following Aquinas and his predecessor Aristotle. For example, it has been described as Neoplatonic, partly as a result of his omission of the notion of epiphany, partly as a result of Stephen's yoking of beauty and truth, partly as a result of Joyce's suspected use of an *Encyclopaedia Britannica* article colored by Neoplatonism.[4] It has also been said to have its ultimate commitments or sources in Kant and Hegel[5] and to draw upon the "romantic concept of the poetic act as the foundation and resolution of the world."[6] Stephen is not aware of these sources and thus seems to modernize Aquinas without knowing it. The portrait that emerges from the alternative source hunting is that of a Stephen not quite in control of his intellectual materials: his philosophic puffery has been deflated, revealed for what it is.

The perceived failure of Stephen's theory as theory has opened up a rich vein of interpretation. If Stephen's theory is not actually a theory, then it must be something else. What that something else is depends on the theoretical "lens" through which one views Stephen's theory. From a contextualist point of view, it is a sign of "aesthetic hubris." It shows how out of touch Stephen is with his intellectual world: the theory lacks what "every proper Victorian critic knew"—an awareness that "the final end of art is social."[7] Coming after Stephen's vision of the bird girl, the theory might—from a psychoanalytic-feminist viewpoint—be a manifestation of "the silencing of the mother, the erasure of her subjectivity, and the creation of the m/other who exists for and in the discourse of the son who thereby takes his place in the symbolic order of the father."[8] The sight of fleshly beauty inspires Stephen but also rekindles his discomfort with the flesh. Stephen's theory is a response to this discomfort: it reduces the feminine "from subject to object in a male economy of desire."[9] Perhaps more positively, the theory is a sign that Stephen has reincorporated "within his now indisputably masculine identity the 'female' self that he has repressed, mourned, and surreptitiously kept alive."[10] In one place his language—"artistic conception, artistic gestation and artistic reproduction"[11]—suggests that an artist has a "symbolic womb."[12] Then, again, the theory might be a psychological defense mechanism, "a means of escape from entrapment by the past and by crippling fixations." It is Stephen's way of proving that "art can be isolated from intense personal feelings."[13] Or, to adopt a political point of view less focused on Stephen, the theory may be, as Declan Kiberd has suggested, a commentary on the revivalist movement in Ireland: an aspiring artist is forced to turn from a failed native culture to an intellectual dead end.[14]

Such metaphorical interpretations, with their "minimalist" approach to Stephen's achievement, might seem to have some biographical warrant: Budgen's frequently reported notion that Joyce emphasized the words *as a young man* when speaking of *A Portrait*.[15] In support of the minimalist approaches to Stephen, Joyce might have meant that Stephen was merely a young man, not an artist. Or, more positively, he might have meant that Stephen was an artist who was also a young man. The title does read: a portrait of the artist *as a young man*. If Joyce had intended the former reading, he might have entitled the book: "a portrait of a young man before becoming an artist."

To be sure, there are times in the book when Stephen's actions are subject to ironic qualification. His responses to his feelings of guilt over his supposed gluttony and sexual misconduct, for example, are described with ironic detachment: the comicality of his acts of self-mortification comes through from their excessiveness (see *P,* 150–51). But Stephen later comes to appreciate his excessiveness, rejecting the institution whose standards induced his sense of guilt. Stephen's aesthetic theory fits into this pattern of growth. His use of Aquinas may support a less dismissive, more positive view of his development. The theory he advances (*P,* 204–15) shows that he understands Aquinas better than he is usually given credit for. It is not only defensible as an extension of notions in Stephen's avowed source materials but also logically coherent. Thus, two grounds for discounting Stephen's theory as theory become suspect. The contextual argument against it can be met by a contextual argument for it, and, similarly, as will be seen below, the argument against its intellectual defects can be met by an argument for its intellectual coherence. The metaphorical interpretations mentioned above, interesting though they are, thus seem to be critical deflections that are not quite warranted. To adopt a principle of critical jurisprudence modeled after one supposed to operate in the Anglo-American legal tradition, unless there are good grounds for denying that something is what it purports to be, one should try in fairness to understand it in its own terms. In the case at hand the terms of Stephen's aesthetic will be revisited.

Many of the allegations of deficiencies in Stephen's thinking might not have arisen if his ideas had been organized more systematically. The logic behind Stephen's aesthetic becomes clear if it is divided into three parts: one dealing with the object or work of art itself, another dealing with the perceiver's response to the work, and a third concerned with the artist's relationship to the work (see schema of the proposed structure).

With regard to the art object itself, Stephen specifies three requisites for beauty: *integritas, consonantia,* and *claritas,* terms that he renders as "wholeness," "harmony," and "radiance." These three Latin terms derive from Aquinas's discussion of beauty in *Summa Theologiae:* "Beauty must include three qualities: integrity or completeness [*integritas*]—since things that lack something are thereby ugly; right proportion or harmony [*consonantia*]; and brightness [*claritas*]—we call things bright in colour beautiful."[16] Aquinas leaves these three terms to a large extent undefined: he does not specify their denotation with the same degree of precision he does, for example, the four

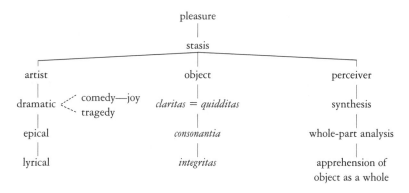

Schema of Stephen Dedalus's Aesthetic Theory

levels of meaning. The three terms, after all, are hardly unique to Aquinas but, as Edgar de Bruyne has documented, common to most if not all discussions of beauty during the medieval period.[17] What has been recognized as Aquinas's contribution to aesthetic theory is his treatment of the psychological effects of beauty, his relating of beauty to intellectual processes: "[T]he good being 'what all things want,' is that in which the orexis [appetite] comes to rest; whereas the beautiful is that in which the orexis comes to rest through contemplation or knowledge. . . . 'Beautiful' therefore adds to 'good' a reference to the cognitive powers . . . 'beautiful' refers to that which gives pleasure when it is perceived or contemplated" (*ST,* 1a2ae.27,1).

Stephen would thus seem justified in applying Aquinas's theory of cognition to his theory of beauty as a way of developing the second part of his theory dealing with the perceiver's response. In his account of the three requisites for beauty, Stephen makes it clear that he thinks they correspond to phases in one's aesthetic response to beauty. According to Stephen, *integritas* denotes the object's existence as a "selfbounded and selfcontained" whole, *consonantia* the harmonious relationship of part to part and of part to whole, and *claritas* "the luminous silent stasis of esthetic pleasure" (*P,* 212–13). William T. Noon argues that Stephen errs by treating the three requisites for beauty as if "they belong to the act of apprehension."[18] Umberto Eco concurs, saying that to interpret *integritas* in this fashion is "to strip it of its original ontological character."[19] What Stephen actually suggests, however, is only that the three essential qualities of beauty correspond—which is not synonymous with "belong"—to three stages in the apprehension of beauty. The first stage is the recognition of the object as a whole—of its *integritas*. This recognition is followed by whole-part analysis: "You apprehend it as complex, multiple, divisible, separable, made up of its parts, the result of its parts and their sum, harmonious. That is *consonantia.*" Then follows a "synthesis" by which one apprehends the "clear radiance of the esthetic image," its *claritas,* which Stephen equates with *quidditas,* "the *whatness* of a thing" (*P,* 212–13).

On this last point Stephen might seem to diverge from Aquinas. At one stage in his analysis Aquinas indicates that the intellect first apprehends "only one aspect of a thing"—its "whatness" (*quidditas*), the "primary and proper object of the intellect." This is followed by whole-part analysis, "combining and separating" of parts (*ST,* 1a.85,5). Apprehension of *quidditas,* for Aquinas, would seem to mark an imperfect state of knowledge: in first apprehending a thing, the human intellect does not immediately arrive at complete knowledge. Apprehending *quidditas* would entail no more than recognizing that an object has an existence apart from other things. But elsewhere Thomas identifies *quidditas* with essence (*essentia*) (*ST,* 1a.85,6) and implies that essence cannot be fully apprehended without a knowledge of the object's parts: "[H]uman beings like to know a thing as a complete whole. Now some things cannot be grasped completely in a single instant; in their case, then, change is pleasurable so that, one aspect replacing another, one may come to grasp the whole" (*ST,* 1a2ae.32,2). In addition Aquinas emphasizes that "knowing something which contains many aspects without having a precise knowledge of each of them is a rather confused knowledge of the thing" (*ST,* 1a.85,3). In such cases knowledge of an object's essence, or *quidditas,* if one accepts this equation, occurs as the final step of intellectual apprehension. This is the notion Stephen develops by identifying *claritas*— apprehended at the highest stage of aesthetic apprehension—with *quidditas.* The effect of his apparent divergence from Aquinas is to restrict the meaning of *quidditas* to "essence," as he suggests with his further definition of *quidditas* as "the supreme quality of beauty." An object's beauty is fully appreciated only when one recognizes its essence.[20]

The third part of Stephen's theory, that dealing with the artist's relationship to his work, has generally been regarded as the least Thomistic. Stephen develops this part of his theory by referring to literary forms: the lyrical, the epical, and the dramatic (*P,* 214–15). He discusses them in order of increasing distance between artist and subject. In the lyrical form the emotions expressed are presented as the artist's own: "[T]he artist presents his image in immediate relation to himself." In the epical form the artist narrates events that do not actively involve him: he presents "his image in mediate relation to himself and to others." In the dramatic form the subject of the work is allowed to present itself with no intervening narrative voice. The artist "refines" his personality "out of existence," presenting "his image in immediate relation to others."

In the past this section of Stephen's theory has been separated from the rest on the grounds that Stephen does not claim "the authority of Aquinas" for it and that it is merely "supplementary" and "strikingly inconsistent" with the rest of the theory.[21] Stephen's threefold theory of forms does seem to draw largely from sources other than Aquinas: those cited include Plato and Aristotle, who distinguish three types of mimetic art roughly analogous to

Stephen's; Georg Wilhelm Friedrich Hegel, who thought of art as progressing through symbolic, classical, and romantic forms; Friedrich Wilhelm Joseph von Schelling, who describes a progression from lyric to epic to dramatic art in terms of increasing universality; and Arthur Schopenhauer, who discusses the same progression in a manner similar to Stephen's—in terms of increasing objectivity.[22] It is also true that Aquinas never developed a theory of literary forms and that Stephen, who seems cognizant of this fact, prefaces his discussion of literary forms by saying that he requires a "new terminology" different from Aquinas's. Even so, it does not necessarily follow that this part of Stephen's theory is inconsistent.

Rather, Stephen's theory of literary forms is connected with the rest of his theory by Thomist principles. One can see this connection by reasoning from Aquinas to Aristotle, whom Stephen has previously identified as one of his sources (P, 187). The starting point is Stephen's first citation of Aquinas: "—Aquinas . . . says *Pulc{h}ra sunt quae visa placent*" (beauty is that which pleases the eye) (P, 186, echoed on 207). The Latin is a paraphrase of Aquinas's statement that "we call a thing beautiful when it pleases the eye of the beholder" (*pulchra enim dicunter quae visa placent*; ST, 1a.5,4). This statement is translated in Joyce's notes as "[t]hose things are beautiful the apprehension of which pleases."[23] According to Stephen, the "esthetic pleasure" induced in the perceiver of an object of beauty by its *claritas* is stasis, or arrest: beauty "awakens, or ought to awaken, or induces, or ought to induce, an esthetic stasis, an ideal pity or an ideal terror" (P, 206). Pity and terror, Stephen says, arrest "the mind in the presence of whatsoever is grave and constant in human sufferings" (P, 204). Suffering is often the subject of tragedy, and, according to Aristotle's *Poetics,* the catharsis of pity and terror is the end of tragedy. The connection made by Stephen between pleasure and arrest helps to justify the claim by Aristotle that the pity and terror aroused by tragedy result in pleasure.[24] Joyce himself agrees with Aristotle. In his notes, under the heading "Esthetic," he writes: "It relieves us to hear or see our own distress expressed by another person."[25] Pleasure thus turns out to be an organizing principle of Stephen's aesthetic, connecting beauty to tragedy, an example of the dramatic form.

Noon and Eco question whether Stephen's stress on the stasis induced by art is based on Aristotelian and Thomist premises.[26] Eco, for example, thinks that Walter Pater and Gabriele D'Annunzio have replaced Aristotle. He and Noon seem to have overlooked that Aquinas, like Stephen, conceives of pleasure as a condition of stasis:

> Passion consists in being moved, as Aristotle says. But pleasure consists not in being moved, but in having been moved; for it is caused by some good thing once it has been obtained. . . . From one point of view, then—namely, considering the fact that the pleasurable good which satisfies the orexis is now in its possession—pleasure consists in being at rest. (ST, 1a2ae.31,1)

Aquinas does recognize that pleasure involves movement, but this movement precedes a "new condition" of stasis: "[T]here is also the fact that the orexis is in a new condition which is being brought about by the object actually working on it; and from that point of view, pleasure is a kind of movement" (*ST,* 1a2ae.34,1). The movement of the appetite toward what is good results in stasis when the appetite joins or unites with the good thing: "pleasure is that repose of the orexis in some loved good which comes at the end of some activity" (*ST,* 1a2ae.34,1).[27]

Stephen, though stressing the final stasis, is aware of the kinetic aspect of pleasure and therefore of art. The word *arrest,* which he uses as a synonym for *stasis,* implies the cessation of motion; and, paraphrasing Aquinas, he says, "*Bonum est in quod tendit appetitus*" (*P,* 186). The Latin is explicated in Joyce's notes, which read in part: "The good is that towards the possession of which an appetite tends: the desirable. The true and the beautiful are the most persistent orders of the desirable" (*JJA,* 7:108). Joyce's recognition that satisfaction involves a movement toward what is desirable or good is translated in *A Portrait* into Stephen's conception of tragic emotion as uniting the mind with "the human sufferer" and the "secret cause" (*P,* 204). It would then be misleading to characterize Stephen's theory as an aesthetic of "art as stasis." It is more aptly described as an aesthetic of art as pleasure. Pleasure is not limited to the sensual. Apprehension of the beautiful involves a form of intellection: "In so far as it [a fire] is apprehended by the sight, which I suppose means here esthetic intellection, it will be beautiful" (*P,* 186). Sensual pleasure, he says later, differs from intellectual pleasure in that it is a kinetic, as opposed to static, emotion, and the arts that excite kinetic emotions are "improper arts" (*P,* 205).

It should be clear that Joyce put some care into the formulation of his protagonist's aesthetic, making sure that Stephen's pronouncements were grounded in the statements of his two acknowledged sources. Joyce shows that an aesthetic system is prefigured in Thomist thought, key elements of which are preserved in Stephen's theory. For Stephen and Thomas, the beautiful and the good are virtually identical; ugliness results from a lack of wholeness. Although much depends on perception in the apprehension of beauty, beauty is not entirely subjective: it is not wholly determined by human perceptual equipment or innate conceptual structures. For Stephen and Aquinas, construction is an important aspect of art.[28] Both recognize that poetic art can move us: "[T]he poet's task is to lead us to something virtuous by some excellent description. And all these pertain to the philosophy of reason, for it belongs to reason to pass from one thing to another."[29]

Stephen's aesthetic theory, though carefully constructed, is by no means comprehensive. For example, it does not contain all of Joyce's own extrapolations from Aquinas's thought. Joyce goes further than Stephen in developing an aesthetic of pleasure. In his Paris notebook Joyce elevates comedy over tragedy in contradistinction to what Aristotle implies in *Poetics.* Joyce may have inverted Aristotle's hierarchy in following a neo-Hegelian lead: for Hegel, comedy is the final stage in the development of dramatic art.[30] Or Joyce may have made the inversion because of Aquinas's emphasis on beauty as a source of pleasure. The pleasure, the joy, of comedy, Joyce implies, is higher than that of tragedy, for the terror and pity of tragedy are ultimately excited by "privation of some good":

> All art which excites in us the feeling of joy is so far comic and according as this feeling of joy is excited by whatever is substantial or accidental, general or fortuitous, in human fortunes the art is to be judged more or less excellent: and even tragic art may be said to participate in the nature of comic art so far as the possession of a work of tragic art excites in us the feeling of joy. From this it may be seen that tragedy is the imperfect manner, and comedy the perfect manner, in art. (*JJA*, 7:107)

Why Joyce did not incorporate his own notions about comedy into Stephen's theory is not entirely clear. The omission might indicate that Stephen's theory is lacking something—a neo-Hegelian update. Stephen does seem to paraphrase Hegel at one point, but with no clear indication that he is aware that he is doing so.[31] Alternatively, the omission could have been made for the sake of consistency—not only in Stephen's theory but also in his character. An exaltation of comedy would have been incongruent with Stephen's humorless personality. In any case the omission does not vitiate the coherence of Stephen's theory. Joyce's remarks on comedy are not inconsistent with Stephen's aesthetic of pleasure, and Stephen nowhere says that the ideas he presents make up his complete system. In *Stephen Hero*, an earlier version of *A Portrait*, Stephen implicitly recognizes the theory's incompleteness by stating his intention to write a treatise on beauty (*SH*, 212).

From a theoretical standpoint a more important omission from the theory is the lack of any reference to the relationship of art to reality. This omission may reflect Stephen's sense of isolation from his surroundings—his ultimate rejection of his country, religion, and family. It may also represent an extrapolation from Aquinas, who verges on making art a morally autonomous activity: "The worth of things produced by art, however, does not consist in their being good for human appetite, but in the good of the products of art themselves" (*ST*, 1a2ae.57,4). Jacques Maritain elaborates on this thought:

> Art . . . remains outside the line of human conduct, with an end, rules, and values, which are not those of the man, but of the work to be produced. That work is everything for art,—one law only governs it—the exigencies and the good of the work.
> Hence the despotic and all-absorbing power of art, as also its astonishing power of soothing: it frees from every human care, it establishes the *artifex*, artist or artisan, in a world apart, cloistered, defined and absolute, in which to

devote all the strength and intelligence of his manhood to the service of the
thing he is making.[32]

For the young Joyce, such isolation is a precondition of artistic production: "If
the artist courts the favour of the multitude he cannot escape the contagion of
its fetichism and deliberate self-deception, and if he joins in a popular movement he does so at his own risk" (*CW,* 71).[33]

It is not until Stephen, in accordance with the young Joyce's notions
about the prerequisites for artistic production, rejects the main influences on
his life that Joyce allows him to state his theory—only as much as is needed
for one to abstract its formal structure. Once one does, the theory assumes
symbolic significance. Its triadic structure—mirrored by the three-part structure of each of its subsections—recalls the trinitarian God. This correspondence accords with Stephen's conception of the artist as performing an almost
religious function as "priest of eternal imagination, transmuting the daily
bread of experience into the radiant body of everliving life" (*P,* 221). As a
medieval writer on beauty might say, "every form is beautiful in proportion to
its resemblance to divine beauty."[34] By virtue of its trinitarian form, its symmetrical structure of three triads, Stephen's theory is itself beautiful.

This numerological interpretation of Stephen's theory may seem far-
fetched, but one should remember that Joyce—perhaps mindful of Thomas's
statement, common to many medieval humanists, that art, *techne,* "seems to
be nothing more than a definite and fixed procedure established by reason"[35]—was obsessed with schematization and form. Beauty, Thomas also
says, is "a matter of right proportion" and "involves the notion of form" (*ST,*
1a.5,4). Aquinas may have helped Joyce to become a devotee of the medieval
cult of proportion, "the characteristic beauty of quantity."[36] Joyce's medieval-
ism—often obscured by his reputation for innovation—may have been
acquired not only through Thomas but also through one of the "gods" of
Joyce's youth, another artist influenced by Aquinas—Dante. Joyce alludes to
Dante in *Stephen Hero* and *Dubliners;* the three parts of the short story "Grace"
have been interpreted as mock-parallels to the three parts of the *Commedia.*[37]
Dantean echoes are also heard in *A Portrait.* The three-nine structure of
Stephen's theory may have been an influence of *La vita nuova.*[38] There Dante
says that the number three represents the miracle of the Three in One and
that his beloved Beatrice is accompanied by the number nine so that one
might understand that "she was a nine, or a miracle, whose root, namely that
of the miracle, is the miraculous Trinity itself."[39]

As it does the young artist in Dante's work, the sight of divine beauty in
female form confirms Stephen in his commitment to art. In the chapter following this vision, Stephen articulates his theory as a prelude to the composition of his own poem and the presentation of his diary entries without the
mediation of the narrator. The theory is part of a sequence of developments in

which Stephen tests his growing artistic powers. The literal sense of the novel's title is primary—by the end Stephen is an artist.

The objection that Aquinas did not develop an aesthetic theory—that his discussion of beauty focused primarily on theology—is hardly an objection. In extending the theoretical to the realm of human activity, Stephen does what one would reasonably do to apply Aquinas. It does not matter that Stephen's theory is contextually inaccurate or that Stephen seems out of touch with intellectual currents in his time. In fact, this would seem to enhance his stature: he is asserting his independence from prevailing trends, from the conventional wisdom of his time. In addition, by producing a theory where one did not exist before, Stephen fulfills the function of an artist: making something where something did not exist before is surely reminiscent of the primal act of creation. Stephen's ability to conceive a theory is thus an indication of his increasing maturity as an artist, a sign that he has found his vocation. When he is expounding his theory, he is not merely philosophizing but also engaging in poetic production. This fusion of philosophy and art is consistent with Aquinas:

> Now the reason why the philosopher is compared to the poet is that both are concerned with wonders. For the myths with which the poets deal are composed of wonders, and the philosophers themselves were moved to philosophize as a result of wonder. And since wonder stems from ignorance, they were obviously moved to philosophize to escape from ignorance.[40]

Stephen's own story reenacts what Aquinas describes here. His theory is the actualization, the entelechy, of the potential shown earlier in novel. As a child, Stephen has a questioning mind: he wonders about the world and shows a philosophic bent. He does not take things for granted and seems to recognize a distinction between nature and convention. He often thinks about language, asking why certain words are used, why they mean what they mean. He finds certain things beautiful—roses, a song (both words and music), writing, the word *wine* (P, 12, 24, 43, 46)—the variety of which can reasonably be expected to lead to an attempt to determine what is common to the various applications of the word *beautiful*, in short, to lead to a theory of beauty. During his childhood, Stephen begins to deal with issues of importance to someone wishing to pursue linguistic art.

There is also, as Aquinas leads one to expect, a mythic impulse behind Stephen's choice of vocation—the story of Daedalus:

> Now, at the name of the fabulous artificer, he [Stephen] seemed to hear the noise of dim waves and to see a winged form flying above the waves and slowly climbing the air. . . . Was it . . . a hawklike man flying sunward above the sea . . . a symbol of the artist forging anew out of the sluggish matter of the earth a new soaring impalpable imperishable being? (P, 169)

Those who hold that Stephen has the wrong myth in mind—that he is not Daedalus but the overreaching Icarus—have often pointed to the *Stephen Hero* manuscript. One difference between it and the published version of *A Portrait* is that in *Stephen Hero* the last stage of aesthetic apprehension is termed an "epiphany" (*SH*, 213). In *A Portrait* Stephen implicitly rejects this term, saying that he once thought that *claritas* meant the "artistic discovery and representation of the divine purpose in anything" (*P*, 213). Some would argue that Joyce's deletion of the term from *A Portrait* indicates ironic intent—that Stephen's theory is now deficient.[41] But the notion of epiphany was never precisely defined by Joyce, and the coherence of Stephen's theory does not suffer by its absence. Moreover, in the "Proteus" episode of *Ulysses* Stephen looks back on his use of the term as a symptom of his immaturity, and biographical evidence suggests that Joyce felt the same way. After writing *Dubliners* Joyce never seems to have applied the term to his own work.

The treatments of Stephen's theory in *Stephen Hero* and *A Portrait* differ more significantly in narrative technique. In *A Portrait* the narrator's distance from Stephen seems to have increased. Unlike the narrator of *Stephen Hero*, who shares the task of presenting the theory with Stephen, the narrator of *A Portrait* allows Stephen to present it by himself in a dialogue with Lynch. The narrator's increased distance from Stephen has often been taken as a sign of irony, a sign that Stephen is being held up to silent laughter: "Joyce's displacement of Stephen's aesthetic theory from the president's chambers to the walk with Lynch undermines Stephen's stance as romantic artist-hero in *Stephen Hero* and contributes to the modernist irony of Joyce's self-portrait in *Portrait*."[42] Ironic intent, however, cannot be inferred from narratorial distance alone. Distance would also result from Joyce's application of Stephen's theory: Joyce refines the narrator out of "existence," making a transition from epical to dramatic art.

Still, those wishing to dismiss Stephen's theory, those unwilling to believe that Joyce's theory at some points coincides with Stephen's, may suggest that Joyce's own views are closer to those of Lynch, who describes Stephen's views as "scholastic stink." On the surface Lynch's antics, his witticisms, may seem so amusing that one can feel superior to Stephen, who does not seem to appreciate Lynch's humor. But Lynch hardly represents a worthy alternative to Stephen's theory. Lynch's attempt to reduce the theory to absurdity by showing that desire is involved in his response to art shows that he has missed the point. Stephen's discussion already presupposes that the body is involved in aesthetic response: one needs sense organs to perceive beauty. The experience of beauty, however, is not merely an immediate sensuous response or bodily reaction but an intellectual process: according to Stephen, as well as Aquinas, one does not truly apprehend beauty without intellection. It is this point that Lynch fails to address, and the narrator's physical descriptions of him imply that he is unable to: his skull, for example, reminds Stephen of a "hooded reptile" (*P*, 205).

The narrator's irony thus does not seem to be directed against Stephen, who is already the target of Lynch's sarcasm. Joyce's indirection is more subtle than that. The narrator's silent mockery is aimed at the mocker himself, who attacks the very thing that could raise him out of his bestial existence. By disrupting Stephen's discourse with Lynch's verbal barbs, Joyce in effect issues a challenge to apply the intellect to the imperfectly apprehended theoretical construct, to discover the relationships among its parts, and then to determine its *quidditas*.

Once one has done this, Stephen's heroism emerges: he shows an ability to transcend his circumstances. He is not defined or defeated by them. He may have to use the language of the conqueror, but the source of his theory is not the religious thinker of the conqueror. Stephen's choice of Thomas as master theorist is not as conservative or backward as it might seem at first. By his choice Stephen commits an act of rebellion: socially and politically, at least, he issues a *non serviam*. Seen in this light, his adversary Lynch is just one more feature of an Irish environment so hostile, so unconducive to art that Stephen eventually feels compelled to leave, using exile as one of his weapons.

It seems that the common critical refusal to see Stephen's theory as what it purports to be has not been well grounded: the scholarship and criticism dismissive of the theory has tended to outrun its evidence.[43] Stephen's theory is not so faulty as to warrant the suspicion that it is meant to be undermined, and indeed it is strong enough to be taken seriously. The question of what Joyce thought of it, touched upon above, remains to be resolved, since his intentions bear on the question of how Stephen's theory is meant to be taken. It is conceivable that, despite the strengths of the theory, Joyce found it wanting. But as has already been seen, this claim cannot be justified solely on internal grounds, much less on the basis of the theory alone. Thus those who would support this claim often have recourse to biography, to Joyce the man. But again the case against Stephen can be met. In *Reauthorizing Joyce,* for example, Vicki Mahaffey has proposed that Joyce had more self-awareness than Stephen, implying that he would not have found Stephen's Thomism satisfying: Stephen, in his avowed adherence to Aristotle and Aquinas, does not see himself as a reconciliation of opposites, whereas Joyce, by the time he wrote *A Portrait,* already had this more comprehensive outlook.[44] Against this view, there is Joyce's statement at the time he was completing *A Portrait* that Thomas Aquinas "was the greatest philosopher because his reasoning was 'like a sharp sword,' " and that he read Aquinas in Latin, "a page a day."[45] Furthermore, in his own critical writings, Joyce tries to practice some of what Stephen preaches. In his 1900 article on Henrik Ibsen Joyce denies that Ibsen's plays depend on action for their interest. What "rivets" the attention (note the similarity to "arrest") is the "perception of a great truth, or the opening up of a great question" (*CW,* 63). What Joyce is pointing to might be the radiance of *claritas*. In another piece, written in 1902, Joyce criticizes an Irish poet on more explicitly Thomistic grounds, a lack of *integritas*: "There is no piece in the book which has even the first quality of beauty, the quality of integrity, the quality of being separate and whole" (*CW,* 87). These are statements by a young Joyce, to be sure, but 20 years after completing *A Portrait,* Joyce is still defending his writing with an appeal to an aesthetics of pleasure: "Lord knows what my prose means. In a word, it is pleasing to the ear. And your drawings are pleasing to the eye. That is enough, it seems to me."[46]

Notes

1. Hugh Kenner, *Dublin's Joyce* (1956; reprint, New York: Columbia University Press, 1987), 132.

2. Mark Wollaeger, "Stephen/Joyce, Joyce/Haacke: Modernism and the Social Function of Art," *English Literary History* 62 (1995): 693.

3. Rick Bowers, "Stephen's Practical Artistic Development," *James Joyce Quarterly* 21 (1984): 231.

4. Kenner, *Dublin's Joyce,* 121; Jacques Aubert, *The Aesthetics of James Joyce* (Baltimore: Johns Hopkins University Press, 1992), 105; and Theoharis C. Theoharis, "Unveiling Joyce's *Portrait:* Stephen Dedalus and *The Encyclopaedia Britannica,*" *Southern Review* 20 (1984): 294. Theoharis argues that Joyce drew upon the British scholar Theodore Watts-Dunton's article on poetry, which first appeared in the *Encyclopaedia Britannica* in 1885. In Theoharis's view, Joyce plays a joke on Stephen, and thus Stephen steals "the British oppressor's words" and uses them "fatuously" ("Unveiling Joyce's *Portrait,*" 296).

5. See Thomas F. Staley, "Religious Elements and Thomistic Encounters: Noon on Joyce and Aquinas," in *Re-Viewing Classics of Joyce Criticism,* ed. Janet Egleson Dunleavy (Urbana: University of Illinois Press, 1991), 161; and F. C. McGrath, "Laughing in His Sleeve: The Sources of Stephen's Aesthetics," *James Joyce Quarterly* 23 (1986), 272. As Staley himself points out, however, Stephen "follows the line from Aristotle to Kant *through Aquinas*" (emphasis added).

6. Umberto Eco, *The Aesthetics of Chaosmos: The Middle Ages of James Joyce,* trans. Ellen Esrock (Tulsa, Okla.: University of Tulsa, 1982), 29.

7. Jackson I. Cope, *Joyce's Cities: Archaeologies of the Soul* (Baltimore, Md.: Johns Hopkins University Press, 1981), 54–55. Weldon Thornton also faults Stephen for retreating from his social responsibilities (*The Antimodernism of Joyce's "Portrait of the Artist as a Young Man"* [Syracuse: Syracuse University Press, 1994], 103–5). Thornton argues that Joyce came to understand that becoming an artist did not require "extensive philosophic theorizing" or a "full-fledged theory of art," and thus differed from Stephen. The difficulty here is that few have claimed that Stephen's theory of art is fully developed or extensive. In addition the argument that an artist need not devote much energy to theorizing is not persuasive: it is disappointing when an artist has nothing profound to say about his or her own work. But perhaps this is a bias of an age marked by artist-critics.

8. Here I adapt Susan Stanford Friedman's interpretation of the modernism of *A Portrait* in "(Self)Censorship and the Making of Joyce's Modernism," in *Joyce: The Return of the Repressed,* ed. Susan Stanford Friedman (Ithaca: Cornell University Press, 1993), 35.

9. Friedman, "(Self)Censorship and the Making of Joyce's Modernism," 42.

10. Here I follow Christine Froula's interpretation of Stephen in *Modernism's Body: Sex, Culture, and Joyce* (New York: Columbia University Press, 1996), 60.

11. James Joyce, *A Portrait of the Artist as a Young Man: Text, Criticism, and Notes,* ed. Chester G. Anderson (1968; reprint, Harmondsworth: Penguin, 1977), 209. Cited hereafter in the text as *P.*

12. Froula, *Modernism's Body*, 60.

13. Sheldon Brivic, "The Disjunctive Structure of Joyce's *Portrait*," in *A Portrait of the Artist as a Young Man: Complete, Authoritative Text with Biographical and Historical Contexts, Critical History, and Essays from Five Contemporary Critical Perspectives*, ed. R. B. Kershner (Boston: St. Martin's Press, Bedford Books, 1993), 263.

14. Declan Kiberd, *Inventing Ireland* (London: Jonathan Cape, 1995), 334–37.

15. Frank Budgen, *James Joyce and the Making of "Ulysses"* (1934; reprint, Bloomington: Indiana University Press, 1960), 60.

16. Thomas Aquinas, *Summa Theologiae*, 1a.39,8 (part, question, article). Cited hereafter in the text as *ST*. All quotations from the *Summa* are from the 61-volume edition translated and edited by Thomas Gilby et al. ([Cambridge]: Blackfriars, 1964–1981).

17. Edgar de Bruyne, *The Esthetics of the Middle Ages*, trans. Eileen B. Hennessy (New York: Frederick Ungar, 1969), 47–78. See also Umberto Eco, *Art and Beauty in the Middle Ages*, trans. Hugh Bredin (New Haven: Yale University Press, 1986).

18. William T. Noon, *Joyce and Aquinas* (New Haven: Yale University Press, 1957), 45.

19. Umberto Eco, *The Aesthetics of Thomas Aquinas*, trans. Hugh Bredin (Cambridge: Harvard University Press, 1988), 249, n. 85.

20. For a different view, see *Joyce and Aquinas*, 49–52, in which Noon argues that Stephen's equation of *claritas* and *quidditas* is "questionable." Noon evidently does not distinguish two senses of the term *quidditas*.

21. Maurice Beebe, "Joyce and Aquinas: The Theory of Aesthetics," *Philological Quarterly* 36 (1957): 22; S. L. Goldberg, *The Classical Temper: A Study of James Joyce's "Ulysses"* (London: Chatto and Windus, 1961), 46.

22. See Noon, *Joyce and Aquinas*, 55–56; David Evans, "Stephen and the Theory of Literary Kinds," *James Joyce Quarterly* 11 (1974): 145–49.

23. James Joyce, *The Critical Writings of James Joyce*, ed. Ellsworth Mason and Richard Ellmann (1959; reprint, New York: Viking, 1964), 147. Cited hereafter in the text as *CW*.

24. Aristotle, *Poetics*, chapter 14, trans. Gerald F. Else (Ann Arbor: University of Michigan Press, 1970), 40. The Greek word *phobos*, which Stephen renders as "terror," is translated by Else (and other translators) as "fear."

25. *James Joyce Archive*, ed. Michael Groden et al., 63 vols. (New York: Garland Publishing, 1977–1979), 7:121. Cited hereafter in the text as *JJA*.

26. Noon, *Joyce and Aquinas*, 39; Eco, *Aesthetics of Chaosmos*, 28. Theoharis echoes the same doubt ("Unveiling Joyce's *Portrait*," 292) and locates Joyce's ultimate source in Kant's aesthetics of disinterest.

27. Here there is some convergence between Aquinas and Kant. For Aquinas, as Eco points out, pleasure is a "factor . . . essential to beauty" (*Art and Beauty in the Middle Ages*, 71). For Kant, Jacques Derrida points out, aesthetic arts—among them the fine or beautiful arts—have their "immediate end in pleasure" ("Economimesis," trans. R. Klein, *Diacritics* 11, no. 2 [1981], 8).

28. For much of the material in this paragraph, I am indebted to Armand A. Maurer, *About Beauty: A Thomistic Interpretation* (Houston, Tex.: Center for Thomistic Studies, University of St. Thomas, 1983).

29. Thomas Aquinas, *Commentary on the "Posterior Analytics" of Aristotle*, trans. F. R. Larcher (Albany, N.Y.: Magi Books, 1970), 3.

30. G. W. F. Hegel, *Aesthetics: Lectures on Fine Art*, trans. T. M. Knox, [Oxford: Oxford University Press, 1975], 2:1208. Joyce could have learned of Hegel's aesthetic views from Bernard Bosanquet's *History of Aesthetic* (1892; 2nd ed., 1904), which Joyce consulted, as Jacques Aubert has shown in *The Aesthetics of James Joyce*.

31. In *A Portrait* Stephen says: "—The Greek, the Turk, the Chinese, the Copt, the Hottentot . . . all admire a different type of female beauty" (*P*, 208)—alluding to Hegel's statement that a European beauty would not please "a Chinese, or a Hottentot either" (*Aesthetics*,

1:44). In the *Stephen Hero* manuscript Stephen does not mention the Hottentot while making a similar point (see James Joyce, *Stephen Hero*, ed. Theodore Spencer, John J. Slocum, and Herbert Cahoon, rev. ed. [New York: New Directions, 1963], 212; cited hereafter in the text as *SH*). In *A Portrait* Joyce seems to have changed Stephen's wording to strengthen the verbal parallel between Stephen and Hegel—both see a way out of relativism. For Stephen, it is his theory.

32.   Jacques Maritain, *"Art and Scholasticism" with Other Essays,* trans. J. F. Scanlon (New York: Charles Scribner's Sons, 1933), 7.

33.   A lack of concern with society is not necessarily a mark of the romantic: the romantic Percy Bysshe Shelley, after all, called poets the "unacknowledged legislators of the world." Stephen's isolationism thus does not make him an idealist or a romantic opposed to Joyce the modernist. Joyce himself produced the great bulk of his work after leaving Irish society.

34.   De Bruyne, *Esthetics of the Middle Ages,* 4.

35.   Thomas Aquinas, *Commentary on the "Posterior Analytics,"* 1. See also Thomas's *Commentary on Aristotle's "Metaphysics":* "[A]rt is defined as the reasoned plan of things to be made" (book 1, lesson 1, C 34, trans. John P. Rowan, rev. ed. [Notre Dame, Ind.: Dumb Ox Press, 1995], 12).

36.   De Bruyne, *Esthetics of the Middle Ages,* 56.

37.   See Stanislaus Joyce, *My Brother's Keeper,* ed. Richard Ellmann (London: Faber and Faber, 1958), 225. For a thorough treatment of Joyce's use of Dante, see Mary T. Reynolds, *Joyce and Dante: The Shaping Imagination* (Princeton: Princeton University Press, 1981).

38.   A copy of this work, printed in 1911, is part of the collection Joyce left in Trieste in 1920. See Richard Ellmann, *The Consciousness of Joyce* (1977; reprint, New York: Oxford University Press, 1981), 106.

39.   Dante Alighieri, *La vita nuova,* chapter 29 (trans. Mark Musa, *Dante's Vita Nuova* [Bloomington: Indiana University Press, 1973], 62).

40.   Thomas Aquinas, *Commentary on Aristotle's "Metaphysics,"* book 1, lesson 3, C 55 (p. 19).

41.   See, for example, Kenner, *Dublin's Joyce,* 121. Others have pointed out possible sources for Stephen's adoption of the term. Cope proposes D'Annunzio as at least providing an analogue (*Joyce's Cities,* 49), and Eco offers Pater as the source of the concept, if not the term (*Aesthetics of Chaosmos,* 23). If any of these suggestions are right, then Joyce may have omitted the term from Stephen's theory to make it more consistently Thomistic.

42.   Friedman, "(Self)Censorship and the Making of Joyce's Modernism," 32.

43.   One critic who takes Stephen's theory seriously is Norman N. Holland, who says that the theory is Joyce's way of telling readers how to read his book ("*A Portrait* as Rebellion," in *A Portrait of the Artist as a Young Man: Complete, Authoritative Text with Biographical and Historical Contexts, Critical History, and Essays from Five Contemporary Critical Perspectives,* ed. R. B. Kershner [Boston: St. Martin's Press, Bedford Books, 1993], 289).

44.   Vicki Mahaffey, *Reauthorizing Joyce* (Cambridge: Cambridge University Press, 1988), 86–103. For a differing view, see Sidney Feshbach, "The Magic Lantern of Tradition: On *A Portrait of the Artist as a Young Man,*" *Joyce Studies Annual* (University of Texas) 7 (1996): 61–66.

45.   Joyce in 1913–1914 as recounted by Richard Ellmann in his *James Joyce,* rev. ed. (1982; reprint, New York: Oxford University Press, 1983), 342.

46.   James Joyce to Lucia Joyce, June 1, 1934, in *Letters of James Joyce,* ed. Stuart Gilbert and Richard Ellmann (New York: Viking Press, 1957–1966), 1:341.

The Genesis of
A Portrait of the Artist as a Young Man

Hans Walter Gabler

James Joyce wrote and rewrote the novel that was to become *A Portrait of the Artist as a Young Man* in several phases between 1903 and 1914. He began *Stephen Hero* sometime in early 1903 but, after some seven chapters, attempted a reorientation with the narrative essay "A Portrait of the Artist." This he submitted to the Dublin literary magazine *Dana* in January 1904.[1] Upon its rejection, he fell back with renewed energy on *Stephen Hero* and carried it forward through 25 (of a projected 63) chapters. Broken off in the summer of 1905 in favor of an undivided attention to the writing of the stories for *Dubliners, Stephen Hero* remained a fragment.[2] In September 1907, when the plans for a revision of the fragment had sufficiently matured in Joyce's mind, he began to write *A Portrait of the Artist as a Young Man* in five chapters. This reached the state of an intermediary manuscript during 1907 to 1911.[3] In 1913–14, the novel was completed. It is represented in its final state by the fair-copy manuscript in Joyce's hand now in the possession of the National Library of Ireland in Dublin. Moreover, complete textual versions or fragments of text from each of the major stages of the novel's eleven-year progression are still extant and identifiable. But it is also true that by far the majority of the materials, the plans, sketches, or intermediate drafts which as a body would have borne witness of its emergence, must be assumed to be lost. Nevertheless, close survey and careful scrutiny of those which survive make it possible to indicate some of the essential aspects of the work's genesis.

I

The only surviving textually complete document of *A Portrait of the Artist as a Young Man* is the Dublin holograph manuscript. In it, several strata of compo-

This essay was revised for this volume from "The Christmas Dinner Scene, Parnell's Death, and the Genesis of *A Portrait*," *James Joyce Quarterly,* 1975, and "The Seven Lost Years of *Portrait of the Artist,*" in *Approaches to Joyce's* Portrait, Thomas F. Staley and Bernard Benstock, Eds., © 1976 by University of Pittsburgh Press. This revision is reprinted by permission of the *James Joyce Quarterly* and the University of Pittsburgh Press.

sition may be distinguished. The manuscript comprises 600 $(-1)^4$ leaves in Joyce's hand. Several orders of page-count may be found in the manuscript. The penciled numbering of the pages in Chapters I–III, and perhaps part of that in Chapter V, may be that of Harriet Weaver, who donated the manuscript to the National Library of Ireland. Page totals for each chapter have also been jotted in ink on the back of protective endpapers to Chapters II, III, and IV. They give the page count in a manner similarly found in some of Joyce's later manuscripts, and may be his. Chapter IV has a page numbering in large arabic numerals, mostly in ink, on the verso of the leaves. This numbering runs on without interruption through the first 13 leaves of Chapter V. The sequence begins with "239" for the first text page in Chapter IV and runs to "313" for fol. 13 of Chapter V (*JJA* [10], 741–882).[5]

For a stratification of the manuscript by which to distinguish the order of inscription, and at times of the composition of the text, this page count is the decisive clue. It links all of Chapter IV with the beginning of Chapter V. It also indicates that, inscriptionally, pages "239" to "313" are the earliest section of the Dublin manuscript. The absence of a corresponding page numbering for Chapters I–III suggests that these chapters were inscribed later, an assumption strengthened by the fact that not 238, but 362 manuscript pages precede Chapter IV in the Dublin holograph. Accordingly, it is easy to see that the continuous page count, a vestige apparently of a through numbering of some other manuscript, was abandoned as of no further consequence for the remainder of Chapter V. Inscriptionally, therefore, this would also seem to be later than pages "239" to "313," though why the pattern breaks where it does is not readily discernible. Nor, of course, is it a foregone conclusion that Chapters I–III in their entirety preceded all of the main body of Chapter V in a relative chronology of inscription of the manuscript.

The page numbers "239" to "313" accord with Joyce's numbering habits in the *Stephen Hero* manuscript. To this, however, the numbered pages in the Dublin holograph cannot have belonged, since they follow so clearly from the five-chapter plan of *A Portrait*. They were consequently written at some time after September 1907. Perhaps their text was not conceived before February 1909, though this depends on what precisely Ettore Schmitz (Italo Svevo) read of *A Portrait* in January–February 1909.[6] The actual pages "239" to "313" belonged, I suggest, to the *Portrait* manuscript that narrowly escaped destruction in 1911, the "original" original which when rescued was sorted out and pieced together in preparation of the final manuscript,[7] and in which there were "pages . . . I could never have re-written" (*JJ* 314). Contrary to the view that the fourth and fifth chapters of the novel were not brought into shape until 1914, after Ezra Pound's enquiry about publishable material had rekindled Joyce's desire to complete the novel—supposedly while the early chapters were already getting into print[8]—the evidence of the Dublin manuscript indicates that, in 1911, when *A Portrait* was almost annihilated, Joyce had completed Chapter IV and begun Chapter V. Indeed, Chapter IV, the only section of the Dublin holograph which has come down inscriptionally intact from the earlier manuscript, appears also to be the only part of the final text which represents without significant and extensive changes the novel in the textual state of 1911.

As applied to the pre-1911 leaves actually preserved in the Dublin manuscript, Joyce's posthumously reported remark about pages he could never have rewritten would seem to mean merely pages which he saw no further need to reinscribe. It is surely significant that Chapter IV in the Dublin manuscript is the only chapter which to any marked extent shows traces of Joyce's revising hand. Consider the final heightening of the paragraph, steeped in the symbolism of Pentecost, which begins: "On each of the seven days of the week he further prayed that one of the seven gifts of the Holy Ghost might descend upon his soul" (4.51–53).[9] In the manuscript, it originally ended: "to whom, as God, the priests offered up mass once a year, robed in scarlet." This is revised to read: "robed in *the* scarlet *of the tongues of fire*" (*JJA* [10], 751). Or consider how much denser and richer, how much more both threatening and alluring, becomes the passage which in the manuscript originally read:

> No king or emperor on this earth has the power of the priest of God. No angel or archangel in heaven, no saint, not even the Blessed Virgin herself has the power of a priest of God, the power to bind and to loose from sin, the power, the authority, to make the great God of Heaven come down upon the altar and take the form of bread and wine. What an awful power, Stephen!—

By revisional amplification, this becomes:

> No king or emperor on this earth has the power of the priest of God. No angel or archangel in heaven, no saint, not even the Blessed Virgin herself has the power of a priest of God: *the power of the keys,* the power to bind and to loose from sin, *the power of exorcism, the power to cast out from the creatures of God the evil spirits that have power over them,* the power, the authority, to make the great God of Heaven come down upon the altar and take the form of bread and wine. What an awful power, Stephen!— (4.382–391; *JJA* [10], 793)

Correspondingly, Stephen, in his imaginings of priesthood, as originally worded

> longed for the office of deacon at high mass, to stand aloof from the altar, forgotten by the people, his shoulders covered with a humeral veil, and then, when the sacrifice had been accomplished, to stand once again in a dalmatic of cloth of gold on the step below the celebrant. . . . If ever he had seen himself celebrant it was as in the pictures of the mass in his child's massbook, in a church without worshippers, at a bare altar . . . and it was partly the absence of a rite which had always constrained him to inaction.

But in the text as interlinearly revised in the manuscript, his longings and reflections are enriched and particularized in much detail. Also, as in the preceding passage, the revision results in greater syntactical as well as rhythmical complexity:

> He longed for the *minor sacred* offices, *to be vested with the tunicle* of *sub*deacon at high mass . . . his shoulders covered with a humeral veil, *holding the paten within its folds,* and then, *or* when the sacrifice had been accomplished, to stand *as deacon* once again in a dalmatic of cloth of gold on the step below the celebrant . . . If ever he had seen himself celebrant it was . . . in a church without worshippers, *save for the angel of the sacrifice,* at a bare altar . . . and it was partly the absence of *an appointed* rite which had always constrained him to inaction . . . (4.412–426; *JJA* [10], 795–97)

Anyone familiar with Joyce's revisional habits in shaping *Ulysses* and *Finnegans Wake* will here recognize in rudimentary form the patterns and procedures which reach such complexity in the processes of composition of the later works. Conversely, although the examples quoted are the only passages in which compositional revision clearly manifests itself in *A Portrait,* these examples, together with our general knowledge of Joyce's later working habits, make us more keenly aware of the likelihood of revision, perhaps even extensive revision, in the course of the emergence of *A Portrait* at lost stages of its textual development.

Pages "239" to "313," salvaged intact from the manuscript of 1911, will not have been the only pages which Joyce "could never have re-written." Such others as there were he apparently recopied, taking advantage in the process of the opportunity for revising and expanding his earlier text. Positive evidence derives from Ettore Schmitz's letter of 8 February 1909, that, for example, certain "sermons" as part of the third chapter then existed. Consequently, they were also in the manuscript of 1911. In one form or another they would textually seem to go back even to February or March of 1904. The notes for *Stephen Hero* at the end of the "Portrait" copybook testify to the plan for the inclusion in Chapter XI(?) of "six lectures," in a sequence outlined as:

1) Introductory, evening before   1st Day
2) Death
3) Judgement   2nd Day
4) Hell
5) Hell   3rd Day
6) Heaven morning after   4th Day[10]

In *A Portrait,* by contrast, we have one introduction and three sermons on four consecutive evenings. Of the three sermons, the first, on death and judgment, is not given verbatim, but as reported speech, filtered through Stephen's mind. Only the second and third sermons are fully developed as insets of pulpit oratory. Hell is the subject of both of them; and despite the preacher's promise in his introduction to put before the boys "some thoughts concerning the four last things . . . death, judgment, hell and heaven" (3.277–279), there is in *A Portrait* no sermon on heaven. In the last part of Chapter III, instead, heavenly mercy comes as an immediate and intensely personal experience to Stephen on the morning after the fourth day of the retreat: "The ciborium had come to him" (3.1584). Revision, then, is indicated not merely between the two extreme stages of, on the one hand, the outline plan for Chapter XI of *Stephen Hero* and its unknown realization, and, on the other, the final version of Chapter III of *A Portrait,* but also as a developmental process in the course of the emergence since 1907–08 of the third chapter of the five-chapter *Portrait.*

About the emergence not only of Chapter III, but of the entire pre-1911 portion of the novel, further inferences are possible from Ettore Schmitz's letter. The only third-chapter matter it expressly mentions are "the sermons." It gives no indication of the chapter's conclusion. By its initial reference to a fragmentary ending of the text it is even open, I suggest, to the interpretation that the third chapter was unresolved in the sections of the work in progress that Joyce allowed his pupil and critic to read. Schmitz feels unable to submit a rounded opinion about the work partly for want of competence, but partly also because the text breaks off at a crucial moment: "when you stopped writing you were facing a very important development of Stephen's mind." At the same time, his letter appears to indicate that, in a discontinuous manner of composition, Joyce had by late 1908 or early 1909 already proceeded beyond Chapter III in his rewriting of *Stephen Hero* into the five-chapter *Portrait.* For Schmitz continues: "I have already a sample of what may be a change of this mind described by your pen. Indeed the development of Stephen's childish religion to a strong religion felt strongly and vigorously or better lived in all its particulars (after his sin) was so important that no other can be more so" (*Letters* II, 226).

This is an obscure comment if referring to Chapter III alone, and to nothing of *A Portrait* beyond it. It makes good sense, however, if considered as a reflection on the first section of Chapter IV which precisely describes "a strong religion felt strongly and vigorously or better lived in all its particulars (after [Stephen's] sin)." Without a knowledge of the subsequent offer and rejection of priesthood and the culminating scene on the beach, Schmitz would not have grasped the ironic implications of the fourth chapter's opening section; nor would he have realized that Stephen's way lay toward art, not religion. But he saw accurately enough that Joyce was "facing a very important development of Stephen's mind." The reference to having a sample of Stephen's altered mind described by Joyce's pen suggests that Schmitz had read a textual fragment drafted for the continuation of the novel beyond the point where Joyce had "stopped writing." Together with the subsequent explicit mention of the sermons, it suggests that, as Schmitz read it, the third chapter ended with the sermons and the dejection and contrition they caused in Stephen, and that Joyce in 1909 had not yet formulated the last transitional section which by way of Stephen's confession, absolution, and communion links it to the opening of Chapter IV.

With the hindsight of our reading experience, the thematic and narrative logic of that transition seems so clear that it is hard to conceive of any great problems encountered in the writing of it. However, several observations converge which may suggest that Joyce did not achieve it easily. The most important of these derives physically from the Dublin manuscript itself and indicates that the end of Chapter III as we now have it is a very late piece of writing. On fol. 100 of Chapter III in the Dublin holograph, the communal prayer which concludes the last of the hell sermons ends, with Joyce's characteristic three asterisks marking the sectional subdivision, halfway down the page. Below, the final section opens with a clear paleographic break: the pen, the ink, the slope of the hand, and the typical letter formations which remain identical from here on for the last 29 leaves of the chapter are all distinctly different from the style of inscription of the preceding 100 pages, and particularly of that of the two hell sermons on fols. 40–100. As will be seen, there is a distinct paleographic link between Chapter III, fols. 40–100 (*JJA* [10], 557–667), and Chapter V, fols. 112–120 (*JJA* [10], 1089–1105). If, as was argued earlier, the main body of Chapter III was itself retranscribed after 1911 (and probably revised, and perhaps augmented, in the process), the evidence now shows that the final section was inscribed, and therefore added to the main transcription, at yet a later stage. It is conceivable that the end of Chapter III was among the latest sections to be inscribed in the Dublin holograph.

In a first draft, Chapters I–III of *A Portrait* were written between September 1907 and 7 April 1908 (*JJ* 264, 270). They are the chapters that Ettore Schmitz comments on in his letter of 8 February 1909. He praises the second and third chapters, but he criticizes the first: "I think it deals with events devoid of importance and your rigid method of observation and description does not allow you to enrich a fact which is not rich by itself. You should write only about strong things" (*Letters* II, 227). The physical evidence of the Dublin manuscript shows that, in consequence, not only were Chapters I–III written out anew after the near destruction, in 1911, of the earlier *Portrait* manuscript; by inference from the page numbering in the leaves which survive from it, the initial chapters were also augmented by a total of 124 manuscript pages. Beyond a recopying of salvaged text, this bespeaks thorough, and probably extensive revision.[11]

We know from an entry in Stanislaus Joyce's diary that in September 1907, Joyce's plan for rewriting *Stephen Hero* was "to omit all the first chapters and begin with Stephen . . . going to school" (*JJ* 264). This was the way out of the difficulty over the first chapters of *Stephen Hero* which Joyce had commented on before to his brother (*Letters* II, 90). The new conception was realized. In the first school episode, the incomplete alteration of the name Mangan to Moonan in the early pages of the Dublin manuscript demonstrates positively a copying from earlier papers.[12] That would put at least this episode of Stephen's illness at Clongowes among the matter contained in the 1911 manuscript, and hence probably into Chapter I as read by Ettore Schmitz in 1909, and, consequently, as written between 8 September and 29 November 1907. No new chapters dealing with Stephen's childhood were written then or later to precede this beginning.

The first chapter of the novel as we now have it, however, opens with a brief section of great significance which on the narrative level relates Stephen's childhood. It represents the final expression of Joyce's original intention to encompass the earliest years in his hero's life. Its consummate artistry, resulting from a great concentration and condensation of thought, imagery, symbolism, and meaning, has often been admired and commented upon.[13] In the manifold attempts at elucidating the complexity of the opening of *A Portrait,* there seems to be an agreement that, to adopt Hugh Kenner's musical terminology, it functions as an overture anticipating the main themes and developments of the novel. As such, it gives every impression of having been written in view not only of the whole as planned, but of the whole of the subsequent composition as executed, or largely executed, in the details of its narrative progression and symbolism. Though no positive textual proof for this is available, I venture to suggest that the opening section of Chapter I was written at a late stage of the textual genesis of the novel. It had found its shape and place by late 1913, of course, when from the Dublin holograph originated the novel's transmission into print via the typescript prepared from the manuscript. But the opening section with which we are familiar may have formed no part, and (though this is speculation only) may have had no textual equivalent or alternative in Chapter I as read by Ettore Schmitz in 1909 and as contained in the manuscript of 1911.

A general paleographic impression gained from the Dublin holograph is that the final inscription of Chapter II preceded that of Chapter I. An assumption of this order of revision gains support from the observation that at some stage in the seven-year textual history of *A Portrait,* the Christmas dinner scene was moved from Chapter II to Chapter I. This was a revision of utmost significance, to which we shall return. Suffice it here to say that, by all available evidence, Chapter I acquired its final shape in stages, and that Joyce's awareness of its potential for meaning grew over an extended period of composition. Nor would the internal textual evidence of the chapter's growth seem inconsistent with an assumption that Ettore Schmitz's criticism added incentive to the revising of it. Schmitz could hardly have denied "strength" to a Chapter I opening as the present one does, and including the Christmas dinner scene.

Therefore, the act of revision by which the Christmas episode was transferred from Chapter II to Chapter I appears to have been undertaken after

February 1909. A still later dating is suggested by Joyce's "Alphabetical note-book." Among its materials, which in their majority are projections for Chapter V of *A Portrait,* and for *Ulysses,* there are just a few entries which indicate that both the Christmas dinner scene and the novel's second chapter were still on Joyce's mind in 1909–10. Under the heading "Pappie," and after an entry which can be dated to Christmas 1909,[14] we find these further entries:

> He calls a prince of the church a tub of guts . . .
> He offers the pope's nose at table. . . .
> He calls Canon Keon frosty face and Cardinal Logue a tub of guts.
> Had they been laymen he would condone their rancid fat.[15]

At some time after Christmas 1909, then, the dialogue of the Christmas dinner scene must have been revised sufficiently to put these quotations from John Stanislaus Joyce into the mouth of Simon Dedalus. Three further entries in the notebook—one under "Pappie," and two under "Dedalus (Stephen)"—point to Chapter II. The names of Pappie's college friends[16] provide material for the Cork episode; and I take the entries for Stephen Dedalus which read, "The applause following the fall of the curtain fired his blood more than the scene on the stage" and "He felt himself alone in the theatre," to refer, respectively, to the Whitsuntide play, and to the scene in the anatomy theatre in Cork. Taken together, this evidence suggests a late revision of Chapters I and II, possibly sometime in 1910, or, indeed, in the course of assembling the novel after its near destruction in 1911.

II

The last of Joyce's *Dubliners* stories, "The Dead," has been widely interpreted as signaling a new departure in his art, leading to achievements such as the first chapter of *A Portrait.* The two have commonly been viewed in close temporal sequence, since it is known that *A Portrait* was begun in September 1907, immediately after the composition of "The Dead" (*JJ* 264). From the account here given of the state of the final manuscript and of the stages of composition and revision to be reckoned with in the novel's initial chapters, it follows, however, that only Chapter IV can be safely assumed to have existed before 1911 as it survives in the completed novel. Chapters I–III, by contrast, attained their final shape only after that date, and are therefore, in the form in which we possess them, five or more years removed in time from *Dubliners,* and the consummation of its art in "The Dead." Paradoxically, it is Chapter V, although presumably the last to be written, which from the vantage point of the finished *Portrait,* and on the evidential basis of the textual documents still extant, reaches back furthest into the novel's textual history and Joyce's artistic development.

Materials from the textual history have been preserved more amply for the fifth chapter than for the earlier ones. They bear witness to the fact that the transformation of the extant *Stephen Hero* fragment (the chapters which Joyce himself called the "University episode" of that novel) into Chapter V of *A Portrait* passed through several stages of experiment. Since the first thirteen pages of the chapter in its final form were contained in the *Portrait* manuscript of 1911, it appears that the earliest traceable attempts at rewriting preceded its attempted destruction. They seem to have been aimed at only a slight modification-by-condensation of the *Stephen Hero* materials which, one may assume, would have preserved their essentially additive narrative structure. At the end of Chapter XV and midway through Chapter XVIII in the *Stephen Hero* manuscript, we find the entries "End of First Episode of V" and "End of Second Episode of V" (*JJA* [8], 95 and 239). The final *Portrait* text does not realize the linear revisional plan that these entries point to. What materials have been salvaged from the *Stephen Hero* university episode—e.g., the fire-lighting incident with the dean of studies, the music-room scene with Emma Clery, the episode of the Stephen-Emma-Father Moran triangle, as well as numerous brief descriptive and characterizing phrases earmarked for transfer in the *Stephen Hero* manuscript—now reappear out of their earlier order, changed and integrated into different settings and contexts.[17]

Against the foil of the original *Stephen Hero* incidents and scenes, Joyce searched for a new novelistic technique and new forms of expression through language and style. Increasingly, the narrative was internalized. The hero's mind and consciousness became a prism through which the novel was refracted. Characters were functionalized as correlative to theme. A workshop fragment happens to have survived which paradigmatically reveals the inner logic of the process of artistic reorientation.

The document in question is one (and the only genuine one) of the two "Fragments from a Late *Portrait* Manuscript."[18] An external, purely orthographic indicator, though by its nature a significant one, of the fact that it distinctly postdates *Stephen Hero,* is the revised spelling "Dedalus" (for earlier "Daedalus") of Stephen's family name. It also postdates *Stephen Hero* by its introduction of Doherty, alias Oliver St. John Gogarty. The fictional name appears as early as the Pola notebook entries for *Stephen Hero* of 1904.[19] But when Joyce in the summer of 1905 discontinued the writing of *Stephen Hero,* he had not yet reached the point where he would have brought Gogarty into the narrative—although his friends in Dublin who were granted the privilege of reading the finished chapters were eagerly awaiting that moment (*Letters* II, 103). Doherty is not finally cast as a character in *A Portrait,* but reappears as Buck Mulligan in *Ulysses.* The Doherty fragment therefore has justly been viewed as an early vestige of *Ulysses.*[20] But by its situational context, it has a place more immediately within a *Portrait* ambience.

The Doherty episode of the preserved fragment constitutes a section of a kitchen scene between Stephen and his mother. On the manuscript leaf, it is preceded by the last half-sentence from a paragraph which, as A. Walton Litz has observed, appears to be the end of a new rendering of the episode that concluded Chapter XIX (in Joyce's numbering) of *Stephen Hero*.[21] The pencil addition to the end of Chapter XIX in the *Stephen Hero* manuscript, "If I told them there is no water in the font to symbolise that when Christ has washed us in blood we have no need of other aspersions," is reflected in the fragmentary phrase "shed his blood for all men they have no need of other aspersion." The kitchen scene to which the Doherty episode itself is genetically linked followed, after some pages, in Chapter XX (in Joyce's numbering) of *Stephen Hero*. Vestigially, therefore, the manuscript fragment gives evidence of an attempt at linear rewriting of *Stephen Hero* by a foreshortening of its episodic sequence.

Yet technically and stylistically, at the same time, the fragment exemplifies a breakthrough toward the narrative mode of the final *Portrait*. It begins in the middle of Stephen's mental reflection on his own mixed feelings toward Doherty's habits of mocking and blasphemous self-dramatization, and it breaks off as mother and son, confronting one another over the dregs of a finished breakfast in the midst of general disorder in the kitchen, embark upon a dialogue which would appear to be heading toward a new version of the conversation, in *Stephen Hero,* about Stephen's neglect to make his Easter duty. There, as they talk, Stephen is made to reveal his inner state at length, while his mother is only gradually brought to a realization and awareness of the fact that he has lost his faith. After four wordy pages, the dialogue ends:

> Mrs Daedalus began to cry. Stephen, having eaten and drunk all within his province, rose and went towards the door:
> —It's all the fault of those books and the company you keep. Out at all hours of the night instead of in your home, the proper place for you. I'll burn every one of them. I won't have them in the house to corrupt anyone else.
> Stephen halted at the door and turned towards his mother who had now broken out into tears:
> —If you were a genuine Roman Catholic, mother, you would burn me as well as the books.
> —I knew no good would come of your going to that place. You are ruining yourself body and soul. Now your faith is gone!
> —Mother, said Stephen from the threshold, I don't see what you're crying for. I'm young, healthy, happy. What is the crying for? . . . It's too silly . . .[22]

From this conclusion, Joyce in the fragment distills the new beginning of an exchange of words:

> —It is all over those books you read. I knew you would lose your faith. I'll burn every one of them—
> —If you had not lost the your faith—said Stephen—you would burn me along with the books— (*JJA* [10], 1221–2)

Within the fragment as it stands, however, this beginning (there is no telling where it would have led, since Joyce himself does not seem to have seen his way to following it up; the fragment ends at the top of its last manuscript page) is only the conclusion of a thoroughly internalized scene. It is primarily Doherty, and not his mother, who is Stephen's antagonist, and he is present not in person, but in Stephen's thoughts. It is in Stephen's mind that his coarse and boisterous blasphemies are called up, the "troop of swinish images . . . which went trampling through his memory" (*JJA* [10], 1219). The particulars of Doherty's self-dramatization "on the steps of his house the night before," as remembered by Stephen, all function for Joyce as the artistically objective correlative of Stephen's rejection of church rituals and Christian beliefs. Together with the subsequent description of the dirt and disorder in the kitchen they serve to create the mood of Stephen's dejection and weariness—totally different from the defiant "Mother . . . I'm young, healthy, happy. What is the crying for? . . . It's too silly" of *Stephen Hero*—out of which the dialogue grows, and then breaks off.

The technique in the act of rewriting is one of inversion in several respects. From being displayed in external dialogue, the theme of the episode is presented as a projection in narrative images (centered on the antagonist) of the protagonist's mind and memory. The facts and attitudes which emerged only gradually in the fully externalized scenic narration by dialogue, are now anticipated by the economy of poetic indirection. The fragment of conversation which remains begins on the note, and, in foreshortening, on the very word with which its model ended. Mood and atmosphere are enhanced and incidentally altered; the effect of condensation is great on all levels of thought, language, and character presentation. The overall gain in intensity is enormous. Constituting as it does a point of intersection between the earlier episodic pattern of *Stephen Hero* and the new evolving narrative principles and techniques, the "late *Portrait* fragment" thus reveals the significance of Joyce's intermediary *Portrait* experiments.

What presumably remained problematic, however, was to adhere to the device of presenting as a scene at all the crucial moment in the process of Stephen's separation from home, fatherland, and religion. As a scene, it may have been felt to give still too much personal and emotional bias to an essentially intellectual conflict and decision. In the fragment, of course, it depends, additionally, on the introduction into the larger narrative context of the new and essentially insincere character Doherty. The experiment of using him as a correlative and a mocking projection of Stephen's serious rejection of Christian values was abandoned. This meant that the scene between Stephen and his mother could not take even the shape into which it was tentatively revised. In the final text of *A Portrait,* by further radical narrative condensation, the confrontation of mother and son over the question of the Easter duty was deleted altogether, entering the novel only by way of report in Stephen's final conversation with Cranly.

The elimination of the kitchen scene has broader implications, for it appears that the narrative progression of Chapter V as ultimately achieved is determined no longer by scenes, but by conversations and reflections. This seems to be the result of the later revisional experiments of which, now, the notation of the text in the pages of the Dublin fair-copy manuscript itself bears witness. The final chapter of the novel divides into four sections. They are no longer "episodes" in the manner of the Christmas dinner scene, or the Cork episode, or Stephen's flight to the seashore at the end of Chapter IV. "Movements" may perhaps be an apter term for them. The second and fourth movements, essentially static, are given to the composition of the villanelle and to Stephen's diary excerpts. It is only in the more dynamic first and third movements that, by a complex sequence of thematically interlocking conversations, the narrative is effectively carried forward.

As with the novel as a whole, so with Chapter V in particular, the Dublin manuscript helps to distinguish phases of inscription which permit inferences about the order of composition of its parts. Of fols. 112 ff, for example (beginning "What birds were they?" [5.1768; *JJA* [10], 1089]), Chester G. Anderson has suggested, from observations on variations in Joyce's handwriting, that they may have been among the first to reach the form they have in the Dublin holograph.[23] This is incorrect insofar as Chapter IV is inscriptionally clearly the earliest part of the fair-copy manuscript. Nevertheless, Anderson's guess conforms with an impression, gained from further comparison, that the particular variation in Joyce's handwriting observable in fols. 112–20 (through the entire passage that ends "went up the staircase and passed in through the clicking turnstile" [5.1863–4; *JJA* [10], 1105]) recurs also in fols. 39–100 of Chapter III, that is, throughout the two hell sermons (3.538–1170). At the bottom of fol. 39, the new hand sets in with the paragraph beginning "The chapel was flooded by the dull scarlet light" (3.523; *JJA* [10], 555). The change of hand on the same page clearly puts the inscription of fols. 1–39 before that of fols. 39–100. Thereafter, the second obvious inscriptional discontinuity in Chapter III after fol. 100 (*JJA* [10], 677), together with the paleographic likeness of the hell sermon section with fols. 112–20 of Chapter V, suggests—in addition to strengthening the earlier argument for a later inclusion of the final transitional section of Chapter III—that Joyce at this point proceeded directly from the third chapter to faircopying the nine-page opening of the fifth chapter's third movement. This, as will be remembered, is a passage which richly orchestrates the novel's symbolism. In tone and imagery, it is particularly close to the latter half of Chapter IV. Since the hell sermons to which in the inscription of the Dublin holograph it is paleographically linked represent text essentially salvaged from the *Portrait* manuscript of 1911, the text of fols. 112–20 in Chapter V, too, may be of pre-1911 origin.

The remainder of the third movement in Chapter V may then not only have been inscribed later, as the change in the style of the hand after "and passed through the clicking turnstile" on fol. 120 indicates; it may also have been written appreciably later. When the textual continuation was ready to be faircopied and Joyce returned to the middle of fol. 120 to join it on where he had left off writing, the beginning of the last preceding paragraph read: "A sudden brief hiss was heard and he knew that the electric lamps had been switched on in the readers' room." This was revised to "A sudden brief hiss *fell from the windows above him*" (5.1860; *JJA* [10], 1105) to correspond to the parallel phrase which occurs within the subsequent text on fol. 131: "and a soft hiss fell again from a window above" (*JJA* [10], 1127). The manner of the revision, undertaken interlinearly on the manuscript page, is reminiscent of the similar revisions observed in Chapter IV and may well support a view that, here as there, Joyce was only after a passage of time returning to text earlier inscribed.

A manuscript section in Chapter V clearly set off as an insert from its surroundings is that of the villanelle movement. Its sixteen manuscript pages are (but for the last one) inscribed with a different ink and a different slope of the hand on different paper. The verso of fol. 95 (*JJA* [10], 1055), which ends the chapter's first section, is smudged and has yellowed. Similarly, fol. 112 (*JJA* [10], 1089), the first page of the third movement, shows traces of having been outer- and uppermost in a bundle. From this evidence it would appear that, for an appreciable time, sections one and three of the chapter existed separately and apart, and that the villanelle movement was later inserted between them. Further observation shows that the last of the sixteen manuscript pages of the villanelle movement is again on paper similar or identical to that used for the rest of the chapter (although this in fact is a mixed batch). Moreover, the leaf (fol. 111; *JJA* [10], 1087) is also heavily smudged on its verso and bears the mark of a huge paper clip. But for the two lines of running prose at the top, it contains only the complete text of the villanelle as concluding the movement. A closer inspection of the preceding leaf reveals that the words in its last two lines are spaced out uncommonly widely and are not brought out as far to the right edge of the paper as the text on the rest of the page. The article "the" which is the first word on fol. 111 could easily have been accommodated at the bottom of fol. 110. Therefore, fol 110 was inscribed after fol. 111, or, in other words, fol. 111 appears to be the last leaf of the villanelle section from an earlier inscriptional (and probably textual) state.

That this section in its final state was inserted in its present position in the Dublin manuscript only after the preceding ninety-five pages of text as written were finally faircopied—and appreciably later at that, as witnessed by the smudged appearance of fol. 95v—is clear from the fact that it opens, with the paleographic break described, in the lower third of fol. 95. That the final transcription of the villanelle movement also postdates the writing of fols. 112–20 is rendered similarly probable by the other physical evidence referred to: the different paper of the insert, and the smudging of fol. 112 itself. But whether the second movement in its original conception is later than the other parts of Chapter V is less easy to determine. On the contrary, considering the marks of wear and tear on fol. 111v, it is not even out of the question that the villanelle section in an earlier unrevised state also belonged to the pages of the rescued 1911 manuscript which Joyce "could never have rewritten." But this, from the evidence, cannot be demonstrated. What the inscriptional stratification in Chapter V of the Dublin manuscript shows, however, is that Joyce did what he later claimed to have done, assembling the chapter by piecing together sections of manuscript. The chapter was by no means inscribed in the fair-copy manuscript in the regular order of the final text (as the other four chapters apparently were in themselves, though they were not written out in the regular order of the chapters), nor was it probably composed in that order.

On the whole, the indication is that the final shape and structure of Chapter V of *A Portrait of the Artist as a Young Man* evolved gradually as Joyce was working on the diverse materials which in the end he succeeded in unifying in this final chapter of the novel. In it, the villanelle interlude on the one hand, and, on the other hand, the orchestration of the novel's imagery and symbolism in the opening pages of the chapter's third movement, are seen from the evidence of their inscription in the fair-copy manuscript to have early roots in the chapter's conceptual genesis. The narrative framework which structurally supports these poetically highly imaginative passages is anchored in the sequences of conversations in the first and third movements and their relation to one another. Their relationship, which, as indicated, appears to reflect Joyce's final experiments at shaping the chapter, may also be seen in terms of a history of the text.

It is movements one and three in Chapter V that reuse the largest quantity of *Stephen Hero* materials; and of the two, the first takes the greater share. This section is also that part of the chapter where greatest emphasis is on establishing and maintaining narrative progression in action and in time. That such narrative progression is structured by a sequence of conversations, and no longer by episodes, becomes clear precisely from the fact that *A Portrait* salvages (though often with significant modification) dialogue from *Stephen Hero,* while abandoning the loose episodic framework to which it was there tied. The altercation developing from the fire-lighting by the dean of studies, or the exposition of Stephen's aesthetic theories, are outstanding examples. The close adaptation of a dialogue in dog Latin from *Stephen Hero* to comment upon the issue of signing or not signing the declaration for universal peace in *A Portrait* points to the revisional principle. The corresponding dialogue in *Stephen Hero* counterpoints the reading and reception of Stephen's paper on "Art and Life," an incident which does not recur in *A Portrait.* Significantly enough, this is the only instance where *Stephen Hero* materials have been reused in *A Portrait* totally divorced from their earlier context. The original unity of episode and dialogue has been dissociated.

It is the achievement of the opening movement of Chapter V to develop Stephen's attitudes to church, university, and Jesuits; to show how he scorns the emotional and unreflected idealism which motivates alike the declaration for universal peace and the arguments for Irish nationalism; and to set forth his aesthetic theories all in a sequence of encounters with persons he talks to in the course of half a day's wandering through Dublin, from half-past ten in the morning in his mother's kitchen to sometime in the mid-afternoon on the steps of the National Library. This wandering movement, at the same time, is a narrative representation of Stephen's leaving his home and family and finding the theoretical basis for his art. The first section of the chapter takes him halfway into exile.

The third movement, by contrast, while of course gravitating toward Stephen's final encounter and conversation with Cranly, reflects upon and heightens imaginatively and symbolically the attitudes and the positions he has secured in movements one and two. It will be noted that the third movement begins in place and time where the first ended, on the steps of the National Library in the late hours of an afternoon. Its action consists simply of Stephen's seeking out Cranly and separating him from the group of fellow students in order to walk alone with him and talk to him. The device is so similar to Stephen's sequestering one by one the dean of studies, Cranly, Davin, and Lynch earlier in the chapter as to suggest that at some stage in the genesis of Chapter V there existed a provisional and experimental plan for tying all the conversations on the issues he faces, and his going away from home into exile, to the narrative sequence of Stephen's wanderings through Dublin in the course of one day. It would have been in embryo the plan realized in *Ulysses*.

But the renouncing of church and faith in the final conversation with Cranly could then not have been linked to Stephen's falling out with his mother over his refusal to make his Easter duty. For that, Stephen would have had to be brought back home once more in the course of the day, which would have broken the chapter's continuous outward movement. Perhaps a sequence was temporarily considered which would have brought all conversations into one day without sacrificing this directional principle. The unfinished revision of the Easter duty conversation in the "Fragment from a late *Portrait* Manuscript," by the reference to Doherty's "standing on the steps of his house the night before,"[24] would seem to be set in the morning. Perhaps it should be seen as a workshop alternative to the kitchen scene at the beginning of the chapter, which by the evidence of the continuous authorial page numbering in Chapters IV–V was in the 1911 manuscript and, therefore, possibly predates the fragment. It would, however, have very heavily weighted the opening of the chapter which, as it stands, begins so casually; and the different thematic order of the ensuing conversations it would have demanded may well have proved too difficult to bring into balance.

By retrospective inference from *Ulysses* we may catch a glimpse of yet another workshop alternative considered but rejected for Chapter V. The beginnings of *Ulysses,* we know, grew from overflow *Portrait* materials. Not only did the projected but abandoned Martello tower ending for *Portrait* provide the opening for *Ulysses.* Notably early during the *Ulysses* years, Joyce also had a "Hamlet" chapter in store (*cf. Letters* I, 101). This eventually became "Scylla and Charybdis." Even as we possess it in the text of the fair copy as completed on New Year's Eve 1918, it is pivoted on Stephen Dedalus, centered on his aesthetics, and devised as a sequence of conversations. With these characteristics, it may in early conception date back to Joyce's experiments over the structure and text for the fifth *Portrait* chapter. Set as it is in the National Library, it would have fitted between the chapter's first movement ending on the library steps going in, and its third movement opening on those steps going out. It would indeed also have fulfilled the one-day time scheme for Chapter V that we have speculatively postulated. It would, however, have shown up the starkness of such a scheme. As an Easter duty conversation in the family kitchen would have unduly weighted the chapter opening, so a heady exchange about Hamlet, Shakespeare, and aesthetics would have overfreighted its middle. The chapter's progression, without the contrast in tone and mood of the villanelle movement, would have been utterly relentless.

Within the four-part composition of Chapter V as ultimately achieved, several structural principles are simultaneously at work, of which the organization of the thematic and narrative progression in the first and third movements by means of a logical sequence of conversations is the dominant one. Each exchange requires an intellectual counter-position, and Stephen's dialogue partners are accordingly functionalized as Doherty is in the "late *Portrait* fragment," though not as strenuously internalized. Of the inferred structural experiments, namely the attempt at confining the chapter's action to one day, and the sustaining of a continuous outward direction of Stephen's movements, neither was completely abandoned, or wholly sacrificed to the other. Although the villanelle movement stands between the first and third sections, thereby indeterminately lengthening the chapter's time span, the third movement still continues in time (late afternoon) and place (steps of the National Library) where the first ends. Simultaneously, by a subtle avoidance of definite place, the illusion at least is maintained of a continuous movement away from home and into exile. The narrative is so devised that once Stephen leaves his home by the kitchen door in the morning of the day on which the chapter opens, he is never visualized as returning there again. Care is taken not to localize his awakening to compose the villanelle in a bedroom of the family house. The Easter duty conversation, which—regardless of its place in the chapter—would have required a setting in Stephen's home, is eliminated from the narrative altogether. Nor is a specific home setting given for Stephen's discussion with his mother about the "B.V.M." in the diary entry of March 24. Both physically and spiritually, in the end, his departure into exile is represented as an unbroken outward movement sweeping through the entire fifth chapter.

A few but quite specific textual observations finally help to establish the relative chronology of the chapter's four movements. The initial thirteen manuscript pages (of 1911) bring Stephen out of his mother's kitchen and start him on his wanderings across Dublin. The entire first section of the chapter draws copiously on *Stephen Hero*. Once the structural plan for a sequence of conversations had been decided upon, the remainder of the first movement would have followed materially and logically from the chapter's beginning The third movement, in the integral shape of its final version, is distinctly later than the first, and as it stands in the Dublin holograph it may postdate the original conception of the villanelle movement. Significantly, it is only in the text of the third movement that Stephen is given his (*Ulysses*) attribute of an ashplant.[25] Also, the Gogarty figure who commonly goes by the name of Goggins is here once called Doherty (5.2534), indicating a relation of the third movement to the experiments of composition to which the "Fragment from a Late *Portrait* Manuscript" directly, and perhaps the "Scylla and Charybdis" episode of *Ulysses* remotely, bear witness. There is no indication of when the finale of the chapter, the diary section, was planned or written. Though ending the manuscript, it may not have been last in composition. It was the villanelle movement, though perhaps drafted early, that in its final version was last inserted in its predetermined position in the holograph, to complete the fair-copy manuscript, and the entire novel.

III

In its four-part structure, the fifth chapter of *A Portrait of the Artist as a Young Man* is the exact symmetrical counterpart to the first. The childhood overture and two Clongowes episodes, separated by the Christmas dinner scene, are the mirror image of the two movements of Stephen's wanderings through Dublin, separated by the villanelle episode, and the diary finale. Genetically, the novel's beginning and its end appear closely interdependent.

It seems that it was a decision to abandon the sequential or cyclic narrative by episodes as used in *Stephen Hero* in favor of a chiastic center design that broke the impasse in which Joyce found himself over *A Portrait* (and which may have contributed to the desperate action of the attempted burning of the intermediary manuscript in 1911). The textual history of Chapter V documents this momentous change in the compositional concept, and there is much reason to believe that from the fifth chapter it retroactively affected the entire work. Discounting the overture and the finale, which functionally relate as much to the entire novel as they do to their respective chapters, the first and last chapters are each chiastically centered on the Christmas dinner scene and on the composition of the villanelle.

Of the three middle chapters, Chapters II and IV are in themselves still basically narrated in a linear sequence of episodes. So is Chapter III, although here the sequential progression is stayed by the unifying and centralizing effect of a concentration on the single event of the religious retreat. But the chiastic disposition of the novel's beginning and end alters the functional relationships within the middle chapters. Chapters II and IV take on a centripetal and a centrifugal direction, and the religious retreat becomes, literally and structurally, the dead center of the novel. If it has been correct to infer an earlier state of Chapter III where four, five, or even six sermons were given verbatim, and therefore of necessity in an overtly sequential manner, then the revision, which essentially left only the two hell sermons as rendered in the preacher's own words, was undertaken to emphasize the chapter's midpoint position in the chiastic structure of the book. Within Chapter III, divided by Joyce's familiar asterisks into three parts, the beginning in Nighttown and the close in Church Street chapel stand in obvious symmetrical contrast. From the close of Chapter II, the Nighttown opening leads naturally into the hell sermon center. The long search for a satisfactory chapter conclusion to lead out of it, indicated by the late inclusion of the final twenty-nine manuscript pages, may reflect Joyce's awareness of how essential for the work's inner balance it was to give the narrative exactly the proper momentum at the onset of its centrifugal movement.

But Joyce's concern in the final shaping of *A Portrait of the Artist as a Young Man* was not structural only. It was also one of thematic and symbolic heightening. To this the reorganisation of Chapters I and II bears witness that can be inferred from close textual scrutiny.

In the novel's first chapter, three boyhood episodes follow the overture. The first and the last of these involve the reader intensely in Stephen Dedalus' sufferings away from home at Clongowes Wood College. In between, the Christmas dinner scene stands out in contrast. At the same time, several devices of narrative design, poetic patterning, and thematic development serve to anchor this scene in its given position. Its opening sentence, "A great fire, banked high and red, flamed in the grate" (1.716), appears as the reversal of the preceding fire-to-water modulation of "The fire rose and fell on the wall. It was like waves. . . . He saw the sea of waves, long dark waves rising and falling, dark under the moonless night" (1.696, 700). The night, in Stephen's vision and dream, is that of Parnell's last return to Ireland. It is thus on Parnell that the first Clongowes episode mystically culminates. The motif is taken up and developed as a central theme of the Christmas dinner controversy. In its course, the anti-Parnellite incarnate among the characters is Dante. Consequently, the repeated instances where she and her symbolically green and maroon-colored attributes (brushes first, then [1.713–14] dress and mantle) were introduced, also provide structural support and thematic preparation for the Christmas dinner scene.

By means of anticipations and projections of later developments, the episode equally points beyond itself in the novel. Stephen, unable to understand who is right and who is wrong in the dispute arising over the Christmas dinner, recalls by association that Dante "did not like him to play with Eileen because Eileen was a protestant" (1.999–1000). Here, in repeating to himself the question—"How could a woman be a tower of ivory or a house of gold? Who was right then?" (1.1003–1005)—he provides himself with the words from which, in the second Clongowes episode, the epiphanous identification of Eileen with the Virgin will spring (1.1257–60). A similar connection is established in Stephen's thoughts between the Christmas turkey and Mr. Barrett's pandybat: "Why did Mr Barrett in Clongowes call his pandybat a turkey?" (1.801–2). Here the main motif of the chapter's concluding section is announced for the first time. Furthermore, the Christmas dinner scene, as it introduces the persons of the inner family circle into the action proper, characterizes not only Dante, whose presence in the novel ends with this scene, and Mr. Casey, who is here given his only appearance, but also Stephen's father and mother, to whom as characters in the novel our relationship is to a considerable extent determined by their roles in this scene. And it gives us a glimpse, at least, of uncle Charles. At the opening of Chapter II, he will be seen to be of similar importance as friend and mentor to Stephen in his later, as Dante was in his earlier, childhood.

It is not certain that the reader would stop to wonder why uncle Charles should first, and somewhat flatly, be introduced directly into the action of the Christmas dinner scene without bringing with him the full stature of one of the early novel's important "round" characters which he so vividly acquires later. Yet, surely, many details which we later learn about him—his serene and peace-loving nature, and his sincere piety—would help to explain (as they do in retrospect) his attempts to pacify Simon Dedalus and Mr. Casey, as well as his own calm restraint during the heated argument. The reference to Mr. Barrett at Clongowes and his pandybat, however, must give pause. It appears as a genuinely false lead, for within the fiction of *A Portrait*, it is not Mr. Barrett but Father Dolan who wields the pandybat at Clongowes. While it is true that in the course of the second Clongowes episode "old Barrett" (1.1293) is mentioned in passing as being somehow connected with the disciplinary system in force at Clongowes, there is here, it would seem, a contextual discrepancy sufficient to provide a clue to the discovery not only of successive revisions to the Christmas dinner scene, but also to its repositioning, in the final structuring of the novel, from a place it originally held in the second chapter, to its present location in the first chapter, of *A Portrait*.

To trace the compositional process, it is necessary to go back to the planning notes for *Stephen Hero*. As entered on the blank leaves in the copybook containing the manuscript of the 1904 narrative essay "A Portrait of the Artist," these provide for a "Christmas party" in the eighth chapter, in a central position between "Business complications," "Aspects of the city" and "Visits to friends," "Belvedere decided on."[26] In a letter of 7 February 1905, furthermore, James Joyce reminds his brother Stanislaus that "Mrs Riordan who has left the house in Bray returns . . . to the Xmas dinner-table in Dublin" (*Letters* II, 79). If the wording "Christmas party" in the notes may leave room for doubt,[27] the letter is unequivocal in giving a Dublin setting to the Christmas dinner episode in *Stephen Hero*. It was doubtless assigned to the Christmas of 1892, a few months before Stephen (like James Joyce) entered Belvedere College. It is probably significant that Sullivan[28] identifies Mr. Barrett of *A Portrait* as Patrick Barrett, S.J., a scholastic stationed at Belvedere College. The name would seem to point to the survival into *A Portrait* of textual vestiges from *Stephen Hero*.

In the *Portrait* paragraph immediately preceding Stephen's recollection of the name Mr. Barrett had for his pandybat, the purchase of the Christmas turkey is related. Stephen's father "had paid a guinea for it in Dunn's of D'Olier Street" (1.797), a poulterer and game dealer in Dublin's finest shopping district. But, as the family is still living in Bray at the time of the Christmas scene in *A Portrait,* one wonders—while not discounting Simon Dedalus', *alias* John Joyce's, predilection for living in style even in progressively adverse circumstances, which would presumably stretch to buying the Christmas turkey from only the choicest of poulterers—why the bird could not have been procured from somewhere nearer home. At least, Dun's of D'Olier Street, a ten-minute walk at the most from 14 Fitzgibbon Street off Mountjoy Square, the first of the Joyce residences in Dublin (*JJ* 35), would be a more natural place to buy it if the family were already living in the city, as the Daedalus family was at the time of the Christmas dinner episode in *Stephen Hero.* When the Christmas dinner scene was rewritten for *A Portrait,* therefore, materials of the *Stephen Hero* Christmas dinner episode appear to have been reused.

From the evidence of various textual details, it may be assumed that, as *Stephen Hero* was rewritten to become *A Portrait,* the scene initially retained the position it held in *Stephen Hero.* In fact, the very survival of the narrative detail about Dunn's of D'Olier Street is the more easily accounted for if the episode was originally cast in Dublin surroundings not only in *Stephen Hero,* but in *A Portrait* also. Similarly, John Casey's opening of his story "about a very famous spit" amuses by the unbashful expedient employed to relate the story to a new setting for the scene in the novel. "It happened not long ago in the county Wicklow" is how John Casey might have begun in Dublin; "It happened not long ago in the county Wicklow where we are now" (1.964–66) is how he begins in Bray. Also, that sentence about Mr. Barrett, "Why did Mr Barrett in Clongowes call his pandybat a turkey?" (1.801) would cause no disturbance at a point in the novel corresponding to the episode's position in *Stephen Hero*. One is struck by the specification "Mr Barrett in Clongowes" and its reinforcement, as if in afterthought: "But Clongowes was far away." (1.803) This is just a little curious when Clongowes is the only school Stephen has so far experienced and from which he is away for a brief Christmas leave only. It would better fit the situation in Chapter II where he has left Clongowes never to return. At that point, too, Stephen's recollection of Mr. Barrett's pandybat would not, as in the final text, have the signalizing force of a first mention of the pandying motif. Rather, it would appear as but an incidental memory of the disciplinary atmosphere of Clongowes, introduced only when, as readers, we had already shared Stephen's gruesome experience of unjust punishment at Father Dolan's hands. At the same time, a passing reference to "old Barrett" in the boys' conversation, establishing that Father Dolan was not the only punishing agent at Clongowes, would have prepared us for Mr. Barrett. There would be no danger of reacting to him as to a false lead in the novel.

The strongest reason for assuming that the Christmas dinner scene was still set in a Chapter II context in an early *Portrait* draft is the way in which, even in its final form, it presents uncle Charles. He is essentially not characterized in the scene itself, and there is almost no previous indication that he belongs to the family circle. His proper introduction follows at the beginning of Chapter II. Here, in the summer after the Clongowes events, he energetically does all the shopping at Bray, and often covers ten or twelve miles of the road on a Sunday with Stephen and his father (*cf.* 2.73–76). In the autumn, he moves with the family to Dublin, where he soon "[grows] so witless that he [can] no longer be sent out on errands" (2.220–21). The uncle Charles of the Christmas dinner scene is this feeble old man, confined to the house, left behind when Simon Dedalus and John Casey go for their Christmas day constitutional. He sits "far away in the shadow of the window" (1.723–24) and does not join in the other men's banter; nor is he given a thimbleful of whisky to whet his appetite. When all take their seats for dinner, he has to be roused gently: "Now then, sir, there's a bird here waiting for you" (1.784).

The novel's final text still shows the episode's initial place:

> He went once or twice with his mother to visit their relatives: and, though they passed a jovial array of shops lit up and adorned for Christmas, his mood of embittered silence did not leave him. . . . He was angry with himself for being young and the prey of restless foolish impulses, angry also with the change of fortune which was reshaping the world about him into a vision of squalor and insincerity. Yet his anger lent nothing to the vision. He chronicled with patience what he saw, detaching himself from it and tasting its mortifying flavour in secret. (2.243–52)

Here is the right time of year; and the violent quarrel between Dante, Mr. Casey, and Simon Dedalus, all dear to Stephen in their several ways, may very well have served as the crowning epiphany to alter Stephen's view of the world about him. It is indeed Stephen's mood and state of mind at this point which provide the final clue that it was the first *Portrait* version of the Christmas dinner scene removed from Chapter II (and not its *Stephen Hero* prototype taken directly from that novel's eighth chapter) which was inserted, with careful, though not flawless adaptation, into the episode's final position in Chapter I. Stephen's detachment and his role of patient chronicler as here described explain admirably the style and point of view which make the scene stand in such striking contrast to the Clongowes episodes which now surround it.

In speculating (for there is not sufficient evidence to support safe inferences) about the shape of the novel's second chapter in detail before the Christmas dinner scene was removed from it, two alternatives, basically, may be considered. Either the present sequence of three disjunct epiphanies (2.253–356), exemplifying what Stephen saw and detachedly chronicled, was inserted to fill the gap; or else, the narrative units coexisted in a climactically additive structure, culminating in the disastrous Christmas dispute. The latter view gains support from a comparison with the notes for Chapter VIII of *Stephen Hero*. All materials which were there planned for narrative execution are contained in the second *Portrait* chapter in its final state, plus the Christmas dinner scene. This would imply that, in terms of its narrative structure, the initial draft of the second *Portrait* chapter was not radically distant from its *Stephen Hero* prototype. By retaining a markedly episodic pattern it would have held an intermediary position comparable to that of those lost stages of composition occurring in the process of remolding Chapter V.

When, however, the Christmas dinner scene was repositioned, the shape of the new novel's second chapter changed, and despite the evidence suggesting that Chapter II was simply foreshortened by the length of an episode, we need not assume that in its final form it represents merely a torso of the narrative structure of the earlier version. At least one paragraph in the final text suggests revision after the Christmas dinner scene's removal which involved a reproportioning of the chapter possibly extending to a substitution or addition of text. The paragraph in question concludes the present sequence of epiphanies and describes Stephen's attempt, unsuccessful for hours, to write a poem to E—— C—— the morning after their parting on the steps of the last tram the night before. As he doodles, he remembers himself similarly "sitting at his table in Bray the morning after the discussion at the Christmas dinnertable, trying to write a poem about Parnell . . ." (2.367–69). He failed (as Joyce, in the corresponding autobiographical situation, reportedly did not). The presence of this reminiscence in the final text suggests that the Christmas dinner scene in at least one of its earlier forms, and so possibly in its first *Portrait* version, was followed by the description of a scene in which Stephen wrote a poem about Parnell. It is possible even that the paragraph in the present final version preserves in part the text of that description. The writing of the poem to E—— C—— would appear to be a substitution for the writing of the poem about Parnell. The event which occasions the poem to E—— C—— must be considered to hold the structural place of the Christmas dinner scene before its removal. That is, the epiphany about Stephen and Emma on the steps of the tram moved into this position by the same act of revision that removed the Christmas dinner scene.

Considering the Christmas dinner scene in its present revisional position, one may note several textual details still betraying that the episode was not original to Chapter I. From the portrayal of Dante in it, for example, references to her green and maroon-colored attributes are conspicuously absent. The green and maroon mark young Stephen's way of grasping the opposition in Dante's shifting allegiance to Michael Davitt and Charles Stewart Parnell. Since the colors are otherwise so consistently associated with the Parnell motif in Chapter I, it is not easily conceivable that they should not in some manner have been woven in if the Christmas dinner scene form the beginning had been written to follow the first Clongowes section and had been evolved directly from it.

On the other hand, it appears that three passages, at least, were added wholly or in part to adapt the scene to its Chapter I setting. They are 1.802–9, or possibly 802–16 (that is, all of the paragraph after "But Clongowes was far away," and possibly much of the subsequent paragraph, too); 1.990–1011, and 1.1058–1073. These passages extend the point of view established as Stephen's and maintained throughout the remainder of the first chapter. They display the schoolboy's thought pattern, his stream of consciousness triggered by smells, warmth, the sensation of "queerness," the sound of a voice, things nice or not nice, and his worry over the meaning of words, and over the rightness or wrongness of things. Without them, the episode is constructed almost wholly by dialogue which, with the emotional reactions of all the characters to it (including Stephen's), is told by a narrator, verging on the omniscient, from the vantage point of an outside observer.

By inference, the dialogue structure, still predominant in the episode's final form, represents the shape of the scene before it was adapted to fulfill the functions of its Chapter I position. Yet the adaptation did not apparently leave the dialogue entirely untouched. Simon Dedalus' emphatic outburst, in response to John Casey's suggestion that the Irish priests "hounded" Parnell into his grave: "Sons of bitches! . . . When he was down they turned on him to betray him and rend him like rats in a sewer. Lowlived dogs!"(1.943–5) is imaginable in an earlier foreshortened form confined to canine imagery alone. The phrase "and rend him like rats in a sewer" is a reference to the square ditch at Clongowes (cf. 1.126–7 and 269–70; and see below) and would thus appear a late addition. Moreover, near this point in the dispute we find two further utterances of Simon Dedalus' which would seem to be late additions to the *Portrait* text because, from the evidence, they were made by John Joyce only at Christmas 1909 when James Joyce was at home in Dublin from Trieste. In his "Alphabetical notebook.," below an entry datable to Christmas

1909, Joyce reminded himself about several of his father's idiosyncrasies and characteristic remarks.[29] "He offers the pope's nose at table," and "He calls a prince of the church a tub of guts," "He calls Canon Keon frosty face and Cardinal Logue a tub of guts" are the entries which refer to "There's a tasty bit here we call the pope's nose" (1.903) and "Respect! . . . Is it for Billy with the lip or for the tub of guts up in Armagh [i.e., Cardinal Logue, archbishop of Armagh]? Respect!" (1.923–4) Just how much altogether the earlier dialogue of the Christmas dinner scene was retouched or rewritten cannot be determined. From the instances that can be made out, however, it is clear that the episode was adapted with some care to its new position in Chapter I.

In James Joyce's childhood, the quarrel between John Joyce, John Kelly, and Hearn Conway which grew so noisy that it was heard by the Vances across the road, broke out over the Christmas dinner in 1891, when the Joyce family was still living in Bray (*JJ* 34). It was by an act of "poetic license," developing and responding to the narrative logic of *Stephen Hero* as it unfolded before him, that Joyce there gave the Christmas dinner scene a setting in 1892 and in Dublin, molding it into the experience of an older Stephen who had, we may assume, an increased understanding of the events he witnessed. That is the direction the scene's exposition still points to: "And Stephen smiled too for he knew now that it was not true that Mr Casey had a purse of silver in his throat" (1.733–34). Exact autobiographical correspondence was not Joyce's primary concern. This circumstance should be borne in mind when, in *A Portrait,* the episode again takes place in 1891. 1891 was the year of Parnell's death. In the final *Portrait,* Chapter I is a chapter as much about Parnell and Ireland as about Stephen and Clongowes, and its strength derives from this thematic correspondence which establishes significant reference to areas its schoolboy world by itself does not reach.

It is Parnell's death and burial which provide the symbolic focus for the beginning of the novel. In order to make the historical event assume structural control over the fiction, the two and a half years, from September 1888 to April 1891, which James Joyce spent at Clongowes Wood College are condensed into Stephen's one year, autumn 1891 to spring 1892, at that school. James Joyce and Stephen Dedalus were at no time contemporaries at Clongowes. In Stephen's year there, the action proper of the novel opens on the day when he changes from "77" to "76" the number in his desk indicating the days which remain until he will rejoin his family. Christmas Eve is the day which the *Portrait* text, by means of Stephen's dream on the night when his fever develops, establishes as the date of reference for his calculation: "Holly and ivy for him and for Christmas" (1.476–77). According to the calendar, then, the novel opens on a day which falls exactly between the day of Parnell's death (October 6th) and that of his burial (October 11th). There can be no doubt about the significance; nor indeed of the fact that Joyce intentionally established the correspondence. For in the Dublin holograph of *A Portrait,* he erased the numerals which were first given as "thir(ty?)-seven" and "(thirty?)-six and wrote in their stead "seventy-seven" and "seventy-six" (1.101–2 and 282–3; *JJA* [9], 19, 45).

The seventy-sixth day before Christmas is October 9th. The next day Stephen is taken to the infirmary. He has a fever fantasy of his own death. They give him no medicine, but in the evening, as the fire rises and falls on the wall, he sinks into a recuperative sleep. In it, he has a dream or vision which synchronizes his time and Parnell's. The scene which he sees under the dark moonless night is that of Parnell's return to Ireland's shore as the ship which carries his body approaches the pierhead. The harbor is Kingstown; the time is daybreak of 11 October 1891, the day when the Irish buried their dead hero. By extension of the sequential numbering, it is the morning of the 74th day before Christmas. Thus, at the end of the first *Portrait* episode Stephen does not die like Little; he recovers. There are for him no "tall yellow candles on the altar and round the catafalque" (1.598–99). In Stephen's sleep of convalescence, Parnell's death stands for his own: "He is dead. We saw him lying upon the catafalque" (1.709). Parnell dies so that Stephen may live. That is why, in the novel, Parnell's return across the waves of the Irish Sea to be mourned by his people and buried in Ireland's soil, and Stephen's return to life from a sickness-to-death (as he imagines it) are synchronized to take place during the same night and early morning hours of 11 October 1891.

From the vantage point of this moment of structural significance, one may discern patterns in the fictional web and their links with real events. It was the seventy-seventh day before Christmas, the first day specifically mentioned in the story (though the action proper does not set in until the next day), which saw the incident that caused Stephen's illness: "Wells . . . had shouldered him into the square ditch the day before . . . It was a mean thing to do; all the fellows said it was" (1.265–69). According to the calendar, this was October 8th. The narrative development of *A Portrait of the Artist as a Young Man,* then, proceeds from the meanness and injury Stephen suffered at the hands of a schoolfellow, and fellow Irishman, on the first post-Parnellite day in Irish history.[30] And it was on October 8th of another year, 1904, that a young Irish couple, James Joyce and Nora Barnacle, left Dublin's North Wall for a life of exile. With the superior touch of the artist in full control of his narrative, Joyce thus ensures that in a novel which leads into exile the beginning prefigures the end.

Here, to be sure, the allusion is indirect and thoroughly submerged. But the synchronization of Stephen's and Parnell's time on the morning of October 11th is tangibly present in the narrative. It suggests further significant correspondences among the events from which it derives. It is true that, if the novel's succession of events is directly projected onto the historical calendar, they are not simultaneous. But it is worth observing that a day or date for Parnell's death is not given in *A Portrait.* If time may be thought to be condensed (silently, in the fiction) into the three days which in Christian countries are customarily observed between a death and a burial in remembrance of the three days of Christ's crucifixion, harrowing of hell, and resurrection, then time at the opening of *A Portrait* is seen to be moralized to link Parnell's betrayal and death with Stephen's fall, at the hands of Wells, into the square ditch at Clongowes. There, "a fellow had once seen a big rat jump plop into the scum" (1.126–7 and 269–70). In the Christmas dinner scene, as we have seen, Simon Dedalus is made to say of Parnell: "When he was down they turned on him to betray him and rend him like rats in a sewer." On Stephen's side of the equation, the assumed parallelism of significant action is strangely supported by the actual fact that, in 1891, October 8th, the day Stephen is shouldered into the square ditch, was a Thursday; October 9th, the day he falls ill and, in the evening, hurries to undress for bed saying his prayer quickly quickly "before the gas was lowered so that he might not go to hell when he died" (1.405–6) was a Friday;[31] October 10th, the day in the infirmary, a Saturday; and October 11th, when Stephen revives at the break of day, a Sunday. On Parnell's side, a similarly significant patterning of the events is prohibited by historical fact: Parnell died on October 6th and was buried on the sixth day thereafter. All the novel can do—and does—is not to relate such fact when it does not tally with the symbolically charged patterns of the fiction. Only pure fiction would permit a narrative of pure significance. But by the patterned interaction of history and fiction as found at the opening of *A Portrait,* and throughout the novel, not only historical event and calendar time are moralized. The fiction, too, Stephen's early schoolboy experience (thoroughly insignificant by itself), acquires symbolic stature.

Significant structure, then, derives here not from an analogy of Joyce's autobiography and the fiction, but from an interaction of history and the fiction. The distinction needs stressing, since it has been through biographical bias that earlier criticism has failed to perceive clearly the meaningful and precise interrelationship of historical event, calendar time, and the narrative in Chapter I of *A Portrait.*[32] It remains most remarkable, of course, that the narrative detail by which everything falls into place, that is, the "right" number of days which separate the events of the first Clongowes episode from Christmas, and thus also from the Christmas dinner, was not present in the text until introduced by revision in the faircopy manuscript. Only then was the chapter's symbolic potential finally realized. James Joyce creatively responded to the disposition of the narrative and the juxtaposition of episodes that he had brought about. The observable act of revision in the final manuscript thus additionally contributes to proving that the Christmas dinner scene only late in the novel's textual history found its present position in Chapter I. Before it did, no particular significance would have attached to the numbers in Stephen's desk; any numbers would have served.

IV

To sum up: from Stanislaus Joyce's testimony we know that James Joyce began to write *A Portrait of the Artist as a Young Man* in September 1907. By 7 April 1908, he had finished three chapters. These, we must assume, were first drafts of the novel's first half which do not as such survive. During the remainder of 1908 no more than partial drafts of Chapter IV appear to have been written. In February of 1909, Ettore Schmitz's praise and criticism of the three completed chapters, plus, apparently, an additional early stretch of narrative of Chapter IV, gave Joyce encouragement to continue with the novel. The only certain knowledge we have of his work between 1909 and sometime in 1911 is that he completed Chapter IV and entered upon the composition of Chapter V. All of Chapter IV and the first thirteen manuscript leaves of Chapter V survive intact in the Dublin holograph from the *Portrait* manuscript which was nearly destroyed in 1911.

Notes or draft materials for Chapters I–IV of *A Portrait* are generally absent, and all of Chapters I–XIV of the *Stephen Hero* manuscript, in particular, is lost. If an inference from these fact is possible, Chapters I–IV of *A Portrait* were by 1911, or even perhaps as early as sometime in 1909, considered essentially completed. Joyce's "Alphabetical notebook" contains materials used almost exclusively in Chapter V of *A Portrait,* and in *Ulysses.* Its inception appears to date from the months of Joyce's visit to Dublin in 1909,[33] where, while he was separated from his manuscript, his memory of persons and incidents would have been refreshed and enriched.

By Joyce's own dating in retrospect, the incident of the near destruction of the *Portrait* manuscript occurred in the latter half of 1911. This was a true moment of crisis in the prepublication history. The "charred remains of the MS" (*Letters* I, 136) remained tied up in an old sheet for some months, and thus it was in 1912 that the writing of *A Portrait of the Artist as a Young Man* entered its culminating phase. According to the mark of division set by the manuscript pages that were transferred physically into the Dublin holograph, Joyce's post-1911 labors were threefold. He composed all of Chapter V, or approximately the last third of the book, in its final form. From it, he devised an essentially new structural plan for the entire book. This involved a reorganisation of Chapters I and II, centered on repositioning and revising the Christmas dinner scene, that intensified symbolical historic and mythic correspondences in the text. Chapters I–III were recopied in their entirety. The operations were interrelated and interdependent, and the creative achievement, one may well believe, was on a scale that would have required the best part of two years' work.

In 1913, when the title page of the Dublin holograph was dated, the end appears to have been well in sight. On Easter Day 1913, Joyce himself envisaged finishing his novel by the end of the year (*Letters* I, 73). He may, however, as so often, have underestimated the time he would need to complete it. He signed the final manuscript page "Dublin 1904 Trieste 1914," and the sections of text which apparently were last included in the manuscript, such as the end of Chapter III and the revised villanelle episode, may not have reached their final form much before they were required as copy for the Trieste typist in, presumably, the summer of 1914. But it is a conclusion from the preceding genetic critical approach that, in essence, the novel attained the shape and structure in which we now possess it during 1912 and 1913. Despite all vicissitudes and misfortunes of his day-to-day life,[34] these were two years of concentrated creativity for James Joyce, as he was forging and welding together *A Portrait of the Artist as a Young Man*.

Notes

1. The narrative essay appears to have given the origin for the date-line at the end of *A Portrait of the Artist as a Young Man:* "Dublin 1904/Trieste 1914." A photoreprint of "A Portrait of the Artist" is available in [vol. 7] of *The James Joyce Archive* [*JJA*]. (New York and London: Garland Publishing, Inc., 1978), pp. 70–94. It has been reprinted, with many oversights and errors, in *A Portrait of the Artist as a Young Man: Text, Criticism, and Notes,* eds. Chester G. Anderson and A. Walton Litz, Viking Critical Library (New York: Viking Press, 1968), pp. 257–68. In a more reliable text, it appears in Robert Scholes and Richard M. Kain, eds., *The Workshop of Daedalus: James Joyce and the Raw Materials for* A Portrait of The Artist as a Young Man (Evanston: Northwestern University Press, 1965), pp. 60–68.

2. From freshly assessed evidence, I argue in the "Introduction," pp. 1–2, to James Joyce, *A Portrait of the Artist as a Young Man,* edited by Hans Walter Gabler with Walter Hettche (New York and London: Garland Publishing, Inc., 1993), that Joyce indeed began his autobiographical novel sometime in the first half of 1903, that is, almost a year earlier than has hitherto been assumed. That he probably wrote just the first seven of the projected nine times seven (=63) chapters before setting down the narrative essay in January 1904 is indicated by the fact that the notes on the blank leaves of the "Portrait of the Artist" copy-book concern *Stephen Hero* from Chapter VIII onwards. If taken with these modifications, the "Appendix" to Hans Walter Gabler, "The Seven Lost Years of *A Portrait of the Artist as a Young Man,*" in: Thomas F. Staley and Bernard Benstock (eds.), *Approaches to Joyce's* Portrait. *Ten Essays.* ([Pittsburgh:] University of Pittsburgh Press, 1976), pp. 53–56, should remain essentially valid. A subsequent in-depth study, however, is Claus Melchior, "*Stephen Hero:* Textentstehung und Text. Eine Untersuchung der Kompositions-und Arbeitsweise des frühen James Joyce." Diss. München, 1988.

3. Richard Ellmann, *James Joyce* (New York: Oxford University Press, 1982), pp. 264, 314, subsequently cited as *JJ.*

4. The one missing leaf is the first of the "Fragments from a Late *Portrait* Manuscript" (*Workshop,* p. 107), now at the British Library. It has been incorporated in its proper place in the photoreprint of the Dublin holograph (*JJA,* vols. [9] and [10]).

5. The actual numbers are 239–41, 243–313. But, with no lacuna in the text, this is apparently a simple error in the numbering, as Harriet Weaver noted when she checked the manuscript: "evidently a mistake for 242. H.S.W."

6. *Letters of James Joyce,* vol. II, ed. Richard Ellmann (New York: Viking Press, 1966), pp. 226f. [*Letters* II]

7. *Letters of James Joyce,* vol. I, ed. Stuart Gilbert (1957; New York: Viking Press, 1966), p. 136. [*Letters* I]

8. On this point Anderson (Chester G. Anderson, "The Text of James Joyce's *A Portrait* . . .," *Neuphilologische Mitteilungen* 65 [1964], pp. 182–84) and *JJ,* 354, basically agree. I follow these authorities in "Zur Textgeschichte und Textkritik des *Portrait,*" in Wilhelm Füger, ed., *James Joyces Portrait: Das "Jugendbildnis" im Lichte neuerer duetscher Forschung* (Munich, 1972), p. 22; and also—though with a cautionary footnote after first looking into the fair-copy manuscript—in "Towards a Critical Text of James Joyce's *A Portrait of the Artist as a Young Man,*" *Studies in Bibliography* 27 (1974): 28.

9. All references (by chapter.line numbers) are to James Joyce, *A Portrait of the Artist as a Young Man,* edited by Hans Walter Gabler with Walter Hettche (New York and London: Garland Publishing, Inc., 1993; and New York: Vintage International, Vintage Books, 1993). Italics indicating revisions are mine.

10. *JJA* [7], p. 86; *Workshop,* p. 69.

11. Quantitatively, however, it is unlikely that the earlier text was augmented by a full 50 percent, as the addition of 124 pages to the original 238 might suggest. As compared to the inscription of Chapter IV, the columns of text in the freshly inscribed chapters are distinctly narrower, especially so throughout Chapter I. This factor alone would account for many more pages in the new manuscript portion.

12. As noted in Anderson, "The Text," p. 170n.

13. See especially Hugh Kenner, *Dublin's Joyce* (London: Chatto and Windus, 1955), pp. 114–16.

14. "He gave me money to wire to Nora on Christmas Eve." *JJA* [7], p. 145, and *Workshop,* p. 103.

15. *JJA* [7], pp. 145–6, and *Workshop,* p. 104.

16. Ibid.

17. In his 1944 edition of *Stephen Hero* (New York: New Directions), Theodore Spencer judged Joyce's red and blue crayon markings in the manuscript to be cancellations. See his "Editorial Note," p. 18. The evidence has meanwhile been thoroughly reconsidered by Claus Melchoir (see above note 2).

18. *JJA* [10], pp. 1219–1222, and *Workshop,* pp. 107–08.

19. *Workshop,* p. 85.

20. A. Walton Litz, *The Art of James Joyce* (London: Oxford University Press, 1964), Appendix B, pp. 132–35.

21. *The Art of James Joyce,* p. 137.

22. *Stephen Hero* (New York: New Directions 1944; 1963), p. 135; *JJA* [8], 441–43.

23. "The Text," p. 179n.

24. *JJA* [10], p. 1220, and *Workshop,* p. 107.

25. Four times, at 5.1770, 1805, 2069 and 2233.

26. *JJA* [7], p. 92 and *Workshop,* p. 73.

27. "Party" is an odd word to use for the family Christmas dinner; the reference just might be to the children's party of which Epiphany no. 3 (*JJA* [7], p. 54 and *Workshop,* p. 13) gives the conclusion, subsequently slightly, if significantly, varied in 2.322–49.

28. Kevin Sullivan, *Joyce among the Jesuits* (New York: Columbia University Press, 1958), p. 92. Curiously, "Mr" Barrett of *A Portrait* is titled "Father" Barrett in the Dublin holograph, and even in the original inscription of the typescript copied from the manuscript. The change from "Father" to "Mr" is one of the very few alterations Joyce himself made in the typescript. The late revisional touch establishes particularly clearly that the character subsequently referred to in *A Portrait* as "old Barrett" (1.1293) and "Paddy Barrett" (1.1450) is thought of as "a scholastic not yet admitted to the priesthood" (*cf.* Chester G. Anderson and A. Walton Litz (eds.), *A Portrait . . .: Text, Criticism, and Notes* [New York: Viking, 1968], p. 494) and would seem to confirm Sullivan's identification of the historical character prototype.

29. *Cf.* above, note 15.

30. Parnell died in England on 6 October, but the news only reached Ireland on the 7th (see, impressively, *Workshop,* pp. 136–37). October 8th, therefore, can properly be said to be the first post-Parnellite day in Irish history.

31. In bed, "the yellow curtains"—yellow like the candles round the catafalque—"shut him off on all sides" (1.422–23). Stephen hears the prefect's shoes descending the staircase. They guide his feverish imagination to a black dog with eyes as big as carriagelamps, and the ghosts of inhabitants of the castle long deceased. The prefect comes back the next morning to take Stephen to the infirmary. Is he, by fleeting association, Stephen's guide, as in a *Divina Commedia,* in a descent to hell?

32. Arnold Goldman, "Stephen Dedalus's Dream of Parnell," *JJQ* 6 (Spring 1969), 262–64, anticipates important elements of the present argument, but remains puzzled by inconsistencies between Joyce's biography and the fiction.

33. The notebook gives the appearance of having been arranged, and begun with a run of its first entries through most of the alphabetical headings, at one time. Consequently, the dateable entry under "Pappie" (see above, note 14) takes on significance for the dating of the whole notebook.

34. *JJ,* chapters 20 and 21 *passim.*

STRUCTURE, IMAGE,
SYMBOL, MYTH
◆

[Joyce's *Portrait* and Flaubert's *L'Education Sentimentale*]

David Hayman

In 1901, nearly two years before he began work on the first version of *A Portrait of the Artist as a Young Man,* James Joyce wrote concerning George Moore:

> Mr. Moore is really struggling in the backwash of the tide that has advanced from Flaubert through Jakobsen to D'Annunzio: for two entire eras lie between *Madame Bovary* and *Il Fuoco.*[2]

There is more to this rather pontifical statement than the value judgment of a nineteen-year-old initiate. Here, for the convenience of later critics, Joyce has listed some of the major literary forebears of his own first novel, and, perhaps unwittingly, he has charted the course to be taken by his later work. Flaubert, Jacobsen and D'Annunzio, through their several *Bildungsromane* furnished Joyce not only with theories, images, points of style and an occasional sequence or scene; they also combined to supply precedents for a significant number of the traits which make *A Portrait of the Artist as a Young Man* a new departure in the English novel. In D'Annunzio's *Il Fuoco,* with its curious blend of symbolist and realist techniques, Joyce found a model for the *Portrait*'s suggestive, almost transitionless narrative method, a method which permits the author to deal with units of experience in a variegated prose style weighted with metaphors and parallels designed to define the artist-hero's experience in terms of his ego as opposed to his environment. More specifically, Joyce may well have derived from this novel, whose first half is significantly entitled the "Epiphany of the Flame," crucial images like that of the labyrinth and the faun, the Daedalus-Icarus identity of Stephen and the extraordinarily effective though extravagantly mannered style which expresses Stephen's mental processes in the *Portrait*'s third chapter. Jens Peter Jacobsen's great novel *Niels Lyhne* is by contrast a lean and spare account of the childhood and sentimental education of a dilettantish poet It is remark-

Originally published as "*A Portrait of the Artist as a Young Man* and *L'Education Sentimentale:* The Structural Affinities" in *Orbis Litterarum* 19, no. 4 (1964): 162–75. Reprinted with the permission of the author.

able for its singlemindedness, its superb dramatic timing and its frank treatment of controversial themes. Joyce seems to have modeled Stephen's religious agony, as depicted at the close of the retreat chapter, after Jacobsen's portrayal of the repentence of Fennimore Refstrup, an adulterous woman mourning the death of her husband.

In Flaubert (whose every word Joyce claimed to have read)[3] the Irish writer may have discovered precedents for the *Portrait*'s architectonic structure, its brilliant and subtle balance of ironies, its "impersonal" narrator whose point of view is only apparently identical with that of the protagonist. The flaubertian precedent stands at the beginning of and controls the direction taken by Joyce's metaphorical tide, but the character of Flaubert's influence is as hard to fix as the affinities are pervasive; for, apart from a near-masochistic perfectionism and from some pregnant theories which Joyce was not alone in appropriating, Flaubert, like Joyce, is most remarkable for his experiments with style and structure.

Although it is not the greatest of these experiments, *L'Education Sentimentale,* the novel of whose structure Flaubert was most proud, is, perhaps more than either *Madame Bovary*[4] or *La Tentation de Saint Antoine,* the logical precurser not only for *Niels Lyhne* but also and in a different way for the *Portrait.* If the multiple amours of Jacobsen's ineffectual hero recall the career of Flaubert's Frédéric and hence the subject matter of *L'Education Sentimentale,* Flaubert's methods (or manner) as well as his matter find important parallels in Joyce's first *puriste* novel. Of these methods one in particular could not have been transmitted by any secondary source: *L'Education Sentimentale* is built upon a framework composed of systematically paired antithetical sequences, that is, lyrical moments (epiphanies) followed in due time by lucid ones (anti-epiphanies), sequences designed to clarify the hero's motives without authorial intervention, to measure his progress and to relate his aspirations to his achievement. The method represents one solution to the problems raised by the dogma of impersonality. By demonstrating that Joyce, when faced with problems similar to those of Flaubert, made use of an identical framework, I hope to establish the *Portrait* more firmly within the tradition which he himself outlined.

Broadly speaking, *L'Education Sentimentale* and *A Portrait of the Artist as a Young Man* are fictionalized autobiographies treating ironically the emotional development of self-deceiving questers who follow idealistic and illusory visions toward unrecognized goals, moving from untenable position to untenable position through a half perceived world. In each case the plot concerns two aspects of the hero's experience: his growth in relation to his environment and his progress toward self-fulfillment.

Frédéric Moreau spends his adult life pursuing the married woman who combines in his romantic imagination the paradise of the flesh and the chaste muse. The pursuit of this faustian ideal draws him increasingly into the currents of his age where successively he finds as surrogates: youth, riches and women. When, finally, after 27 years of frustration and emotional *cache-cache,* his Helen offers herself, aging and no longer attractive, a symbol of his misspent youth, he is forced to abandon his dream of *volupté*-to-come so that he may discover in the now-distant past his land of milk and honey.

Like Frédéric, the boy Stephen Dedalus ends his quest with a paradoxical return to innocence. But whereas the currents of life move the passive Frédéric through the real world, Stephen is driven by disappointments and growth towards the experience of himself. One by one he tests each of his powers beginning with his will. Building through five stages to a knowledge of the combined resources of his being, shucking at each stage the futile husk of former illusions, he succeeds in metaphorically recreating himself, in being reborn. Metaphorically, by leaving home, he discards the mother image and the ties which have haunted his childhood and adolescence; but he fails to recognize the nature of the metaphor, of the cumulative effects of his quest or of his internal commitments.

In order to dramatize the immutability of their protagonists' natures and to measure their progress towards self-realization, if not self-recognition, both authors make systematic use of the device which I shall call the epiphany: a lyrical and wish-fulfilling moment during which the illusory is made to appear *as* immediate and valid as the real. Such moments are given a form which approximates or counterfeits the lyrical in Joyce's sense of that term: "the form wherein the artist presents his image in immediate relation to himself."[5] Thus, during epiphanies the prose of the third person narrator seems to be fused with or, as Richard Ellmann puts it, "infected by the hero's mind."[6] I am deliberately limiting my use of the term to those passages which Joyce himself would have called the crucial or climactic epiphanies: moments of illusion which are nevertheless instants of illumination or radiance for both the protagonist and the reader. Joyce's term is of course more inclusive, but its implications are too complex to treat here.[7] For Joyce the epiphany is first of all the final stage in the apprehension of beauty *by the viewer* who discovers in a work of art an object or a circumstance, an aesthetic significance or radiance which he has not previously perceived. The object or circumstance may be apprehended objectively or subjectively, that is, its radiance may be partially equated with its subjective impact upon the observer, but no matter what the source, the experience should be both pleasurable and static. To use the author's words, it "arrests the mind" in the presence of beauty. Joyce himself extends this fundamental definition (the one given in *Stephen Hero*) of the epiphany as a moment of perception to include the artifact which records and transmits the pure experience. In *Ulysses* he has Stephen speak mockingly in a fit of depression of "epiphanies on green oval leaves . . . to be sent . . . to all the great libraries of the world . . ."[8] Hence, the passages from the *Portrait* and *L'Education Sentimentale* which I have called epiphanies may be viewed as both art and event: Stephen and Frédéric have a subjective and semi-mystical moment of truth, the reader is permitted at once to share the hero's experience and to view it as an aspect of the aesthetic whole. For the reader the epiphany is static by virtue, among other things, of the double focus. His experience is paradoxically one of detached involvement. For the protagonist the *moment* is static to the extent that it interrupts the action as would a fainting spell; it is what Stephen describes as "an enchantment of the heart" and as such it curtails the logical processes, stopping time and transcending it. But such moments generate a kinetic reaction, providing the anti-aesthetic impulse to action by stimulating in the hero a desire to sustain the illusion. Stephen is neither attracted nor repelled by his bird-girl (chapter four); Frédéric contemplates in awe his "vision" in chapter one of section *I*. Yet both boys set out in quest of the vision's actuality.

I shall use the term *epiphany sequence* to denote the tripartite development during which the hero moves from a relatively detached position as uncomprehending witness to his own depressing experience of the world to a full-blown subjective euphoria, losing himself in the vision, identifying for one blinding instant reality and the dream. This moment of bliss or blindness, this epiphany is succeeded by a relatively lucid interval: the anti-climax, during which objective and subjective elements are combined to the detriment of the latter. Though there is some interpenetration of mood and motifs, the three aspects are clearly differentiated. Flaubert, whose subject matter is failure, locates the epiphany in the first chapter of each of his three sections and includes all three elements of the sequence in each of his epiphany chapters: relating the hero first to the world as he sees it, then to the vision and finally to the vision in conjunction with the world. Joyce, whose subject is illusory or impermanent achievement and whose structure is climactic, places the epiphany in the last section of each chapter and locates the anti-climax at the beginning of the succeeding chapter. In each instance the lyrical impulse which has established the shape of the hero's dream survives intellectually the anti-climax only to be discredited toward the middle of the section or chapter during the passage which I shall call the anti-epiphany.

The least alloyed lyrical passage in *L'Education Sentimentale* occurs in chapter one of section *I* during the eighteen-year-old hero's river voyage from Paris to Montereau. The young aesthete, Frédéric Moreau, after having failed to nourish his romantic muse upon the unsavory aspect of his fellow passengers achieves without warning what Stephen Dedalus would call the "birth of his soul." Pushing open the gate of the first class section, he sees Marie Arnoux under circumstances recalling Faust's vision of his ideal in the mirror of the *Hexenküche*. Without knowing who she is or where she comes from he gives her an imaginary identity, spins a dream about her which neither the atmosphere of the boat, the noise and tawdriness, the uninspiring landscape or the boorish behaviour of her mephistophelian husband can dissipate:

Il y avait dans le ciel de petits nuages blancs arrêtés,—et l'ennui, vaguement répandu, semblait alanguir la marche du bateau et rendre l'aspect des voyageurs plus insignifiant encore.

A part quelques bourgeois, aux Premières, c'étaient des ouvriers, des gens de boutique avec leurs femmes et leurs enfants . . . Le pont était sali par des écales de noix, des bouts de cigares, des pelures de poires, des détritus de charcuterie apportée dans du papier; trois ébénistes, en blouse, stationnaient devant la cantine; un joueur de harpe en haillons se reposait, accoudé sur son instrument; on entendait par intervalles le bruit du charbon de terre dans le fourneau, un éclat de voix, un rire . . . Frédéric, pour rejoindre sa place, poussa la grille des Premières, dérangea deux chasseurs avec leurs chiens.

Ce fut comme une apparition:

Elle était assise, au milieu du banc, toute seule; ou du moins il ne distingua personne, dans l'éblouissement qui lui envoyèrent ses yeux . . .

Elle avait un large chapeau de paille, avec des rubans roses qui palpitaient au vent derrière elle. Ses bandeaux noirs, contournant la pointe de ses grands sourcils, descendaient très bas et semblaient presser amoureusement l'ovale de sa figure. Sa robe de mousseline claire, tachetée de petits pois, se répandait à plis nombreux. Elle était en train de broder quelque chose; et son nez droit, son menton, toute sa personne se découpait sur le fond de l'air bleu.[9]

[A few small white clouds hung motionless in the sky; boredom, vague yet pervasive, was abroad; the movement of the boat seemed slower and the passengers looked even more insignificant than before.

These, apart from some richer folk in the first class, consisted of workmen and shopkeepers with their wives and children . . . Nutshells, cigar ends, pear skins, and the remains of sausage meat wrapped in newspaper befouled the deck. Three cabinet makers in blouses lounged in front of the bar; a harpist, in rags, was resting, with his elbow on his instrument; from time to time one caught the sound of the coal in the furnace, a burst of voices, or a roar of laughter . . . Frederic pushed open the grating that led to the first-class deck, upsetting two sportsmen with their dogs.

It was like a vision.

She was seated all alone in the middle of the bench; or at least he could distinguish no one else in the dazzling light which her eyes shed upon him . . .

She was wearing a wide straw hat, with pink ribbons that fluttered in the wind behind her. Her black hair was parted into two broad tresses that brushed the corners of her heavy eyebrows, and, hanging low on her cheeks, seemed to caress the oval of her face. Her dress of pale sprigged muslin billowed out in a multitude of folds. She was working at a piece of embroidery; and her straight nose, her chin, her whole form, stood out in relief against the background of blue sky.]

The equating sentence: "Ce fut comme une apparition," and the subsequent mingling of objective detail with the hero's subjective reactions to Marie render the illusion equal to the reality with which it competes on the scale of values. So true is this that, though the events described are banal, we often forget that the view we receive of Marie is a product of the astigmatic vision of a naïve ephebe. When, shortly after this encounter, the ragged harpist mentioned in the previous citation begins to play for Marie's daughter, both he and his performance are transformed by the presence of the lady who has already become Frédéric's muse. We may compare the two descriptions of the musician to see how much the adolescent's consciousness impinges upon the texture of the narrator's prose, imposing itself even upon his choice of naturalistic detail:

> C'était une romance orientale, où il était question de poignards, de fleurs et d'étoiles. L'homme en haillons chantait cela d'une voix mordante; les battements de la machine coupaient la mélodie à fausse mesure; il pinçait plus fort; les cordes vibraient, et leurs sons métalliques semblaient exhaler des sanglots, et comme la plainte d'un amour orgueilleux et vaincu. Des deux côtés de la rivière, des bois s'inclinaient jusqu'au bord de l'eau; un courant d'air frais passait; Mme Arnoux regardait au loin d'une manière vague. Quand la musique s'arrêta, elle remua les paupières plusieurs fois, comme si elle sortait d'un songe. (*Œuvres,* page 38)

> [It was an eastern serenade—all about daggers, flowers, and stars. The man in rags sang this in a harsh voice; the beat of the engine formed a discordant background to the melody; he plucked harder, the strings vibrated, and it was as if the metallic notes were sobbing out the plaint of a proud and vanquished love. On either side of the river woods leaned down to the very edge of the water; a fresh breeze blew; Mme Arnoux looked vaguely into the distance. When the music ceased she moved her eyelids several times, as though she were waking from a dream.]

We need not be surprised to find that, after he has taken leave of the attractive bourgeoise to whom he has never spoken, Frédéric compares her to "women in romantic novels." His quasi-mystic experience has "enlarged his universe." Perhaps it has even made a man of him:

> Il n'aurait voulu rien ajouter, rien retrancher à sa personne. L'univers venait tout à coup de s'élargir. Elle était le point lumineux où l'ensemble des choses convergeait; . . . il s'abandonnait à une joie rêveuse et infinie. (*Œuvres,* page 41)

> [He wanted nothing added to her, and nothing taken away. The universe had suddenly expanded. She was the focal point of light at which the totality of things converged; . . . he gave himself up to an infinite, dreamy felicity.]

Stephen Dedalus' crucial epiphany takes place at the end of the *Portrait*'s penultimate chapter as he walks along the beach one evening shortly after his graduation from Belvedere college and his rejection of the priesthood. His walk is marred at first by a residue of puritanical shame and a fear of life which leads him to dwell upon the ugliness of his surroundings. At the end of the first half of the sequence the sound of his own name identifies him with his namesake, the artificer Daedalus, and his profound depression gives way to euphoria. He experiences the sensations of flight, imagines himself released from the grave of adolescence, at one with life, and finds confirmation for his mood in the sudden appearance of the bird-like girl described in the following paragraphs:

> A girl stood before him in midstream, alone and still, gazing out to sea. She seemed like one whom magic had changed into the likeness of a strange and beautiful seabird. Her long slender bare legs were delicate as a crane's . . . Her bosom was . . . slight and soft as the breast of some darkplumaged dove . . .
> She was alone and still, gazing out to sea; and when she felt his presence and the worship of his eyes her eyes turned to him in quiet sufferance of his gaze, without shame or wantonness . . .
> —Heavenly God! cried Stephen's soul, in an outburst of profane joy.
> He turned away from her suddenly and set off across the strand. His cheeks were aflame; his body was aglow . . . Her image had passed into his soul for ever and no word had broken the holy silence of his ecstasy. (*Portrait,* page 171)

This silent communion with a girl whom Stephen has endowed with magical qualities consistent with his own desires is generally thought to be the climactic moment of the novel. Like Frédéric's, Stephen's complete commitment to the illusion is conveyed by means of a dramatic shift from apparent objectivity to controlled and deepening subjectivity. The narrator disarms his reader by at first describing objectively the hero's dejection, his confusion, discontent, indecision and revery, allowing this medley of moods to color the descriptions. In doing so he relies heavily upon simile words which give his suggestive images plausibility and internal logic, creating the impression that Stephen is actually watching himself feel the emotions the narrator describes. As the passage progresses and both Stephen's and the narrator's critical faculties are sublimated, the similes grow sparser and the logic of the outer world gives way discreetly to that of the vision. Thus the girl who was *like* a bird is transformed in his imagination, becoming, without benefit of the words *like* or *as,* "a wild angel of mortal youth and beauty."

Not only the manner but also the matter of these two epiphany passages reveals, upon examination, unmistakable parallels. Frédéric and Stephen, two adolescent boys, both about to enter the university, both with artistic pretensions, experience beauty: the one on a river, the other by the sea. Each encounters an isolated female figure who is made to embody some transcendental aspect of his own dream. Neither hero converses with his ideal or lusts after her though she is in each case sensually appealing and though both feel an immense and quasi-religious joy in her presence. Each experiences a rite of passage into manhood and, in a faustian context, a stimulus to action. Similarly, in both instances, the illusion rises from the muck of reality and seems to return there. Thus Frédéric's departure is ignored by Mme Arnoux; his return home after the boat trip is characterized by ineptitude and prose. Stephen's epiphany is immediately followed in chapter V by a description of his breakfast table with its pool of drippings and its louse-stained pawn tickets, components of his newly discovered worldly estate.

Equally important are the clues which point to the paradoxical nature of the dream, to its lack of inner consistency, to its false relationship to reality, and to the probable outcome of the hero's aspirations. Previous to seeing the bird-girl, Stephen has identified with the "hawk or eagle," Daedalus, declaring himself and his soul delivered not only from "fear", "incertitude" and "shame" but also from adolescence and the church. Yet his reaction to the bird-girl, herself a combination of dove and crane, reflects, like Frédéric's reaction to Marie, an unstable compound of material and spiritual ideals. His appreciation of his vision is voiced in the words "Heavenly God!" which the narrator qualifies as "an outburst of profane joy." The dreamer who has conceived of himself as free to wander to the ends of the earth exhibits towards the end of the epiphany an ambivalent attitude toward the time and space he has previously discarded when he asks himself "How far had he walked? What hour was it?" The components have begun to sunder even before the moment has been consummated.

The structural complement of the epiphany is the anti-epiphany: a sequence whose function is to provide the hero with insights which will pave the way for the next epiphany by furthering or completing the destruction of the illusion surviving the previous one. Whereas the epiphanies are markedly irrational, partaking of the nature of hallucinations or dreams, climaxed by moments of lyrical inspiration rather than insights, the anti-epiphanies are composed of intensely conscious moments during which the hero receives an insight, witnesses rather than experiences an unveiling. In general such passages systematically reverse not only the imagery of the lyrical epiphany but also its action and mood. Here the events are narrated in detail; the hero's thoughts are noted, but the insight is communicated not through his emotional reaction but through a combination of carefully arranged descriptive details and dialogue upon which the hero is occasionally permitted to comment. By focusing and crystallizing his disillusionment the anti-epiphanies restore balance and consolidate the hero's gains. They give him, along with an awareness of the nature of his illusion, a partial understanding of the lesson learned, and therefore they make possible further progress towards enlightenment. Just as the epiphanies are compounded of vision and blindness, anti-epiphanies join negative and positive insights. If the epiphany drives the hero out in quest of fulfillment, the anti-epiphany forces him back into himself, enabling him to take stock of his position. Thus the fleshly component of Frédéric's ethereal vision is made available to him during an anti-epiphany which also serves to reënforce the positive thrust of the original experience. Similarly, Stephen's romantic error in dedicating his whole soul to the limited world represented by Ireland and symbolized by a Dublin street girl is exposed in a sequence which serves to broaden his vision and deepen his understanding of his situation, sending him out into the world where he must inevitably face new disillusionments.

The anti-epiphany passages in *L'Education Sentimentale* are the visit to the Alhambra dance-hall (pages 101–108), the races at the Champ de Mars (pages 232–245), the auction of Mme Arnoux' belongings (pages 434–448). In each of these passages Frédéric paradoxically realizes some good whose possession was desired at the time of the vision. Paradoxically, because the reality belies the promise. The same may be said with few qualifications for Stephen's moments of insight. The latter occur in all but the third chapter of the *Portrait* where the emotional context limits clarity of vision. It might be said that the entire retreat sequence serves the purpose in that chapter which the shorter anti-epiphany sequences serve in other chapters. Stephen experiences anti-epiphanies in chapter one during the Christmas dinner, in chapter two during the trip to Cork, in chapter four during the interview with the Director of Belvedere and in chapter five during the evening of the interview with Cranly.

The anti-epiphany for Frédéric's vision of Marie Arnoux falls in the fifth chapter of section one during an otherwise uneventful and even sordid visit to the Alhambra dance-hall. Frédéric, who has come to console himself for his inability to seduce Marie, suddenly discovers her husband under circumstances which ironically recall those of the first epiphany. Pushing through some bushes where formerly he pushed through the first-class gate, he sees, not the Spanish-looking Marie sitting *alone,* but Mlle Vatnaz, the Spanish procuress, who is "seul avec Arnoux." Instead of being dazzled by Marie's gaze, he is forced to admire the Vatnaz' "admirables yeux, fauves avec des points d'or dans les prunelles, tout pleins d'esprit, d'amour et de sensualité" (*Œuvres,* page 104). Instead of listening to the ragged harpist while he watches Marie gaze dreamily ashore, Frédéric, well aware of the contrast, listens to the *cabotin* Delmas singing affectedly *le Frère de l'Albanaise* while Vatnaz exhibits sensual joy:

> Les paroles rappelèrent à Frédéric celles que chantait l'homme en haillons, entre les tambours du bateau. Ses yeux s'attachaient involontairement sur le bas de la robe étalée devant lui. Après chaque couplet, il y avait une longue pause,—et le souffle du vent dans les arbres ressemblait au bruit des ondes.
>
> Mlle Vatnaz, en écartant d'une main les branches d'un troène qui lui masquait la vue de l'estrade, contemplait le chanteur, fixement, les narines ouvertes, les cils rapprochés, et comme perdue dans une joie sérieuse. (*Oeuvres,* page 105)

[The words reminded Frederic of those which the ragged man had sung on the boat, between the paddle boxes. He fastened his eyes involuntarily on the hem of the dress spread out in front of him. After each verse there was a long pause—and the breath of the wind in the trees was like the sound of waves.

Mlle Vatnaz, drawing aside with one hand the branches of a privet that was impeding her view of the stage, gazed fixedly at the singer, her nostrils dilated, her eyes half closed, lost, as it seemed, in a sober delight.]

Following this experience, Frédéric leaves the Alhambra and wanders to Arnoux' street to stare at the wall of Marie's house in an effort to refurbish the tarnished illusion. But here too he is forced to acknowledge his deception. The vision has been reversed. Marie can no longer be isolated from her ubiquitous husband:

> Maintenant, sans doute, elle reposait, tranquille comme une fleur endormie, avec ses beaux cheveux noirs parmi les dentelles de l'oreiller, les lèvres entre-closes, la tête sur un bras.
> Celle d'Arnoux lui apparut. Il s'éloigna, pour fuir cette vision. (*Œuvres,* page 108)

> [Now, doubtless, she was resting, peaceful as a sleeping flower, with her lovely black hair spread over the lace of her pillow, her lips half open, her head on her arm.
> Arnoux's face came into view. He hurried away, to escape from this apparition.]

Within this same anti-epiphany there are equally elaborate and ironic parallels with the next epiphany: the masked ball at Rosanette Bron's during which Rosanette makes love to Delma but takes Arnoux' neighbour, Mr. Oudry, as her lover. Among the elements foreshadowing this sequence are the factitious Moorish setting of the Alhambra, the presence of Delmas, Vatnaz and Arnoux, the fact that Arnoux is at the Alhambra to arrange for Rosanette to become his mistress. It seems appropriate that the first chapter of section *II* should culminate in Frédéric's dream: "il lui semblait qu'il était attelé près d'Arnoux, au timon d'un fiacre, et que la Maréchale [that is, Rosanette], à califourchon sur lui, l'éventrait avec ses éperons d'or" (*Œuvres,* page 159). Over this vision hover the eyes of Madame Arnoux "légers comme des papillons, ardents comme des torches . . ."

In a like manner the penultimate segment of the *Portrait*'s fifth chapter, through its objective treatment of spoiled friendships, isolation, flight and departure and of Stephen's rejection of his mother, Ireland, and the church, reverses the bird-girl epiphany. At the same time it foreshadows the final epiphany, revealing Stephen's indecision and doubts. Chapter five's anti-epiphany opens with an evocation of a flock of small birds, but the bird image has lost some of its savour, and Stephen, in spite of his newly acquired knowledge of the occult, feels lonely, weary and deceived:

The colonnade above him made him think vaguely of an ancient temple and the ashplant on which he leaned wearily of the curved stick of an augur. A sense of fear of the unknown moved in the heart of his weariness, a fear of symbols and portents, of the hawklike man whose name he bore soaring out of his captivity on osier woven wings, of Thoth, the god of writers . . . (*Portrait,* page 225)

This mood is sustained as Stephen watches the sterile "monkeyshines" of his friends, silently observes EC as she greets Cranly, the priest of the world, to whom he later "confesses." Specific parallels with the beach epiphany are not lacking. The "crane" and "dark-plumaged dove" embodied in the bird-girl are here metamorphosed into Cranly and EC, both of whom pointedly ignore Stephen. The suggestion of an Icarian or Luciferian fall which followed Stephen's Daedalian flight in chapter IV ("—O, Cripes, I'm drownded!—") is given new force when Stephen misquotes Nash's "*Brightness falls from the air.*" Likewise, the elation and light which characterize the earlier scene are turned here into depression and darkness. The young hero's ecstatic and quasi-religious dedication to the world proves most ironic when Cranly, his best friend, shows himself to be a hypocrite and a betrayer, and when EC, the chaste bird-girl's flirtatious and seductive surrogate is found to possess the *bat*like soul of her people.

Though somewhat less mechanical than in Flaubert's anti-epiphanies, the reversal of images which occurs in the following passage is reasonably evident. Note that the flush which formerly colored Stephen's cheek is now seen on that of Cranly, that the rosy light imagery of the beach sequence is reversed to accord with Stephen's rimbaldian mood, and that the crucial confrontation has been replaced by a slight: "She passed out from the porch of the library and bowed across Stephen in reply to Cranly's greeting. He also? Was there not a slight flush on Cranly's cheek? . . . The light had waned. He could not see" (*Portrait,* page 232). Instead of rushing off elated and alone as he did after the bird-girl epiphany, Stephen loiters under the colonnade thinking lustful thoughts as he waits for Cranly like some loyal acolyte or serf:

She had passed through the dusk. And therefore the air was silent save for one soft hiss that fell. And therefore the tongues about him had ceased their babble. Darkness was falling.
> *Darkness falls from the air.*
A trembling joy . . . played like a fairy host around him. But why? Her passage through the darkening air or the verse with its black vowels . . .
He walked away slowly towards the deeper shadows at the end of the colonnade, beating the stone softly with his stick to hide his revery from the students . . .
. . . Vaguely first and then more sharply he smelt her body. A conscious unrest seethed in his blood . . .

A louse crawled over the nape of his neck . . . (*Portrait,* pages 232–234)

Brittle, alert to the dangers of self-deception, he withdraws rather than expose himself to the world. Like Frédéric, Stephen in the anti-epiphanies is at least half aware of the ironic parallels. Both are witnesses as much to their thoughts as to the events; both see mocking mirrors held up to their fleeting lyrical impulses.

While underlining the ironic relationships of epiphanies to anti-epiphanies, we must not fail to note the non-ironic linkage of epiphany to epiphany and anti-epiphany to anti-epiphany, a suggestive device which clearly states in each novel the parallel functions of the subdivisions, sections and chapters. In section *II* of *L'Education Sentimentale* the crowds, the deceptions, Frédéric's moods and even the principal event from the horse-race anti-epiphany parallel the mood, action, language and imagery of the Alhambra scene of section *I*. Here, for example, is Flaubert's description of the horses racing at the Champ de Mars: "revenant bien vite, ils grandissaient; leur passage coupait le vent, le sol tremblait, le cailloux volaient; l'air s'engouffrant dans les casaques des jockeys, les faisait palpiter comme des voiles . . ." (*Œuvres,* page 237). His description of the dancers doing the *galop* at the Alhambra does more than capture the same rhythm: "Haletants, souriants, et la face rouge, ils défilaient dans un tourbillon qui soulevait les robes avec les basques des habits; les trombones rugissaient plus fort; le rythme s'accélérait . . ." (*Œuvres,* page 106).

In the *Portrait* the Director of Belvedere's interrogation of Stephen in chapter four parallels Cranly's interrogation of him in chapter five in that both men are in effect confessing to Stephen, the unwilling confessor. To emphasize this fact, Joyce first describes the Director's head as a *memento mori:* "The priest's face was in total shadow, but the waning daylight from behind him touched the deeply grooved temples and the curves of the skull" (*Portrait,* pages 153–154). Later Cranly is described in his role as "the decollated precursor": ". . . in the shadow of the trees Stephen saw his pale face, framed by the dark, and his large dark eyes" (*Portrait,* page 245).

Once these complex but consistent interrelationships are recognized and we are aware of the function of epiphanies and anti-epiphanies as markers along the road of experience, we may assume that a study of these passages in sequence will reveal the nature of that road and its extent.

The progress of the epiphanies in *L'Education Sentimentale* may be gauged in terms of action, of imagery or in terms of Frédéric's dream. For example, we note that each succeeding epiphany chapter takes up its action metaphorically where the preceding sequence ends. Thus Frédéric's anti-climactic carriage-ride home, at the end of chapter one, is reflected in the coach trip to Paris which opens the second epiphany, while the orgy which follows the glamour of the masked ball is in its turn reflected in the masquerade of pomp and the orgy of destruction during the revolutionary sequence which opens section *III*.

If we study the river-of-life imagery which dominates the first third of each epiphany chapter, we find that Frédéric moves from a boat in the center of the Seine in section *I* to a coach drawn by wavy-maned horses in section *II* and that in section *III* he is carried by the surging crowd of revolutionaries. Passive in all things, Frédéric is drawn along by the increasingly turbulent stream, forced to participate in a reality which he fails to understand. A similar progression is evident in his dream or quest object which is first seen through a vision of Marie Arnoux as a romantic ideal: chaste but appealing. In the second epiphany, Marie's image is refined to a hovering kiss which haunts the hero as he lusts after the dancers at the masked ball. At last, in section *III,* reality triumphs as Frédéric attempts, amidst dead luxury at Versailles, to renew his dream in the company of his mistress, Rosanette. Appropriately, in that section's anti-epiphany, Frédéric sees his dream fall under an auctioneer's hammer to the possessive Mme Dambreuse.

In the *Portrait* each of Stephen's epiphanies marks a stage in his development, teaches him the nature of another of his powers after he has been purged of past error. Thus, the unmerited punishment which the boy receives in chapter one destroys his faith in the power of innocence, leading him to discover his will as a moral force. In the next epiphany his will is punished by desire and he is led to discover the power of his senses through intercourse with a whore. He learns to control his lust in chapter three after the retreat sermons which force him to discover the power of his emotions. In chapter four he purges himself of his adolescence and of his emotional commitments to the church, witnessing the birth of his soul or spirit which finally takes wing in chapter five to carry his creative intellect out of Ireland. Each experience destroys his faith in some aspect of that environment of which he will paradoxically become the mirror, adds something to the mask which he exposes to the world, and contributes to the making of the artist.

With each succeeding epiphany Stephen becomes increasingly the agent of his own seduction; the vision or illusion becomes first more and then less and less the product of his participation in the world. Hence the Rector of Clongowes seduces Stephen with a soft word, a look and a handclasp; the harlot seduces him with an embrace; the bumbling capuchin permits him to cleanse his conscience through a confession; the sirenlike bird-girl simply endures Stephen's rapturous gaze; and finally, the diary provides a sounding board for his disjunct musings. Contrarywise, the successive anti-epiphanies show Stephen to be increasingly involved with the world, increasingly aware of his own position in it. The distance spanned in five chapters may best be gauged by comparing Stephen, the mute and nearly uncomprehending observer of his elders' behavior in chapter one's Christmas dinner, to Stephen in chapter five, observing as an equal (or superior) the behavior of his comrades, judging and calibrating his own emotional reactions.

Like Flaubert, then, Joyce has used the epiphanies and the anti-epiphanies as keystones of a complex and well-ordered structure, a means of imposing upon his narrative the rhythm of Stephen's growth, a means of defining the hero's quest and his achievement in terms of a constant and seemingly inevitable pattern of experience. Like the father of realism, he has used the lyrical moments to deepen, enrich and embellish an uncompromisingly realistic and often brutally ironic account of the hero's experience. It would be wrong however to equate the two uses of the epiphany without underlining Joyce's contributions to the device, contributions which derive in large part from his fundamentally serious (as opposed to Flaubert's comic-satiric) intention. The *Portrait*'s irony, for example, is not designed to destroy Stephen, to render him insignificant, but rather to help the reader to achieve a balanced view of a character who is not everyman but every artist as a young man. Accordingly, Flaubert's anti-climactic structure and crushing irony emphasize reality to the detriment of Frédéric's aspirations and make reader identification unlikely; Joyce's climactic structure and his severely limited perspective lead to reader empathy, while his mute irony underlies the positive aspects of Stephen's' development, gives voice to a sublimated reality. Working within what is generally described as the combined realist and symbolist traditions, Joyce has used the epiphany with more daring and greater subtlety. He has refurbished the device and adapted it to his purposes, married it to other devices and new techniques; but the essential character of the sequence has not changed and by its existence in the *Portrait* the epiphany along with the anti-epiphany testifies to a commitment on Joyce's part to a particular sort of organic structure and implicitly to a theory of the nature of experience as a clue to identity. The tide has "advanced from Flaubert through Jakobsen" and D'Annunzio to Joyce.

Notes

1. A somewhat shorter version of this article was presented before the Comparative Literature Section *I* of the Modern Language Association in Chicago, December 1961.

2. "The Day of the Rabblement" in *James Joyce, The Critical Writings,* edited by Ellsworth Mason and Richard Ellmann (New York, 1959), p. 71.

3. See Stuart Gilbert, *James Joyce's Ulysses* (New York, 1952), p. 92. Joyce's knowledge of Flaubert's works can be reasonably well documented from his juvenilia, his notebooks, his letters and his comments to friends conserved in biographies and memoirs. Thus, for example, bookseller's bills reproduced by Richard Ellmann in his biography indicate that, along with eighteen other items purchased between October 1913 and May 1914, the chronically impecunious author purchased both Flaubert's *Saint Antoine* and his *Premières Œuvres* (Richard Ellmann, *James Joyce,* New York, 1959, p. 788.). Among the notes taken in 1913 in preparation for the writing of the play *Exiles* we find the following: "Since the publication of the lost pages of *Madame Bovary* the centre of sympathy appears to have been esthetically shifted from the lover or fancyman to the husband or cuckold . . . This change is utilized in *Exiles* although the union of Richard and Bertha is irregular . . ." (*Exiles,* London, 1952, p. 165). Again, in Ellmann we read that in 1920 Joyce was able to point out errors in the French of *Trois Contes* to the Swiss writer, Edmond Jaloux. All of the major critics have noted Joyce's use of flaubertian

ideas, techniques and theories, though to date only Haskell Block in an unpublished *doctorat* thesis has attempted to treat them in depth. We read of the influence of *Trois Contes* upon the style of *Dubliners;* of Flaubert's letters upon the aesthetic theory expressed in *A Portrait of the Artist as a Young Man* and of Flaubert's theories and life upon Joyce's attitudes as an artist; of *Madame Bovary* and *Bouvard et Pécuchet* upon the subject matter of *Ulysses;* and of the *Tentation de Saint Antoine* upon the form and matter of the Circe chapter of *Ulysses*. Most suggestively, we find in *Finnegans Wake* notebook VI.B.8 (*James Joyce Archive* 30) three entries dating from 1924 in which Joyce seems to acknowledge (and mitigate) an influence: "Flaub treatment of language as despair/ J.J contrary" (p. 42); J[ohn] S[tanislaus] J[oyce] can rest having made me/ G[ustave] F[laubert can rest having made me] (p. 71); "Larbaud result of J[ames] J[oyce] & G[ustave] F[laubert]"; (I have studied the implications of these lines in two other essays: "Toward a Post-Flaubertian Joyce" in *James Joyce: "Scribble" 2: Joyce et Flaubert,* eds. Claude Jacquet and André Topia (Paris: Les Lettres Modernes, 1990, pp. 13–32; "A Desimplified Heart: Flaubert through a Joycean Optic," in *Modes of Narrative: Approaches to American, Canadian and British Fiction,* eds. Reingard M. Nischik and Barbara Korte (Würtzburg: Königshausen & Neumann, 1990, pp. 45–56).

4. It should be noted that Flaubert has in effect perfected for *L'Education Sentimentale* a structure first used in *Madame Bovary* and that less elaborate examples of the devices which I shall deal with in this paper are to be found in that book. *L'Education Sentimentale* by virtue of its polish and its subject matter seems to me to be the more likely source for Joyce's epiphany sequences.

5. *A Portrait of the Artist as a Young Man* (New York, Viking Press, 1956), p. 213.

6. Ellmann, p. 150. Mr. Ellmann is referring to a passage from Joyce's early essay "A Portrait of the Artist" in which he quite accurately sees the germs of Joyce's later development.

7. In applying this term to a device used by both Joyce and Flaubert I am not implying that the two writers shared a theory of epiphanies. It should be clear that Joyce invented a term and a theory but not an experience or a technique.

8. *Ulysses* (New York, Modern Library, 1934), p. 41. Given this application we may even use the term epiphany to describe Joyce's books, seeing the *Portrait* or *Ulysses* as sequences of epiphanies linked together to form the larger epiphany which is the novel. (See S. L. Goldberg's extended treatment of Joyce's aesthetic theory in *The Classical Temper* (London, 1961)). Thus the book becomes, like Mallarmé's "poème" a *metaphor:* a metaphor composed of metaphors, a sort of total expression or communication.

9. Flaubert, *Œuvres;* (NRF, vol. 2, Paris, 1951, pp. 36–37). [All the passages translated into English are to be found in Gustave Flaubert, *Sentimental Education,* trans., with introduction and notes, Anthony Goldsmith (London and New York: J. M. Dent and E. D. Dalton), 1941.]

[A Slow and Dark Birth: A Study of the Organization]

SIDNEY FESHBACH

—*The soul is born, {Stephen} said vaguely, first in those moments I told you. It has a slow and dark birth, more mysterious than the birth of the body.*[1]

In July 1907 Joyce was hospitalized with rheumatic fever; he returned home in August but did not feel fully well until the middle of September.[2] According to Richard Ellmann, "The period of his illness . . . had actually been for James a time to concentrate on what he wanted to do. During his illness and the three months that followed, he plotted his literary life for the next seven years. On September 6 he had almost completed 'The Dead.' . . . On September 8 he informed Stanislaus that as soon as he had completed the story he would rewrite *Stephen Hero* completely. 'He told me,' Stanislaus noted in his diary, 'he would omit all the first chapters and begin with Stephen . . . going to school and that he would write the book in five chapters—long chapters.' " Mr. Ellmann accounts for Joyce's discovery of a "principle of structure"[3] of five chapters in the occasion of Lucia Joyce's birth on July 26. "His decision to rewrite *Stephen Hero* as *A Portrait* in five chapters occurred appropriately just after Lucia's birth. For *A Portrait of the Artist as a Young Man* is in fact the gestation of a soul, and in the metaphor Joyce found his new principle of order."[4] Mr. Ellmann is correct in seeing the novel as the "gestation of a soul"; but he does not say why the gestation period should be five chapters, even long ones.

In this essay, I will show how the principle of the gestation of Stephen's soul is correlated with the principle of the organization of the novel. The gestation follows a very precise schematic order with the novel possessing the same order.[5]

This essay was originally published in the *James Joyce Quarterly*, Vol. 4.4 (Summer 1967), and is reprinted with permission.

I

In each of *A Portrait*'s five chapters a cry occurs as the climax of a sequence of physical and psychological events that usually follow a single pattern or narrative rhythm: a situation, such as punishment, provokes an internal response that intensifies until it forms a cry in Stephen's mind; the cry seeks expression and then, under increased pressure, it is released.[6] The first important outburst occurs when Father Dolan punishes Stephen.

—Lazy idle little loafer! cried the prefect of studies. Broke my glasses! An old schoolboy trick! Out with your hand this moment!

Stephen closed his eyes and held out in the air his trembling hand with the palm upwards. . . . A hot burning stinging tingling blow like the loud crack of a broken stick made his trembling hand crumple together like a leaf in the fire: and at the sound and the pain scalding tears were driven into his eyes. His whole body was shaking with fright, his arm was shaking and his crumpled burning livid hand shook like a loose leaf in the air. A cry sprang to his lips, a prayer to be let off. But though the tears scalded his eyes and his limbs quivered with pain and fright he held back the hot tears and the cry that scalded his throat.

—Other hand! shouted the prefect of studies.

Stephen drew back his maimed and quivering right arm and held out his left hand. The soutane sleeve swished again. . . . The scalding water burst forth from his eyes and, burning with shame and agony and fear, he drew back his shaking arm in terror and burst out into a whine of pain. His body shook with a palsy of fright and in shame and rage he felt the scalding cry come from his throat and the scalding tears falling out of his eyes and down his flaming cheeks.

—Kneel down, cried the prefect of studies. (50–1)

With some variation this pattern is repeated in Chapters 2, 3, 4, and 5.

The verses passed from his lips and the inarticulate cries and the unspoken brutal words rushed forth from his brain to force a passage. . . . The cry that he had strangled for so long in his throat issued from his lips. (99–100)

Stephen, his tongue cleaving to his palate, bowed his head, praying with his heart. . . . To say it in words! His soul, stifling and helpless would cease to be. . . . Then, bowing his head, he repeated the *Confiteor* in fright. (143)

His throat ached with a desire to cry aloud, the cry of a hawk or eagle on high, to cry piercingly of his deliverance to the winds. . . . An instant of wild flight had delivered him and the cry of triumph which his lips withheld cleft his brain. (169)

The rhythm died out at once; the cry of his heart was broken. . . . The heart's cry was broken. (218)

These five distinct events, prominent in the novel because of their emotional power and theatrical placement, are the grounding in experience for Stephen's theories of the origins of poetry. Poetry in history and in the individual begins with the cry: "The lyrical form," he says to Lynch, "is in fact the simplest verbal vesture of an instant of emotion, *a rhythmical cry* such as ages ago cheered on the man. . . ." (214. Italics mine.) And in his summary of the process of maturing as artist, he states, "The personality of the artist, *at first a cry or a cadence or a mood* and then a fluid and lambent narrative, finally refines itself out of existence, impersonalizes itself, so to speak." (217. Italics mine.) Comparable statements are found in *Stephen Hero:* "He read Blake and Rimbaud on the values of letters and even permuted and combined the five vowels to construct cries for primitive emotions." He "caught glimpses of emergent art. . . . He seemed almost to hear the simple cries of fear and joy and wonder which are antecedent to all song. . . ." (*SH,* 32, 33) However important Stephen's own cries are for understanding the basis of his theories, his theory suggests that his own cries indicate his development into a poet and his movement toward the creation of poetry. Another look at the ambience of these cries, such as the language, thought, action, or mood which express, accompany, contain, or surround them, will discover that they form that specific traditional progression called the "chain of being" or "the ladder of perfection"[7]; in the order in which they occur, the five cries are vegetative, animal, rational, angelic, and divine.

The first cry is plant or vegetative. "His whole body was shaking with fright, his arm was shaking and his crumpled burning livid hand shook like *a loose leaf* in the air." (My italics in these quotations.) The second is animal or bestial. "The inarticulate cries and the unspoken *brutal* words rushed forth from his brain to force a passage. . . . He moaned to himself like some baffled prowling beast." (99) That the third cry is human or rational can not be illustrated briefly, for its rational quality is not immediately apparent.[8] Rational, though, means here "ratio," such as are found in this chapter of the novel in the precise ratios of the ordering of the days of the retreat, the rhetorical organization of the sermon on Hell, and the construction of Hell's time and place; furthermore, rational implies without body, just as the Jesuits, who come to represent sterile reasoning, are human but have "an inhuman voice." (169) The fourth cry is angelic or intellectual. "When she felt his presence and the worship of his eyes turned to him in quiet sufferance of his gaze, without shame or wantonness. . . . —Heavenly God! cried Stephen's soul, in an outburst of profane joy. . . . Her image had passed into his soul forever. . . . A wild *angel* had appeared to him, the *angel* of mortal youth and beauty. . . ." (172) And the fifth cry modulates from the angelic into the divine or imaginative. "In a dream or vision he had known the ecstasy of *seraphic* life. . . . O!

In the virgin womb of the *imagination* the *word* was made flesh." (217) The cries measure precisely Stephen's development. How they are caused follows a specific psychological sequence: the first is sensation caused by external stimulus (pandybat), the second is fantasy caused by physiological changes (sexual desire), the third is understanding caused by verbal commands (sermon), the fourth is vision caused by intellectual adoration (sight of beauty), and the fifth is ecstasy caused by and in purified imagination (poetic annunciation). Similarly the cries themselves are a progression from a gross word-sound through increasing articulation to culminate in the logos and the "Villanelle." The differences distinguishing these crucial cries make them into signs of Stephen's chronological development into a poet; the cries and the development they signify control the organization of the novel. Their similarities indicate they are analogous events within a larger pattern: that is, the cries form a *scala verborum* that is the procession of Stephen's soul. Joyce in a more literal rendition of Aristotle has made Stephen's soul the soul and form of the novel.

II

The idea that the human soul comprises the vegetative, animal, and rational souls is found in Aristotle's psychology, the "De Anima," which Stephen implies he has used in constructing his theories of art. (176, 187) The idea of the gestation of the human soul as a progression through three souls is found in Thomas's *Summa Contra Gentiles,* which has an embryological schedule, "a kind of ontogenitic evolution *in utero,*" where the vegetative soul, "infused at the moment of conception," is replaced by the sensitive soul and, finally, the rational.[9] Although Aristotle's three souls are insufficient in number for the five chapters of *A Portrait,* they may be accommodated with such further distinctions as conation and spontaneous motion. Thomas's embryology is also partly applicable because even though Stephen is not *in utero,* he may be so symbolized, as Joyce says in his letter to Frank Budgen about the Lying-in chapter of *Ulysses:* Joyce wrote that "Bloom is the spermatozoon, the hospital the womb, the nurse the ovum, Stephen the embryo."[10] (In this chapter of *Ulysses,* Stephen says, "also how at the end of the second month a human soul was infused. . . ."[11]) Where *A Portrait* homologizes the embryology of the soul with personal poetic development, *Ulysses'* Lying-in chapter homologizes the embryology of the body with national literary history.

Both Aristotle and Thomas are necessary for an analysis of details; and they are important sources for other elements of the novel's organization— they will be discussed in later essays on *A Portrait.* However, the idea of the five stages of the soul most easily utilized in this study of the larger units of *A Portrait* can be found in the tradition of Neoplatonism, where, beginning with

Dionysius the Areopagite, the cosmic chain of being was increased to include orders of angels and the spiritual ladder of perfection was extended to include degrees of soul ranging above the rational to the reaches of the divine. A particularly suitable Neoplatonic summary is found in the manifesto, "The Oration on the Dignity of Man" by Pico della Mirandola, who is mentioned in *Ulysses* by Stephen as someone whose intent was similar to his own.[12] To man, Pico wrote in "The Oration,"

> it is granted to have whatever he chooses, to be whatever he wills. . . . On man when he came into life the Father conferred the seeds of all kinds and the germs of every way of life. Whatever seed each man cultivates will grow to maturity and bear in him their own fruit. If they be vegetative, he will be like a plant. If sensitive, he will become brutish. If rational, he will grow into a heavenly being. If intellectual, he will be an angel and the son of God. And if, happy in the lot of no created thing, he withdraws into the center of his own unity, his spirit, made one with God, in the solitary darkness of God, who is set above all things, shall surpass them all.[13]

However, Joyce's attitude of regarding a person's life as a sequence going from the lowest materialism to the highest divinity was clearly expressed at least as early as 1903, which was about the time he wrote the manuscript "A Portrait of the Artist" and began *Stephen Hero*. In his review of a book on Bruno, Joyce described the philosopher as moving toward God: "Inwards from the material universe, which . . . [was] his opportunity for spiritual activity, he passes, and from heroic enthusiasm to enthusiasm to unite himself with God."[14] And ten years later Joyce had Stephen say to Cranly in the fifth chapter, "I tried to unite my will with the will of God instant by instant. In that I did not always fail." (240) I have found too many possible sources in both the Aristotle-Aquinas and the Augustine-Pico traditions to say with confidence that any one source is the only one. I am saying only that it is likely that Joyce's decision to organize his novel in accord with these five stages was determined by the coincidence of a specific event, such as the birth of Lucia, and a specific reading, such as "The Oration" of Pico; in 1907, Joyce's mind was particularly ready for this meeting of event and idea in that it was during his wife's pregnancy that he prepared and delivered his long talk called "Ireland, Island of Saints and Sages," which mentions within two pages the *Summa Contra Gentiles* of Thomas Aquinas, the mystical theology of Dionysius the Areopagite, and the "translations from Plato made in the time of Pico della Mirandola."[15]

By analogy with Pico's view that the ways of life are seeds or germs which bear fruit, we can say that each of Stephen's cries is a realization of a spiritual condition or an actualization of a potential in his soul. Thus each chapter, bringing to tentative maturity an appropriate seed, is a stage in the gestation of Stephen's soul, until the fifth chapter when Stephen achieves the quintessential condition and—in Pico's words—"happy in the lot of no created thing," he writes in his diary that "I desire to press in my arms the love-liness which has not yet come into the world." (251) If it can be shown that each chapter reflects in its smaller details or in its larger sectional units a spe-cific stage of Stephen's spiritual gestation, then each chapter can be described as *a mode of becoming*. Thus, in the vegetative mode of Chapter One, the leit-motif of real and symbolic flowers—wild rose blossoms, little green place; canker of plants, cancer of animals; war of the roses; the green rose; the holly and the ivy; Stephen's hand and body shaking and burning like a leaf in a fire—are details harmonious with the larger sections of the chapter which can be understood in the light of the faculty psychology of Aristotle, who asserts that the minimal requirements of the vegetative soul are growth, reproduc-tion, and nutrition, especially, nutrition.[16] Stephen's vegetative need for nourishment is stressed by more or longer scenes involving food in this chap-ter than in any other; the food is eventually for his soul, and his nausea in the refectory and his terror at the Christmas dinner express the privation of his vegetative soul. Aristotle says that the animal possesses a sensitive soul, which has the function of movement and perception and desire (appetition) and which expresses phantasia and memory.[17] In the animal mode of Chapter Two, Stephen, with his family or alone, is kept constantly in motion by run-ning around a race-track, wandering through Dublin and suburbs, and riding with the milkwagon; his trip to Cork with his father is a movement into the city of memory, where the word "Foetus" shocked him to find in the outer world a trace of what he deemed till then a *brutish* and individual malady of his own *mind*. His monstrous *reveries* came thronging into his memory." (90) In this mode, Stephen is transformed into the half-man, half-animal, the Minotaur, who hunts in his maze of Dublin's red-light district.

In the rational mode of Chapter Three, as I have already indicated, the entire chapter is composed of ratios. We should note that Pico says if the seeds are rational, then man will grow into a heavenly—but not an angelic or divine—being; "heavenly," in this case, would mean the priesthood, with the rational to be distinguished from the intellectual or angelic of Chapter Four and from the imaginative or divine of Chapter Five. The rational soul engages in thinking and knowing, and it acts on the images of "phantasia"[18]; so we find that the introductory statements of Father Arnall, echoing St. Ignatius's *Spiritual Exercises,* emphasizes that the retreat is to examine, to reflect, to understand, to know, and to remember. Father Arnall says, "He who *remem-bers* the last things will *act* and *think* with them always before his eyes. He will live a good life and die a good death, *believing* and *knowing*. . . ." (111) Some of Joyce's revisions of the translation of Pinamonti's *Hell Opened* are the addition of the word "remember" or, as was remarked by Elizabeth Boyd in her study of the Sermon, the change from Pinamonti's simple advice to a more intense "imagine."[19] "Consider. . . . Imagine. . . . Imagine. . . . And then imagine. . . . Imagine all this. . . ." (120) The priest directs his "kinetic" words to a lower and important function of the rational soul.

In the angelic or intellective mode of Chapter Four, the first section, in which Stephen participates in the *Spiritual Exercises,* may correspond to the angelic *intellectus practicus*[20] in which the soul seeks to perform good acts, the action being a sequence of devotions and mortifications. The second section in which Stephen evaluates the life of the priesthood and chooses the life in his father's house (". . . this disorder, the misrule and confusion of his father's house and the stagnation of *vegetable life,* which was to win the day in his *soul"* (162)) may correspond to the angelic *intellectus speculativus* in which the soul apprehends knowledge and discriminates between the true and false. The third section is the passage from these lower and more "terrestrial" angelic concerns to the higher and more "astral" angelic joys. In this section, where the soul is winged or is represented in bird-metaphors, his soul achieves its angelic condition; his epiphany of the hovering winged Daedalus, whose art-work is angelic—a "being" that is "new soaring impalpable imperishable" (169)—transports his soul "beyond the world" and his body "was commingled with the element of the spirit." (169) His sight of the bird-girl ("Her image had passed into his *soul* forever. . . . A wild *angel* had appeared to him, the *angel* of mortal youth and beauty." (172)) increases the height of the soul's angelic flight until his soul swooned "into some new world," i.e., an angelic sphere in waters above the firmament, "fantastic, dim, uncertain as under sea, traversed by cloudy shapes and beings. . . ." (172) The angelicizing of Stephen's soul follows in part Plato who says that the sight of beauty impels the soul to reach its proper realm. One of several explanations of why the girl on the beach is "mortal beauty" can be derived from Erwin Panofsky's discussion of Pico's three categories of sexual love[21]: the prostitute of the animal mode would correspond with the *Venere Volgare;* the girl on the beach with a worldly or, as suggested by Stephen's terms, "profane" and "mortal" *Venere Celeste;* and the temptress of the "Villanelle" with the transcendent *Venere Celeste,* whose proper mode is the divine of Chapter Five. This suggests that Stephen's secularism in *A Portrait* has its degrees from the basest to the highest, and that the "profane" beauty of Chapter Four is also to be transcended or transformed into an even more "radiant body of everliving life." (221)

In Chapter Five, completing his transition from the intellectual and angelic mode to the imaginative and divine mode, Stephen presents his Summa Poetica, in imitation of Thomas Aquinas the Angelic Doctor; in this discourse, Stephen says, "I too am an *animal.* . . . But now we are in a *mental* world." (206) The next section of Chapter Five shows his sublime beatific inspiration in an amalgamation of the (angelic) seraphic vision and the (divine) logos. "In a dream or vision he had known the ecstasy of *seraphic* life. . . . O! In the virgin womb of the *imagination* the *word* was made *flesh.*" (217) In this section Joyce uses some of the language, psychology, and form of Dante's *Vita Nuova,* which presents an analysis and representation of the creative process in terms of spiritual faculties (*lo spirito della vita, lo spirito animale, lo spirito naturale*),[22] and in a form of mixed prose and poetry; the title, "New

Life," is, obviously, particularly appropriate for this climactic stage of the gestation of Stephen's soul. Stephen, at the end of Chapter Four, has further to go in his ascent. As Gregory of Nyssa says of Paul, "Yet even after listening in secret to the mysteries of heaven, Paul does not let the graces he has obtained become the limit of his desire, but continues to go on and on never ceasing his ascent." The characterization of Chapter Four is preliminary to Chapter Five's radical consolidation of spiritual and social qualities. From the beginning of the angelic mode of Chapter Four to the writing of the "Villanelle," Stephen's soul had been mounting the ladder of perfection from the rung of the *intellectus practicus* through the seraphic vision to the divine imagination. (We recall Stephen's defense in *Stephen Hero* that "Ibsen has the temper of an Archangel."[23]) The chapter's divine mode suggests that Stephen's final appeal to the "old father and old artificer" is directed not only to Ovid's Daedalus, but also to Plato's more divine demiurgos, who, in Jowett's translation of the Timaeus, is called father and artificer[24]; in *Ulysses,* for example, Stephen thinks of "Los Demiurgos," a Spanish-sounding junction of Blake and Plato.[25]

Just as the actualization of a potential occurs in each chapter, so an actualization of one chapter (the *terminus ad quem*) must be the potential of the next (the *terminus a quo*): the result is that an action central to one mode may be displaced in another. For example, in the vegetative mode, Stephen's getting justice from the rector of Clongowes becomes laughable in the value system of the animal mode. The physical lust after flesh in the animal mode becomes mental torture in the rational mode. The highly organized spiritual exercises of Ignatius Loyola in the rational mode become in the angelic mode subject for caricature. And the intoxication of the discovery of vocation in the angelic mode becomes luxurious and precious when seen from the viewpoint of the divine mode where the expanded soul yearns for fuller, more permanent, and more intensely true signs and experiences of vocation and dedication. Thus, interspersed throughout Chapter Five are references to the divinity of the imagination, the messianic creation of conscience, and the godlike creation of a totally new beauty. With these phrases, with "I tried to unite my will with the will of God instant by instant. In that I did not always fail" (240), with "I do not fear to be alone" (247), and with his departure *into* the diary as well as *away from* Dubliners, Stephen's soul is revealed in the divine mode of this chapter as something like Pico's quintessential soul: "And if, happy in the lot of no created thing, he withdraws into the center of his own unity, his spirit, made one with God, in the solitary darkness of God, who is set above all things, shall surpass them all."

This description of the gestation of Stephen's soul, the birth of his divine soul, or the chapter's divine mode does not contradict, but complements Hugh Kenner's characterization of Stephen or the content of the fifth chapter as "priggish, humourless," "a final balance," "development . . . ended," "equilibrium," "unusual integrity," and "freedom."[26] These terms are correct enough; they can be better understood in the light of Aristotle's description in the "Nicomachean Ethics" of the highest level of happiness possible to man and of the happy man himself. Instead of a quotation from Aristotle the following summary analysis by Victor White in *God and the Unconscious* will serve to connect Stephen and the happy man: the happy man, at the top of a hierarchy of lesser men is "Aristotle's 'magnanimous' prig: free, self-sufficient, unsocial, even anti-social . . . the acme of humanity, the 'theoretician,' the godlike contemplator of the divine . . .; he is passion-free, and seeking a godlike life among men in self-sufficient isolation."[27] Thus, outer "priggish, humourless" action is informed by a divinized soul. Or, the outer stability of the magnanimous man reveals and embodies the inner action of the quintessential soul, and while Stephen argues for happiness, freedom, and isolation, his soul seeks to act—"to discover the mode of life or of art whereby [his] spirit could express itself in unfettered freedom," and "to forge in the smithy of [his] soul the uncreated conscience of [his] race." (246, 253)

And it cannot be forgotten—it must not be forgotten!—that Stephen, a "happy man" with a "divinized soul," can still suffer. This idea is served by the analogy in Chapter Five of Stephen to Jesus. At the end of *A Portrait* as at the beginning, Stephen's body is still subject to its pains and his soul to its perturbations.

CONCLUSION

In this conclusion, I present a half-dozen implications to be drawn from my analysis of the novel's organization. They are about the control and freedom given by the ladder of perfection—in the revision of *Stephen Hero* into *A Portrait of the Artist as a Young Man;* in the integration of the development of Stephen's poetic spirit with the reality of Dublin; and in the location of the novel in the center of European culture.

1. The ladder of perfection is the organizational principle that transformed the amorphous *Stephen Hero* into *A Portrait of the Artist as a Young Man.* It ordered the mass of details and encounters of *Stephen Hero* not just by giving categories within which Joyce could place mechanically the data, but by giving a teleology to each category and to the whole novel; the result was that each scene could retain its own significance, as a specific "real" experience, have its dramatic value, as a specific "theatrical" gesture, and function symbolically, as a participant, in the total work. It ordered or schematized without creating, for example, the uncomfortable artificiality of the categories of *Ulysses.*

2. By spiritualizing every event, the ladder of perfection intensified the novel's atmosphere of subjectivity; but, at the same time, by organizing the events of Dublin and environs in modes appropriate to condition of the spirit, the ladder correlated the objective world with the subjective experience and

interpretation. As Joyce wrote of Bruno, "the material universe . . . [was] his opportunity for spiritual activity. . . ." This pairing of the objective and the subjective is clear in these two statements made by Stephen. "This race and this country and this life produced me, he said. I shall express myself as I am." "I mean, said Stephen [later], that I was not myself as I am now, as I had to become." (203, 240)

3. The integration of character and action, spirit and flesh, mind and world, occurs with special clarity in certain points of fusion, in the cries, "which are," as Stephen says in *Stephen Hero,* "antecedent to all song": the *scala verborum* shows the flesh made word and then, in climax, the word is fleshed out in a poem. The self and the world become poetry.

4. The technique of analogy, used to "telescope" the lengthy *Stephen Hero* into *A Portrait,* can also telescope *A Portrait,* for its five chapters seem one action in five modes. And, as the quantity of five chapters corresponds to the quality of the process of the soul through five stages, so the novel's emphasis on the technique of analogy corresponds to the way Stephen's spirit functions. A brief example to illustrate this important point is found in Stephen's diary: "Item, he eats chiefly belly bacon and dried figs. Read locusts and wild honey." (248) The combination of the assimilation of Stephen's extensive reading, his impulse to find analogies, and the novel's structure of analogies creates a very complex nexus of literary references, allusions, and analogues. The construction of *A Portrait* in every aspect is consistent with—in Northrop Frye's phrase—the "learned mythopoeia" of the "Villanelle for a Temptress" or the "Proteus" chapter, in which Stephen indulges his soul's habit of analogization of himself and his landscape; indeed, *A Portrait* is consistent with the "learned mythopoeia," the transformations by analogy, of *Ulysses* and *Finnegans Wake.*

5. Along with its spiritual categories and dynamics, the ladder of perfection has a highly *conventional* vocabulary; and by revising into this vocabulary, the obviously autobiographical notes and episodes of *Stephen Hero* were placed at a distance, objectified, fictionalized, and stylized. *A Portrait* is a translation of the provincial *Stephen Hero* into the language of Europe.

6. While *A Portrait*'s structure of analogical modes enforces a very tightly bound reflexive coherence, its sequence of modes allows variety, movement, and change. By repeating words in leitmotif or in clusters and by changing the "tonal key" in accord with the different modes, Joyce could alter radically or slightly, but *at will,* the meanings and values of the events; without losing the basic feeling that every character and scene is an analogy of another, he could advance the narrative. Thus the ladder renders the novel kinetic, in sequence, and static, in analogy. This paradox of novelty and repetition is reflected in a note in the diary: "I go to encounter for the millionth time the reality of experience. . . ." In sum, the novel possesses symmetrical formalism and passionate realism, or "classical" stability and "romantic" energy.

After this romance of idealistic striving for godlikeness, after this excitement and strain of the individuation of the soul in *A Portrait,* the subdued stoicism of *Ulysses* is at best a world in which there is a steady mood of some loss: Stephen's soul, born slowly and darkly in five stages of twenty years, must now find its way in the labyrinth of the present; his ladder of perfection has brought (not his vegetable, animal, rational, or angelic soul, but) his godlike soul to encounter in *Ulysses* this "vegetable world . . . the now, the here."[28]

Notes

1. [James Joyce, *A Portrait of the Artist as a Young Man* (New York: Viking Press, 1964), 203; hereafter cited in the text.] The main ideas of this essay were presented in a talk before the James Joyce Society at the Gotham Book Mart, April, 1965. I was much aided at the beginning of my research by friends at the University of Hartford, Bill Brayfield, historian, and Albert Hamel, philosopher.

2. Richard Ellmann, *James Joyce* (New York, 1959), p. 272.

3. Ellmann, p. 274.

4. Ellmann, p. 307.

5. There are some things I have not done in this essay. I do not try to establish a source for the scheme, but to study the organization of the novel and to merely indicate the vast tradition to which it belongs; without Joyce's personally specifying his source, I do not think it is possible to reduce to a reasonable number the probable sources. Nor can I do more than indicate here how the scheme is present in the details: a detailed analysis will be given later in a longer study of the novel. Furthermore, I have not touched on the problem of irony; I believe that the analysis offered here demands a serious review of that problem. The problem of irony will also be discussed in a separate essay.

   After this essay was written, *Studies in Structure: Stages of the Spiritual Life in Four Modern Authors* by Robert J. Andreach appeared. Mr. Andreach writes, "The novel is built upon the stages of the fivefold division of the spiritual life with a difference—the order of the stages is reversed and the individual stages are inverted." A comparison of Mr. Andreach's scheme and the one in this essay will show that the reversals and inversions are easily straightened out.

6. I am now writing an article explicating this pattern and relating it to theories of linguistic and poetic origin.

7. The tradition of the chain of being is presented in A. O. Lovejoy, *The Great Chain of Being: A Study of the History of an Idea* (New York, 1960) and a catalogue of ladders of perfection is given in Mircea Eliade, *Shamanism: Archaic Techniques of Ecstasy,* trans. W. Trask (New York, 1964), pp. 487–90.

8. Because there is much other evidence to support a *ratio* hypothesis, e.g., "The equation on the page of [Stephen's] scribbler began to spread out a widening tail . . .," (*P* 102–3) I have no doubt that this chapter is "rational"—but I wish my argument could be simplified by more immediately apparent evidence.

9. The quoted phrases are taken from C. R. S. Harris, *Duns Scotus* (New York, 1959), vol. 2, p. 255.

10. James Joyce, *Letters,* ed. Stuart Gilbert (New York, 1957), p. 139.

11. James Joyce, *Ulysses* (New York, 1934), p. 383.

12. *Ulysses,* p. 41. For discussion of Pico and Stephen, see William M. Schutte, *Joyce and Shakespeare* (New Haven, 1957), pp. 56–7.

13.   Giovanni Pico della Mirandola, "Oration on the Dignity of Man," trans. E. L. Forbes in *The Renaissance Philosophy of Man,* eds. E. Cassirer and others (Chicago, 1948), p. 225.

14.   James Joyce, *Critical Writings,* eds. E. Mason and R. Ellmann (New York, 1954), p. 134.

15.   *Critical Writings,* pp. 160–1. In a letter to me, J. S. Atherton reminded me of Joyce's confusion of people (see *Critical Writings,* p. 161, n. 2) and suggested a French dictionary encyclopedia as the probable source for Joyce's lecture.

16.   Aristotle, *De Anima,* 415a–b.

17.   Aristotle, 414b, 427b.

18.   Aristotle, 433a–b.

19.   Elizabeth F. Boyd, "Joyce's Hell-fire Sermons," in *Portraits of an Artist,* eds. W. E. Morris and C. A. Nault, Jr. (New York, 1962), p. 261.

20.   These speculations on angelic *intellecti* are based on the comments on angelology in Henry Corbin, *Avicenna and the Visionary Recital* (New York, 1960), p. 360.

21.   Erwin Panofsky, *Studies in Iconology: Humanistic Themes in the Art of the Renaissance* (New York, 1962), p. 144, n. 51. The faculties of the soul to correspond with the Venuses are not those I find for *A Portrait.* At this time I do not find the differences important but they may be.

22.   Dante, *Vita Nuova and Canzoniere* (London, 1948), pp. 3, 5.

23.   *Stephen Hero,* p. 93.

24.   Plato, *Timaeus,* trans. B. Jowett, para. 41.

25.   *Ulysses,* p. 38. The association of Stephen's "old father, old artificer" with Los is noted by Northrop Frye, who arrived here by another route; he writes, "This father, the spiritual or imaginative Dedalus who built the labyrinth and then flew out of it, is a figure very close to Blake's Los, the prophetic blacksmith who builds the Mundane Shell." In "Quest and Cycle in *Finnegans Wake," Fables of Identity: Studies in Poetic Mythology* (New York, 1963), p. 261.

26.   Hugh Kenner, *Dublin's Joyce* (Bloomington, 1956), pp. 131, 112, 121, 122, 132. Whether agreeing or disagreeing with Mr. Kenner's attitudes, all serious criticism of *A Portrait* is a footnote to his commentary.

27.   Victor White, O.P., *God and the Unconscious,* intro. by C. G. Jung (New York, 1961), p. 122.

28.   *Ulysses,* p. 148.

The *Portrait* as Portrait:
Joyce and Impressionism

Maurice Beebe

Considering how much has been written on James Joyce's *A Portrait of the Artist as a Young Man,* it is surprising that critics have almost entirely overlooked an Italian writer's review of the novel on which Joyce placed his own stamp of approval. He took the trouble to translate a commentary of Diego Angeli and to see that it was published in a 1918 issue of *The Egoist,* the periodical in which the *Portrait* had been serialized. Called in the original "Un Romanzo di Gesuiti," Angeli's critique offers a number of keys to the interpretation of a book that is seen to be both rebellious in its thought and traditional in its use of analytical techniques, which Joyce learned in Jesuit schools. But what strikes me as particularly original in Angeli's description of the *Portrait* is the comparison he draws between Joyce's art and that of the Impressionist painters. "The brushwork of the novel," says Angeli in the English words of Joyce, "reminds one of certain modern paintings in which the planes interpenetrate and the external vision seems to partake of the sensations of the onlooker. . . . The naturalism of Mr. Joyce is impressionist, the profound synthetic naturalism of some pictures of Cézanne or Maquet, the naturalism of the late impressionists."[1]

This affinity with the visual arts is one of the things Joyce probably meant to suggest through his use of the word "portrait" in his title. Because critics have always disagreed on whether Stephen Dedalus is to be taken seriously or viewed ironically, more attention has been devoted to the relative importance of the words "artist" and "young man" in Joyce's title than to the significance of what is after all the key word of that title. Considering what "portrait" implies in terms of the artistic tradition dominant when Joyce began writing may enable me not only to be quite specific about the kind of novel he wanted to write, but also to show how Impressionism profoundly influenced the style and imagery of the novel, the theory of aesthetics expounded by Joyce through Stephen, and certain important aspects of theme and form. Such an approach may even help to resolve the conflict between those who see Stephen as only a "young man" with limited artistic talent and those who feel that he is already a true "artist."

Reprinted from *Irish Renaissance Annual* 1:1 (1980): 13–31, with the permission of the editor.

"Portrait" implies a picture, and to a young man of cultivated artistic interests around the turn of the century pictures would imply the several kinds of visual art prevalent then which could be placed under the general heading of Impressionism or Post-Impressionism. Although I cannot trace a direct line of influence from the early Impressionist painters of the 1870s to Joyce's first efforts at fiction, he seems to have been almost as strongly attracted to the visual arts as to music and to have been so knowledgeable about current trends and fashions in painting that he made use of pictorial themes and archetypes in his writing.[2] As for the literary Impressionists, Joyce was well acquainted with the work of Henry James and probably borrowed the title "A Portrait of the Artist" from *The Portrait of a Lady*. We have long known that Joyce admired such Impressionist writers as Gustave Flaubert, George Moore, and Walter Pater; and when he sent the first chapter of the *Portrait* to Ezra Pound, that most perceptive of readers sent it on to *The Egoist* and told Joyce that he could not "usually read prose at all not anybody's in English except James and Hudson and a little Conrad."[3]

Even if Joyce had never heard of Impressionism in art and literature, he would have been affected by the movement. T. S. Eliot said, "Our sensibility is constantly changing as the world about us changes";[4] and the prevailing sensibility when Joyce was growing up and learning the literary craft was shaped by Impressionism. Arnold Hauser calls it "the last universally valid 'European style'" and asserts that "the whole philosophy of the last decades of the [nineteenth] century is dependent on it."[5] William Fleming sees Impressionism as a cultural force that united painting, sculpture, architecture, literature, music, and philosophy during the last quarter of that century,[6] and when the first centennial of Impressionist painting was celebrated in a 1974–1975 exhibition, which broke attendance records in both Paris and New York, René Huyghe of the Académie Francaise was able to look back on the phenomenon from a hundred-year perspective that enabled him to see that the Impressionist Era was distinguished by a "collective intellect," which profoundly altered the thinking behind not only the visual arts, literature, and philosophy, but also history and science.[7]

The early Impressionists issued no group manifestoes, and therefore "impressionism" may be defined in many ways. Most explanations of the movement rely, however, on two basic and related assumptions—first, what Monsieur Huyghe calls "the death of matter"; and second, the fusing of subject and object in a way that blends together the one who sees with what he sees. It was fitting, Huyghe says, that "the Impressionists liked to paint the breaking up of ice on rivers and streams," for such scenes reflected a "new understanding of nature . . . : all that connoted the inert and stable was increasingly supplanted by the fluid and impalpable; nature lost its attributes of weight, density, and hardness" until eventually "the Fluid supplanted the Solid."[8] This was true of time as well as space. In the Heraclitan concept of life as flux Arnold Hauser finds the essence of the Impressionist movement:

"The dominion of the movement over permanence and continuity, the feeling that every phenomenon is a fleeting and never-to-be-repeated constellation, a wave gliding away on the river of time, the river into which 'one cannot step twice,' is the simplest formula to which impressionism can be reduced."9

With the death of matter and the breakdown of a belief in permanence came increasing scepticism about the realness of the world outside the self. Visually everything began to seem misty, contours were blurred, and for the early Impressionist painters "there were no longer any firm, straight lines. Lines floated and moved."10 As Maria Kronegger puts it, "A world arises in which everything seems to have lost its natural identity. . . . Impressionists are caught up in the transitoriness of all things. The painter Monet, when painting Rouen cathedral, did not directly catch its gothic structure, but an air envelope of a certain density, through which the cathedral could be seen and by which its appearance was modified with every shift of light."11 In seeking to capture the transitory, evanescent scene before them, the Impressionist painters came to realize that the integrity of their work depended not only on that particular object seen while standing there in that spot at that particular time of day through whatever quality of light the climate of the day and season provided, but also on the person doing the seeing. The true Impressionist, Jules Laforgue insisted, is "a modernist painter endowed with an uncommon sensibility of the eye."12 When Monet wrote to a friend in 1880 that he was seeking "*instaneity,* above all, the envelopment, the same light spread over everywhere," he apparently thought that he had to wait for just the right light before continuing work on a painting already started. He could not have known then that there would come a time when, virtually blind, he would have to paint largely from memory. But implicit throughout the Impressionist aesthetic is the assumption that "the act of perception is more important than either the perceived or the perceiver. No longer is there ME . . . on the one hand, and that tree on the other hand; there is only my seeing, retaining, or remembering that tree."13 In turn the tree becomes a painting of a tree, and if one is truly to comprehend that tree as the artist saw it, he must have powers of vision as intense as those of the artist. Conrad's ringing statement of his mission, "My task . . . is, by the power of the written word to make you hear, to make you feel—it is, before all, to make you *see,*"14 reminds us that Impressionism implies collaboration between artist and audience. As Albert Guerard puts it, "The . . . central preoccupation of Conrad's technique, the heart of the impressionist aim, is to invite and control the reader's identifications and so subject him to an intense rather than passive experience."15 The way in which "external vision seems to partake of the sensations of the onlooker" that Diego Angeli had in mind when writing his review of the *Portrait* strikes close to "the heart of the impressionist aim."

One would suppose that Joyce's *Portrait* has been often seen against the rich tradition of the Impressionist era. Such is not the case. Although critics have acknowledged the "impressionistic" qualities of Joyce's style, they have failed to consider the broader implications of his association with the tradition. Even on the matter of style they are rather vague in their understanding of the term. For some an "impressionistic" style seems to imply nothing more than one that is sensuously rich, a mellifluous flow of descriptive images like those to be found in Pater's prose. As early as 1918, however, Scofield Thayer tried to be more specific when he wrote:

> The great Frenchman [Flaubert] did his best to depict things as he saw them, and that is all the word "impressionist," at least in literature, heretofore implied. Joyce has become impressionist in a much more subtle sense. He gives us, especially in *Ulysses,* the streaming impressions, often only subconsciously cognate to one another, of our habitual life—that vague, tepid river of consciousness to which only our ephemeral moments of real will or appetite can give coherence.[16]

And William York Tindall implied a proper understanding of the term when he wrote, "The first three stories of *Dubliners* and *A Portrait of the Artist* are presented impressionistically through the consciousness of Stephen, who is made to seem both subject and object."[17] If it is the fusion of the observer with what he sees that largely determines an impressionistic style, then Joyce's frequent use of a Jamesian reflector or center-of-consciousness would be almost enough in itself to justify calling him a literary Impressionist. William A. Harms could have been thinking of Joyce when he offered this definition: "Literary Impressionism is a style of writing which gives aesthetic evidence of an author's profound absorption in life as a diaphanous flow of internalized feelings."[18]

Joyce makes use of several stylistic devices associated with writers of the late nineteenth century who tried to achieve effects similar to those in Impressionist art. Commenting on how George Moore's work reflects "the approach of the impressionist painters wherein vivid details are momentarily accentuated against a moving blur of undelineated background," Benjamin Giorgio cites this passage from *A Mummer's Wife* to illustrate his point: "The two women looked down into the great pit, through which the crowd was rolling in one direction, a sort of human tide, a vague tumult in which little was distinguishable; a bald head or a bunch of yellow flowers in a woman's bonnet flashed through the darkness for an instant like the crest of a wave."[19] The use of a part to suggest the whole may at times result in rather extravagant use of synecdoche, especially when parts of the human body are made to act in a peculiarly autonomous way, as in Moore's " 'What have you got for us?' said four red lips as Kate entered" or "she made a sign to the ladies, and the room was left to the flat chests and tweed coats." But the device can be effective when it is used to suggest a fragmentary or disoriented view of a larger scene. Joyce uses the device effectively at the beginning of the *Portrait* when Stephen "was caught in the whirl of a scrimmage and, fearful of the flashing eyes and muddy boots, bent down to look through the legs. The fellows were struggling and groaning and their legs were rubbing and kicking and stamping. Then Jack Lawton's yellow boots dodged out the ball and all the other boots and legs ran after."[20]

Joyce's choice of imagery seems strongly influenced by Impressionist practice in his extensive use of water, shadows, clouds, windows, and mirrors. Some art historians date the beginning of Impressionism as a movement from that moment in 1869 when Monet and Renoir met at La Grenoillère and each painted three pictures of the Frog Pond which, though distinguished by individual style, are very much alike in the impression they convey. "Water was the key element to be studied," Howard Greenfeld says of these celebrated paintings, "the movement of water and the varied reflections on water. . . . A study of the play of sunlight in the water, too, gave them deeper insights into the uses of color."[21] According to William Fleming, the early Impressionists liked to paint scenes of water because of "its fluidity, its surface reflections, the perpetual play of changing light"; and with the help of new technical theories about color, they were able to "to step up the luminosity of their canvases so as to convey the illusion of sunlight sifted through a prism."[22] It is no accident that the moment of Stephen's consecration as an artist takes place against a setting which Joyce describes as a seascape, but long before then Joyce has made effective use of Impressionist imagery. For instance—

> How pale the light was at the window! But that was nice. The fire rose and fell on the wall. It was like waves. Someone had put coal on and he heard voices. They were talking. It was the noise of the waves. Or the waves were talking among themselves as they rose and fell.
> He saw the sea of waves, long dark waves rising and falling, dark under the moonless night. A tiny light twinkled at the pierhead where the ship was entering. . . . [26–27]

Irish climate being what it is, there are few sunny scenes in the *Portrait,* but Joyce achieves much the same shadowing effect through the use of firelight. At one point "the firelight flickered on the wall and beyond the window a spectral dusk was gathering upon the river" (67–68), and at another

> The chapel was flooded by the dull scarlet light that filtered through the lowered blinds; and through the fissure between the last blind and the sash a shaft of wan light entered like a spear and touched the embossed brasses of the candlesticks upon the altar that gleamed like the battleworn mail armour of angels. [116]

Windows are important in such passages. As Stephen travels with his father by the night train to Cork, he sits in a corner of the railway carriage and gazes out the window:

He saw the darkening lands slipping past him, the silent telegraphpoles passing his window swiftly every four seconds, the little glimmering stations,
manned by a few silent sentries, flung by the mail behind her and twinkling for
a moment in the darkness like fiery grains flung backwards by a runner. [87]

Here Joyce achieves an effect of movement which a painter would have difficulty attaining. It is as if the train were still and what is outside the window
were moving ("the silent telegraphpoles passing his window swiftly"), but
that feeling gives way to a sensation of rapid movement through time as well
as space. Commenting on the "kaleidoscopic effect" of this passage, Maria
Kronegger notes that "Joyce creates the impression of blurred images passing
before his eyes in total silence by repetition of key words (flung), and by his
use of the gerund and adjectival participles. Words take the place of objects:
darkening, slipping, passing, glimmering, twinkling, etc."[23] Because the
effect of words ending in –ing is to suggest a process of becoming rather than
static, fixed being, the reader participates as he himself seems to "travel"
through Joyce's narrative.

The Impressionist painters were fond of using pictures within pictures as
well as windows and mirrors in order to create an illusion of internal depth.
They felt that the use of pictures, mirrors, windows, and doorways served to
draw the viewer into the painting by calling attention to the artificial aspects
of the larger picture and by subtly reminding the spectator that he is himself
taking part in a visual experience. Similarly, it is difficult to read the passage
quoted above without being forced to share vicariously Stephen's sensations,
for we have all experienced the illusion of both moving and remaining still as
we have watched the horizon slip by from a moving vehicle. This is but one of
several ways in which Joyce's adaptation of Impressionistic techniques
enables him to achieve a sense of identification among artist, character, and
reader that helps to justify the world-within-world of his reflexive art.

In addition to being able to depict a progression through space and
time, the writer has a further advantage over the painter in that he can make
use of other senses than sight. In what amounts to an Impressionistic credo
for the literary artist, Conrad insisted that

the artistic aim when expressing itself in written words must . . . make its
appeal through the senses, if its high desire is to reach the secret spring of
responsive emotions. It must strenuously aspire to the plasticity of sculpture,
to the colour of painting, and to the magic suggestiveness of music—which is
the art of arts. And it is only through complete, unswerving devotion to the
perfect blending of form and substance; it is only through an unremitting
never-discouraged care for the shape and ring of sentences that an approach
can be made to plasticity, to colour, and that the light of magic suggestiveness
may be brought to play for an evanescent instant over the commonplace surface of words.[24]

How "the shape and ring of sentences" can evoke both the plasticity of visual images and the musical effect of the auditory is well illustrated by this key passage in the *Portrait:*

> He drew forth a phrase from his treasure and spoke it softly to himself:
> —A day of dappled seaborne clouds.
> The phrase and the day and the scene harmonised in a chord. Words. Was it their colours? He allowed them to glow and fade, hue after hue: sunrise gold, the russet and green of apple orchards, azure of waves, the greyfringed fleece of clouds. No, it was not their colours: it was the poise and balance of the period itself. Did he then love the rhythmic rise and fall of words better than their associations of legend and colour? Or was it that, being as weak of sight as he was shy of mind, he drew less pleasure from the reflection of the glowing sensible world through the prism of a language manycoloured and richly storied than from the contemplation of an inner world of individual emotions mirrored perfectly in a lucid supple periodic prose? [166–67]

Here auditory effects blend with the visual imagery. Throughout his reveries Stephen moves easily from one sense to others. Thus the sound of the word "suck" evokes the visual image of water draining from the wash basin of a lavatory in the Wicklow Hotel, and when he remembered "the white look of the lavatory" and the faucets marked hot and cold, "he felt cold and then a little hot" (11). And if words have colors, sounds may have feelings: "There were different kinds of pains for all the different kinds of sounds. A long thin cane would have a high whistling sound and he wondered what was that pain like. It made him shivery to think of it and cold" (45). If the reader too feels a tremor as he reads the sentence, then Joyce has tapped what Conrad calls "the secret spring of responsive emotions" and thus achieved one of the aims of Impressionist prose.

Several aspects of the aesthetic theory presented in *Stephen Hero* and the *Portrait* seem to be closely related to Impressionism. Stephen's explanation of the three essential qualities of beauty—wholeness, harmony, and radiance—is particularly significant in this regard. By showing that these three qualities correspond to three stages of aesthetic apprehension, Joyce equates the objective beauty of the art work with the subjective process by which it is seen, thus insisting that a collaboration between the artist and his viewer is necessary to art. As Stephen expounds his theory to his friend Lynch in the *Portrait,* he uses a basket as his example of an object to be perceived, but when he says that "the first phase of apprehension is a bounding line drawn about the object to be apprehended," it is as if he were describing a framed picture:

> . . . the esthetic image is first luminously apprehended as self-bounded and selfcontained upon the immeasurable background of space or time which is not it. You apprehend it as *one* thing. You see it as one whole. You apprehend its wholeness. That is *integritas.* [212]

Stephen moves on easily to the second quality:

—Then, said Stephen, you pass from point to point, led by its formal lines; you apprehend it as balanced part against part within its limits; you feel the rhythm of its structure. In other words the synthesis of immediate perception is followed by the analysis of apprehension. Having first felt that it is *one* thing you feel now that it is a *thing*. You apprehend it as complex, multiple, divisible, separable, made up of its parts, the result of its parts and their sum, harmonious. That is *consonantia*. [212]

But he hesitates over the third term he has borrowed from Aquinas. In *Stephen Hero* Joyce acknowledged a religious dimension to art when he had Stephen define *claritas* in terms of "epiphany," equating the radiance of the art object with its "soul" and using other religious imagery in defining the final stage of apprehension of that "moment" which is the artwork: "Its soul, its whatness, leaps to us from the vestment of its appearance. The soul of the commonest object . . . seems to us radiant. The object achieves its epiphany."[25] In the *Portrait* version, however, words like "epiphany," "soul," and "vestments" are avoided as Stephen offers an entirely secular definition of *claritas*. He tells Lynch that he has rejected Aquinas's notion that

claritas is the artistic discovery and representation of the divine purpose in anything or a force of generalisation which would make the esthetic image a universal one, make it outshine its proper conditions. But that is literary talk. I understand it so. When you have apprehended that basket as one thing and have then analysed it according to its form and apprehended it as a thing you make the only synthesis which is logically and esthetically permissable. You see that it is that thing which it is and no other thing. The radiance of which he speaks is the scholastic *quidditas*, the *whatness* of a thing. [213]

Hence, in keeping with Joyce's initial insistence that art is a form of stasis rather than a kinetic force propelling the observer to something beyond the art work itself, Joyce now rejects all implications of symbolism or idealism as he equates the radiance of the work of art with its simple, objective whatness.

Although Joyce himself rejected the idea of epiphany, it remains a valid concept in literary criticism. It is a convenient term to apply to those moments of sudden insight which mark, for instance, the climaxes of the stories in *Dubliners*. Judging, however, from the modest collection of *Epiphanies* which Joyce himself wrote, he was less likely to find epiphanies in dramatic or significant actions than in those "minor, unimpressive, random events" which Erich Auerbach considers one of the hallmarks of modern literature.[26] Joyce's epiphanies are closely related to the images of Pound's Imagism, the "airblown grains" of Henry James, the "essences" of Marcel Proust, and Virginia Woolf's "moments of being." But it does not seem to be widely recognized that an emphasis on separate moments of perception in twentieth-century literature may owe much to the revolution in the visual arts which occurred during the era of Impressionism. From the constantly changing flux of life, the Impressionist painters attempted to capture in that flash perception they called *vistazo* an isolated snapshot of reality. Painters have always had to deal with single instants, but whereas earlier artists preferred to depict moments of intense dramatic action or to freeze life in a way that would suggest significance beyond the object represented, it was "only the Impressionists," John Rewald tells us, who "pursued the instant for the instant's sake, not as the climax of biblical or historical or mythological events, not as a symbol, not as a distillation of intimate visions, but as the immediate response of their retinas and brushes to their observations of nature."[27]

The reluctance of the Impressionists to depict significant scenes, preferring instead what often seemed to be only random or trivial, is one reason why initial public and critical response to their work was hostile. Similarly when Stephen Dedalus of *Stephen Hero* offered some of his ideas about aesthetics before the Literary and Historical Society of University College, his listeners were unsympathetic because his insistence on the formal autonomy of art would absolve the artist from moral and patriotic obligations. That separation is, of course, one of the main points of Stephen's aesthetic. Joyce knew that in the realm of ethics art is not to be confused with artist, but as far as art itself is concerned, he did indeed insist that what matters is the simple, static presence of the art work rather than any abstract meaning or lesson that might be found in it. The Impressionist painters annoyed philistine visitors to their exhibitions by demanding that their paintings be viewed not as windows on the world, but simply as paintings. Clement Greenberg makes a significant statement about this aspect of their work:

> Realistic, illusionist art had dissembled the medium, using art to conceal art. Modernism used art to call attention to art. The limitations that constitute the medium of painting—the flat surface, the shape of the support, the properties of pigment—were treated by the Old Masters as negative factors that could be acknowledged only implicitly or indirectly. Modernist painting has come to regard these same limitations as positive factors that are to be acknowledged openly. Manet's paintings became the first Modernist ones by virtue of the frankness with which they declared the surfaces on which they were painted. The Impressionists, in Manet's wake, abjured underpainting and glazing, to leave the eye under no doubt as to the fact that the colors used were made of real paint that came from pots or tubes. Cézanne sacrificed verisimilitude, or correctness, in order to fit drawing and design more explicitly to the rectangular shape of the canvas.[28]

It is not far from the Impressionist painters to those writers who insist on calling attention to the media and materials with which they work. In *The Pound Era* Hugh Kenner says that a distinguishing feature of Modernist literature is its insistence on "space-craft." We may think of Henry James's *The Ambas-*

sadors, for example, as a narrative occupying a period of time, but the book itself "is a hundred cubic inches of wood pulp."[29] Henry James would not have put it so bluntly, but the first of the major Impressionist writers certainly saw his novels as physical blocks of matter which were to be divided into units called paragraphs and chapters.

Applying Joyce's notion of *claritas* to *Portrait* and thereby emphasizing the *whatness* of the work helps to justify certain aspects of the novel's form. In spite of the fact that the narrative proceeds chronologically from Stephen's infancy to early manhood, the *Portrait* is a much more static work than its predecessor. Whereas *Stephen Hero* was written mostly in conventional summary narrative, the *Portrait* is developed largely by means of distinct scenes. This is widely recognized, of course, but we can better understand why the novel is written scenically if we place it against the context of the Impressionist era and realize that in fiction Impressionism was found not only in works by James, Conrad, and other writers who used a center-of-consciousness technique or filtered everything seen through a detached narrator, but also in the *vistazo*-like slices of life depicted by Chekhov, Katherine Mansfield, and, of course, the Joyce of *Dubliners.* If we say that the contents of that collection seem more like "sketches" than stories, it is partly because there is an obvious analogy between those works and the visual arts.

The *whatness* of the *Portrait* begins literally with the words "A Portrait" in its title. The story begins in a ragged, rough-edged way with Stephen in infancy, his mind a confused jumble of baby-talk, but little by little as the novel progresses he emerges as a clearly distinct character until finally his essential nature is, as it were, distilled. In an important article on "The Imaginary Portrait: Fin-de-siècle Icon," Jan B. Gordon has shown how "at the conclusion of *A Portrait* there is no longer the voice of a character but of a Stephen who, as surely as Dorian Gray, victimized by another Portrait, has refined himself out of human existence. He literally *is* his art."[30] We are given a set-piece demonstration of Stephen the artist by means of the villanelle he composes, a romantic lyric which bids farewell to romantic yearning, and finally at the end of the work there are extracts from Stephen's diary. Why Joyce's *Portrait* ends in this way has never been fully explained, but the device may be understood in part as a heritage from the Impressionist tradition. Commenting on the use of diaries in fiction by the French Impressionist writers, Maria Kronegger points out that "writers of diaries, notebooks, and memoirs have the advantage of making everything proceed from a certain instant: according to the moment, they can change writing styles, that is the manner of suggesting reality; they can change points of view in order to capture the most volatile moments of life together with nuances of color and tone, and to seize in passing the variations in aspect which the same scene assumes at different moments."[31] In other words, short diary entries can be seen as verbal equivalents to the *vistazos* recorded visually by Impressionist painters. Appropriately therefore one of Stephen's diary entries is almost like a little Frog Pond painting. We have seen that earlier in the novel Stephen speculated on the implications of the phrase "a day of dappled seaborne clouds" as something of a touchstone for the kind of art he wanted to create. Now he again combines images of clouds, waves, and even an apple orchard, but in a much more concise way which seems to offer his own objective demonstration that he has become an artist committed to life as seen:

> 5 *April:* Wild spring. Scudding clouds. O life! Dark stream of swirling bog-water on which appletrees have cast down their delicate flowers. Eyes of girls among the leaves. Girls demure and romping. All fair or auburn: no dark ones. They blush better. Houp-la! [250]

That little set-piece may or may not be a convincing example of Stephen as artist, but if I have presented enough evidence thus far to support the claim that the novel could have been titled "A Portrait of the Impressionist Artist as a Young Man," some of the problems readers have encountered in dealing with Stephen may be explained away. It seem to me obvious enough that Joyce intended us to see a progression towards some kind of artistic maturity in Stephen. That progression is represented through certain key episodes which revolve around the theme of vision, beginning with the traumatic episode of Stephen's broken glasses and proceeding through such phases as his deliberate attempt "to mortify the sense of sight" by making it "his rule to walk in the street with downcast eyes" (150) until finally during his moment of consecration as artist he proceeds from a sense that "darkness was falling" over the scene before him until he realizes that "it was not darkness that fell from the air. It was brightness" (232–34). Recognizing this progression from varying degrees and kinds of blindness to seeing things not necessarily clearly but brightly should help us to realize also the way in which Impressionism influenced the point-of-view used in the novel. Just as the Impressionist painters insisted that it was their superior vision rather than just the objects they depicted which justified their work, Joyce located *claritas* not only in the whatness of the work of art but in the eye of the beholder. We have seen that throughout his exposition of the three qualities of beauty Stephen equates *integritas, consonantia,* and *claritas* with the three stages of aesthetic apprehension. In *Stephen Hero* he was even more specific than in the *Portrait,* in the earlier work using not a basket but the clock of the Ballast Office as his example of an aesthetic object:

> —Imagine my glimpses at that clock as the gropings of a spiritual eye which seeks to adjust its vision to an exact focus. The moment the focus is reached the object is epiphanised. It is just in this epiphany that I find the third, the supreme quality of beauty.[32]

Stephen does not achieve that kind of focus until near the end of the novel in which he appears. Until then the method carefully used by Joyce enables him to depict not so much his mature view of his younger self as Stephen's own view of himself and the world around him. The often maligned style of the *Portrait* may thus be defended as Joyce's quite brilliant effort to show how life might have been viewed by an archetypal young artist at the turn of the century who had not yet found his own separate and unique identity.[33] If that artist was, as I have tried to show, an Impressionist, it was to be expected that what he viewed might often appear to be shimmery, diaphanous, and evanescent.

Notes

1. Reprinted in *James Joyce: The Critical Heritage,* ed. Robert H. Deming, 2 vols. (New York: Barnes and Noble, 1970), 1:115–16. Angeli's critique was first published in *Il Marzocco* (Florence) 22 (12 August 1917): 2–3.

2. See, for example, Archie K. Loss, "The Pre-Raphaelite Woman, the Symbolist *Femme-Enfant,* and the Girl with Long Flowing Hair in the Earlier Work of Joyce," *Journal of Modern Literature* 3 (February 1973): 3–23.

3. Ezra Pound to James Joyce, January 1914, in *Pound/Joyce: The Letters of Ezra Pound to James Joyce, with Pound's Essays on Joyce* (New York: New Directions, 1966), p. 24.

4. T. S. Eliot, "The Social Function of Poetry," in *On Poetry and Poets* (New York: Farrar, Straus and Cudahy, 1957), p. 10.

5. Arnold Hauser, *The Social History of Art,* 2 vols. (New York: Knopf, 1951), 2: 869–926.

6. William Fleming, *Arts and Ideas,* 3rd ed. (New York: Holt, Rinehart and Winston, 1968), pp. 477–500.

7. René Huyghe, "Shifts in Thought During the Impressionist Era: Painting, Science, Literature, History, and Philosophy," in *Impressionism: A Centenary Exhibition* (New York: Metropolitan Museum of Art, 1974–75), pp. 14–32.

8. Huyghe, pp. 18–21.

9. Hauser, *Social History,* 2: 872.

10. Huyghe, "Shifts in Thought," p. 22.

11. Maria Elisabeth Kronegger, *Literary Impressionism* (New Haven, Conn.: College and University Press, 1973), pp. 45–46.

12. "Impressionism," in Linda Nochlin, ed., *Impressionism and Post-Impressionism, 1874–1904: Sources and Documents* (Englewood Cliffs, N.J.: Prentice-Hall, 1966), p. 15.

13. Kronegger, *Literary Impressionism,* p. 40.

14. Joseph Conrad, "Preface" to *The Nigger of the "Narcissus."*

15. Albert J. Guerard, *Conrad the Novelist* (Cambridge, Mass.: Harvard University Press, 1958), p. 152.

16. "James Joyce," *Dial* 65 (19 September 1918): 201–03.

17. William York Tindall, *James Joyce: His Way of Interpreting the Modern World* (London: Scribner's, 1950), p. 40.

18. William A. Harms, "Impressionism as a Literary Style" (Ph.D. diss., Indiana University, 1971), p. 35.

19. Benjamin David Giorgio, "Stephen Crane: American Impressionist" (Ph.D. diss., University of Wisconsin, 1969), p. 17ff.

20. *A Portrait of the Artist as a Young Man* (New York: Viking Press, 1965), pp. 9–10. Subsequent references are included parenthetically in the text.

21. Howard Greenfeld, *The Impressionist Revolution* (Garden City, N.Y.: Doubleday, 1972), p. 67.

22. Fleming, *Arts,* p. 485, 483.

23. Kronegger, *Literary Impressionism,* p. 78.

24. Conrad in "Preface" to *The Nigger of the "Narcissus."*

25. James Joyce, *Stephen Hero,* ed. Theodore Spencer (New York: New Directions, 1955), p. 213.

26. As cited by Morris Beja, *Epiphany in the Modern Novel* (Seattle, Wash.: University of Washington Press, 1971), p. 17.

27. John Rewald, *The Impressionist Brush* (New York: Metropolitan Museum of Art, 1974), p. 54.

28. Clement Greenberg, "Modernist Painting," in Gregory Battock, ed., *The New Art: A Critical Anthology,* new rev. ed. (New York: E. P. Dutton, 1973), pp. 68–69.

29. Hugh Kenner, *The Pound Era* (Berkeley and Los Angeles: University of California Press, 1971), p. 28.

30. Jan B. Gordon, "The Imaginary Portrait: Fin-de-siècle Icon," *University of Windsor Review* 5 (Fall 1969): 99–100.

31. Kronegger, *Literary Impressionism,* p. 51.

32. Joyce, *Stephen Hero,* p. 211

33. This view of the novel is argued persuasively by James Naremore in "Style as Meaning in *A Portrait of the Artist," James Joyce Quarterly* 4 (Summer 1967): 331–42.

[Davin's "Strange Woman" and Her Biblical Prototypes]

NEHAMA ASCHKENASY

In Chapter V of James Joyce's *A Portrait of the Artist as a Young Man,*[1] Stephen Dedalus recalls a haunting story that was related to him by his friend Davin, the "peasant student." Young Davin, we are told, is a worshipper of the "sorrowful" legends of Ireland, whose imagination has been fueled by stories from Irish myth. Davin's friends have added a heroic aura to his figure, casting him in the role of a "young Fenian." Stephen Dedalus, on the other hand, is now in the process of divorcing himself mentally and spiritually from family, home, and country, and has been labeled "an antisocial being" by his peers. Stephen is seen as selfish and self-immersed, denouncing all the claims that church, country, and family may have on him. In an attempt to transcend the squalor of his everyday reality and dissociate himself from it, Stephen indulges in an intellectual and artistic search for the essence of beauty and for an aesthetic muse that would replace these social and religious institutions that have controlled his life so far.

Davin's story is presented to the reader through Stephen's eyes, yet it has not lost its power of dramatic immediacy. While Stephen may have rearranged and reshaped the tale, he allows Davin's voice to actually narrate it, and it is clear that Davin is still in the grips of its disturbing effect. It happened after a hurtling match, when Davin missed the last train home and was forced to walk through the countryside at night. He walked along the lonely road in total darkness until he spotted a light in the window of a small cottage. Davin knocked at the door and a voice answered. He asked for a glass of water, and after a while a "half-undressed" young woman, apparently pregnant, came out and gave him a big mug of milk. The woman then began chatting with Davin, telling him that her husband had gone for the night, and finally inviting him to come in and spend the night in her house. Davin thanked her, declined her invitation, and feverishly rushed away, leaving the young woman standing at her door.

Reprinted, with modified title, from *Modern Language Studies* 15, no. 4 (Fall 1985): 28–39, with the permission of the author.

To Stephen, the woman in Davin's story evokes the memory of other peasant women he has seen, standing at their doorway, as the college car drove by. He regards her "as a type of her race and his own, a batlike soul waking to the consciousness of itself in darkness and secrecy and loneliness and, through the eyes and voice of a woman without guile, calling the stranger to her bed" (P 183). The peasant woman represents for Stephen eternal womanhood in her dual role as the provider of food and comforts, as well as the remote, mysterious, and dangerous "other." The young woman's breasts and shoulders are bare, her hair is hanging, and she is pregnant; in other words, she stands for erotic promise and procreative fulfillment. In her role as nurturer, she generously gives the young man "a big mug of milk" instead of the humble "glass of water" that he has asked for. As a peasant, "a type of her race and his own," she is close to the land, and in her pregnant state she is "Mother Earth" herself. Yet she is also a seductress, trying to lure the young man to her bed, where he might find not only sexual satisfaction but also danger and probably death. Like the earth that she represents, the woman has the power to bring forth life, but she can also entrap and devour, turning from shelter into grave.

For the feverish Davin, who experiences "this strange thing," as he calls it, as well as for the intellectual Stephen, who contemplates the event coldly and analytically, the peasant woman stands for everything that is eternally fascinating and terrifying in womanhood. She can give life, nourishment, pleasure, and warmth, yet she is treacherous ("her husband had gone . . ."), secretive, dangerous, and frighteningly inhuman ("batlike"). The adolescent Stephen, confused as he is by his own budding sexuality, commutes Davin's confrontation with the young woman into a universal paradigm of the paradoxical nature of the male-female relationship. It is the utmost expression of the human life-force, on the one hand, and a death-like experience in which man loses control of himself and surrenders to the frailties of his body, on the other. If "reproduction is the beginning of death," as Stephen's friend Temple argues, quoting Hegel (P 231), then the pregnant stranger is a reminder not only of life and procreation but also of decay and mortality. As a symbol of physical temptation, she epitomizes for Stephen the treachery of the body and underlines his terror of woman as well as of his own sexual needs.

The archetypal power of this enigmatic and disquieting event is reinforced once we realize that Joyce has incorporated in this episode two Biblical scenes which he has meshed together and used as an archaic support for his narrative. While the Davin tale seems to belong to the lore of the land, with the mysterious woman as a demon from Celtic legends, it derives its vitality from Biblical imagination. The first obvious Biblical source is the story of Jael and Sisera in Judges chapter 4, which is tied to the Davin episode through the motif of "milk instead of water." Davin's fear of the woman is not consciously fear of death; rather, the young man's panic is caused by his anticipation of the erotic encounter, perhaps also by the adultery involved, and only remotely is it related to the husband who might surprise the couple and take revenge. But to any Bible reader the theme of "milk instead of water" immediately evokes the image of another woman, Jael, the wife of Heber the Kenite, who, in ancient times, also lured a man into her house, answered his plea for water with a mug of milk, and then killed him. The episode occurred after the defeat of the Canaanite army by the children of Israel, when Sisera, chief of the Canaanite forces, fled the battlefield by foot. This is how the Bible tells the story:

> Howbeit Sisera fled away on his feet, to the tent of Jael the wife of Heber the Kenite: for there was peace between Jabin the king of Hazor, and the house of Heber the Kenite. And Jael went out to meet Sisera, and said unto him, Turn in, my lord in to me, fear not. And when he had turned in unto her, into the tent, she covered him with a mantle. And he said unto her, Give me, I pray thee, a little water to drink, for I am thirsty. And she opened a bottle of milk and gave him drink, and covered him. . . Then Jael Heber's wife took a nail of the tent, and took a hammer in her hand, and went softly unto him, and smote the nail into his temples, and fastened it into the ground: (for he was fast asleep, and weary;) so he died. (Judges 5:17–19, 21)

The similarities between the Joycean episode and the Biblical tale are obvious. Table I illustrates the parallelism between the two scenes by placing side by side their corresponding elements. We should remember, however, that the chronological sequence of the ancient tale is slightly different from that of the Davin episode. In the Biblical narrative the man asks for water only after he has entered the woman's tent; in the modern episode, Davin asks for water while he is standing outside the cottage. The events in the Bible column in Table I are therefore numbered in accordance with their chronological progression.

TABLE I

A Portrait, Chapter 5	*Judges,* Chapters 4 and 5	
—A "hard fight" between "Croke's Own Boys" and the "fearless Thurles."	—Battle between the Israelites and the Canaanites.	(1
—Davin is forced "to foot it out."	—Sisera "fled away on his feet."	(2
—He spies a "little cottage."	—Sisera arrives at Jael's tent.	(3
—Davin asks for "a glass of water."	—Sisera asks for "a little water."	(5
—Woman gives him "a big mug of milk."	—Jael "opens a bottle of milk."	(6
—Woman invites Davin to come in and says: "you've no call to be frightened."	—Jael invites Sisera to come in and tells him "fear not."	(4
—Davin declines and leaves.	—Sisera comes in, falls asleep, and is killed by Jael.	(7

—Erotic tension throughout the scene (woman is "half undressed," and her breast and shoulders are bare).	—Erotic element emerges in Deborah's song: "At her feet he bowed, he fell, he lay down" (5:27). In Hebrew: "Between her feet" (or: "legs").
—Commentary of a third person (Stephen the artist)	—Commentary of a third person (Deborah the prophetess and poetess) (8
—Stephen the man condemns the woman for her "batlike" qualities and concludes that she represents "her race."	—Deborah, a woman, commends Jael for her courage and, indirectly, blesses Jael's whole tribe.

Both incidents start with a man departing from what is an exclusively male activity. In the Biblical tale, Sisera flees the battlefield; in Joyce's story, Davin leaves a hurtling match which, while not a real battle, is depicted in the language of fierce combat. In both scenes, the man finds himself alone at night, and when his solitude is finally broken, it is in his encounter with a woman, the social and psychological "other." The woman stands at her door and offers a haven from danger, alleviation of hunger and thirst, and the other comforts of home and hearth. While the man ostensibly asks for water only, he is, in fact, asking for more. Since ancient times, water symbolized the totality of womanhood, and breast, milk, and rain belonged together in mythological apperceptions of early man.[2] In both episodes, it is the woman who interprets, and expands, the male's request for water, by offering him milk and asking him in. The theme of "milk instead of water" is central in both narratives, and represents the female as supplier of the basic sustenance needed for life, milk. The prophetess Deborah harps on the milk motif, and even allows herself the poetic license of exaggeration in her victory ode: "He asked water, and she gave him milk / She brought forth butter in a lordly dish" (Judges 5:25).

In the Davin episode, the threat of death is not immediately apparent. Young Davin's panic may be due to the fact that the pregnant young woman who offers him milk and appears the epitome of motherhood, suddenly reveals a different side and becomes a seductress. The inexperienced youth is also terrified of his own sexual agitation; but beyond that, he is filled with an unidentified primeval fear, embedded in his male consciousness, the origin of which he does not entirely comprehend. Consciously Davin is not afraid for his life. Subconsciously, however, he is reenacting an archetypal male experience, in which the female is conceived of as a threat and a mortal enemy. The Biblical story, which ends with the death of the trusting man at the hands of the treacherous woman, substantiates and explains Davin's fear. By declining the temptress' invitation, Davin avoids Sisera's fate and survives.

In both texts, the female protagonist has stronger roots in the land than the third person who later comments on the event. Jael belongs to a Canaanite tribe which, at least chronologically, is closer to the Land of Canaan than the Israelite invaders. Similarly, the peasant woman in Davin's story is more intimately connected with the Irish soil than the alienated, intellectual Stephen. The identification of the woman with the land is Stephen's contribution to the story. If for Davin the woman stands for the paradoxical nature of femininity, for Stephen she stands for the race, the people, and the soil; in short, she is no less than Mother Ireland herself. The woman as symbol of the land, and the wanton woman as the unfaithful and treacherous soil are Biblical images. One example out of many is the verse in Hosea: "And the Lord said to Hosea, Go, take unto thee a wife of whoredoms, and children of whoredoms: for the land hath committed great whoredom, departing from the Lord" (Hosea, 1:2). The centrality of Davin's tale in Stephen's present frame of mind is now clear. In his attempt to sever his emotional ties with his country and to cast off the yoke of Mother Ireland, just as he has rejected both physical mother and Mother Church, Stephen identifies the seductive and deadly peasant woman with his homeland. The alluring but treacherous nature of his country is a mental rationalization that Stephen is using in trying to justify his feelings of estrangement towards his homeland and his eventual departure from it.

In another conversation between Stephen and Davin, the latter claims not to understand Stephen's coldness towards the cause of Irish independence: "Too deep for me, Stevie, he said. But a man's country comes first. Ireland first, Stevie. You can be a poet or a mystic after" (P 203). Stephen answers with an image that his peasant friend might understand: "Ireland is the old sow that eats her farrow." While taken from his friend's frame of reference, Stephen's analogy is also a paraphrase of the Biblical verse in which the spies who returned from Canaan describe the land to Moses and the people; it is, they say, "a land that eats up its inhabitants" (Numbers 13:32). The feminine gender of the noun 'erets, land, in the Hebrew language determines the whole image: the land is seen as a predatory female. Stephen picks up the feminine identity of the noun "land" in the original phrase and goes a step further: he likens the land to a female animal that eats its young.

Stephen's paraphrasing of the Biblical verse, as well as his recreation of the Jael and Sisera episode, are characterized by the young artist's deliberate reversal of the meaning of the verse and the scene in their original contexts. Stephen's description of his homeland as the old sow that eats its farrow is conceived by the young man as a truthful and correct reflection of reality that cuts through the hypocrisy of sentimental patriotism. However, in the incident cited in the Book of Numbers, the spies' indictment of the Land of Canaan as a soil that devours its inhabitants is considered a slanderous distortion of the truth, perpetrated by the spies in order to demoralize the people and undermine Moses' authority. The spies remain in Biblical memory the epitome of malicious liars and they suffer God's retribution for their false portrayal of the Land of Canaan as a treacherous soil. Similarly, in the story in the Book of Judges, Jael is seen as a divine instrument through whom God rescues his chosen people from the hands of their enemies. Jael's act is praised as moral and right, and the woman herself is exalted as a model of courage and loyalty. In the confrontation between the woman, Jael, and the man, Sisera, the woman exhibits a sound and rational judgment by aligning herself with the right side, God's people, while the man is the enemy, the stranger, who has to be defeated. In Stephen's rendering of the Davin episode, however, the young woman becomes the cosmological other, depicted as almost demonic, "batlike," and as the enemy that the young man has to overcome.

Stephen's treatment of both the Biblical drama of the formidable Jael, which he transplants to the Irish landscape, and the spies' harsh statement about the Land of Canaan, which he modifies and applies to his own homeland, reflects the complexity and ambivalence of his present state of mind. The Jael and Sisera drama and the acerbic Biblical verse that indicts the land, are summoned for the purpose of vindicating the young man's repudiation of femininity, of his own mother, and of Mother Ireland. If women are treacherous and the land is a killer, then Stephen is justified in withdrawing into the rarefied realm of the self and cultivating his own artistic nature. Furthermore, by distorting and misrepresenting the moral and historical significance of the two Biblical texts which underlie his narrative, the rebellious Stephen expresses his individualistic reading of the ancient words, thus rejecting ecclesiastical tradition and authority. At the same time, by evoking the original Biblical narratives, the young artist puts himself in an ambiguous position. Stephen reads the Biblical stories from a non-traditional perspective by identifying with the man, Sisera, rather than with the woman, and by sympathizing with the spies' stand. Thus, he puts himself in the position of the enemy of justice, Sisera, and of the prototypical slanderers, the spies. The Biblical underpinning of Stephen's narrative, which is supposed to defend and validate the young man's anti-social and unpatriotic stand, also reveals his doubts regarding his position as the remote, alienated observer. The truthful, objective recorder of scenes and events may be a self-serving, egoistic slanderer and falsifier of the truth.

Stephen's recreation of the Biblical narratives thus serves at least three conflicting purposes. First, the Biblical structure that underlies the modern point of view provides an archaic precedence for the young man's experience and lends a universal and archetypal reinforcement to his subjective, individualistic positions. Secondly, by perverting the moral and historical significance of the original documents, Stephen asserts the supremacy of his own reading over the traditional interpretation of these ancient texts. Thirdly, though the Biblical tales are being read by Stephen from a new, non-traditional perspective, the powerful ancient verses assert themselves in their original meaning, thus casting doubt on the validity of the young man's position, and turning him from seeker of absolute truth to a reembodiment of the archetypal slanderers.

In the Biblical story of Jael and Sisra the erotic element is suppressed and is handled only symbolically and euphemistically in the water requested by the man and the milk handed to him by the woman. The sexual undertones of Jael and Sisera's encounter are made more explicit in Deborah's verses: "At her feet he bowed, he fell, he lay down / at her feet he bowed, he fell / where he bowed, there he fell down dead" (Judges, 5:27). Early Jewish exegetes noticed the sexual implications of these verses, especially since the Hebrew reads: "Between her feet (or: legs) he bowed, he fell."[3] However, the anonymous Biblical narrator who records the story chooses to be silent on Jael's sexual tactics and concentrates on the woman's swift and brave action. Davin's tale brings the submerged sexual tenor of the "milk instead of water" motif to the foreground. But the full meaning of Davin's experience as a reenactment of the archetypal sexual tension between man and woman is provided by Stephen when he remembers Davin's story and broods over it.

The analogy between Davin's story and the Biblical episode does not end with the young man's last minute escape from the fate that befell the ancient Sisera. Both episodes, the Biblical and the modern, receive their fullest artistic treatment from other persons who did not witness the actual event but who recapture the dramas in a poetic way and crystallize them in the realm of aesthetic expression. In Deborah, who is earlier known as a prophetess and a judge, the event now awakens her poetic powers and she composes a memorable victory ode which celebrates and glorifies the rescue of the people of God from the hands of their enemies and extolls the courageous Jael. If the event itself, in which the woman baits the man and then kills him, may instill in the male reader a primeval terror of women, Deborah puts the woman's action in the context of divine justice by describing Jael as a tool at the hands of God and Sisera as the oppressor of the people of God.

Furthermore, Deborah's ode pays homage to femininity as a powerful theological and political factor. Deborah congratulates herself for her role as a woman-leader: "Until that I Deborah arose / that I arose a mother in Israel" (Judges 5:7). She also panegyrizes and blesses Jael, and, through her, Jael's whole tribe: "Blessed above women shall Jael the wife of Heber the Kenite be" (Judges 5:24). Deborah's ode thus enfolds three different testimonials: it is a reflection of the prophetess' poetic abilities, a national and theological manifesto, and a tribute to women's power and their role in the community. Deborah's poem reflects the singer's harmonious view of the scheme of things where the individual's creativity is enhanced by his or her national commitment and the woman can be an integral part of her nation's life and its destiny.

Obviously, Davin's experience creates in Stephen opposite sentiments; or rather, Stephen's response to Davin's tale is very different from Deborah's reaction to the Jael and Sisera event. While Stephen, like Deborah, is stimulated into putting the experience in a poetic-literary frame, he is also prompted by the tale to further set himself apart from his environment and cultural roots, and to split his world into different and hostile fractions. Instead of the cohesive vision offered by Deborah, Stephen's recounting of Davin's tale underlines the eternal enmity between male and female, man and the earth, native and his homeland, the artist and his environment.

The second Biblical image incorporated in the Davin episode is that of the "strange woman" (or: "stranger woman"), which is a frequent subject of discussion in The Proverbs. This is how the poet of The Proverbs depicts the prototypical seductress:

> For at the window of my house / I looked through my casement
> And beheld among the simple ones / I discerned . . . a young man
> > void of understanding.
> Passing through the street near her corner / and he went the way
> > to her house.
> In the twilight, in the evening / in the black and dark night.
> And behold, there met him a woman / with the attire of an harlot
> > and subtil of heart
>
> . . . .
> So she caught him, and kissed him / and with an impudent face,
> > said unto him,
> I have peace offerings with me / this day I have paid my vows.
> Therefore came I forth to meet thee / diligently to seek thy face,
> > and I have found thee.
> I have deckt my bed with coverings of tapestry / with carved works,
> > with fine linen of Egypt,
> I have perfumed my bed / with myrrh, aloes, and cynamom.
> Come, let us take our fill of love until the morning / let us solace
> > ourselves with loves
> For the good-man is not at home / he is gone a long journey.
> He hath taken a bag of money with him / and will come home at the day
> > appointed.
> With much fair speech she caused him to yield / with the flattering of
> > her lips she forced him.
> He goes after her straightway / as an ox goeth to the slaughter, or as
> > the fool to the correction of the stocks,
> Till a dart strike through his liver / as a bird hasteth to the snare,
> > and knoweth not that it is for his life.
>
> . . . .
> Her house is the way to hell / going down to the chambers of death.
> > (Proverbs 7:6–27)

This Proverbial female figure is indeed the eternal woman, using all her wiles to get the young man to come into her house and meet his doom. The woman is not named, nor is she anchored in any particular historical reality. Table II illustrates the parallelism between Davin's tale and the verses in The Proverbs:

TABLE II

A Portrait, Chapter 5	*Proverbs* 7:6–23
—Davin stops by the young woman's cottage.	—Young man passes by woman's house.
—"It was pitch dark almost."	—It happens "in the black and dark night."
—Young woman is half undressed, her breast and shoulders are bare and her hair is hanging.	—Woman is dressed like a harlot.
—Young woman gives Davin a big mug of milk.	—Woman offers the young man food and luxuries.
—"She asked me . . . would I like to stop the night there."	—Woman seduces the young man: "Come, let us take our fill of love until the morning."
—"She said . . . that her husband had gone that morning to Queenstown . . ."	—"For the good-man is not at home, he is gone a long journey."
—Davin declines the young woman's offer and leaves.	—Young man follows woman into her house and meets his doom.
—Scene is followed by Stephen's conversation with the dean of studies who is dressed like "a levite of the Lord," instructs Stephen in "one of the useful arts," and talks about good and evil.	—Scene is followed by chapter on Wisdom (Proverbs 8) as a female figure who admonishes men to stay away from "wickedness."

In another verse, the young man is exhorted by the Proverbial teacher to beware the "strange woman": "For the lips of the strange woman drop as an honey comb / and her mouth is smoother than oil. But her end is bitter as wormwood / sharp as a two-edged sword. Her feet go down to death / her steps take hold on hell" (Proverbs 5:3–5).

In other instances, the "strange woman" is identified as the "woman Folly" or "a foolish woman," as in the following verses:

A foolish woman is clamorous / she is simple and knoweth nothing.
For she sitteth at the door of her house on a seat / in the high
places of the City:
To call passengers who go right on their ways:

. . . .

Stolen waters are sweet / and bread eaten in secret is pleasant.
But he knoweth not that the dead are there / and that her guests
are in the depths of hell.
(Proverbs 9:13–18)

The young woman in Davin's tale shares many qualities with the Proverbial "strange woman" or "woman Folly." She meets the young man at her door and urges him to commit adultery. She offers the young man food and comforts but she is actually an envoy from hell and would lead the young man to damnation and death. She claims to stand for the pleasures of the body and to be a life-giving force, but she is actually a life-destroying, death-dealing creature. Davin's tale seems to be modeled, in its dramatic structure, after the scene described in The Proverbs 7:6–23. While the woman in The Proverbs is more direct and brazen than the peasant woman in Davin's story, she shares with the latter some essential traits. Both women are married and claim that their husbands are away; both conduct the seduction in the dead of the night, and both are dressed in a suggestive way. Davin's experience thus seems to be a particular case of the generalized, prototypical scene depicted by the Proverbial teacher.

It is hard to see in the "strange woman" the epitome of the Proverbial conception of womanhood. To balance the image of woman as a wanton seductress, the Book of Proverbs offers the poem on the "woman of valor," as well as many other verses describing positive female images, such as the delightful "wife of your youth," and Wisdom as a female figure. The "strange woman" is only one aspect of womanhood, that of the deadly harlot. Beyond that, the Proverbial seductress stands for all the dangers and temptations of the world, not necessarily those connected with women only, which the young man is instructed to avoid. Similarly, the female figure in Davin's episode embodies for young Stephen, who is about to embark on adulthood, all the various temptations of life, as well as the difficult decisions he has to make. The anxiety that fills Davin's and Stephen's heart is fear of experience. The peasant woman offers Davin initiation into life with all its mysteries and dangers. As a female, a mother to be, and a peasant, the young woman in Davin's episode stands for the familiar and known that Stephen has rejected, that is, women, mother, and country. But in her sheer feminine "otherness" she also stands for the unknown in Stephen's future experiences, his awakening sexuality, with which he is still uncomfortable, as well as his ventures into art and foreign landscapes. Thus the Biblical image of the "strange woman" that underlies Davin's encounter with the peasant woman expands the meaning of the female to include the totality of life's mysteries and pitfalls.

For both Stephen and the poet of The Proverbs, the figure of the "strange woman" who solicits young men is a sponge that absorbs all of life's deadly lures, obstacles, and evils. But for Stephen, the peasant woman stands also for all the constrictions imposed on him by his environment. The female figure is not only a fleshly reminder of corruption and decay, but also a symbol of all the forces—home, country, and bodily lust—that have coalesced to paralyze the young artist and imprison his free spirit.

However, while The Book of Proverbs de-emphasizes the woman's femininity and uses it only as an image that stands for worldly evil, for Stephen, the woman's primary meaning and identity are anchored in her femininity. Thus, while the Bible counterbalances the debased vision of the "strange woman" with another feminine emblem, that of the exalted Wisdom, Stephen's antidote for the seductive peasant woman is the celibate dean of studies, whom he encounters after recalling Davin's story, and finds him busy lighting a fire. The sexless, elderly dean is the polar opposite of the voluptuous young peasant woman. He also embodies the total expendability of the female, exuding an air of self-sufficiency, reinforced by his adeptness at the domestic chore of lighting a fire, which he brands "one of the useful arts" (P 185). Dressed as a "levite of the Lord," he stands for the victory over the flesh and the female element.

But the renunciation of the female is not a sufficient solution for Stephen, nor is the Biblical option of morality and ethical conduct—embodied in the figure of Wisdom—a satisfying remedy for the tormented, sensitive young man. The female figure still looms large as a source of physical generation as well as bodily lust, and as a constant testimony to human animality, decay, and death. The only way of overcoming the eternal female's threat with all its repercussions is through the sublimation offered by art. In a different scene, Stephen rejects MacCann's theory that Venus' popularity was anchored in her implied powers of reproducing and nurturing:

> I see however two ways out. One is the hypothesis: that every physical quality admired by men in women is in direct connection with the manifold functions of women for the propagation of the species. It may be so. The world, it seems, is drearier than even you, Lynch, imagined. For my part, I dislike that way out. It leads to eugenics rather than esthetic. It leads you out of the maze into a new gaudy lectureroom where MacCann . . . tells you that you admired the great flanks of Venus because she would bear you burly offspring and admired her great breasts because you felt that she would give good milk to her children and yours. . . . There remains another way out . . . all people who admire a beautiful object find in it certain relations which satisfy and coincide with the stages themselves of all esthetic apprehension. (P 208, 209)

If the terrifying eroticism and the awesome reproductive powers of the female are transformed into a thing of beauty, and transferred into the realm of art, they are no longer a source of anguish and fear. Once the female no longer belongs to the sphere of nature but of art, that is, once Stephen was able to commute Davin's frightening experience into a beautifully narrated tale, the eternal feminine becomes a static, nonphysical image and loses her menacing force.

A further way of overcoming the female threat is by assuming her pro-creative powers; thus the artist becomes a procreator: "When we come to the phenomena of artistic conception, artistic gestation and artistic reproduction I require a new terminology and a new personal experience" (P 209).

It seems that the Biblical vision of the "strange woman" not only invigo-rates and energizes Stephen's imagination, but also instills in him a certain amount of gynophobia. The Proverbial teacher avoids turning the "strange woman'" into an unbearably fearsome image by balancing her with admirable female figures as well as by describing her frivolity in a comic way: "She is loud and stubborn / her feet abide not in her house: Now she is with-out, now in the streets / and lieth in wait at every corner" (Proverbs 7:11, 12). He therefore never renounces women, but a certain type of woman, just as he never condemns the whole world, but a certain kind of worldly evil. Stephen, however, is so obsessed with the pernicious power of the female that his only solution is repudiating women and usurping their generative powers.

Finally, another ancient female figure incorporated in the image of the peasant woman is that of Lilith, the winged she-demon. The legend of Lilith, the precurser of Eve, was developed in post-Biblical Judaic literature, and later reappeared in the works of Jewish mystics. Lilith also entered Western European writings and surfaced in the poetry of Dante Gabriel Rossetti, Robert Browning, and others. While for Davin the peasant woman is a real flesh and blood figure, Stephen attributes to her a demonic dimension and divests her of realistic qualities. For him, her feminine body is just a disguise; actually, she is a spirit, "a batlike soul waking to the consciousness of itself in darkness and secrecy and loneliness, and, through the eyes and voice and ges-ture of a woman without guile, calling the stranger to her bed" (P 183). Without naming Lilith, it is clear that Stephen has a Lilith-like figure in mind. Like the demon Lilith who flies at night on a mission of evil and destruction, the peasant woman is a "batlike" soul who appears out of nowhere in the thick of the night and tries to seduce the young man. Further-more, the mythic Lilith is known by her long hair, and it is significant that though it is very dark, Davin notices that the young woman's hair "is hang-ing." Interestingly, in the Walpurgis-Night scene in Goeth's *Faust,* Meph-istopheles points Lilith out to Faust, who has regained his youth, and warns him to beware of her, because she lures young men with her beautiful hair and never leaves them alone (*Faust* 1, 4119–4123).

The Davin episode exhibits Joyce's ambivalent attitudes towards women and his tendency to portray them exclusively in relation to men.[4] Further-more, Stephen's obsession with Davin's tale and his interpretation of it reveal the young artist as a misogynist who equates women with the physical life, the chaotic, and even demonic, and for whom gaining mastery over the world and asserting his artistic nature mean rejecting the female and relegating her to an inferior sphere of being. Beyond that, this episode exemplifies once again Joyce's power of creating a labyrinthine world of images and associations whose roots extend into the depths of Western cultural memory. Davin's short tale thus emerges as a juncture where some very powerful ancient images converge to reinforce its archetypal dimension and haunting impact.

Notes

1. James Joyce, *A Portrait of the Artist as a Young Man* (New York: The Viking Press, 1968). All quotations are from this edition, referred to as P. Bible references are to the AV.

2. See Wolfgang Lederer, *The Fear of Woman* (New York: Grune and Straton), p. 127. Lederer shows how women, water, and milk have been tied together in the male mind from early antiquity. He also reminds us that in Egyptian hieroglyphics the water jar is a symbol of femininity.

3. The Bible commentator R. David Kimhi (Radak), in his discussion of Judges 5:27, mentions an old midrash that suggests that there was sexual intercourse between Jael and Sisera.

4. For insightful discussions of Joyce's portrayal of women see: Suzette Henke and Elaine Unkeles, eds. *Women in Joyce* (Urbana: University of Illinois Press, 1982).

[Daedalus and the Bird Girl: Classical Text and Celtic Subtext]

F. L. RADFORD

> Once upon a time and a very good time it was there was a moocow coming down along the road and this moocow that was coming down along the road met a nicens little boy named baby tuckoo. (P 7)

Hugh Kenner has reminded us that, if we have Daedalus on our minds when rereading the opening lines of *A Portrait of the Artist,* we must pick up an echo of the tale of Pasiphaë and the Daedalian wooden cow.[1] But the book starts out in the manner of the *shenachie,* the Irish teller of tales, and the first pages speak of two Irish heroes, Davitt and Parnell, before they imply an allusion to Daedalus (in Nasty Roche's "What kind of a name is that?"—*P* 9). Now, if we have Irish hero tales on our minds, we may recall lots of moocows led down many roads. Not least are the moocows of the Ulaid driven by the armies of Queen Maeve in *Táin Bó Cúailnge,* which climaxes the Ulster cycle of heroic tales. The "nicens little boy" whom the raiders met on that occasion was Cú Chulainn (who is generally presented as being both smaller and younger than his heroic colleagues, as Stephen is at Clongowes). The earliest version of that notable "moocow" story is in a book itself called *Lebor na huidre* (*The Book of the Dun Cow*)—because of its binding rather than its content—a fact that would have appealed to Joyce's delight in correspondences. Certainly, to think of the *Táin* is no more of a leap than to imagine Stephen's moocow occupied with the panting Pasiphaë, whose object of attention was a white bull, as Maeve's, for different reasons, was a black bull.

It is revealing that Don Gifford explains the source of the moocow story as a tale told by Joyce's father, versions of which are still current in the west of Ireland, telling of a magical white cow that takes children to an island where they are "magically schooled as heroes before they are returned to their aston-

This essay was originally published in the *James Joyce Quarterly,* Vol. 25.1 (Fall 1987), and is reprinted with permission.

ished parents and community."² The young Cú Chulainn also crosses to an island where he receives the final schooling in his vocation as hero from a magical woman warrior. Likewise, Stephen Dedalus crosses to the island of The Bull, where he is confirmed in his vocation as the "priest of eternal imagination" (*P* 221). If we look at *A Portrait* from this perspective, we see beneath the surface of classical allusion a complex of ancient Irish themes and motifs that has a quite different significance.

Having made this assertion, one must comment on the likelihood of Joyce's knowing the sources that are to be cited. For a long time the received opinion on Joyce's knowledge and use of Irish sources could be summed up by the comment of Mason and Ellmann in *The Critical Writings* that "When, in his own last book, he deigned at last to make use of the materials of Irish folklore, he showed himself to be as much in tune with them as either Lady Gregory or Yeats" (*CW* 102). Presumably this harmony was not learned in Paris in the 1920s. In both the original and the revised editions of his *James Joyce*, Ellmann plays down the importance of Joyce's Irish studies in Dublin, but this seems at variance with the remarks of Stanislaus Joyce that James "studied Irish for a year or two" and that his sympathies "extended in Ireland from Mangan and Yeats to the unlettered poets of the rugged glens, where a few years later Synge was to stake out his claim."³ This suggests that Joyce may have been more receptive than has been generally surmised to Synge's conversation about Irish studies when they met in Paris in 1903. Synge had studied extensively under Henri d'Arbois de Jubainville in Paris, even acting as his assistant for a time.⁴ If Synge mentioned d'Arbois de Jubainville to Joyce, the latter could have found his lectures in either the Bibliothèque Nationale or the Sainte-Geneviève, the two libraries most frequented by Joyce at this time. Even a brief acquaintance on Joyce's part with the first few volumes of the twelve-volume *Cours de Littérature Celtique* would give a context to Stephen Dedalus' sneer at the translator, Richard Best, as "Mr. Second-Best Best" in the library episode of *Ulysses,* where the translated second volume is called "Jubainville's book." Elsewhere, there were many sources available to Joyce. For example, the tale of "Bricriu's Feast"—which will be referred to in some detail later—was available in versions ranging from Lady Gregory's popularization, in *Cuchulain of Muirthemne,* to Professor George Henderson's scholarly bilingual edition for the Irish Texts Society in 1899. We may be fairly sure that Joyce knew the Lady Gregory version and that it is unlikely that he knew Henderson's version, but some of the parodies in the "Cyclops" episode of *Ulysses* are so close in style to Henderson's translation that knowledge of this text cannot be ruled out. Much the same may be said of Alfred Nutt's scholarly edition of Kuno Meyer's *Voyage of Bran* for the Grimm Library series in 1895–97, with its inclusion of important linked essays on "The Irish Vision of the Happy Otherworld" and "The Celtic Doctrine of Rebirth," both of which have apparent correspondences with some of Joyce's usage. Of course, given his retentive memory, Joyce could have gotten the sense of much of this material from general conversation and discussion during the period of his interest in Irish studies in Dublin.

There is one rather unexpected source of scholarly material that is virtually sure of having been known to Joyce and that includes almost all of the works to be cited in this paper. From 1901 to 1903, Arthur Griffith's paper, *The United Irishman,* undertook what is clearly a highly conscious effort to educate its readership in the content of the Irish mythological and heroic cycles in a manner that would draw attention to the extent and scholarly respectability of Irish Studies. It was here that Best's translation of d'Arbois de Jubainville's second volume, *The Irish Mythological Cycle and Celtic Mythology* had its first publication, uncut and complete with scholarly notes. This was followed by a series on "Tara of the Kings" and then by an extensive series of "Old Irish Bardic Tales," again with complete scholarly apparatus, calling upon the work of such important scholars as Jubainville, Whitley Stokes, Kuno Meyer, Standish O'Grady and P. W. Joyce. We know that Joyce had a long-standing interest in *The United Irishman* from his University College days until the paper's demise. In the 1902–03 period, he may have missed issues because of his stays in Paris, but he also had a special interest in the paper at this time because its annoyed response to his criticism of William Rooney's poems gave his review prominent attention.

It would seem obvious to ask here why Joyce did not use Irish bardic material openly in *A Portrait* if he was so knowledgeable. After all, Finn was a poet and diviner as well as a warrior and could have made a good analogy for the aspiring Irish poet as hero.[5] Stephen's visions and his concept of himself as poet-priest recall the druidic poets whose works mediate continually between the world of common experience and the unseen world of transcendent immortality. In their useful book, *Celtic Heritage,* Alwyn and Brinley Rees seem to be making a reverse allusion to Joyce when they say of Finn and Cú Chulainn that their development "from infancy to young manhood could appropriately be described as successions of epiphanies."[6] But we have only to think of *A Portrait* with Daedalus and Lucifer removed as conscious self-images for Stephen, and with Finn and Cú Chulainn put in their places, to realize how impossible it was for the young Joyce to make overt use of any figure from Irish tradition.

In *Ulysses,* Joyce shows us an Englishman who is learning Irish as being more acceptable to the Celtic Revival group than is Stephen Dedalus. Lady Gregory collects Kiltartan tales and sayings; Synge collects sayings and tales of the West; Yeats collects Sligo folktales, and Haines wants to make a collection of the sayings of Stephen Dedalus, whom Mulligan calls "the bard Kinch" and "wandering Aengus of the birds" (*U* 214). Stephen is not a colleague in these researches; he is a subject. His Irishness is too embedded for self-study, but it must inform his art if he is to succeed. As he is forced to acknowledge of his race in "Proteus," "Their blood is in me, their lusts my waves" (*U* 45). But he is also creating his artistic identity and can subject it neither to the patriotic self-censorship demanded by the Gaelic League nor to the theory-tormented efforts of the Irish Literary Revival to bring about a renaissance of English writing in Ireland through an exploitation of indigenous materials.

One thing to keep in mind is that the Daedalian image is the character's own conscious self-concept, an obvious one for Stephen Dedalus to choose, given his name. It is also an ideal choice for the young writer who is Irish in his subject matter but European in his ambitions. We should also remember that Joyce does not tell his characters everything. *Ulysses* is full of allusions and parallels consciously evoked by either Stephen or Bloom, or sometimes both, but neither of them is aware of the Ulysses/Telemachus/Penelope parallels. This is not to say that the Daedalus allusion is only useful to Stephen and not to Joyce. The multiple implications of Daedalus (and Icarus) are of obvious and continuing value to Joyce, not only for their blend of the heroic and the ironic, but as a means of avoiding direct use of Irish heroic allusions that would mark his work as that of either a disciple of the Gaelic League or an acolyte of Yeats.

II

Though it is the classical Daedalus who is directly invoked as Stephen's father-in-art, the theme of fosterage and multiple parentage that runs through *A Portrait* is as much Irish as classical in its evocations. Stephen's queenly "nice mother" with her "jewelly slippers" (*P* 9–10) shares her motherhood with the fierce Dante Riordan, who "hit a gentleman on the head" (*P* 37) when he uncovered for "God save the Queen" and who defeats the Fenian hero, Mr. Casey, in the Christmas dinner battle of words. Like the warrior woman, Scáthach, who gives Cú Chulainn his final training in arms, Dante is connected with distant parts and transmits esoteric knowledge: "the name of the highest mountain in the moon" (*P* 11). Stephen's father sends the small boy off to Clongowes Wood College, where the Jesuit fathers are analogous to the druid foster fathers of the Irish tales. Later, Stephen feels outside his own family and related to them only "in the mystical kinship of fosterage, fosterchild and fosterbrother" (*P* 98). This intuition leads to the appearance in Stephen's imagination of Daedalus as the spiritual father who governs the heroic destiny of the artist, matching the supernatural father from the Other World who so often shares in the begetting of the Celtic hero, the god Lug in some versions of Cú Chulainn's story, and the birdman of the *sidhe* in the story of Conaire Mór, for example.

The first chapter, with its evocation of the small child's consciousness— half in the external world, half in his own imagination—is full of echoes of the bardic tales. Stephen's fevered vision of Dante Riordan walking proudly by the water's edge, in a maroon velvet dress with a green velvet mantle, recalls the many women of Irish myth and legend who appear by water, dressed in green or in green and crimson, bringing fateful consequences for the hero. Given the association of Stephen's vision with the death of the hero, Parnell, and with Stephen's illness and fever, the closest analogy is probably the opening part of "The Only Jealousy of Emer" sometimes called "The Wasting Sickness of Cú Chulainn." As told by Lady Gregory, in a version certainly known to Joyce, Cú Chulainn seeks to capture two magic birds on a lake but misses his aim for the first time. He sinks into a sleep and while sleeping sees two women approach: "one of them having a green cloak about her, and the other a five-folded crimson cloak."[7] The women, who are clearly transformations of the birds and from the Otherworld, beat Cú Chulainn with rods, and he falls into a coma that lasts for a year. This is the first sign of the decline of the hero's powers. The development of the tale introduces the theme of adultery that is central to Parnell's fall also.

In *A Portrait,* Stephen's illness and fever are conflated with the death of Parnell and the enmity of Dante Riordan. In her capacity as a "spoiled nun" (*P* 35) and self-appointed spokeswoman for priests and bishops, Dante has an aura of the magical or druidic. Stephen recalls his vision in the midst of the Christmas dinner quarrel where Dante defeats Mr. Casey, the Fenian hero: "—Devil out of hell! We won!" she shouts, while Mr. Casey collapses in grief, crying "—Poor Parnell! My dead king!" (*P* 39). In Cork much later, Stephen remembers his illness and again joins himself with Parnell: "But he had not died then. Parnell had died" (*P* 93). This conflation is typical of the rebirth patterns in Irish legend. One version of the birth of Cú Chulainn makes the latter the rebirth of the god Lug who is "at once father and son."[8] In the story of Mongan, a historical king of the seventh century, Mongan is not only the son of Fiachna Lurga, king of Ulster, and Manannan, the sea god, but also "a re-birth of Finn, son of Cumall, or rather, to put it as the Irish story-teller does, Mongan was Finn, though the latter had been supposed to be long dead."[9] The idea of Stephen as hero is united with the image of Parnell as the dead King of Erin. Parnell's death as a kind of scapegoat to Dante's narrow morality substitutes for that of Stephen. In Stephen's imagination the image of Parnell as the type of the betrayed Irish hero is placed in the context of the bardic heroes and the total conflation is transferred to Stephen himself.

When Father Dolan bursts into Stephen's class and threatens to be back to punish them "every day" (*P* 49), he is like the giant churl who bursts into the hall at Emain Macha in the story of "Bricriu's Feast." The churl promises to return each night to challenge one of the champions to submit to beheading. His role is to give Cú Chulainn the chance to prove his claim to be Champion of Ulster, as Father Dolan gives Stephen his first chance at heroism. In the ancient tale there is even a curious analogy to the moment when the prefect of studies pauses to straighten Stephen's hand before striking:

when Cú Chulainn lays his head on the block, the churl complains that his neck is too short and bids him stretch it out further.

As in many of the Celtic tales and the best of the chivalric romances that were rooted in them, Stephen's is a display of both moral and physical courage. Besides risking the heightened anger of Father Dolan, in protesting to the rector Stephen must undertake a journey similar for his age to those made by the heroes who seek aid in the Otherworld. He first must cross "the threshold of the door" (P 55) that divides his path from those of his fellows. He must then enter "the low dark corridor that led to the castle" (P 54). Then he passes two doors to reach the rector's office. The corridor is like a dark cave, and caves and thresholds are points of entrance to the Celtic Otherworld. Stephen's way "through the gloom" (P 55) is lined with images and historical memories of heroes of the Catholic and Irish past. Finally reached, Father Conmee, with his impressive surroundings of learning and the skull on his desk, carries the full aura of a druid king of the ancient tales. In "Bricriu's Feast" Cú Chulainn must similarly pass through many trials to reach the druid king, Curoi Mac Daire, for help in establishing his claim to be Champion of Ulster. At the end of that tale, we learn that it was Curoi himself who magically changed his shape to become the giant churl and offer Cú Chulainn the last and crucial challenge. Likewise, the rector and the prefect of studies are conflated in Stephen's father's report of the story as told by Father Conmee: "—Father Dolan and I, when I told them all at dinner about it, Father Dolan and I had a great laugh over it" (P 72).

It should not be thought, as it sometimes is, that the rector's story destroys the heroism of the young Stephen, any more than Cú Chulainn's heroism is lessened by the revelation that the threatening churl was really Curoi. At the end of Chapter I, Stephen did truly return from his adventure to be a hero among his people, who happened at that time to be the small boys of Clongowes Wood College. From his father's deflating story, he just learns more about the mechanics of the heroic and the necessary interweaving in life of the ideal and the ironic, which the artist must understand (as Stephen is beginning to understand it in Chapter V). Father Conmee does not merely give us the material for ironic deflation; he confirms the heroism at the level at which it took place: "*Manly little chap!* he said" (P 72).

In Chapter II, Vincent Heron greets Stephen as "the noble Dedalus!" (P 75). He has "a bird's face as well as a bird's name" (P 76) recalling, in an ironic context, the prophetic birdmen of Irish legend. He and Stephen are friendly enemies and they are "the virtual heads of the school" (P 76) as Cú Chulainn and his friend Ferdiad were rivals and chief heroes of Scáthach's school for warriors. Is it coincidence that Joyce has Heron say to Stephen, "—You're a sly dog, Dedalus!" and repeat three lines later, "But I'm afraid you're a sly dog" (P 76)? Cú Chulainn, of course, means "the hound of Culain."

Towards the end of *A Portrait* we have a more sophisticated version of the interlacing of echoes of Daedalus and the Irish heroes that open the book.

The moocow makes its reappearance in the library when the noisy group of students must leave to escape the anger of a priest:

> Dixon folded the journal and rose with dignity, saying:
> —Our men retired in good order.
> —With guns and cattle, added Stephen, pointing to the titlepage of Cranly's book on which was printed *Diseases of the Ox*. (P 227)

Daedalus seems fairly distant here, but there is a sufficient echo of the *Táin,* the Cattle Raid of Cooley, and it is evoked by the words and imagination of Stephen, the would-be Irish bard. As the opening of *A Portrait* speaks of the moocow of experience "coming down along the road" (P 7) to meet the little boy, so the conclusion speaks of the young man going forth on "the white arms of roads" (P 252) like the wandering heroes (or the *peregrini,* the wandering monks) of ancient Ireland, to encounter experience and perfect his vocation.

There is much of the Irish Otherworld in the first chapter of *A Portrait*— in Stephen's fevered vision and in his heroic journey to the rector's office. Throughout *A Portrait,* it is in the evocation of the Otherworld as a state of being parallel to the world of concrete reality, rather than separate from it, that Joyce is closest to the ancient Celtic sensibility. The easy coexistence of the two worlds is seen by many authorities as the element that distinguishes the Celtic Otherworld from those of Graeco-Roman and Christian belief.

The Otherworld is outside time: a state of permanence that abolishes time, of simultaneous being and non-being, no past or future, but a different state not explainable through words or traditional logic. In his important 1895 study of "The Happy Otherworld in the Mythico-Romatic Literature of the Irish," Alfred Nutt makes the distinctions that the Otherworld over or under sea has a largely female character, while the Otherworld within the hills has a male character; in one case, the messengers tend to be female, in the other male. The land Otherworld may or may not insist upon the immortality of its denizens or on the absence of strife. There is often no danger in return to the ordinary world. The sea Otherworld is more insistent upon the immortality of its inhabitants and the distortion of time that makes it dangerous for the traveler to return to the mortal world. The beings of the sea Otherworld are more amorous and "a portion of the land is dwelt in by women alone." The two versions of the Irish Otherworld are linked by such characteristics as "the amorous nature of the dames of Faery" and the "definite connection of the magic land with water."[10] In their more recent summary of the characteristics of the Celtic Otherworld, Alwyn and Brinley Rees argue that its interaction with the ordinary world "is similar in many ways to the interaction between the 'conscious' and 'unconscious' mind as described by modern psychologists."[11] They point out that the supernatural power breaks through into this world at dividing lines such as thresholds, beaches, rivers, fords, bridges, islands, caves, mist, night, dawn, dusk, and the borders of sleep.[12] We have only to look at the last part of "The Dead" or at Stephen's fever-vision in Chapter I of *A Portrait,* his vision of his personal hell in Chapter III, or his "morning inspiration" (*P* 217) in Chapter V, to see how often in Joyce moments of intense psychic experience take place in the borderline state between sleeping and waking. Rivers and sea beaches are also important places of vision throughout Joyce's works. Joyce parallels the suspension of normal time and space with moments of poetic vision that transcend time and space.

In parts of *A Portrait* the Otherworld is openly mentioned—in those "moments" that Stephen later tells Davin are the times when the "soul" has its "slow and dark birth" (*P* 203). In Chapter II, when Stephen traverses the "maze of narrow and dirty streets" (*P* 100) that lead to Nighttown, he is first quite lost, then finds himself in a magic realm which seems to be inhabited entirely by women whose only desire is to please him (an echo of Otherworld voyage tales of the Island of Women, or the *sidhe* mound within which the nightbound hero finds bright light and is welcomed by beautiful women). *Celtic Heritage* tells us that "it is when the voyagers have lost their course and shipped their oars—when they are not going anywhere—that they arrive in the wondrous isles."[13] From the moment Stephen enters the brothel district until his sexual initiation by the "young woman" at the end of the chapter, all that is sordid drops out of the description, and the experience is presented with a unique lack of guilt or shame. It is more like the pagan initiation of the young hero to sexual mysteries (the warrior sorceress grants the young Cú Chulainn the "friendship of her thighs" as part of the learning of his mystery), or the totally guilt-free union of the voyaging heroes with the women of the islands of the Otherworld in the ancient Irish tales. Joyce's description has unmistakable echoes of the Otherworld tradition of the Celtic sagas:

> Women and girls dressed in long vivid gowns traversed the street from house to house. They were leisurely and perfumed. A trembling seized him and his eyes grew dim. The yellow gasflames arose before his troubled vision against the vapoury sky, burning as if before an altar. Before the doors and in the lighted halls groups were gathered arrayed as for some rite. He was in another world: he had awakened from a slumber of centuries. (*P* 100)

Alfred Nutt evokes these qualities when he comments:

> One special characteristic of the Irish Otherworld may be cited as exemplifying, in the strongest manner, the primitive nature of the conception. Quatrain 41 of Bran's Voyage gives a picture of the island Elysium from which one gathers that it must have resembled Hampstead Heath on an Autumn Bank Holiday evening. The trait is not confined to Bran's Voyage. Unlimited lovemaking is one of the main constituents in all the early Irish accounts of Otherworld happiness. . . . Alien to Judaism . . . the absence from Heaven of all that con-

cerns the physical manifestations of love is, like so much else in Christianity, of Greek origin.[14]

III

The collection of Irish Bardic Tales published by *The United Irishman* in 1902–03 was preceded by an announcement that cited available texts and bibliographical aids and recited the traditional classification of the tales, including "*immrama,* or Navigations, *echtrai,* or Adventures, and *fís,* or Visions."[15] In form, Stephen's journey to the rector's office in Chapter I; his journey through the city to the Otherworld of Nighttown in Chapter II; his journey to find "grace" at the end of Chapter III (with an old woman as his guide); his beach journey in Chapter IV; and even his journey through the city to encounter the dean of studies, the false druid in the "theatre" in Chapter V, all partake of two formal categories of the ancient Irish tales: *echtrai* (adventures, with a strong ingredient of the marvelous, similar to the formal meaning of "adventure" in the later chivalric romances which have their roots in the Celtic sagas) and *immrama* (marvelous voyages such as those of Maeldúin and Bran). As Alfred Nutt points out, it is usual in the older *immrama* that the Happy Otherworld of the Oversea type should figure in the journey. In *A Portrait,* the marvelous is supplied by the working of the poetic imagination. This lends to the climactic passages, especially the beach journey, the qualities of the third type cited above, the *fís,* or vision, which also figures in Stephen's visions of Parnell's funeral in Chapter I, of Hell in Chapter III, and of the lascivious E—— C—— in Chapter V.

From start to finish, Stephen's adventure on the beach is infused with themes and motifs of the Celtic Otherworld and of druidic magic. He leaves the pub where his father is arranging his worldly future to "set off abruptly for the Bull" (*P* 164) having escaped "by an unseen path" from "the sentries" who have controlled his boyhood and seek to subject him to their purposes. Now "a new adventure" is "about to be opened to him." He seems to hear "notes of fitful music" forming "an elfin prelude" (*P* 165). In the ancient Celtic tales, the hero, separated from his companions on a hunt or other occasion, unwittingly crosses the dividing line between the worlds; the sound of music "often heralds the approach of the supernatural, and by means of it the *síd*-folk place men and women under enchantment."[16] Stephen's adventure, which is to give him a visionary revelation of his vocation as a poet, takes place by the sea after a crossing of water, and we are told that the ancient "Irish poets deemed that the brink of water was always a place where *éicse*— wisdom, poetry, knowledge, was revealed" and that crossing water "always implies change of state and status."[17] The Irish heroes undergo similar tests and transitions at streams, fords and islands. Cú Chulainn, for example, must cross a perilous bridge to reach the island of Scáthach, the warrior druidess who will teach him the final mysteries of his vocation.

The tests that Stephen faces are psychological. The "thin wooden bridge" that he must cross to reach the island of the Bull is "trembling and resounding" from the passage of a "squad of christian brothers" (*P* 165) who remind him of his efforts at "humble and contrite" devotion (*P* 166), testing his refusal to "obey the call" that "he had so often thought to be his destiny" (*P* 165). He defeats his misgivings with "a phrase from his treasure" (*P* 166) that reasserts his devotion to poetry and passes safely "from the trembling bridge on to firm land again" (*P* 167). The island gives him a supernatural feeling of being outside of time, and he sees the city in a distant haze "across the timeless air" like "a scene on some vague arras" which evokes the ancient past of Ireland from the first "host of nomads on the march" (*P* 167) to the days of the Viking thingmote. The Otherworld music comes again:

> He heard a confused music within him as of memories and names which he was almost conscious of but could not capture even for an instant . . . and from each receding trail of nebulous music there fell always one longdrawn calling note. . . . A voice from beyond the world was calling. (*P* 167)

There is an abrupt fall when the mystic voice turns into the calls of his bathing friends. They call to him as Daedalus, but it has been pointed out that the content of their cries invokes Icarus: "—O, cripes, I'm drownded!" (*P* 169); it is certainly not clear that Stephen is Icarus, however, although he would be if he joined them. The "drowning" calls are addressed to each other; only "—Stephanos Dedalos! Bous Stephanoumenos! Bous Stephaneforos!" (*P* 168) is addressed to Stephen. What he takes from the calls out of the waters of the Bull are their appeals to "his mild proud sovereignty" and an imaginative vision of Daedalus as "a hawklike man flying sunward above the sea" carrying a prophecy of Stephen's destiny as an artist (*P* 168–69). The world of the imagination is again presented as being outside of time, like the Celtic Otherworld: "So timeless seemed the grey warm air, so fluid and impersonal his own mood, that all ages were as one to him" (*P* 168).

The imaginative content of Stephen's adventure on the beach seems to echo the ancient Irish tale of "The Destruction of Da Derga's Hostel" which appears to have been known to Joyce.[18] The High King of Ireland has died and a new ruler must be found for Tara. There is a bull feast and, after drinking the waters of a bull broth and falling into a prophetic sleep, a druid dreams a description of the new king and his coming which matches the looks and arrival of Conaire. In the meantime, the young Conaire has wandered away from his comrades, following a flock of strange birds to the sea. They become fierce birdmen who at first attack him, before their leader reveals himself as "King of your father's birdflocks"[19] sent to tell Conaire of his noble destiny (Conaire's supernatural father was a birdman of the *sidhe* who flew in the window of his mother's secret refuge shortly before his earthly begetting by King Eterscel, the great-grandson of a former king of Tara). The Irish parallel here explains the prophetic function of Stephen's "hawklike man" which is missing from the classical parallel.[20]

As he walks the beach, Stephen becomes more isolated from his fellows, and it is when he is "alone amid a waste of wild air and brackish waters" (P 171) that he sees the birdgirl. Placed as she is, at a moment when Stephen feels his soul reborn and "soaring in an air beyond the world" (P 169), the union of his artistic soul with her image is a variant of many Irish tales of lovers who unite as birds (such as Midhir and Étaín who fly away from Étaín's husband in the forms of "two swans high up in the air, linked together by a chain of gold"[21] and escape to the Otherworld). In the effect of the wading girl on Stephen there is also an echo of the Otherworld woman whose beauty strikes the hero to the heart and distracts him from worldly duty and fellows. The opening of "Da Derga's Hostel" has such a description, summarized as follows by Professor Miles Dillon:

> I first heard of it from A. E. who told me of this wonderful description to illustrate what he called the incandescent imagination of Irish story-tellers:
>
> > He saw a woman at the edge of a well . . . washing in a silver basin in which were four birds of gold. . . . She wore a purple cloak of good fleece . . . and a smock of green silk with gold embroidery. . . . The sun shone upon her, so that the men saw the gold gleaming in the sunshine against the green silk. . . . She was undoing her hair to wash it, so that her arms were out from beneath her dress. White as the snow of one night were her hands, and her lovely cheeks were soft and even, red as the mountain foxglove. . . . The blushing light of the moon was in her noble face, a lofty pride in her smooth brow. The radiance of love was in her eyes; the flush of pleasure on her cheeks, now red as a calf's blood and changing again to snowy whiteness. . . . They thought she was of the fairies.[22]

What Stephen is feeling might well be termed the product of "incandescent imagination," and the description of his magic girl belongs in the same realm as the description of Étaín just quoted. In the climax of the beach section of *A Portrait,* the interlacing of classical, Celtic, and Christian symbolism—which has been loosely evident all through the book—becomes as tightknit as the interlacing of Christian and pagan motifs in a carpet page of *The Book of Kells.* The interweaving of Christian elements in the sensual description of Stephen's birdgirl has often been pointed out as a secularization of the Holy Virgin symbolism that has been a dominant guiding image in Stephen's life. It is notable that the Virgin never again appears in this role. The magic bird image set against the dove image; the "emerald trail of seaweed" that "had fashioned itself as a sign upon the flesh" of her legs, set against the blue and white of her clothing and the "ivory" of her thighs; and her role as a magical "envoy" from a new realm of experience that stresses more intense life (*P* 171–72), are all typical of Irish hero-saga.

Stressing the importance of waterbird transformations in Celtic legend, Alwyn and Brinley Rees say:

> There is no suggestion that a swanform is the norm in the Otherworld. The implication is rather that the form of a swan—perhaps because it is that of a creature of land, water and air, a creature whose milieu has no boundaries—is appropriate for communication *between* two worlds.[23]

The hero is frequently conceived in this transitional zone as Stephen's poetic soul has its rebirth confirmed in the creative union between his imagination and his perception of the girl as seabird. Stephen's birdgirl is not likened to a swan, but her legs are "delicate as a crane's" (*P* 171) which evokes an Irish myth that seems relevant to his vision of his destiny. Cranes were said to make letters in the sky, carrying the code of the first Irish alphabet. The wife of the God of the Land Undersea, Manannan, was magically changed into a crane and was punished for stealing the code and giving the secret of language to mankind.[24] That a young man who treasures a hoard of words and conceives himself to be a poet in the making should be inspired on the seashore by a crane-like woman—and led "into some new world, fantastic, dim, uncertain as under sea" (*P* 172)—places him well in the tradition of the Irish heroes who marry their vocations in their union with magical women. If the undersea reference implies Stephen's fall as Icarus, his fate afterwards is not that of the drowning youth but of the Irish hero, whose "lust of wandering" (*P* 170) has brought him to the realm of Manannan, the magic islands of the sea and the female country of the land-under-wave. A pattern is being set up, in which failure is implied in the ironic Icarus suggestion of the Daedalus legend, and success is implied in the hidden identification with Irish heroes.

If we look at the insistence upon rebirth of the soul "from the grave of boyhood" (*P* 170) in the beach episode; upon the girl as "an envoy from the fair courts of life" (*P* 172); upon Stephen's reborn soul as the figure of "the great artificer whose name he bore" (*P* 170); and upon his visionary entry into a new "undersea" world, then Alfred Nutt's study of the Irish Otherworld is again revealing. The Otherworld messenger who summons Connla across the sea is "a damsel in strange garb" who "comes from the land of the living, where is neither death, nor sin, nor transgression." Nutt points out that there is a frequent "connection of the two conceptions of the Happy Otherworld and of Rebirth" and that wisdom and poetry originate in the Otherworld: "Thus the *dinnshenchas* of Sinnan: 'Sinend . . . went to Connla's Well which is under sea to behold it. That is a well at which are the hazels of wisdom and inspirations, that is, the hazels of the science of poetry.' "[25]

By the time we reach Chapter V, the material of Irish heroic tradition has been absorbed into Stephen's way of thinking, though he is not consciously aware of this and he would probably consciously deny it. As Joyce's Trieste lectures show—and his letters from Rome about the time of writing "The Dead"—he is much more reconciled with his Irish background than the Stephen who is departing for Paris at the end of *A Portrait of the Artist*. It is part of the complex irony of *A Portrait* that Joyce builds into the character of Stephen a coherent pattern of Irish heroic analogues which move parallel to the character's self-conscious patterning according to the classical analogue of the Daedalus legend. The soul-as-bird motif is picked up in Stephen's famous assertion that he will "fly by" the nets of "nationality, language, religion" (*P* 203), which we can assume is consciously referring to the escape of Daedalus from Crete, but which, after the birdgirl episode of the previous chapter, must also include hidden echoes of the many bird stories of Celtic legend, especially when the assertion includes such strong allusions to birth. In Stephen's description, the body is born of earthly parents; the soul is born of experience. This seems to correspond to the supernatural begetting of the superhuman element of the heroes in the ancient tales. In his response to Stephen's ideas, Davin unconsciously evokes the combination that Stephen is to use later when raising his vocation as hero/poet to a priestly elevation: "Ireland first, Stevie. You can be a poet or mystic after" (*P* 203).

Stephen's conception of the creative experience, in his "morning inspiration" in Chapter V, parallels the Celtic experience of the Otherworld, including the motifs of "faint sweet music" and "cool waters" sensed on the edge of sleep. His image for the fertilized imagination—"Gabriel the seraph had come to the virgin's chamber" (*P* 217)—is a Christian analogue of the bird-man entering the chamber of Étaín to beget Conaire. As with the birdgirl on the beach, his imagination again unites with a winged image to produce a moment of poetic ecstasy. The interlacing of allusive elements here may explain the confusion of the sensuous and the holy in the perplexing villanelle. As with the ecstatic conclusion of Chapter IV, the element of still air, transitional time (here dawn rather than dusk), music, birds, and "roselight" mark the climax of creative inspiration (*P* 217–18). On the steps of the library, birds return in prophetic form. Once gain, the first image they evoke is that of Daedalus: "the hawklike man whose name he bore soaring out of his captivity on osierwoven wings" (*P* 225). Stephen's train of thought moves to the symbolism of birds as prophetic creatures through the ages, from the auguries of Rome, back to Greece, and to Egypt and the birdgod of writers, Thoth. But he only remembers the name of Thoth because it is "like an Irish oath" (*P* 225), and in Stephen's imagination the birds come to rest in the Irish context of Yeats's poetry in *The Countess Cathleen*. In a passage that again echoes Stephen's *echtra* on the beach, he feels the peace "of oceanic silence, of swallows flying through the seadusk over the flowing waters" (*P* 225). Once again the Otherworld elements of dusk, sky, waters, birds, and music are united with Stephen's artistic destiny as the birds turn into the music of poetic vowels:

> A soft liquid joy flowed through the words where the soft long vowels hurtled noiselessly and fell away, lapping and flowing back and ever shaking the white bells of their waves in mute chime and mute peal and soft low swooning cry; and he felt that the augury he had sought in the wheeling darting birds and in the pale space of sky above him had come forth from his heart like a bird from a turret quietly and swiftly. (*P* 225–26)

The last phrase recalls again the birdman who flies in at Étaín's window to beget Conaire Mór and then departs as he came. But now the power of shape-changing lies in words and imagination, and the druid is the poet.

Between his "morning inspiration" and his prophetic observation of the birdflight at the library, Stephen had thought of himself as "a priest of eternal imagination, transmuting the daily bread of experience into the radiant body of everliving life" (*P* 221), a concept that we know from his letters to Stanislaus as being part of Joyce's own self-image when he was writing *Dubliners*. This concept is closer to that of the ancient Irish *filid* than to any other cultural analogue:

> In Ireland there was a special class, which may be regarded as a sub-class of nobles, the *oes dána*, whose art ennobled them. The *oes dána*, or learned class, included as most important of all, the poet (*fili*), who seems to have inherited much of the prestige of the druid of pagan times. . . . The *fili* was honoured and feared, like the brahmin in India. He was no longer a priest in this Christian society, but he had means of divination akin to magic. Or at any rate, he had had them in the pagan past, and the tradition of his magical power survived.[26]

In his 1899 edition of *Fled Bricrend*, George Henderson notes that Druidism was not fully established and organized in Ireland before the coming of Christianity and therefore, "the *filidh*, 'seer, poet,' cognate with Cymric *gwelet*, 'to see, sight; vision'; preceded the druid by many centuries as the chief minister of religion."[27] D'Arbois de Jubainville claims that the *filid* remained strong after the coming of Christianity and often contested successfully with the priests for the confidence and admiration of the people.[28] It is notable that when Stephen thinks of himself as "priest of eternal imagination" it is in opposition to the "young priest" (*P* 220) who has attracted E.C. away from him. This suggests another reason for the abstraction of the young woman, who may thus more easily acquire the traditional identity of Ireland as woman. Shortly before, Stephen has conflated her image with those of other Irish girls who have angered him with their disdain or betrayal.

As with so much else in *A Portrait*, the elaborate interweaving of classical and Celtic that is sketched out in the opening passages is reworked in

Stephen's diary at the end of the book. The winged beings who call to Stephen are more like the fierce birdmen of Conaire Mór than like Daedalus: "And the air is thick with their company as they call to me, their kinsman, making ready to go, shaking the wings of their exultant and terrible youth" (P 252). But the call, in the last line of *A Portrait*, to "Old father, old artificer" (P 253), seems to allude clearly, and only, to Daedalus. The flight of Daedalus is for Stephen a conscious image for the escape of his artistic soul from the labyrinth of family, church, and nation into the broader and freer European tradition. But he also yearns for his flight as the Irish birdman to carry him back to his people as their "priest of eternal imagination" who will create "the uncreated conscience of [his] race" (P 253), presumably teaching them to value art more than dogma and life more than afterlife. At the end of *A Portrait*, Stephen is between becoming and being, governed by potential and desire. He is poised between the wish to abandon forever all that has shaped him and the wish to return triumphant (a fairly common adolescent state, I suspect).

The desire for departure is governed by the male genius, Daedalus, but in accordance with the inspirational role of woman at each stage of Stephen's *echtra*, it is the mother who is putting Stephen's "new secondhand clothes in order" (P 252), supplying him with the feathers for his flight, in effect.

Irish sovereignty is most clearly evoked in the diary. Stephen recalls his last remark to Davin: "Told him the shortest way to Tara was *via* Holyhead (P 250). However consciously sardonic the remark may be, it has a prophetic implication that conforms with the other Celtic allusions in *A Portrait* and asserts a return in triumph. But this seems to be overwhelmed by the last invocation of Daedalus which has special weight as the last sentence of the book and sums up the duality of the classical allusion "Old father, old artificer, stand me now and ever in good stead" (P 253). By confirming Stephen's identity as Icarus, this seems to look forward to his sense of a pitiful return in *Ulysses*. But even here there may be a submerged and triumphant Celtic reference that parallels the Cú Chulainn allusions earlier in *A Portrait*. There is no doubt that Joyce knew Richard Best's translation of d'Arbois de Jubainville's *Le Cycle Mythologique Irlandais* (referred to by Best as "Jubainville's book" in the library episode of *Ulysses*). In that book, Cú Chulainn's divine father, Lug, claiming entry to Tara, is called "the young artist" and calls himself "an excellent artificer."[29]

What we may infer, then, is that the overt classical allusive pattern in *A Portrait* predicts the failure of a first attempt at artistic flight which rejects Stephen's Irish identity. But this is countered by a Celtic subtext which predicts heroic success in the acceptance of that identity. It is notable that there is no evidence of any similar pattern of Celtic themes and motifs in what remains of *Stephen Hero*. It appears that the drastic revision of form and content that produced *A Portrait of the Artist as a Young Man* included Joyce's deeper awareness (already implied in "The Dead") that his subject matter must be Irish and that his Irish identity was ineluctably part of his artistic identity.

IV

The significance of the Celtic subtext of *A Portrait of the Artist* goes beyond an ironic counterpoint to the main character's self-concept. It also supports the opposition of life and death forces that informs the novel, with the life forces identified with the poetic imagination and the death forces associated with the nets of nationality and religion that Stephen tells Davin he will "try to fly by" (*P* 203). The skull on Father Conmee's desk; the Hell evoked by Father Arnall; the face of the director of Belvedere, with its "mirthless reflection of the sunken day" (*P* 160), and the "livid" faces of the marching Christian Brothers, all associate the conventional priesthood with death in order that Stephen's priesthood of "eternal imagination" may take over the task of "transmuting the daily bread of experience into the radiant body of everliving life" (*P* 221). In another death association, Davin, who tells Stephen "Ireland first, Stevie. You can be a poet or mystic after" (*P* 203), is described as having a "rude Firbolg mind" (*P* 180). Less than a page away, Thomas Moore, called "the national poet of Ireland," is described as "a Firbolg in the borrowed cloak of a Milesian" (*P* 180). Presumably Joyce does not use this term twice without having some knowledge of the meaning given to it in his time.

The August 2, 1902 *United Irishman* installment of "Tara of the Kings" mentions the Firbolgs, "whose characteristics, physical and mental, are still apparent in the inhabitants of certain portions of Connacht," as an inferior race to the Tuatha De Danann who "were a race of artists and philosophers with a sublime and beautiful religion" but who were also "intellectually haughty and possibly for that reason obnoxious to the Firbolgs." Jubainville cites a seventeenth-century report by the annalist Duald MacFirbis of people in the West of Ireland claiming to be descendants of the Firbolg. He repeats several times that their ancient gods were the Fomorians, who were anti-life and anti-art, while the De Danann religion worshipped light and life and the gods of music and literature. It is notable that when Stephen decides not to respond to the director's invitation to join the Order, the activating circumstance is the priest's failure to respond with joy to the "agile melody" and dancing step of the young men with the concertina seen from the school steps. Jubainville also reports that the most ancient tradition has the Tuatha De Danann coming to Ireland "on the wings of the wind" without ships, out of heaven. On his beach journey, disheartened by the sight of Dublin across the water, "old as man's weariness," Stephen is cheered by the "clouds, dappled and seaborne . . . a host of nomads on the march" (*P* 167). He hears "a confused music within him as of memories and names which he was almost conscious of but could not capture even for an instant" (*P* 167). Instead he is called back to reality by the voices of his bathing school companions with their "corpse-white" bodies (*P* 168). Jubainville gives the opposition universal significance:

> The Tuatha De Danann are the most exalted representatives of one of the two principles that divide the world. The more ancient of these is negative—death, night, ignorance, evil; the second, which proceeds from the first, is positive—namely, day, life, knowledge, goodness. In the Tuatha De Danann we find the most brilliant expression of the latter principle; and from them emanate the lore of the druids and the science of the *file*.[30]

Thus, the large issues of *A Portrait* are reflected and supported by its hidden Irish dimension.

The questions of authorial voice and parody are raised in relation to Stephen's moments of vision by such elements as the sudden bathetic fall from Stephen's "voice from beyond the world" (*P* 167) to the call of his school friends in the water, or the fall from the lush romanticism of the undersea vision at the end of Chapter IV into the dregs of watery tea and the boghole of yellow dripping in the first lines of Chapter V. Though these sharp transitions from visionary sensuality to the coolly realistic show an artist in strict control of his medium, one of the things that Joyce has done in converting *Stephen Hero* into *A Portrait of the Artist as a Young Man* is to render the authorial voice more ambiguous. Joyce's new title must lead us to the sister art of painting where such titles always mean that the work is by the artist of the title. This encourages us to think of *A Portrait* as an autobiographical work, but as the autobiography of Stephen Dedalus, not Joyce, however closely they may be related. If this is so, the ironic narrative stance is that shown by the older Stephen in *Ulysses* and cannot be as savage as has recently been argued. In fact, the title implies a circular argument which asserts that, if Stephen Dedalus is viewed ironically in the romantic extremism of his artistic ambition and the extravagance of his language, the superb control of these elements within a context of precisely evoked realism is simply more evidence of the excellence of the artist-to-be. In this way *A Portrait* is supremely self-reflexive. The artist at the end of the book will create the book and only by reading to the end are we ready to read again from the beginning, realizing that the superior art of the mature narrator both validates and deconstructs the self-concepts of his younger self.

So we have a strong central consciousness that sees other characters and events and judges its experience according to its own prejudices and aspirations. This is a progressively more educated consciousness capable of elaborating for itself a satisfying and justifying symbolic complex. Against this is the narrating consciousness which subjects the character's romantic aspirations to the test of sordid reality and which sets up a counterpoint of conflicting images. Thus the character Stephen constantly thinks of the analogy between himself and Daedalus, but never of Icarus. When he does think of a fall, it is the grander one of Lucifer, who does not merely disappear beneath the waves. But the narrator ensures by a repeated pattern of bathetic fall that if Stephen does not think of Icarus, the reader does. And, of course, the later Stephen of *Ulysses,* who is to be the putative narrator of *A Portrait,* thinks of himself as that neglected Daedalean relative, "Lapwing" (*U* 210). Likewise the character's conscious rejection of Irish roots in favor of the European cultural tradition is countered by the narrator's insertion of the Irish mythic pattern which reinforces the character's Irish identity and is the disguised essential element in his own self-concept as "priest of eternal imagination" and as one who aspires to "forge . . . the uncreated conscience of [his] race" (*P* 253).

Joyce proceeds by a series of deferrrals of artistic consummation, reinforced by the tension between allusive meanings. From early in *A Portrait,* Stephen has a desire to reach a sensed goal, expressed in term of encounters with experience. The apparently climactic encounter—whether with the prostitute or the girl on the beach or the vision of E.C.—is constantly achieved only to have its meaning for the artist deferred by the device of rise and fall. At the end of the book, Stephen is leaving Ireland "to encounter for the millionth time the reality of experience" (*P* 253) without realizing that the substance of his art lies already at hand in the experience he has had in Ireland, as *A Portrait* itself confirms. At the end of *Ulysses,* Stephen is again preparing to leave, without realizing that his encounter with Bloom has just given him the experience for a masterpiece. It is in the disguised Irish allusions that the narrator hides the potential for success. The flight of Daedalus is an ending, as is the fall of Icarus, but "the shortest way to Tara" is a beginning.

Notes

1. Hugh Kenner at the James Joyce Symposium, Frankfurt, 1984. See also Clive Hart, *James Joyce's "Ulysses"* (Sydney: Sydney Univ. Press, 1968), p. 36.

2. Don Gifford, *Joyce Annotated* (Berkeley: Univ. of California Press, 1982), pp. 131–32.

3. Stanislaus Joyce, *My Brother's Keeper* (New York: Viking, 1958), pp. 171, 123.

4. Toni O'Brien Johnson, *Synge: The Medieval and the Grotesque* (Gerrards Cross: Colin Smythe, 1982), pp. 6ff.

5. Alwyn and Brinley Rees, *Celtic Heritage* (London: Thames and Hudson, 1961), p. 67; Lady Gregory says of Finn in *Gods and Fighting Men* (London: John Murray, 1904), that "he was a king and a seer and a poet; a Druid and a knowledgeable man," p. 145.

6. Rees, p. 247.

7. Lady Gregory, *Culchulain of Muirthemne* (London: John Murray, 1902), p. 211.

8. Alfred Nutt, "The Celtic Doctrine of Re-Birth," in *The Voyage of Bran,* ed. Kuno Meyer (London: David Nutt, 1895), II, 42, 55–56.

9. Nutt, II, 22.

10.   Alfred Nutt, "The Happy Otherworld in the Mythico-Romantic Literature of the Irish," in *The Voyage of Bran,* I, 229, 232.

11.   Rees, pp. 308–09.

12.   Rees, p. 83.

13.   Rees, p. 346.

14.   Nutt, I, 290–91.

15.   *The United Irishman,* 11 October 1902.

16.   Rees, p. 137.

17.   Rees, pp. 345, 107; see also Lady Gregory, *Gods and Fighting Men,* p. 141.

18.   John V. Kelleher argues for Joyce's use of the later part of this tale in "The Dead." See "Irish History and Mythology in James Joyce's 'The Dead,' " *Review of Politics,* 27 (July 1965), 414–33. Janet Grayson considers Stephen's relationship to the sovereignty of Ireland in " 'Do You Kiss Your Mother?': Stephen Dedalus' Sovereignty of Ireland," *JJQ,* 19 (Winter 1982), 119–26. She deals with the kiss of sovereignty, most notably in the tale of Niall and the hag of the well, but sees Joyce's treatment of the theme as more humbling to Stephen, totally denying him the sovereignty that I argue he is merely postponing.

19.   Máirín O Daly, "Togail Bruidne Da Derga," in *Irish Sagas,* ed. Miles Dillon (Cork: Mercier, 1968), pp. 107–08.

20.   Nutt, II, 56, notes that "Da Derga's Hostel" contains the earliest post-classical European example of the supernatural lover in bird shape.

21.   Gregory, *Gods and Fighting Men,* p. 95.

22.   Miles Dillon, "Tochmarc Étaíne," in *Irish Sagas,* pp. 25–26. I cite Dillon's more recent version here, rather than Lady Gregory or *The United Irishman,* because the allusion to AE demonstrates the informal transmission of knowledge among those engaged in the Irish cultural revival, as Joyce was (at least peripherally) for a time.

23.   Rees, pp. 235–36.

24.   See Robert Graves, *The White Goddess* (New York: Farrar Straus, 1966) which parallels the Irish myth with "the legend of Mercury's return to Greece from Egypt with the Pelasgian alphabet" and says that "Hermes is credited with having invented the alphabet after watching the flight of cranes," pp. 233–34. Graves expands on this in a later book, *The Crane Bag* (London: Cassell, 1969). Here Graves argues that "This Crane Bag stood for a complex and secret system of poetic discipline based on the ancient Pelasgian Greek alphabet imported from Spain to Ireland in the late second millennium," and that "Cranes were, in fact, totem birds of the poetically educated priests who gave counsel to Queens and Kings and ranked above mere warriors," pp. vii, 4.

25.   Nutt, I, 145, 176n, 213–14.

26.   Nora Chadwick and Myles Dillon, *The Celtic Realms* (London: Weidenfeld and Nicolson, 1967), p. 129.

27.   George Henderson, ed., *Fled Bricrend: The Feast of Bricriu* (London: The Irish Texts Society, 1899), p. 215.

28.   Henri d'Arbois de Jubainville, *Introduction à L'Étude de la Litterature Celtique* (Paris: Albert Fontemoing, 1883), p. 320.

29.   Henri d'Arbois de Jubainville, *The Irish Mythological Cycle and Celtic Mythology,* trans. Richard Best (Dublin: Hodges Figgis, 1903), pp. 99–100.

30.   Best's "Jubainville," Chapter VII. The notes to the serialization in *The United Irishman* point out that the work "is based entirely upon the 'Leabhr Gabhala,' or 'Book of Invasions' as it is contained in the 'Book of Leinster.' " It is interesting that Maria Tymoczko finds much evidence of Joyce's use of *The Book of Invasions* in *Ulysses:* "Symbolic Structures in *Ulysses* from Early Irish Literature," *JJQ,* 21 (Spring 1984), 215–30.

The Art of the Labyrinth

DIANE FORTUNA

James Joyce's *A Portrait of the Artist as a Young Man* introduces the reader to the world of Stephen Dedalus, a world that is at once Irish, Catholic, political, and aesthetic. Joyce indicates these themes in the first pages of his narrative, runically transcribing Stephen's experience at the age of two or three. The reader knows by the end of this short initial section that the child's name is Stephen, but Joyce gives no surname until Stephen goes away to school, presumably at age six. At the school, Clongowes Wood College, Stephen's first conversation concerns his name and his father's profession. Nasty Roche, one of his schoolmates, asks:

> —What is your name?
> Stephen had answered:
> —Stephen Dedalus.
> Then Nasty Roche had said:
> —What kind of name is that?[1]

Nasty Roche's question is well taken. What kind of a name is that? The name is like a Latin word, *daedalus,* from the Greek *daidalos,* "skillfully or cunningly wrought," a word derived from the name of the Greek mythic artist, Daedalus, inventor of axes, plumb lines, masts of ships and dolls—especially those used as votive offerings; sculptor who first separated the legs of statues; and architect of the labyrinth built for the Cretan king, Minos.

Nasty Roche continues his interrogation by asking Stephen, "What is your father? . . . Is he a magistrate?" Joyce is again pointing to the myth here, for Mr. Dedalus's first name, Simon, is an anagram for Minos and, as Homer tells us in the *Odyssey,* Minos eventually became a judge of the dead, a magistrate, in Hades.

In order to understand how deliberately, particularly, and extensively Joyce uses the legend of Daedalus, the reader needs a full account of the myth at this point. Minos, son of Zeus and Europa, refused to sacrifice a white bull that Poseidon had sent to him for that purpose. Poseidon punished the king

This essay was condensed and revised for this volume from "The Labyrinth as Controlling Image: James Joyce's *Portrait of the Artist as a Young Man,*" *Bulletin of the New York Public Library* 76 (1972): 120–80. Reprinted with permission of The New York Public Library.

for this act of simony by causing Pasiphaë, the wife of Minos, to lust after the white bull. She begged Daedalus, the court artisan, to create a hollow wooden cow within which she might consummate her passion with the bull. To hide her shame, Minos concealed the offspring of this union, the Minotaur, within the labyrinth built by Daedalus. A monster with the body of a man and the head of a bull, the Minotaur became the bovine god of Crete to whom, every eight years, seven Athenian youths and seven Athenian maidens were sacrificed.

Daedalus had designed the labyrinth so that no ordinary person, having once entered and proceeded to the center where the Minotaur was kept, could find his way out. It was a prison into which Minos threw Daedalus himself and Daedalus's son, Icarus, as a punishment for having created the wooden cow. Daedalus's craft was put to the ultimate test by his imprisonment within his own creation. According to Ovid, even if Daedalus were to find his way out of the labyrinth, he could not escape; Minos had blocked all exits from Crete by land and sea. Daedalus solved both problems by inventing waxen wings for himself and Icarus. But despite his father's warning, Icarus flew too close to the sun, his wings melted, and he plunged into the sea.

Only two persons ever escaped from the labyrinth and lived: Daedalus and the Athenian prince hostage, Theseus. Minos's daughter, Ariadne, fell in love with Theseus; fearing that he would become the sacrificial victim of the Minotaur, she gave Theseus a skein of thread by means of which he wound his way to the center of the maze, slew the Minotaur, and escaped.[2]

Thus the full myth rehearses acts of simony, lust, imprisonment, betrayal, and sacrificial deaths, themes that Joyce returns to again and again in his writings. Stopping to interpret at this point, the reader might assume that Joyce has named his character for the first artist of the classical world in order to confer Daedalus's authority on Stephen, a young Irishman attempting to forge a skillfully wrought aesthetic. And the identification of Simon Dedalus as a latter-day, albeit diminished, Minos at least partially explains Stephen's increasing alienation from his father. But such interpretations avoid a basic issue: why did Joyce choose a mythic figure to start with? And why, of all the extant stories of legendary artists, did Joyce single out the Daedalus myth?

The question at the beginning of this essay—what's in a name?—needs revision: what might Joyce have known about myth in general during the years of his apprenticeship, and what might have led to his particular interest in the Daedalus myth?

THE REDISCOVERY OF THE LABYRINTH, 1900–1911

At the turn of the century, Dublin was a city steeped, in fact and in fiction in, the classical tradition. Schoolboys, like Joyce, could be expected to turn out translations of Horace; Irishmen like John Joyce did quote Virgil to the ends of their lives; Gabriel Conroys would compliment aging aunts as the Three Graces; and Buck Mulligans might authentically boast of Hellenizing Ireland. Gerard Manley Hopkins had lately held the chair of Classics at University College; J. P. Mahaffey did not limit himself to writing standard works on the silver age of Greece but, fascinated by contemporary archaeology, also edited the Petrie papyri (1891–1905). Classical studies came to include discussions of archaeology, anthropology, myth, and initiatory rituals not only in Dublin but all over the continent.

From the turn of the century through 1911, a whole literature of initiation grew up, largely stimulated by the writings of James Frazer, Jane Harrison, and Arnold Van Gennep among others.[3] During the same period, efforts to document the validity of myth and a separate but not unrelated exploration in Crete coincided to keep one myth in particular—that of Daedalus and the labyrinth—constantly before the public. Before 1900, little more was known about labyrinths and their function than had been known to the ancient world. After 1900, the literature derived from the exploration at Knossos and interpretations supplementing those findings are astounding both in their detail and their sheer volume.

The Daedalus myth became the focus of widespread scholarly and public excitement in mid-April 1900, when the *Times* of London carried the dramatic news that Arthur Evans had discovered the ancient palace of Minos. In an unprecedented series of events and over an amazingly short period of time, the world learned that Evans, until then a relatively obscure archaeologist and keeper of the neglected Ashmolean Museum, had privately purchased a piece of land in Crete. Within a week, he had recovered a maze of columns and courtyards that he identified as the royal palace at Knossos. Within three weeks, the excavations revealed an extensive series of terraces and staircases that in their intricacy were clearly the remains of what the ancient world had called the labyrinth of Daedalus. Delighted, Evans wired the *Times* on April 10, and a second communication appeared in the *Times* on April 18 under the heading "Remarkable Discoveries in Crete." Overnight, as it were, Evans became as famous as his boyhood idol, Heinrich Schliemann, discoverer of Troy and excavator of Mycenae.

The turn of the century proved to be an annus mirabilis for archaeology. By the end of the year, the British School at Athens turned over the major part of its *Annual* to Evans so that all his findings could appear. Less than a year after he had first put spade to earth, Evans published what had been obvious from the very first:

There can be little remaining doubt that this vast edifice which in a broad sense we are justified in calling the "palace of Minos," is one and the same as the traditional "labyrinth." A great part of the groundplan itself,—its bewildering system of small chambers does in fact present many of the characteristics of a maze.[4]

The excavations, moreover, supported details of the myth. The palace apartments were strewn with images of sacral double axes, frescoes of huge bulls, and artifacts inscribed with bull-headed figures, thus accounting for the growth of the Minotaur legend. Conclusive evidence of a ritual drama based on bull worship dominated the early discoveries.

Scholarly honors followed: in 1901 Evans was made a Fellow of the Royal Society and received two honorary degrees, one from Edinburgh and the other, significantly enough, from the University of Dublin. At the time, Joyce was in his third year at University College a quarter of a mile away. Evans's name and the general import of his discoveries may have become known to Joyce at this time.

For the next ten years, Evans's contributions to archaeology were constantly before the public: scholarly journals summarized his own extensive publications; semi-scholarly magazines such as *Scientific American* and *Nature* carried accounts of the excavations in Crete; and journals devoted to literature and fine arts, among them *Current Literature* and the *Athenaeum,* reported his findings. Under the titles "Mycenaean Pompeii," the "Labyrinth of Crete," and the "Land of Minos and the Labyrinth," even the more popular British and American magazines, the *Gentlemen's Monthly,* the *Nation,* and the *Fortnightly Review* (in which Joyce had published his review of Ibsen in 1900) publicized the discoveries. The *Athenaeum* in particular carried extensive summaries and together with the *Times* did more to popularize the subject than any other single source. Reviews stressed the underlying truth of ancient tradition and in the most laudatory terms conveyed the excitement of Evans's achievement to a large reading public.[5]

Perhaps the high point of public interest in the labyrinth of Minos was reached in London during the winter of 1902–1903 when, under the auspices of the Royal Society, Burlington House exhibited Evans's collection of Cretan art. Joyce was in London for a day en route to Paris, December 1–2, 1902, to see William Butler Yeats and Arthur Symons. A little over a year later, Joyce was calling himself Stephen Daedalus, signing that pseudonym to letters and his first published short stories, and using the name for the main character in his first novel, *Stephen Hero,* which was probably conceived in 1903 and written between 1904 and 1906.[6]

So extensive were the newspaper and magazine accounts of the Burlington House collection that Ronald M. Burrows, professor of Greek at Cardiff University, was moved to write a popular account of the discoveries in Crete.[7] Of particular interest is Burrows's bibliography; by 1907 he had access to over 150 separate publications that dealt with ancient civilizations, at least half of them written between the years 1885 and 1905. Included in the list are W. Helbig's *La Question Mycenienne* (1896), Evans's *Mycenean Tree and Pillar Cult* (1901) and *Prehistoric Tombs of Knossos* (1906), H. R. Hall's *Oldest Civilization of Greece* (1901), and R. Dussaud's *Questions Myceniennes* (1905). Burrows also used Frazer's *Pausanius' Description of Greece* (1898) and referred extensively to Victor Bérard's *Les Phéniciens et l'Odyssée* (1902–1903; a favorite source for Joyce), and Jane Harrison's *Prolegomena to the Study of Greek Religion* (1903).

Another popularizer of Evans's work, the Reverend James Baikie, claimed that the discoveries at Knossos had "revolutionized all ideas as to the beginnings of European civilizations."[8] Baikie's assessment is valid; voluminous commentaries of other writers ascribed the origin of initiation ceremonies to the Cretan labyrinth.

From the evidence of the actual excavations, Evans was able to pinpoint three parts of the "mysteries" performed within the labyrinth: lustration, ritual dance, and sacrifice. In the Throne Room of the palace, he unearthed a square pit that must have been an impluvium used to sanctify the body of the king with oil in periodic rites of lustration.[9] Lustral wells, fonts, and ditches were an essential part of the mysteries enacted in Egyptian burial tombs, in the Eleusinian celebrations, and in the rites of Cybèle. In Egypt the well of Osiris was meant to refresh thirsty souls as they began the journey of the dead.[10] At the Eleusinian, initiates, upon entering, "blessed themselves at the vase of sacred water placed near the door."[11] And in Asia Minor as part of the *taurobolium,* devotees of Cybele descended into a pit and were "baptized" in a bath of bull's blood.[12]

Cretan mysteries also included ritual dance—that much was evident from the frescos of dancing women that adorned the palace of Knossos, especially in the Theatral Area uncovered in 1903. Evans was sure that the tiled pavement was the dancing floor of Ariadne, the famous "choros" of Homeric tradition.[13] In a moment of exhilaration, he invited his workmen and their wives to a celebration. Within Minos's theatre, they performed ancient Cretan dances. Watching them, Evans felt as though the past had been recaptured. The sinuous meandering course of the dancers, as they were led hand in hand by the chief performers in each set, was curiously appropriate to the ancient traditions of the spot. Of such a kind, we are told, was the *geranos* dance mimicking the mazy turns of the Labyrinth.[14]

Ritual sacrifices had undoubtedly attended the bull cult. Had the story of the Athenian captives a basis in fact? Had there been human sacrifices to a bull-headed god? Or had the bull been substituted for a human victim to ensure the renewal of the king?

Sir James Frazer and Jane Harrison answered these questions and added that the labyrinth had been the scene of a sacred marriage and a sacred birth. The circumstances of the Minotaur's conception and birth seem to Frazer to describe a ritual marriage. He comments: "The legend appears to reflect a mythical marriage of the sun and moon, which was acted as a solemn rite by the king and queen of Knossos, wearing the masks of a bull and cow respectively" (II, 71). Frazer also believes that the bull or crane dance performed by the Athenian hostages was a preliminary to their sacrificial deaths in honor of the Minotaur. Both the dance and the sacrifices were essential steps in a purgative rite that ensured the renewal or rebirth of the king (II, 74–78). The labyrinth, therefore, housed the awesome ritual of "he who must die"—it provided another variant to the rite of the King of the Wood at Nemi, to the legends of the dying kings, Attis, Adonis, and Osiris.

In *Prolegomena to the Study of Greek Religion* (1903), Jane Harrison forcefully establishes that Hellenic initiations had originated in Crete, "the mother of the mysteries." To Crete and, by implication, to the labyrinth, Harrison traces the beginnings of Orphic ceremonies and the Eleusinian mysteries. She notes that Strabo (x.iii.13) "knew that the orgies of Thrace and Phrygia and Crete were substantially the same" (Harrison, 481). In her discussion of Cretan worship, Harrison concurs with Frazer: ritual wedlock had resulted in the birth of the Minotaur, to whom sacrifices were offered and who in turn was himself sacrificed: "Of the ritual of the bullgod in Crete, we know that it consisted in part of the tearing and eating of a bull, and behind is the dreadful suspicion of human sacrifice" (Harrison, 481).

This bloody communal feast originated in Crete, but it became an essential element in the Orphic mysteries. Known as the Omophagia, the "feast of the raw flesh," it was dedicated to the infant god variously called bull-Dionysus and Zagreus. It consisted of the following ceremonies: (1) the bull-god's initiates smeared themselves with white clay (cleansing with mud or pitch was also common in rites of purification); (2) the worshippers summoned the bull-god to appear, in a step repeatedly called an epiphany: "It was this Epiphany, outward and inward, that was the goal of all purification, of all consecration, not the enunciation or elucidation of arcane dogma, but the revelation, the fruition, of the god himself" (Harrison, 515); (3) they then sacrificed the bull in order to eat him; (4) celebrated a sacred marriage to the sacred bull-god; and (5) announced the sacred rebirth of the bull-child.[15]

> The monstrous complex myth is obviously aetiological through and through, the kernel of the whole being the ritual fact that a sacrificial bull, or possibly a child, was torn to pieces and his flesh eaten. Who tore him to pieces? In actual fact his worshippers. . . . (Harrison, 490)

The Orphic initiate pronounced himself one with the divine by eating of the god and, through this union, believed that he had attained immortality.

At Eleusis, the Omophagia disappeared, but the sacred marriage and the sacred birth were retained. Harrison once again considers the Cretan influence, especially that "of the Mother," on these mysteries. She cites Evans's description of a dove cult dedicated to the Minoan Great Mother Goddess. Evans proposed that the goddess was related to Aphrodite and Rhea in Greece and to Cybele in Asia Minor;[16] all were variants of Isis (Frazer, VI, 202, 212). This indigenous goddess, Evans wrote, "belongs to the very ancient class of Virgin Mothers."[17]

In summary, based on Evans's researches, the interpretations of James Frazer and Jane Harrison established the Cretan labyrinth as the primary site of an initiatory ritual. The design of the building derived from the Egyptian labyrinth, and the mysteries celebrated in Crete bore striking similarities to Egyptian bull cults dedicated to Osiris, as well as to the analogous rites of Attis in Asia Minor. Similarly, the Cretan Mother Goddess was related to Isis and to Cybele. In Crete, the ceremonies were conducted by priest-kings to ensure their renewal and included lustration; ritual dances; sacred marriage; coronation and its corollary, ritual death; and ritual rebirth. Tests, riddles, and graffiti figured as parts of the mysteries.

The myth adumbrated these details: the Minotaur was the bull-god of Crete, sacred child of a sacred marriage between a divine bull and a queen. Dances and human sacrifices to him probably did take place, though at some stage bulls were killed in lieu of human victims. And, finally, Crete, the mother of the mysteries, had given rise to Hellenic initiations that in their most primitive form were based on bull worship. From this source, the mysteries of Orphism and Eleusis took shape. Cretan rituals enacted in the labyrinth, therefore, were part of a vast symbolic drama that, celebrated under the names of various local deities, had encompassed the entire ancient world.

THE LABYRINTH AND THE TOPOGRAPHY OF THE UNDERWORLD

The researches of Evans, Frazer, and Harrison represent the most widely known and encyclopedic sources for information about the Cretan labyrinth available to James Joyce. Just as important as their research was the revolutionary study of the patterns of initiation and the topography of these rites contained in Arnold Van Gennep's *The Rites of Passage* (1908). Van Gennep was fascinated by the fact that initiatory ceremonies marking the various stages of life were essentially the same. In a passage that might be applied to describe the patterns of repetition found in *Portrait,* Van Gennep presents his thesis:

> . . . there are ceremonies whose essential purpose is to enable the individual to pass from one defined position to another which is equally well-defined. . . . Thus we encounter a wide degree of general similarity among ceremonies of birth, childhood, social puberty, betrothal, marriage, pregnancy, fatherhood, initiations into religious societies and funerals. (2–3)

Not only are the rites attending various stages similar but, as an almost universal pattern, these initiations figure as symbolic journeys through hell.

Thus, primitives consider the neophyte dead during the period of transition or passage from one stage to another. He "dies" in order to put behind him forever his former life and world. After a transitional period that includes instruction and testing, the novice rejoins the community in a ceremony always considered a resurrection from the dead (Van Gennep, 74–75, 80–81). Van Gennep goes on to explain that the same pattern occurs in the "journey of the dead" of the Mysteries and in the descent into the Underworld of various heroes (91).[18] Initiations, therefore, are not only conducted from one stage of life to another but from one life to the next.

Van Gennep himself did not comment on the specific topography of these regions, but later commentators did.[19] Labyrinths whose purposeful complexity had hidden the sacred mysteries of the here-now symbolized the tortuous route to the House of Hell that concealed the secrets of the hereafter. But the young Joyce may have reached that conclusion as early as 1902.

That year, Joyce bought a most curious book, W. Marsham Adams's *House of the Hidden Places: A Clue to the Creed of Early Egypt from Egyptian Sources* (1895). In describing the Great Pyramid, Adams accounted for its abrupt descents and ascents by relating its construction to the Egyptian journey of the dead: the soul first purified itself at a lustral font, went through a series of purgational descents, then, judged and cleansed, it ascended through a series of chambers and corridors to a sacred room at the apex of the pyramid where it found eternal rest.[20] Anyone familiar with the description of the Cretan labyrinth would have seen a parallel to it in the structure of the Great Pyramid.

Outside of Egypt, initiatory journeys of the dead took place in palace-like structures, temple-tombs, or caves and were associated with actual *daedalia,* art works or votive dolls ascribed to Daedalus. Accounts of the Eleusinian mysteries, of the ritual at the oracle of Trophonius, and of the descent of Aeneas into the Underworld were all available to Joyce. Van Gennep explains that at Eleusis the initiates' final ordeal was to undergo a journey of the dead that "included a voyage through a hall divided into dark compartments which each represented a region of hell, the climbing of a staircase, the arrival in brightly illuminated regions, and entrance into the megaron where sacra were displayed" (90–91).

Jane Harrison had recorded a similar rite in 1903. According to Pausanius (IX.39.5–14), before initiates at the oracle of Trophonius descended into an elaborate artificial cave, they were shown an image which Daedalus had made. The ritual that followed, Harrison notes, was "of course a descent into the underworld" (578–80).

Virgil seems to present his hero as an initiate in the sixth book of the *Aeneid,* widely considered a description of the Eleusinian mysteries as early as the eighteenth century.[21] Aeneas, too, sees a work of art made by Daedalus, an architectural representation of the labyrinth itself, blazoned on the portals of Apollo's temple. For Virgil, the labyrinth symbolizes hell: Aeneas is previewing the devious path that he will shortly follow; the Sibyl has to urge him along; then, like the novice at the oracle of Trophonius, Aeneas enters the cave to Tartarus and descends through gloomy windings.

Initiatory rituals of death and rebirth, then, found their most poetic utterance in the Minoan legend of Daedalus and the labyrinth. But wherever the rituals of life and death are dramatized, actual labyrinths or symbolic designs of labyrinths appear, often figuring as symbols for hell. Joyce was fully cognizant of that drama's relationship to Christianity. He was also aware of the labyrinth's structure and its development as an art convention.

THE STRUCTURE OF THE LABYRINTH

A Portrait of the Artist as a Young Man is essentially a mythic novel because Joyce draws both its structure and its imagery from contemporary accounts of the labyrinth and its legend. No novel has ever wound itself through so many repetitions of prior incidents, so many recapitulations of terms associated with winding corridors, threads, and mazes, so many deliberate passages in which the protagonist seems to be involved in an intricate initiation that includes caves; gates; staircases; riddles; circling dances; divination; auguries; ritual birth, death, and rebirth; nets; snares; hidings; escapes; and finally ascension.

Many early commentators use the term *labyrinthine* as a metaphor to characterize *Portrait*.[22] In France, Jean Paris first explored the literal implications of the term. In 1957 he devoted a full chapter to the labyrinth in his work *James Joyce par lui-même*.[23] He aptly prefixes to his discussion a reproduction of Brancusi's portrait of Joyce—a five-fold spiral reminiscent of the anatomical labyrinth of the inner ear—and includes nine illustrations: of Celtic interlaces from the Book of Kells, of mazes from the Bibliothèque Nationale, and of a bas-relief depicting Daedalus fashioning wings for Icarus. He writes, "La tradition représente Dédale captif du Labyrinthe qu'il avait construit lui-même: ne faut-il voir ici l'artiste aux prises avec son oeuvre et qui ne peut s'en libérer qu'en la reniant?" (Paris, 103).[24] Paris further identifies the table under which Stephen hides on the second page of the novel with the entry into a punitive existence. Extending the range and importance of the image, Paris argues:

> Le Labyrinthe est donc, avant tout, une punition. Il est donc la prison symbolique de l'existence, la condamnation à un voyage sans horizon. Il est l'enfer dont Stephen entendra bientôt un effroyable description, et dont Grimmelshausen, parodiant Virgile et Dante, nous apprend que, s'il est fort aisé d'y descendre, "il faut suer sang et eau pour en remonter." (Paris, 105)[25]

In *Portrait* to be born is to be plunged into the labyrinth. In wetting the bed, dancing the hornpipe, wanting to marry Eileen, and being forced to apologize, Joyce is already indicating through Stephen the basic elements of an initiatory ritual that includes lustration, dance, marriage, and sacrifice. No rebirth occurs on these first pages, just as at the novel's end Stephen's flight from Ireland fails to give him a "new life." In the interim, he walks along the most symbolic of roads.

Harry Levin and Dorothy Van Ghent have both noted that the central action of *Portrait* is Stephen's continual walking.[26] But Stephen not only walks, he creeps along the fringe of the line; files in and out of winding corridors; circles; ascends; descends; runs round the park track; makes rounds with the milkman; takes turns riding the tractable mare around the field; circles nearer and nearer to the quarter of the brothels; feels his mind wind itself in and out of curious questions; circles about his own center of spiritual energy; notes with dismay (at this time perhaps dizzy from the activity) that Jesuits do much cycling and that Clongowes was where Jesuits walked round the cycle track; and attends a physics lecture on theories of coils, winding ellipses, and ellipsoids. In short, in noting that Stephen does a great deal of walking, critics have missed the far more important point that (like Theodore Roethke's lovely woman) he "moved in circles, and those circles moved."

When these circles lead Stephen from the road on which he meets the moocow to a confrontation with a bovine God; when his father's name is an anagram for Minos; when he has traveled from Clontarf Chapel (the Meadow of the Bull) past the Bull Wall and is there identified as Bous Stephanoumenos and Bous Stephaneforos; when Dublin's Nighttown and the process of art itself are characterized as mazes; when Aquinas, rather than Ariadne, leads him out of the maze; when, a modern Theseus, he hits the bull's eye twice with his aesthetic theories—then the geographical and spiritual orbit that Stephen circumscribes can be nothing but a labyrinth. Stephen's ambulatory dialectical journey is a quest through the labyrinth of the world to the paradise of the heart.

David Hayman was the first American scholar to focus on Daedalian imagery. Examining the labyrinth, minotaur, and wings motifs, Hayman points out that Stephen's ambivalence toward these images tends to reverse itself as he matures and notes "that Stephen shares his identity not only with Icarus and Daedalus but also with a number of other figures."[27] Hayman recognizes that "meaningful repetitions and cross references enable Joyce to reinforce the idea that his hero is repeatedly remaking himself through a series of deaths and rebirths which can hardly end with Stephen's departure from Ireland" (52). But he does not connect the reversed values of the images or Stephen's opposing identities with either the structure or the ritual of the labyrinth.

Critics and laymen alike have ignored the shape of the labyrinth because they have assumed that it is only a chaotic linear path nearly always ending in blind alleys. But this is a modern misunderstanding. The labyrinth as a symbol had been stylized very early. When represented in art, especially in mortuary seals, signet rings, and coins, it appears as a spiral enclosing a bull. In fact, this form of the labyrinth seems to be universal; it appears as a crenelated ring with a bull at the center in Egyptian mortuary seals, as a spiral surrounding a bull on Cretan coins and on the walls of Pompeii, and in connection with descriptions of the Game of Troy that was played all over Europe.[28]

Whether or not Joyce consulted any of the numerous contemporary commentaries on the Cretan labyrinth (it is highly unlikely that an artist attempting to write a modern novel about a character named after Daedalus would not do so), he knew that the labyrinth had been represented by the two-dimensional spiral with a bull at its center. He also had the example of Dante's three-dimensional gyre-labyrinth, most impressively established in the *Inferno*. There, hell "is pictured as a huge funnel-shaped pit, situated beneath the northern hemisphere and running down to the center of the earth."[29] This tundish is constituted of nine major circles, the last very small in diameter and covered with ice. Figured two dimensionally, Dante's hell is a spiral of concentric circles, like Brancusi's portrait of Joyce or the inscribed symbol on ancient artifacts described above. Figured three-dimensionally, Dante's underworld is a gyre-labyrinth, whose circles had merged into one another until Christ the Hero harrowed hell, destroying the connections between levels. Since then, Virgil tells Dante, leaps or some form of unnatural descent have to be made from one circle to the next. In locating Christian themes and patterns within the framework of the labyrinth, moreover, Dante establishes that topography as the Christian way or path and presents Christianity itself as an initiatory rite dealing with birth, baptism, tests, coronation, trials, sacrifice, and rebirth.[30] Anyone familiar with the shape of the labyrinth, as Joyce was, could easily recognize that structure in Dante's *Inferno*.

As spiral or gyre or winding hell, these circular structures are symbolic forms of the labyrinth and appear as the defining structure of *Portrait*. The circles that Stephen circumscribes in the course of his walks are parts of the successive spirals of the labyrinth.

Aside from the initial subsection of *Portrait,* each of the subsequent 18 divisions of the novel presents at least one image of rolling, cyclical, or circling motion. Van Ghent was perfectly right in describing them as circles of ever-expanding radius.[31] They radiate from the isolated little community of Clongowes to Dublin, from Dublin to the whole globe, and eventually throughout the entire universe. Virgil's winding Tartarus and, even more importantly, Dante's gyre-like hell are the literary antecedents for Joyce's conception of the labyrinth's form.

Stephen begins his windings on the outside fringe of the labyrinth. The linear progress around these circles describes Stephen's movement into the center and his subsequent movement back out of the maze. The retreat sermons, largely devoted to a discussion about hell, are composed of three subsections and form the middle and third chapter of the book. In the middle subsection of this chapter, Joyce brings Stephen to the center of hell, where the boy sees a bovine god (*P*, 111). In placing a bull in the central section of the central chapter, Joyce certainly was structuring his novel on the principle of the spiral labyrinth.

Stephen's psychological development thereafter becomes more free. Having reached the center, he reverses his course. His mind is gradually released from its burden of sin; he rejects the priesthood in favor of art; and he is ready at the end of the novel to escape the beauty maze and fly beyond the nets of nationality, language, and religion. Circling ever outward through more complex and mature levels, he finds, in aesthetics, the thread that carries him out of the labyrinth.

This reversal of direction explains the double nature of the images in the novel. Birds and water, to name just two of the ambivalent images, at first seem to terrify Stephen. From Chapter IV on, the connotation of the bird-girl and of the swallows of augury reverses and opposes the associations posited in the early chapters with the eagles of Rome, the eagle-like Father Dolan, and the bird-headed Heron, as Hayman has demonstrated (Hayman, 45 ff.). Water, so feared in the early chapters, now becomes, as William York Tindall notes, "good on the whole and unmistakenly a symbol of creation."[32] Similarly, the reversal of direction explains the thematic oppositions: in Chapters IV and V, Stephen rejects sin, repentance, and redemption, which provide key points in each of the first three chapters, and, instead of apologizing, admitting, or confessing, he denies the priesthood and, finally, his home, fatherland, and church.

As many readers have agreed, Stephen's linear progress through the labyrinth seems to be subsumed within the larger circles of each chapter. Dorothy Van Ghent was referring to individual chapters when she used the term "orbits" in her discussion of *Portrait* in *The English Novel* (274). Actually, it was Hugh Kenner who first recognized that the chapters themselves are repetitions of one another on different planes of existence. The subsections of the novel are parts of the larger spiral or plane of each chapter. In that they are all spirals, each chapter is analogous to every other. The pattern of the spiral labyrinth thus incorporates a principle of repetition among its major parts.

Kenner argues that the development of *Portrait* is a psychological and "precise analogical structure that suggests [that] the action of each of the five chapters is really the same action."[33] He also suggests that

the movement of the book is dialectical; each chapter closes with a synthesis of triumph, which in turn feeds the sausage machine set up in the next chapter. The triumph of the appeal to Father Conmee from lower authority, of the appeal to the harlots of Dublin, of the appeal to the Church from sin, of the appeal to art from the priesthood, is always the same triumph raised to a more comprehensive level (129).

What Kenner has so brilliantly seen as a rising and falling motion is actually the function of the successive spirals of the labyrinth. Beginnings of chapters are the initial and lowest point on a new plane. Kenner's "synthesis of triumph" at the end of chapters represents the completion of any single level of the labyrinth as it ascends into the next orbit. Like Kenner, Sidney Feshbach analyzes the climactic cries in each chapter that characterize Stephen's development up to that point, but he does not recognize that the labyrinth's gyre-like shape necessitates the repetition of those analogous moments.[34]

What critics have noted as the essential and controlling form of *Portrait* is only a small part of a larger pattern, the spiral labyrinth. To miss this larger pattern in any of its parts is to ignore the mythic substructure of Joyce's work.

THE LABYRINTH RITUAL

I have considered the spiral labyrinth only as a physical structure, arguing that its circular patterns provide the formal characteristics of *Portrait.* But Joyce was also interested in the labyrinth's assimilation to Hebraic-Christian myth and tradition. That Christianity preserves pagan rituals, especially those based on bull worship, was the implicit and explicit assumption of the cultural anthropologists already cited. Frazer, in particular, traces Christian festivals of Christmas and Easter to the worship of Attis, a Phrygian God whose postulants underwent a baptism in bull's blood. Attis is a syncretic brother of Osiris and, for that matter, of the Minotaur. Christ's resurrection, Frazer explains, coincided exactly with the resurrection of Attis, and the similarity of these celebrations caused many controversies in the early Church (V, 309 ff). Pagan rebirths, then, are akin to the Christian resurrection. Similarly, if lustrations are primitive baptisms, as Harrison and Van Gennep noted, it takes very little imagination to see rites like the Orphic Omophagia, the eating of the sacrificed bull, as heathen communions.[35] The Cretan cult of the Virgin Mother and the sacred birth of the bull-child, likewise, have more spiritualized counterparts in the Christian worship of the Virgin Mary and her Child, mystically conceived by the dove. Literature and art documented this historical continuum further by adapting the ancient labyrinth design to Hebraic-Christian themes.

Sacred bull-child born of the moocow, Christ born in a poor cowhouse; sacrificed bull of the *taurobolium* and crucified Jesus; monstrous animal and first protomartyr; proud Icarus and defiant Lucifer—these are just a few of opposing identities that Joyce adds to that continuum in creating Stephen Dedalus.

Although it is generally assumed that no sophisticated work of art follows the myth and ritual pattern point by point, it was exactly this possibility—that the labyrinth ritual could function contrapuntally—that so attracted Joyce. Mooring his narrative to such a basic pattern would provide an underlying structure for his novel and developmental control for the emerging consciousness of his character. It would thereby eliminate the shapelessness to which Joyce so objected in romantic art.

A myth that itself evolves could also serve as a cultural parallel to another structural device of *Portrait*—embryonic development. Nowhere is Richard Ellmann more convincing than in his description of Joyce's use of fetal differentiation as a structural principle in *Portrait* (Ellmann, 307). Just as rites of Minoan civilization evolve from primitive human sacrifices to the symbolic form of the Mysteries and finally find their highest representation in the Christian sacraments, so the baby's gestation gradually emerges from a virtually amoebic animalistic form to the youth's accretive shape. The development of religion originating in the Cretan labyrinth parallels the individual's physical development. Minoan phylogeny recapitulates Irish ontogeny.

Commenting on such substructures in *Finnegans Wake* many years later, Joyce referred to his use of Vico's cycles as a "trellis" and explained that he was "trying to build many planes of narrative with a single esthetic purpose" (Ellmann, 565–66). No doubt Joyce always worked this way: he seemed unable to rest in the telling of a tale unless he had a complex schema on which to hang his story. He may have discovered this kind of composition only when he decided to abandon the loosely episodic *Stephen Hero* in favor of a five-part novel. In the later work, Joyce regularizes the spelling of Stephen's last name, deftly employs Minoan myth as its narrative substructure, and drops his characterization of Stephen as a hero in order to present him as an ironically drawn victim. In the final lines of the novel, this university student posturing as an authority on aesthetics does not become Daedalus, the fabulous maker, but Icarus, the doomed romantic figure who violates the natural order in his flight to the sun.

Joyce presents each chapter of Stephen's life as a passage from one basically analogous initiation to another. The principle is similar to that presented by Van Gennep in *The Rites of Passage*. Like each near circle of the labyrinth, each chapter reveals an initiatory pattern of lustration, ritual dance, ritual marriage, sacrificial death, and rebirth. Included less extensively are coronations, riddles, and tests. Generally, the successive functions of each chapter include a movement from the cultural initiation of childhood in Chapter I, to the sexual initiation of adolescence in Chapter II. The third chapter outlines religious mysteries; the fourth, the denial of Holy Orders and the awakening of Stephen to art. Not until he passes these stages in development can Stephen engage in the intellectual initiation of young manhood and mythic identification with Icarus that is, in part, the subject of the final chapter of the book. Stephen consciously undergoes the first rite of the labyrinth, lustration, when Wells shoulders him into the square ditch that serves as a drain for the school urinal.[36] Potentially present on the first page when, as a baby, Stephen wets the bed, this image is Joyce's version of the ritual descent and lustration so frequently mentioned in labyrinth ceremonies. It recalls the impluvium in the Throne Room of Minos's palace and W. Marsham Adams's description in the Great Pyramid of the entry Well of Osiris, a square "Chamber of Deep Waters," that combines the notion of ritual descent with a bath-like structure.[37] "Uncleanly" purifications, moreover, were common. As Harrison remarks, initiates often smeared themselves with clay, dirt, and mud (Harrison, 490). It is entirely possible that in some rites excreta may also have been used.

In repeating the image of the square ditch throughout the first chapter, Stephen comes to associate it with his fear of the bath, its turf-colored bog-water, the sea, and other watery places. This complex of images already dimly foreshadows the disastrous end of his Icarian flight at the close of the novel.

Only four pages later, the same Wells asks Stephen if he kisses his mother before he goes to bed. This is a riddle, part of an initiatory test. Unable to answer Wells's question satisfactorily, Stephen repeats his description of the square ditch and remembers his discomfort of the day before. "The cold slime of the ditch covered his whole body; and, when the bell rang for study and the lines filed out of the playrooms, he felt the cold air of the corridor and staircase inside his clothes" (P, 14). The important additional detail here is the association of the square ditch with the corridors and staircases of the college. Clongowes is not the palace of Minos, but the former castle clearly represents the closest correspondence to the labyrinth in Joyce's early experience. With the publication of Arthur Evans's studies at Knossos, the term *labyrinth* could be extended to any building whose purposeful complexity hid the sacred rite of death and rebirth. At Clongowes, the obsequies for both Little and Parnell are celebrated, and Stephen himself, ill in the infirmary, imagines dying and being carried off to heaven.

The association of cesspool, bath, and bog with the labyrinth could be dismissed were it not continually repeated at later stages of the book. Indeed, Joyce refuses to allow the reader to forget it. The structural rationale for this repetition has already been indicated: each chapter represents one spiral of the labyrinth. In each chapter a complete initiation takes place and reference to lustration recurs.

In the second chapter, which broadly concerns sexual initiation, the image of the ditch reappears, most notably in the final section. Unable to gratify his lust, Stephen thinks of grafitti that he had seen in a urinal. Immediately thereafter, he realizes that he has found his way into a maze. Here Joyce explicitly shows that the ditch-urinal prefaces a sexual rite:

He stretched out his arms in the street to hold fast the frail swooning form that eluded him and incited him: and the cry that he had strangled for so long in his throat issued from his lips. It broke from him like a wail of despair from a hell of sufferers and died in a wail of furious entreaty, a cry for an iniquitous abandonment, a cry which was but the echo of an obscene scrawl which he had read on the oozing wall of a urinal.

He had wandered into a maze of narrow and dirty streets. (P, 100)

Joyce knew that the labyrinth had been the topography for a sexual rite: Pasiphaë's lust for the white bull of Poseidon had probably indicated a ritual marriage. With the mention of the word *maze,* Stephen is now initiated into that mystery.

Joyce describes Stephen's encounter with the prostitute in unmistakably mythic terms: the "maze of narrow and dirty streets" echoes the labyrinthine nature of earlier corridors and windings; the "yellow gasflames" burn "as if before an altar"; "the groups" of women are "gathered as for same rite." What altar and what rite, the reader must ask, belong in a maze? No wonder that Stephen feels "he was in another world: he had awakened from a slumber of centuries" (P, 100).

Like an Eleusinian initiate, once in the young woman's room, Stephen sees an artifact ascribed in its origin to Daedalus. "A huge doll sat with her legs apart in the copious easychair beside the bed" (P, 100). Daedalus had not only invented dolls—especially those used as votive offerings and found in profusion at gravesites all through Egypt and the Mediterranean—but he was also the first artist to separate the legs of statues.[38]

The subject of Chapter III is religious initiation, and Joyce now graphically extends the circling labyrinth of prior scenes to the Christian hell described in the retreat sermons. Though devoted to the last four things—death, judgment, hell, and heaven—the sermons stop short of heaven. Once Stephen's old teacher, Father Arnall, begins to preach, it becomes clear that hell is the real subject of his discourses.

As the chapter opens, Stephen's nocturnal visits to the whores' quarter continue. He follows "a devious course up and down the streets, circling always nearer and nearer in a tremor of fear and joy" (P, 102). The image for lustration—fetid water—figures first as a description of Stephen's mental state, a "swamp of spiritual and bodily sloth" (P, 106); then, as the priest gives the introduction to the retreat sermons, the image of the square ditch surfaces again. Stephen recollects his childhood: "the wide playgrounds . . . the square ditch" (P, 108). When Arnall describes hell a few pages later, it is clearly a *malebolge,* to use Dante's word, "a straight and dark and foulsmelling prison," as well as a reeking sewer where all the offal and scum of the world runs (P, 119–20). Repeating the image of the cesspool and the urinal of the first and second chapters, Joyce makes this Gehema bottomless, infinite, and eternal. Woven into Arnall's text is a reference to Daedalus: what does it avail to have been a marvellous inventor if one loses one's soul (P, 113)? Just as the labyrinth was a prison, so is the Christian hell. In addition, the priest characterizes the descent into this prison as a "fall," aligning Stephen's plunge into the square ditch and his swoon into the prostitute's arms with the Christian fall of man.

Like Dante, Joyce was fond of symmetries. Chapter III, made up of three subsections, is the central chapter of the five-part novel. In this chapter's second subsection, which is the chapter's dead center, Stephen's life converges head on with the Minotaur and the myth of the labyrinth.

When Stephen leaves the chapel after the first day of the retreat, mental swamps, windings, and a gluttonous bestiality cloud his thought. "As he walked home with silent companions a thick fog seemed to compass his mind. He waited in stupor of mind till it should lift and reveal what it had hidden" (*P,* 111). The purpose of initiations, Harrison had explained in *Prolegomena,* is the Epiphany, "the revelation, the fruition, of the god" (515). When Stephen's mental fog gradually lifts, he beholds what his benumbed mind had concealed—the hidden god himself. Guilty of the sins of sloth, gluttony, and, above all, lust, Stephen envisions his soul "fattening and congealing into a gross grease, plunging ever deeper in its dull fear into a sombre threatening dusk, while the body that was his stood listless and dishonoured, gazing out of darkened eyes, helpless, perturbed and human for a bovine god to stare upon" (*P,* 111).

If Joyce has at times unobtrusively introduced the strands of Minoan myth in Chapters I and II, his intention is transparent in this central passage. Once the reader identifies the topography of the Cretan labyrinth, the epiphany of the Minotaur becomes unmistakable. Within the labyrinth, a bovine god mirrors Stephen's animal soul. That god, to whom fatty flesh, burnt offerings, and human sacrifices are made, is the Minotaur, himself the product of bestial lust.[39]

And Stephen is a sacrificial victim, for Joyce immediately follows the manifestation of the bovine god with: "The next day brought death and judgment." Poor Stephen dies again: "the hoarse voice of the preacher blew death into his soul. He suffered its agony" (*P,* 112). Just as Stephen has recreated in imagination the burial rites for Parnell and has feared dying himself in Chapter I, just as he coldly perceives that "his childhood was dead or lost" on the trip to Cork with his father in Chapter II, so here his own terrified imagination judges and condemns him, once again, to die.

As if that realization were not sufficiently horrifying, Stephen shortly after has a vision of the personal "hell reserved for his sins" (*P,* 138). With this nightmare, Joyce magnifies and dramatizes the circling images of the labyrinth; even the sentence structure provokes the image of an ever-expanding circle. The topography of the scene is sewerlike, an expansion of the oozing urinal of the first chapter, complete with a foul marshlight that recalls the "vapoury sky" of labyrinthine Nighttown and the mental fog of Stephen's lust:

Creatures were in the field; one, three, six: creatures were moving in the field, hither and thither. Goatish creatures with human faces, horny-browed, lightly bearded and grey as india-rubber. . . . They moved in slow circles, circling closer and closer to enclose, to enclose, soft language issuing from their lips, their long swishing tails besmeared with stale shite, thrusting upwards their terrific faces. . . . (P, 137–38)

While in Chapter III the circling and winding images are used primarily to ally the Christian hell to the Cretan labyrinth, in Chapter IV Minoan references control the development of the narrative. The "mystery" of Chapter IV is Holy Orders, but instead of answering the summons of the Jesuits, Stephen accepts the calling of art. Turning his back forever on the Irish priesthood, Stephen recognizes the consequences of dedicating himself to the world and to the flesh. He reverses direction, as it were, in accepting that "he would fall" (P, 162).

Up to this point in the narrative, two irreconcilable forces—a degrading lust and a guilt-ridden piety—have been the poles of Stephen's existence. He reconciles these oppositions, and rank smells and watery places now become positive images. In accepting the foul laneway that leads to his father's house (P, 162), Stephen takes a crucial step in his development as an artist: neither passionless spirituality nor sensual animality detains him. He commits himself to the world as a sensible material that mediates between his spiritual and sexual nature. This recognition will be the basis for his later, fully conscious theory of art. And he will call it "a way out of the maze." Perhaps not fully aware of the implications, Stephen begins that journey here.

In the last section of Chapter IV, Minoan parallels or their equivalents surface in profusion. While waiting for his father, Stephen plants "his steps scrupulously in the spaces of the patchwork of the footpath . . ." (P, 164), repeatedly moving back and forth between Byron's public-house and Clontarf Chapel. Clontarf is the Gaelic word for the Meadow of the Bull, a meaning that Joyce immediately reinforces by having the impatient Stephen turn seaward at Dollymount and set off for the Bull Wall.

On his way to the Bull, literally and symbolically, Stephen equates the Jesuits with the guards of Minos's island, who had prevented the escape of Daedalus and his son. He "had passed beyond the challenge of the sentries who had stood as guardians of his boyhood and had sought to keep him among them that he might be subject to them and serve their ends. . . . The end he had been born to serve yet did not see had led him to escape by an unseen path" (P, 165). The sacramental act that follows will deliver him to "a new wild life" (P, 170), a rebirth that Joyce ironically undercuts by repeated references to Icarian motifs and drowning.

Faced with the problem of presenting a sacrificial rite when no account exists of the actual ceremonies performed in the labyrinth, Joyce chose to adapt the most famous literary description of a bull cult from Prudentius's

Peristephanon, X, 1106–1150.[40] Joyce establishes his budding artist as both victim and celebrant of the *taurobolium,* a baptismal ceremony older than that of Christianity.[41] He fully recognizes that the Attis bull is a type of the Minotaur as well as of Christ, the sacrificial lamb. The world to which Stephen now passes is pagan in its celebration of this ancient ritual.

According to Frazer, the ceremony consisted of a baptism in the blood of the bull performed in connection with the rites of the Great Mother, Cybele, and the worship of her infant son, Attis, who died and was reborn during Eastertide. This ritual baptism was preceded by a Day of Blood, the 24th of March, on which the priests in their service sacrificed their virility. Frazer gives a detailed account of this savage ceremony and cites for corroboration Catullus's wry poem, "Atys." The god was reborn on the next day, the 25th of March, and his castrated worshipper rededicated himself through the agency of the *taurobolium:* he "had been born again to eternal life and had washed his sins in the blood of the bull" (Frazer, V, 274–75).

As Prudentius records the ritual, the high priest descends "into a trench dug deep in the ground to be made holy . . . his hair clasped with a golden crown." Above him, the worshippers lay planks perforated with many holes where they lead "a great bull . . . wreathed with garlands of flowers. . . . They cut his breast open with a consecrated hunting-spear and the great wound disgorges a stream of red hot blood" through the perforations. Bathed in the blood of the victim, the priest reascends. The worshippers "all stand apart and give him salutation and do him reverence."

In Joyce's version of the Day of Blood, Stephen "turned seaward from the road at Dollymount and as he passed on to the thin wooden bridge he felt the planks shaking . . . a squad of christian brothers was on its way back from the Bull" (*P*, 165). Like Catullus, he commiserates with these humble servants of god. Like the devotees of Attis, they are also "victims" of their piety. The planked bridge is the place of the rite, and Stephen looks down as if he were trying to see the priests in the trench. He does; for in the swirling water, he sees their reflection.

Stephen then crosses the bridge and goes on to the next part of the ceremony. "Again! Again! Again! a voice from beyond the world was calling" (*P*, 167.) In the most explicitly mythic scene in the work, fellow students swimming at the Bull Wall hail him as both the bull who is sacrificed and the high priest of the *taurobolium.* The boys are presented as his followers, shouting his name in Greek: "—Hello, Stephanos—Here comes the Dedalus!"

In Greek, Stephan's name, "Stephanos," means a crown for the head or a crown of martydom and in its widest sense includes "a ring or circle, a thing that encloses," as Harrison notes in her discussion of Orphism. The initiate entered the *stephanos* and then exited to a new birth, new baptism, and new name (Harrison, 592).

Like the followers of the Stephaneforos, a name for the high priest in bull worship,[42] the boys give Stephen salutation: again they call, "—Come along, Dedalus! Bous Stephanoumenos! Bous Stephaneforous!" [Come along, cunning one! Martyred Bull! Crown-Bearing Bull][43] as if urging an animal on. Is Stephen "chilled to the bone at the sight of their corpselike nakedness" and pained "with a swordlike pain to see . . . their pitiable nakedness" because the boys have already participated in the Day of Blood? Joyce's repeated emphasis on "pain" and his compound words, "corpselike nakedness" and "swordlike pain" indicate a sharply inflicted bodily sacrifice.[44]

A third time they call his name: "—Stephanos Dedalos! Bous Stephanoumenos! Bous Stephaneforos!" [Martyr and cunning one! Martyred Bull! Crown-bearing Bull!] (P, 168). Both crowned celebrant and crowned victim, Stephen is the priest about to be bathed in the blood of the bull and the animal about to be sacrificed. In Chapter V Joyce will parallel the opposing and metamorphic identities of this substructure in terms of Christian ritual. There, Stephen, as Catholic celebrant, will perform the sacrifice of the Mass and be identified with Christ crucified.

Hailing the celebrant, Prudentius says, the worshippers of Attis "stand apart" from the *stephaneforos* and "do him reverence." Stephen "stood still in deference to their calls" and "apart from them." The swimmers' banter, Joyce writes in imitation, "flattered" Stephen's "mild proud sovereignty" (P, 168). In Prudentius' account, the followers of Attis cut open the breast of the bull with a consecrated hunting-spear; Stephen experiences "a cry of triumph" that "cleft his brain" (P, 169).

At the sound of Daedalus's name, Stephen has been transfigured, and "the body he knew was purified in a breath." Like the Orphic initiate, he is renamed and rededicated: "He would create proudly out of the freedom and power of his soul, as the great artificer whose name he bore, a living thing." Instantly, "he started up nervously from the stoneblock for he could no longer quench the flame in his blood." Finding a rivulet in the strand, he wades in the seawater, which he had formerly feared. Joyce is obviously referring to a rebaptism. In this most important lustration, his sins are washed away; reborn, "a new wild life was singing in his veins" (P, 169–70).

Stephen's path now leads him to the bird-girl, Ariadne-Cybele, symbol of "the advent of life that had cried to him" (P, 172). She seems like "a strange and beautiful seabird," her bare legs as "delicate as a crane's," her bosom like "the breast of some darkplumaged dove" (P, 171). Ariadne was traditionally associated with the crane, as the dance that Daedalus created for her demonstrates. Further, all the Minoan goddesses were represented by the dove.[45] After leaving Crete, she became the consort of Dionysus, another bull-god, and as such presided over death and rebirth. In this function, she guided the soul through the winding labyrinth of life to freedom and a new existence.[46] And this is exactly how Joyce uses her in this scene, for the girl, like Ariadne, initiates Stephen into the new life of art, a life that throws "open before him in an instant of ecstasy the gates of all the ways of error and glory. On and on and on and on!" (P, 172).

Through the now positive bird imagery, Joyce ties this "angel of mortal youth and beauty" to Minoan myth. Exhausted, Stephen feels that "earth," the Great Mother, "had taken him to her breast . . . "; her "vast cyclic movement" (*P,* 172) propels him to the fifth and most complex circle of the labyrinth.

Thus, in a single scene, Joyce has managed once more to invoke a ritual based on bull worship for his own narrative purposes.[47] Stephen is the bull victim who dies in order to live again. His boyhood is dead, and he is reborn as the artist as a young man, purified of the fear and guilt that has attended his entry into the labyrinth from the beginning of the book. But his triumph is momentary, for in the final chapter, he repeats an equally complex initiatory ritual. This time Joyce invokes a Christian pattern—the historical continuum of pagan worship.

The fifth chapter of *Portrait* begins with another recollection of the bog and bath associated with Clongowes. As Stephen eats breakfast, the pool of partially melted butter in a jar "brought back to his memory the dark turf-coloured water of the bath in Clongowes" (*P,* 174). But now he is unmoved by the recollection. This initial image of lustration, used to indicate the descent into the labyrinth, moreover, has been assimilated to Christian ritual. Chester G. Anderson notes that in this scene Stephen as celebrant is symbolically performing the ritual sacrifice at the heart of the Maundy Thursday Mass.[48] As the chapter progresses, Stephen as Christ, the victim of that sacrifice, reenacts the events of Passion Week. When Stephen washes himself moments later, it is a Christian lustration that he performs—the purification of the fingers at the beginning of the Mass (Anderson, 6).

After breakfast, Stephen winds through the streets of Dublin again, then enters the corridor of the college that is "dark and silent but not unwatchful" (*P,* 184). The language echoes the description of Clongowes' halls early in the book, and in the scenes following, Joyce underscores Stephen's labyrinthine path with enough circles, coils and uncoilings, ellipses, and radiating eddies to rival the Book of Kells. The way out of this final circle of the maze appears when Stephen delivers an aesthetics lecture to Lynch: the beautiful itself is of two kinds—physical and aesthetic.

Physical beauty is mortal and "dangerous"; it leads to eugenics, reproduction, and the creation, as Daedalus learned to his dismay, of the wooden cow with all its sad consequences. Although Stephen admits to being a monster and an animal (*P,* 203), he is no longer consumed by the sensual.

Neither Stephen nor Joyce, however, is suggesting an aesthetic that renounces the sensible. Joyce firmly believed that the greatness of genuine art lay in its capacity to penetrate to the real, to the sensible, and effectively strip it of all accidental qualities derived from blind enmeshment in space and time. This is not the denial of the real but the freeing of it to exist in its perennial and most pure form.

Based on the sensible, Stephen's aesthetic is the other way out of the beauty maze. It is a way that affords him the strong intellectual support of

Aquinas, who, rather than Ariadne, "will carry him all along the line" (*P,* 209); therefore, to Stephen's definitions of the central concepts of *integritas* and *consonantia,* Lynch admiringly responds "Bull's eye!" and "Bull's eye again!" (*P,* 212). In effect, Stephen has slain the Minotaur within himself.

Shortly thereafter, the narrative of *Portrait* concludes, but the novel does not. Joyce ends with what might be called the "chapbook" of the young artist in the form of a diary. It certainly does not represent a falling off of Joyce's inventive powers, nor does it serve merely as a bridge to *Ulysses.* Very simply, the diary completes the labyrinth that Joyce has created in this novel. In it are to be found the clues to every important image and theme.

As one would expect, the ritual structure of the novel outlined above comes to the surface in the diary. Stephen writes about "dark streams of swirling bogwater," the masts of ships (an invention of Daedalus), a strange cavern in which underworld figures of the dead approach and seem to ask questions with their eyes (a direct reference to Homeric and Virgilian descents into Hades and an implicit reference to the initiatory caverns found in all Mediterranean and Northern mythologies).

Most important, perhaps, is Stephen's awareness of myth as the basic structure of his own life, as evidenced in his last diary entry. Ready to fly forth, he invokes Daedalus as "Old father, old artificer, stand me now and ever in good stead" (*P,* 253). These final words of the novel serve to underline the legend of the labyrinth that has patterned it and the ultimate irony of Joyce's characterization. Stephen is the artist as a young man and an Icarus, poised before his fall.

Thus the diary functions structurally in much the same way as the first pages of the book beginning with the story of the moocow. It is a microcosm with language, myth, and image given not as données that the child inherits but as the productions of the artist, albeit young, creating, controlling, and devising symbols that bestow order and coherence on the life that he has known.

In tracing Stephen Dedalus's movements up to that proud flight, I have attempted to show that it is only the last example of lustration, of ascent and descent, of ritual sacrifice, and of disappointed rebirths present from the opening of the novel. Joyce layered his text with Minoan imagery because the labyrinth was the actual topography for an extensive initiation whose full meaning only came to be understood in the years of his apprenticeship.

This paper began with the question: what's in a name? If Stephen is Icarus, who then is Daedalus? However ingenious his language and varied his occupations and avocations, Simon Dedalus is no artist of the beautiful.

As the Irish would say, "Daedalus? Why it's himself, of course."

Like "the old artificer," James Joyce "flew. Whereto?"—stayed there, and went on to write gloriously, in Ovid's words, "of things that change, new being out of old . . . the shifting story of the world."[49]

Notes

1. James Joyce, *A Portrait of the Artist as a Young Man,* ed. Richard Ellmann (New York: Viking Press, 1964), 8–9; hereafter cited in the text as *P.* All citations of *Portrait* are from this edition, which employs the textual corrections of Chester G. Anderson.

2. All aspects of this myth can be found in August Pauly-Georg Wissowa, *Real Encyclopädie der classischen Altertums-wissenschaft* (Stuttgart: J. B. Meltzer, 1894), under the articles "Labyrinthus" and "Daedalus."

3. A similar revolution in thought was occurring on the continent, spearheaded by the work of Émil Durkheim, Paul Rivet, and Lucien Lévy-Bruhl, especially his influential *How Natives Think* (Paris, 1910).

4. Arthur Evans, "The Palace of Minos," *Monthly Review* (London) 2 (January–March 1901), 115–32; reprinted in the Smithsonian Institution, *Annual Report of the Board of Regents* (Washington, D.C., 1900/1901), 420–36. The editor of the *Annual Report* also included a lengthy bibliographical footnote that showed the wide dissemination of Evans's material that first year: "The most scientific account of the exploration of the Cretan labyrinth is the official statement of Mr. Evans in the Annual of the British School at Athens, 1899–1900. The following is a brief list of papers on the subject by men who speak with authority: (1) Paul Walters in Archaeologia, August, 1900; (2) Mr. Evans, Biblia, September, 1900; (3) Mr. Evans and Mr. D. E. Hogarth, Biblia, January, 1901. (See also Biblia, November and December, 1900); (4) Mr. Lewis Dyer, the Nation, August 2, 1900; (5) Mr. Evans, Murray's Monthly Magazine, February, 1901; and (6) Mr. Hogarth in the Contemporary Review, December, 1900. In Biblia, 1901, p. 121–128, Mr. Evans describes the recent discoveries at Knossos up to the middle of May; and the Nation, June 27, 1901, contains extracts from letters of Mr. Evans to the *Times* dated May 16 and June 12, telling of the latest results" (425).

5. *Athenaeum,* July 26, 1902 (July–December, 1902), p. 133. Of the more important early reviews and mentions of Evans's work that appeared in this magazine, see July–December, 1900, 620–21; July–December, 1901, 260; January–June, 1902, 88; July–December, 1902, 35–36, 132, 592; January–June, 1906, 115; July–December, 1905, 651–52.

6. Richard Ellmann, *James Joyce,* rev. ed. (New York: Oxford University Press, 1981), 170, hereafter cited in the text. Letter to Oliver St. John Gogarty, June 3, 1904; letter to C. P. Curran, June 23, 1904; letter to C. P. Curran, n.d. (?), 1904 in James Joyce, *Letters of James Joyce,* ed. Stuart Gilbert (New York: Viking Press, 1957). For date of composition of *Stephen Hero,* see James Joyce, *Stephen Hero,* ed. Theodore Spencer (New York: New Directions, 1944), 7–9.

7. Ronald M. Burrows, *The Discoveries in Crete* (London: John Murray, 1907), v.

8. James Baikie, *Sea Kings of Crete* (London: A. and C. Black, 1911), iii.

9. Evans, "The Palace of Minos," *Annual of the British School at Athens* 6 (1899–1900): 36–42; 7 (1900–1901): 62.

10. Jane Harrison, *Prolegomena to the Study of Greek Religion* (Cambridge: Harvard University Press, 1922), 575–78; hereafter cited in the text.

11. Arnold Van Gennep, *The Rites of Passage,* trans. Monika B. Vizedom and Gabrielle L. Coffee (Chicago: University of Chicago Press, 1960), 90; hereafter cited in the text; originally published as *Les Rites de Passages* (Amsterdam, 1908).

12. James Frazer, *The Golden Bough* (New York: Macmillan, 1935), V: 274ff; hereafter cited in the text.

13. Evans, "Excavations at Knossos," *Annual of the British School at Athens* 9 (1902–1903): 111.

14. Evans, "Excavations," 11–12. The *geranos* is the Crane Dance mentioned by Plutarch, *Theseus,* xxi.

15. This is a summary of "Orphic Mysteries" (Harrison, *Prolegomena,* 478–571).

16. Evans, "The Prehistoric Tombs of Knossos," *Archaeolgia* 59 (1905): 559. See also *Athenaeum* (July–December, 1902): 133.

17.   Evans, "The Palace of Minos," *Annual of the British School at Athens* 9 (1903): 86.

18.   In greater detail than Harrison, Van Gennep describes the Eleusinian Mysteries, then explains the cult of Attis and the survival of pagan elements in Christian ritual.

19.   W. F. Jackson Knight, *Cumaean Gates: A Reference of the Sixth Aeneid to the Initiation Pattern* (Oxford: Blackwell, 1936), 32ff.

20.   W. Marsham Adams, *House of the Hidden Places: A Clue to the Creed of Early Egypt from Egyptian Sources* (London, 1895), 21ff. The fly-title is inscribed "Jas. A. Joyce, 1902," as noted in John J. Slocum and Herbert Cahoon, *A Bibliography of James Joyce* (New Haven: Yale University Press, 1953), 177.

21.   In *Cumaean Gates,* 160, W. F. Jackson Knight quotes William Warburton, *The Divine Legation of Moses,* I (London, 1738): " 'We hope to make it very evident that the masterpiece of the Aeneis, the famous Sixth Book, is nothing else but a description, and so designedly, by the author, of his hero's initiation into one part of the Eleusinian Spectacles.' " See also C. N. Deeds, "The Labyrinth," in *The Labyrinth: Further Studies in the Relation between Myth and Ritual in the Ancient World,* ed. S. H. Hooke (London: Society for Promoting Christian Knowledge, 1935), 42ff.

22.   William T. Noon, *Joyce and Aquinas* (New Haven: Yale University Press, 1957). Noon entitles his second chapter "Daedalus and the Beauty Maze," but he is using "maze" simply as a metaphor to introduce distinctions between Joycean and Aquinian aesthetic. See also Harry Levin, *James Joyce* (New York: New Directions, 1960), 61. Levin considers Stephen at the end of the novel to be more akin to Icarus than to Daedalus and concludes that "his wings take him from the fatherland. The Labyrinth leads to a father." Ellmann writes that in choosing Stephen's name, Joyce planned to create "a labyrinth, a mysterious art based on great cunning" (Ellmann, *James Joyce,* 154).

23.   Jean Paris, *James Joyce par lui-même* (Paris: Éditions du Seuil, 1957), 101–18; hereafter cited in the text. This elegant little book deserves to be better known.

24.   The tradition represents Daedalus as a captive of the Labyrinth which he himself had constructed: mustn't one see here the artist struggling with his own work who can only free himself from it by denying it? (All translations are my own.)

25.   The Labyrinth, then, is above all a punishment. It is the symbolic prison of existence, the condemnation to a voyage without horizon. It is the hell of which Stephen will soon hear a terrifying description, the hell into which Grimelshausen, parodying Virgil and Dante, teaches us that if it is all too easy to descend into it, "one must sweat blood and water to come back up again."

26.   Levin, *James Joyce,* 21; Dorothy Van Ghent, *The English Novel: Form and Function* (New York: Rhinehart, 1953), 274–75.

27.   David Hayman, "Daedalian Imagery in *A Portrait of the Artist as a Young Man,*" in *Hereditas: Seven Essays on the Modern Experience of the Classical,* ed. Frederic Will (Austin: University of Texas Press, 1964), 54; hereafter cited in the text. The opposing identities may stem from Bruno's reconciliation of opposites and/or from the structure of Dante's *Purgatorio.*

28.   Deeds, "Labyrinth," 9; B. V. Head, *Historia Numorum* (Oxford, 1887), 389–91, as quoted by Frazer, *The Golden Bough,* IV, 76. Frazer also relates the spiral labyrinth to church mazes known as "the roads to Jerusalem" and to the garden mazes of the Renaissance.

29.   Dante Alighieri, *The Comedy of Dante Alighieri, the Florentine: Hell (L'Inferno),* trans. Dorothy Sayers (Baltimore: Penguin Books, 1949), 68. Dante's Inferno is a gyre that places the Minotaur in the seventh circle of the lustful. Dante descends into hell by turning to the left; when he reascends to the 10 circles of purgatory, he changes direction and turns to the right. Purgatory is a 10-circle gyre, and purgation itself includes elaborated oppositions. Joyce also uses the gyre, the Minotaur, the change in direction, and elaborate oppositions to structure his novel.

30.   For the relationship of the labyrinth to the Christian way, see Edith Schnapper, *The Inward Odyssey: The Concept of "The Way" in the Great Religions of the World* (London: George Allen and Unwin, 1965), 5–27.

31.   Van Ghent comments that Stephen "moves from one geographical and spiritual orbit to another, walking in lengthening radius until he is ready to take up flight"; *English Novel,* 274–75.

32.   William York Tindall, *The Literary Symbol* (New York: Columbia University Press, 1955), 81.

33.   Hugh Kenner, "*A Portrait* in Perspective," in *James Joyce: Two Decades of Criticism,* ed. Sean Givens (New York: Vanguard Press, 1948), 168; hereafter cited in the text. This essay was later reprinted with minor changes in Hugh Kenner, *Dublin's Joyce* (Bloomington: University of Indiana Press, 1956), 129.

34.   Sidney Feshbach, "A Slow and Dark Birth: A Study of the Organization of *A Portrait of the Artist as a Young Man,*" *James Joyce Quarterly* 4 (Summer 1967): 289–300. Feshbach gives a convincing explanation of the five-part chapter structure; my reading of the larger labyrinth structure complements his.

35.   Harrison traces Orphic baptismal formularies to the sacrament of baptism "in the primitive church" (*Prolegomena,* 596); Van Gennep goes so far as to call the vases used in Eleusinian purifications "our holy water fonts" (*Rites of Passage,* 90) and sees the rites of blood in the worship of Attis as "a baptism in the Christian sense—that is a remission of sins" (93).

36.   What follows is a shortened explication of the ritual pattern in *Portrait.* For a fuller version, see my earlier monograph, "The Labyrinth as Controlling Image in Joyce's *A Portrait of the Artist as a Young Man,*" *Bulletin of the New York Public Library* 76 (1972): 120–80.

37.   Adams, *House of the Hidden Places,* 24.

38.   Joyce seems to be referring to Daedalus as early as 1900 in his University College essay "Drama and Life" (1900), in *The Critical Writings of James Joyce,* ed. Ellsworth Mason and Richard Ellmann (New York: Viking Press, 1959). There, Joyce writes that the advent of drama "made an outburst, as when the first sculptor separated the feet" (41), and, using a familiar metaphor, he characterizes man as having "a further longing to become a maker and moulder" (43).

39.   Compare Hayman, 43, n. 5: "We should note here that Joyce's conception of the minotaur of lust is probably derived from Dante's view of that beast as expressed in Canto XII of the Inferno. There the monster personifies 'violence, bestiality, and lust' and guards the entrance to the seventh circle. The imagery of circles used by Joyce owes much to Dante's vision of hell."

40.   Prudentius, *Peristephanon* [Crowns of Martyrdom], trans. H. J. Thomson (Cambridge: Harvard University Press, 1953). The late Professor Don Cameron Allen of Johns Hopkins University and Professor Edward Epstein, then at Southern Illinois University, called my attention to Prudentius.

41.   The major works on this ritual were published during the period 1901–1906: Grant Showerman, "The Great Mother of the Gods," *Bulletin of the University of Wisconsin* 43, Philology and Literature Series 3 (1901); Hugo Hepding, *Attis, seine Mythen and seine Kult* (Geissen, 1903); and Frazer's own account in *Adonis, Attis and Osiris* (London, 1906).

42.   R. F. Willetts, *Cretan Cults and Festivals* (New York: Barnes and Noble, 1962), 49.

43.   I have translated the terms for readability. Cf. Stuart Curran, " 'Bous Stephanoumenos' ": Joyce's Sacred Cow," *James Joyce Quarterly* 6 (Winter 1968): 163–68.

44.   Joyce seems to be attacking Irish Catholicism in this and related passages for castrating its young men and reducing its young women to batlike souls..

45.   The most substantial work on the dove cult in Crete available to Joyce was Arthur Evans, *Mycenean Tree and Pillar Cult* (London, 1901).

46. Georg Friedrich Creuzer, *Symbolik und Mythologie der alten Volker* (Leipzig, 1819), IV, 166ff. Evans associates Ariadne with Aphrodite, goddess of life and death, in *Archaeologia* 59 (1905): 559.

47. This passage is much more complex than is possible to indicate here. For Joyce's use of Dante, see Barbara Seward, "The Artist and the Rose," originally printed in the *University of Toronto Quarterly* (January 1957) and reprinted in *Joyce's "Portrait": Criticisms and Critiques,* ed. Thomas Connolly (New York: Appleton Century-Crofts, 1962), 167–80. In limiting my discussion to the ritual structure in *Portrait,* I am tracing only one line in Joyce's elaborate spirograph.

48. Chester G. Anderson, "The Sacrificial Butter," *Accent* 12 (Winter 1952): 3–13; hereafter cited in the text.

49. Ovid, *The Metamorphoses,* trans. Horace Gregory (New York: Viking Press, 1958), 11.1–5.

THE IMPACT OF THEORY
◆

[Reading Acts, Reading Warrants, and Reading Responses]

James J. Sosnoski

Imagine three hundred critics in Dublin at a future Joyce symposium each reading a paper on "Joyce's Portrait of Stephen Dedalus." Not *5 Readers Reading;* but 300 readers reading! Early the first morning Barbara Herrnstein Smith gives her reading, then Jacques Derrida gives his reading, then E. D. Hirsch, Jr., then Roland Barthes, then Gayatri Chakravorty Spivak, then Jeffrey, Fredric, Julia, Jon . . . A Jungian reading by Morris Philipson is followed by a Freudian reading by Jacques Lacan. Harold Bloom's reading of the villanelle has Yury Lotman's as its sequel. Hans Robert Jauss follows Robert Weinmann. Richard Ohmann follows David Bleich. And so on.

Many readers sit in the privacy of their homes silently consuming countless texts. And, that readers reading the same text silently enjoy widely disparate readings is of no critical consequence. We expect the reading acts of different critics to differ. Yet, the moment one of the readers, leaving the privacy of his or her study, publishes a claim about his or her act of reading, the situation shifts. Private differences become public disputes.

How can the multiplicity of disputable readings be explained without subverting the study of literature? This question (I hope you will agree) seems a reasonable formulation of the problem presented by 300 readers reading the same text, and it has parallels: philosophers of law have questioned the validity of legal proceedings, philosophers of science have investigated the falsifiability of scientific procedures. Granting that the history of critical discourse is invariably a record of disputes, I believe that only if we, like many philosophers of science, assume that *hypotheses generate evidence,* will we account for the overwhelming diversity of readings without suggesting that the pleasure of reading is a form of self-indulgence. Only if we assume that hypotheses about the nature of texts generate the facts of a given text, will we explain controversies about a specific text. Only if we assume that reading warrants generate reading acts, will we justify readings. In this essay, I have no hope of demonstrating this thesis, but I do hope to persuade you, by an analysis of the controversy about "esthetic distance" in *A Portrait,*[1] that it is heuristic.

This essay was originally published in the *James Joyce Quarterly,* Vol. 16.1/2 (Fall 1978/Winter 1979), and is reprinted with permission.

When Wayne Booth published his *Rhetoric of Fiction,* he called into question ironic readings of Joyce's *Portrait.* "Where do we find, in any criticism of *Portrait* based entirely on internal evidence," he wrote, the ironic "juxtaposition of Stephen's views with the author's superior insight?" (1961, 334; *P* 465). This question is the pivotal point in a dispute which has been described by William Schutte as "the vexed question of esthetic distance over which critics have been arguing ever since Hugh Kenner insisted that Joyce had given us a portrait of a prig" (1968, 14). Taking this issue as a point of departure, I hope to show that, in a changing critical climate, the claims *Portrait* critics made about their *reading act*-ivities during this controversy were inseparable from the *reading warrants* they used to justify their *readings.*[2] I hope to show that the texts they described in their critical discourses were linked to specific kinds and combinations of evidence which, in turn, were linked to specific conceptions of texts. To show this, I will begin, in part one, with some distinctions about the ways in which these critics use evidence in their arguments. Then, in part two, I will link the "groups" of evidence to reading activity as such. Finally, I will advance the hypothesis that a theory of criticism based on a theory of reading offers an explanation of critical disagreements.

I

Sentences in critical essays function as evidence in the context of sentences that state claims. Evidence is often recognized as a quote linked to a claim. For instance, in 1948, having called our attention to the contrast between the style of Book V of *A Portrait* and the preceding sections, Mark Schorer somewhat tentatively claimed that "Joyce is forcing technique to comment" ironically on Stephen. He argued that since "In the last two or three paragraphs of the novel, the style changes once more, reverts from the bare, notative kind to the romantic prose of Stephen's adolescence," . . . "Might one not say that the austere ambition is founded on adolescent longing? That the excessive intellectual severity of one style is the counterpart of the excessive lyric relaxation of the other? And that the final passage of *A Portrait* punctuates the illusory nature of the whole ambition?" (1948, 16) To serve as evidence, he inserted between his first sentence and the concluding series of claims phrased as rhetorical questions the following quote: "Away! Away! The spell of arms and voices: the white arms of roads, their promise of close embraces and the black arms of tall ships that stand against the moon, their tale of distant nations. They are held out to say: We are alone—come." On the other hand in 1948, Hugh Kenner, citing the same passage as evidence though omitting "Away! "Away!," claimed that *A Portrait* is focused and completed in the "exalted" "instance of emotion" "emerging at the end of the book, of freedom, of vocation, of Stephen's destiny . . . the instant of promise on which the crushing ironies of *Ulysses* are to fall" (1948, 149–50; *P* 424). For Kenner, Joyce remained identified with Stephen to the extent that he did not succeed in punctuating "the illusory nature" of Stephen's vision—at least not until the *The Mime of Mick Nick and the Maggies* (1948, 173; 1955, omitted).

Several years later, confident in his view of "the facts of the text," Wayne Booth challenged the reader of *A Portrait* to find any internal evidence of ironic devices or techniques (1961; *P* 465). He pointed out that "ironic readings did not become popular, in fact, until after the fragment of *Stephen Hero* was published in 1944" (1961; *P* 464). Granting textual evidence for an ironic reading of Stephen in this prior draft of *A Portrait,* Booth claimed that readers of the fiction published in 1914 readjusted their anticipations of Stephen's characterization. Such readjustments, he argued, could be warranted only by historical (and therefore external) factors, not by the presence of ironic devices in the text. Here were grounds for dispute.

Beginning with Robert Scholes (1964), critics have been trying to refute Booth for the last fourteen years. During these years, three distinguishable responses to his stipulation that only internal evidence can validate a reader's claim about "esthetic distance" emerged: A. There is sufficient *intra*-textual evidence to establish an ironic reading of Stephen's characterization. B. *Intra*-textual evidence is never sufficient to validate a reading; consequently, *extra*-textual evidence is always required to prove that any given reading is an accurate one. C. *Extra*-textual facts linked to *inter*-textual forms which, in turn, are linked to *intra*-textual features validate readings.

A. Since the publication of Kenner's *Dublin's Joyce* in 1955, many other formalists have read Joyce's portrait of Stephen ironically; but, like Schorer, have found Book V a fitting ending to the fiction. There has been a steady accumulation of *intra*-textual evidence, largely about Joyce's technique, in favor of an ironic reading of Stephen's character. Robert S. Ryf, for instance, argues that *A Portrait* is not authorless, as Booth claimed. One of Joyce's techniques in the novel, he suggests, is to create an "illusion of non intervention on the part of the author" (1962, 95). Also emphasizing stylistic technique, James Naremore, in "Style as Meaning in *A Portrait of the Artist*" (1967), argues forcefully that an analysis of Joyce's style provides the "internal evidence" Booth requires. In the same vein, K. E. Robinson, borrowing from Lee T. Lemon's formal analysis of the "motivation" of the scene with the rector (1967), elaborates upon Mark Schorer's description of *A Portrait* as a juxtaposition of contrasting styles, which are related to a careful "structural use of interior monologues." He writes: "two structural interior monologues form the frames on which Joyce built his irony. . . . If Stephen is the ostensible ironist for the first frame of ironic reference, then Joyce, as narrator in the structural unit of narrated interior monologue, occupies that position for the second" (1971, 75).

B. Robert Scholes disputes Booth's preference for "internal evidence," remarking that "everything about Joyce is relevant in some way to our interpretation of *A Portrait*" (1964: *P* 469). Scholes begins his essay by "reviewing the composition of the poem in its narrative context" (1964: *P* 470), in order to refute Booth's argument by showing that it is possible to know what Joyce intended his readers to understand about the merit of the villanelle. He soon turns to biographical information and manuscript material for confirmation. As his exegesis of the villanelle proceeds, he comments upon the literary conventions and models available to Joyce and concludes that "Joyce intended the poem to be the product of genuine inspiration" and that his intention "can be readily demonstrated by an examination of the manuscripts of Joyce's notebooks" (1964: *P* 479). In other words, Joyce's intention can be established by an historical explanation of conventional forms. Scholes's position is that Joyce intended his fictional character to be like himself in "his ability to play *eiron* to his own *alazon*" (1961, 14).[3]

Like Scholes, Sharpless rejects Booth's stipulation and supports his reading with *extra*-textual evidence. He begins by agreeing with Booth that "the rigorous exclusion of authorial 'presence,' either explicit or implicit, results in "consequent absence of any means of directly controlling the reader's response" (1967, 321). However, such "exclusion" is seen as one of the "special techniques of the novel" (1967, 321), through which we can see Stephen as "wise *and* foolish, callow *and* mature" (1967, 322). We should read the novel with the same "classical temper" (1961: Goldberg) that Joyce recommends elsewhere in his writings. If they were detached readers, both Scholes and Booth would have perceived Joyce's ironic "juxtaposition of a moment of exalted, serious vision, with matter of a lower kind" (1967, 324). In support of these textual juxtapositions, Sharpless offers biographical explanations, extending his description of the classical temper to the development of Stephen's fictive personality.

While Sharpless and Scholes adduce historical reasons in support of their claims, other critics apply psychological and philosophical paradigms to the novel. In his essay, "Stephen's Aesthetic in A Portrait of the Artist" (1964), and then later in his book, *A Scrupulous Meanness* (1971), Edward Brandabur argues for the existence of irony in Joyce's novel on the grounds that, although an amateur, Stephen's creator described his own neurosis accurately enough that it is possible to reconstruct Stephen's character from an explicitly psychoanalytic model of the specific neurosis. "Throughout," writes Brandabur, "I have imagined Joyce's characters as real and I have perceived what he was saying about them in the configurations of psychoanalysis" (1971, 3). Such an analysis implies that Joyce was at a "distance" from Stephen. For Brandabur, this distance parallels the distance between the narrator and the boy in "Araby" (1964, 18) and it allows for "Joyce's subtle irony toward Stephen which redeems the book [*Portrait*]" (1964, 20). Arnold Goldman, in *The Joyce Paradox: Form and Freedom in His Fiction* (1966), perceives Joyce perceiving the nature of existence in terms quite parallel to Kierkegaard's sense of "absolute paradox"—a sense Joyce may well have derived from Ibsen (1966, 71). Evert Sprinchorn (1965) reads *A Portrait* in terms of the archetypal Eleusinian mysteries. James Klein compares a phenomenological description of a neurotic consciousness to Joyce's description of Stephen's consciousness (1976).

In each of the readings of *A Portrait* we have just discussed, an *extra*-textual paradigm is advanced to warrant a claim about the text. The paradigms are derived from analyses of human behavior conducted by scholars in other disciplines. If such formulations "fit" discernible features of the text, the critic offers an explanation of the textual structure in which the features are seen to be derived from motives justified on *extra*-textual grounds, which often include a probable historical link between the "paradigm" and the text. Such arguments are usually based upon critical "methodologies" or "approaches." Complaints about such arguments are celebrated in the expression, "the hermeneutic circle."

C. By 1975, with the publication of Rossman's "Stephen Dedalus' Villanelle," the controversy seemed to come to an end, leaving only matters for critical "mopping up." But, over the years, as critics slowly changed their conceptions of texts, the warrants they used in their arguments slowly shifted. The stock of the "formal" critic plunged; the stock of the "method" critic held steady; but the stock of the "genre" critic was bullish.

Changes take place by degrees. Scattered among the formal arguments for the existence of ironic techniques in *A Portrait* are a number of remarks about comedy. Ryf, for instance, in 1962 in a chapter on "Joyce's Use of Irony," wrote:

> Finally, it is helpful to remember, at the risk of reiteration, that irony is not everywhere and at all times present in the novel. I have described many of Joyce's techniques and rhythms as being patterns of interrupted or intermittent pulsations, and his tone in the *Portrait,* I think constitutes another such pattern. Joyce coins a word in *Ulysses* which seems to fit here. The word is "jocoserious." As we consider the *Portrait,* with its fluctuations of tone pattern, we realize that it is a "jocoserious" novel. Realizing this, we are in a position to see that the comic spirit in Joyce's later writings, now generally recognized, did not originate in a vacuum, and that the seeds of it can be seen in the *Portrait* (1962, 170).

Grayson (1967, 311) and Murillo (1968, 15 & 29) share a similar interest in considering Joyce's ironic techniques in the context of comic conventions.

As Wayne Booth had anticipated, the question of esthetic distance could not be solved without taking into account the genre of *A Portrait*. "If an author chose to write comedy," Booth had argued, "he knew that his characters must at least to some degree be 'placed' at a distance from the spectator's norms. . . . If, on the other hand, he chose to write tragedy, or satire, or elegy, or celebration odes, or whatever, he could rely to some extent on conventions to guide him and his audience to a common attitude toward his characters" (1961: *P* 462).

In retrospect, the first critical insistence upon reading *A Portrait* in its generic frame came from Harry Levin, who, as early as 1941, argued that the book should be understood in the context of the *Bildungsroman* tradition (1941, 41–43). In a talk before the Joyce section of the NCTE convention in Pittsburgh (published in the following year, 1959), Maurice Beebe reminded scholars that Joyce conceived his portrait of Stephen Dedalus as an inheritor of Goethe's *Wilhelm Meister* and suggested that Joyce's attitude toward his fictional counterpart could only be perceived in this light. In 1963, he engaged Edward Brandabur at a conference on Irish Studies at Purdue University, cautioning him that "when we try to establish the degree of irony in an autobiographical novel of the *Bildungsroman* sort, there is a simple test that can be applied. The hero in such books does not find his true self or his proper vocation until near the conclusion; almost always he undergoes a transformation which makes him reject the standards of his past." ". . . if Stephen is a fake artist then irony should be apparent after his consecration" (1964: "Comment," 23). And, the next year in *Ivory Towers and Sacred Founts,* he again argued that the book be put in its appropriate literary context—the *Bildungsroman.* Louis Rubin, in *The Teller in the Tale* (1967), also explored the relationship between the autobiographical content and the conventions of fiction in *A Portrait.* In 1973, Tobin continued this exploration. Two years ago, Ronald Wallace argued that Joyce employed a *Bildungsroman* form as a genre (in Hirsch's terms) in such a way as to parody the romance-comedy genre (in Frye's terms). Quoting E. D. Hirsch, Wallace warrants his claim on the grounds that "an interpreter's preliminary generic *conception of a text* is constitutive of everything that he subsequently understands" (italics mine; 1976, 62). Last year, Jon Lanham took a similar stand in an issue of *Genre,* quoting Roland Barthes to the effect that "The goal of literary work is to make the reader no longer a consumer, but a producer of the text" (1977, 95).

This last group of critics differs from the previous two groups in that they bring *extra*-textual, historical/biographical knowledge of Joyce to the text of *A Portrait* which leads them to read that text from the *inter*-textual perspective of this genre, variously named, which, in turn, brings to light *intra*-textual patterns.

II

We have seen that evidence functions in the context of claims. We need, now, to examine how they are linked. In arguments, warrants, which are law-like, hypothetical statements, provide the links between claims and the evidence for them. In the literary arguments already discussed, it makes sense to speak of the hypothetical generalizations about texts linking quotations to conclusions as "reading warrants" because the dispute is about *how a text should be read* rather than about *how a text should have been written.* Not only do such warrants allow readers to put into words how a given text should be read, but, prior to any critical commentary, these hypotheses provide models for combining distinctive features of a given text which allow readers to perceive "facts of the text" that would otherwise have gone unobserved. To look at a painting does not guarantee that you will see the principles of its composition. To read a book is no guarantee that you will perceive the form of its features.

However confusing the terms of the dispute we have been studying, it is clear that each critic discussed complains that at least one other critic *misreads* part of the text of *A Portrait.* Hugh Kenner, for whom "Criticism is nothing but explicit reading,"[4] variously complains about "the careless reader" and the "insensitive" reader, while avowing that *A Portrait,* like *Ulysses,* "must be read and reread line by line and word by word" and "must be read with unrelaxing attention" because these materials "demand to be read" this way which "the fit reader will be able to see" because "the key . . . for Joyce as for the reader, is the word." In a similar vein, Booth writes:

> Can two readers be said to have read the same book if one thinks it ends affirmatively and the other sees the ending as pessimistic? . . . Most readers, even those who follow the new trend of reading Stephen ironically, seem to have read [his rejection of the priesthood] as a triumph: the artist has rid himself of one of the chains that bound him. To Caroline Gordon, this is a serious misreading. "I suspect that Joyce's *Portrait* has been misread by a whole generation." . . . Well, which *Portrait* do we choose, that of the artistic soul battling through successfully to his necessary freedom or that of the child of God, choosing, like Lucifer, his own damnation? No two books could be further from each other than the two we envision here (1961; *P* 456–59).

In turn, Scholes sees Booth's reading as a misreading. And so on. Granting that Kenner and Booth complain about the way in which the book is written in their essays, both critics aim to describe the way in which it *must be read.* For Kenner, the book necessarily will frustrate any reader, as, in his act of reading, it had frustrated him. For Booth the book necessarily will confuse any reader, as, in his act of reading, it had confused him. Both critics describe their acts of reading in the confidence that their descriptions are accurate and sharable.

Summing up, it seems fair to say that among the critics engaged in the controversy about "esthetic distance" a central issue is: how should Stephen's character be read? Should readers follow a trend of reading Stephen ironically? Should they follow a trend of reading him romantically? Or, as Scholes argues, should we read Stephen as *eiron* to his *alazon?* Or, as Wallace, revising

Scholes, argues, should we read Stephen's character through the lens of romance—comedy? The terms of "irony"/"ironic"/"*eiron*" and "romance"/ "*alazon*" are central to the dispute. What is the relationship between these terms and the acts of reading and misreading the text of *A Portrait*? The pivotal essays of Kenner, Booth, Scholes, and Beebe should contain at least some hint of an answer to this question.

Booth regards an ironic reading as a *misreading.* At the same time he is prepared to concede that Joyce intended an ironic reading. This is puzzling unless Booth is using the word, "misreading," in the sense that readers of *A Portait* are not accurately reporting the cognitive activities stimulated in them when they approach this text as a system of signs. As I understand it, Booth's point is that the distinctive features of an ironic text are not present in *A Portrait.* As a consequence, any reader who reports them is inaccurately reporting the effect which the text has on him. Booth explains how false reports have occurred on such a wide scale by pointing out that because the distinctive features of irony do exist in an earlier draft of *A Portrait* readers are inclined to impose them on the text of *A Portrait* that Joyce published. The question Booth raises is: can any critical reader of *A Portrait* who claims that the form, irony, exists in the text of that fiction, refuse to offer "internal evidence" to support his claim? He asks, "Where do we find, in any criticism of *Portrait* based entirely on internal evidence, the . . . [ironic] juxtaposition of Stephen's views with the author's superior insight?" (1961: *P* 465). These features, Booth argues in his *Rhetorics,* are distinctive of "stable irony." In a sentence, his argument is: If you read *A Portrait* in the light of the concept of "stable irony," then, despite counterclaims, you will not find it ironic. As it is used by Booth in his argument, the concept of irony functions as a *warrant* for the claim that Stephen's character cannot be read ironically. At the same time, because this concept implies *a conception of the text,* that is, a model of some part of the text or a paradigm of characteristic combinations of textual features, it functions, in the privacy of a reading act, as a *preconception of the text* which selects certain features for observation. It has the character of an hypothesis. In Science, hypotheses predict the results of experiments and thereby justify the research. In Criticism, reading warrants predict what readers will or will not find in their acts of reading and thereby justify these readings.

If, as readers, we read *A Portrait* in the fashion of a Hugh Kenner, with a preconception of it as lyric in style, we will discover contrapuntal motifs and controlling images. If, as readers, we come to *A Portrait* with Booth's concept of "stable irony" already in mind, we will not find it ironic. If we read the text in terms of Scholes' conception of Joyce's intention or Beebe's definition of a *Bildungsroman,* we will notice, roughly speaking, the same sets and combinations of textual features. Concepts of texts regulate ways of reading a given text. When you listen to a critic giving a reading of a text, Hugh Kenner, for instance, it is possible to infer his presumptive model of the text from the way he tends to combine disparate features of the text. Or, when you are reading a critic, you can construe the sentences originally written as warrants as norms for your own act of reading, that is, instead of understanding the warrants as descriptions of texts, understanding them to be instructions about how to read *a* text as one text in the group being described. For example, take the following sentence from Kenner's 1948 *Portrait* essay: ". . . like a Chinese ideogram, the whole has a total intelligibility based on the interaction of the parts juxtaposed by association" as an instruction. In fact, virtually the same proposition appears as an instruction in *Understanding Poetry:* "A poem should always be treated as an organic system of relationships, and the poetic quality should never be understood as inhering in one or more factors taken in isolation." It is this aspect of literary studies that allows one reader to teach another how to read the text in a new way. Kenner, whose *Dublin's Joyce* was first drafted as a Yale dissertation under the direction of Cleanth Brooks, describes the critic-pedagogue of the forties and fifties:

> All that is in front of the naive student is the poem, . . . A half-hour spent on the doctrines of romanticism insures that meanwhile a dozen odes will die in their entirety. *Any strategy for entering directly into the text, and encountering the strange capacity of its words for engaging one another and absorbing attention,* is clearly preferable to a pedagogic habit that lingers amid peripheral data, because in no other way the life of the poem be saved, the life that alone confers interest on other orders of lore.[5] (italics mine)

What we identified earlier as a reading warrant in his 1948 essay is now the instruction: Read only the text, allowing your attention to be absorbed by the "interinanimation" of its words!

This kind of schooling in critical reading results in critical schools. And, speaking loosely, we can discern tendencies in changing concepts of the text as well as correlative changes in the demands for evidence.

During the years since Booth challenged the readers of *A Portrait,* there has been a considerable shift in the critical climate. The period immediately prior to the publication of the *Rhetoric of Fiction,* the late forties and the fifties, was the heyday of formalist criticism. Mark Schorer's and Hugh Kenner's 1948 essays were a part of that critical *zeitgeist.* Booth's critique of Schorer, itself, questioned the description and identification of *formal* features of ironic techniques in Joyce's text. During the sixties, however, the critical climate changed. There was widespread interest on the part of critics in "methodological approaches" involving the application of historical, psychological, sociological, phenomenological and Marxist paradigms to literary texts. The formal method of explication was criticized on the grounds that *intra*-textual evidence is never sufficient to validate a reading of a text and that *extra*-textual evidence is inseparably linked to the critic's reading of any text. The seventies have brought us another change in the critical climate. Phenomenological critics have turned to a phenomenology of reading; psychological critics have turned to a psychology of the reader's response; archetypal critics have become structuralists; and formalists have become semioticians. What are the consequences for the critical readers of *A Portrait?*

III

The moral of the [hi]story of this controversy is that one's way of reading the text cannot easily be separated from one's reasons for reading the text that way. How a text is conceived has a good deal to do with the reasons that will be offered in support of a critic's reading of the text. In this section, I will develop two interrelated arguments: in the present critical climate, wherein Jon Lanham, the most recent critic to enter the controversy about "esthetic distance" in *A Portrait,* makes use of Roland Barthes' assumptions about texts to warrant his conclusions, it is predictable that increasing numbers of claims about Joyce's work will be warranted by conceptions of texts developed by semioticians. (This issue is a witness.) Nonetheless, if disputes in Joyce studies are about *how Joyce's texts should be read,* not about *how Joyce should have written them,* then a *reader*-oriented structuralist poetics would provide the most useful set of warrants and a *theory* of criticism would become possible to the extent that we would be able to answer the question: How can the multiplicity of critical readings be *explained* without subverting the study of literature?

Let me begin my argument by trying to characterize the kind of reader-oriented poetics advanced by Jonathan Culler.[6] By analogy with Chomsky's view of "linguistic competence," reading "performances" (reading acts) are seen as "derivable" from a reader's "competence." Chomsky argued that the subject matter of linguistics was not a "corpus" of sentences but the competence of the native speaker who was able to generate the sentences; so, in this poetics, generalizations are not statements about a corpus of texts, but about the rule-governed "literary competence" that allows a reader to generate a meaningful text. This poetic, however, is Chomskian only in inspiration. Unlike Chomsky, Culler does not resist the influence of models derived from semiotic theory, speech act theory, or communication theory in general. Nor is he deaf to critiques of the linguistic models used in the previous decade. Consequently, he introduced an historical perspective. Subscribing to a view of his subject matter that parallels Chomsky's view of the subject matter of linguistics, he attempts to incorporate structuralist thought about literature in his poetics while avoiding recognizable pitfalls.

A "structuralist poetics" like Culler's is a set of potential warrants. As a poetics, it presents a coherent model of the read-text[7] situated in its contexts. As a set of concepts, it supplies a range of useful terms for many "structures," though not all, arranged around the familiar axes of the text *in relationship to* 1) itself, 2) its author, 3) its conventions and traditions, 4) its world and, most significantly, 5) its readers. As a set of warrants, it enters, albeit piecemeal, into the discourse of a reader when he attempts to justify his reading of a text or to refute someone else's. Only warranted claims can be supported by evidence. Though obviously not always, critical discourse is a record of the critic's reading act, conducted in private but formulated in public as an argument for or against a specific reading. *Portrait* criticism is a representative instance.

Any poetics—Aristotelian, Coleridgean, Formalist, Structuralist, whatever—is, therefore, a powerful tool and a powerful weapon. As a tool, it can induce discoveries about texts and resolve anomalies in the discussion of texts. As a weapon, it can destroy previous readings and force compliance with new ones. Considering Culler's "structuralist poetics" as a "research programme" for the study of literature, we can identify at least three of its underlying axioms (its weapon-like tools):

1. To emphasize a description of the performance of reading acts over a theory of competence (i.e., over explanation) results in trivial claims; but to emphasize explanation (the theory) at the expense of description results in arbitrary claims. [Chomsky's impact.]

2. To emphasize the text over its contexts or its codes results in endless or naive claims; but to emphasize contexts or codes at the expense of texts results in groundless or vague claims. [The impact of communication models from speech act theory and semiotic theory.]

3. To emphasize synchronic analyses over diachronic perspectives results in indiscriminate claims; but to emphasize diachronic perspectives over synchronic analyses results in prejudicial claims. [The impact of the "New Literary-historians."]

Such axioms are very helpful in the effort to develop a "balanced" poetics (set of reading-warrants) for the practice of criticism. But, as we all know, programs become platforms. Speaking from a structuralist platform, it might be said that it is axiomatic that "formalists" who eschew theory and history are likely to produce endless, trivial, and indiscriminate results. In an endless series, one formal study supplants the previous one. No one study can be related non-trivially to the history of human attempts to find the meaning of existence. And, axiomatically, it might be said that "methodologists," on the other hand, produce . . . And so on and so on.

It is an easy matter to prescribe ways of reading. And, even in justifiable research programs, such prescriptions are tantamount to privileging one set of warrants over another, or to informing other critics that they have the "wrong method." Hypotheses are inexpensive. It is their consequences that are costly. But, prescriptions are not endemic to research programs. Some hypotheses about criticism are used to account for the way in which critics have misread a text; and others for the ways in which they have read a text. Some are meant as answers to the question, "*Why* did this critic misread this text?"; others to the question, "*How* did this critic read this text?" In the case of the critics of *A Portrait,* it is possible to argue that Kenner, Booth, Scholes, and Beebe, despite their public disagreements, nonetheless make reconcilable claims about Joyce's book, even when their differences are not taken lightly. Let me try to suggest how a reader-oriented theory of criticism, compatible with Culler's structuralist poetics, would account for the reading acts of Kenner, Booth, Scholes and Beebe.

If reading is a rule-governed activity, then such rules can be described. If they can be described, they can be placed in relationship to each other, allowing for distinctions between "reading acts"—or, if you prefer, reading "strategies." I understand this to be the import of Jonathan Culler's discussion of "naturalization" and the "levels of *vraisemblance.*" He writes:

> To assimilate or interpret something is to bring it within the modes of order which culture makes available, and this is usually done by talking about it in a mode of discourse which a culture takes as natural. This process goes by various names in structuralist writing: recuperation, naturalization, motivation, *vraisemblablisation.* . . .
>
> Whatever one calls the process, it is one of the basic activities of the mind. We can, it seems, make anything signify. If a computer were programmed to produce random sequences of English sentences we could make sense of the texts it produced by imagining a variety of functions and contexts.[8]

He goes on to distinguish five "levels of *vraisemblance,*" which he defines as principles of "integration between one discourse and another or several others." Each "principle" or rule identifies a distinctive way of reading a text. (It is interesting that Jon Lanham, who, like Culler, is influenced by Roland Barthes's *S/Z,* reads *A Portrait* in terms of an "integrated" set of conventions.)

In general terms, giving only a sketch of the explanation, a theory of "naturalizing" the text could account for the proximity and dissimilarity of the conflicting readings of *A Portrait* that we discussed in section I. From the vantage point of a theory of integrated levels of complex "reading acts" (my term for modes of *vraisemblance*), Kenner, Booth, Scholes, and Beebe each read the text narrowly, emphasizing a single kind of convention or a simple combination of conventions which results in claims warranted by different but equally uncomplicated conceptions of the text. Kenner reads the "novel" in terms of the conventions of the lyric; Booth, in terms of the conventions of "stable irony"; Scholes, in terms of the conventions of *eiron/alazon* characterization, read in terms of historical conventions of "composition." Kenner, Booth, and Scholes stress technical conventions; and warrant their claims with—to borrow a tactic from Barthes—"written-ly" conceptions of the text. Beebe emphasizes the conventions of genre rather than of technique. As Culler suggests in his discussion of irony in Flaubert's *Madame Bovary,* a reader's comprehension or "naturalization" of a text as ironic depends upon a complex operation in which a sequence of sets of conventions becomes an integrated frame for reading a given sentence. It is a matter of *priority.* Certain conventions must be operative in the reader's consciousness before other conventions can be comprehended. (Lanham makes a very similar point about reading *A Portrait* as an ironic text—1977, 82.) What Culler calls "genre" conventions, for instance, need to be understood before it is possible for readers to perceive sentences in terms of the conventions of irony. This conception of the readability of the text elucidates the dispute about irony in Joyce's characterization of Stephen.

Since reading is a systematic process in which any form functions only in terms of its position in the language system of the text, a central factor in the reader's perception of form in a text is the generic anticipation he brings to the text, which cues him to the specific functions of formal devices. Consider the effect of the text of *A Portrait* on a reader reading in terms of the generic anticipations of tragedy, for example, Hugh Kenner, who in 1948 read the work as lyric in style but tragic in mood. "The *Portrait,*" he wrote, "is throughout a tragedy of ideals without matter; the tragic conflict is always between the dream and life . . ." (1948, 172; *P* omitted). Thus, for him in 1948, the "wet dream" in Book V was inappropriate. His point would have been well taken if the lines, "Towards dawn he awoke. O what sweet music. His soul was all dewy wet. Over his limbs in sleep pale cool waves of light had passed . . ." (*P* 217) were lines written about Hamlet in Act V. Kenner was disturbed by Joyce's portrait of Stephen at this juncture in the fiction. He wrote that "our impulse on being confronted with the final edition of Stephen Dedalus is to laugh; and laugh at this moment we dare not; he is after all a victim being prepared for a sacrifice" (1948, 173; *P* 439). But not all readers read the passage as Kenner read it. Benstock, for example, finds youthful sexuality an appropriate context for the villanelle. For him, there is little to disturb us in the circumstance that a very young poet is inspired by his own eroticism (1976). If a reader came to *A Portrait* with the generic expectations of tragedy, he would, like Kenner, find it inappropriate for the tragic artist-hero to record the incident of a "wet dream," even though there is nothing in the physiology of tragic heroes to make them incapable of wet dreams. But, if we read these lines as lines written about Ernest Pontifex, we would take them with a grain of salt. Since there are reasons for reading Stephen as the hero of a *Bildungsroman,* shouldn't we read the passage with anticipations similar to those we have while reading *The Way of All Flesh*? Consider how the generic anticipations of a *Bildungsroman* structure our sense of the relationship between the hero's final, superior insight and his earlier, inferior understanding. Consider how differently we regard the relationship between a tragic hero's failure in self-understanding in the first and second acts and his final moment of self-understanding. From the perspective of a *Bildungsroman,* if an artist-protagonist like Ernest Pontifex were narrating his life, it would be "consistent" for him to record a wet dream in order to indicate to his readers that he had deflated his own view of himself. (Once again it is interesting that Jon Lanham makes a similar critique of Kenner's reading of the "final edition" of Stephen—1977, 101).

A multiplicity of readings constitutes the controversy about "esthetic distance." Isn't the theory that most of them are "wrong" and only some of them are "right" too simple an explanation? A *writer*-oriented theory of criticism commits us to this view. Yet, are "erroneous" readings explained by hypotheses about artistic intentionality? Does any theory of artistic intentionality explain Hugh Kenner's perception of *A Portrait* as lyric in style and tragic in mood? Does a theory of writing tell us anything about this controversy? Would a theory of criticism, based in a view of language as an accessible public domain, in principle, be distinguishable from Wellek and Warren's *Theory of Literature*? If critics are well-schooled readers, a reader-oriented theory of criticism is the only one likely to have any explanatory force.

A reader-oriented theory of criticism such as the one at which I have been hinting would be timely and useful in that it incorporates a "fuller" (more complete) and "richer" (more complex) conception of the relationships between writer, reader, context, and text than preceding theories have. Secondly, it may have "explanatory force." Moreover, when applied to the controversy about "esthetic distance," it suggests a future direction for the study of *A Portrait,* namely, toward a complete semiotic description of the text. What we most need is a way of relating those three hundred readers reading *A Portrait* to each other. But this is a matter for future issues of this quarterly.

Notes

1. For excellent descriptions of the controversy see Chester G. Anderson's "Controversy: The Question of Esthetic Distance" in his Viking Critical Library edition of *A Portrait;* and Thomas F. Staley's "Strings in the Labyrinth: Sixty Years with Joyce's Portrait" in *Approaches to Joyce's Portrait: Ten Essays,* eds. Thomas F. Staley and Bernard Benstock (Pittsburgh: University of Pittsburgh Press, 1976), pp. 14–16. For the convenience of the reader I have given the bibliographic references to individual essays belonging to this controversy in an appendix so that I may give the page references in the text, keyed to the year in which a specific item was published. Where a given essay is reprinted in the Viking Critical Library volume edited by C. G. Anderson I have the date the item was originally published and a page reference to the Viking Critical Library volume.

2. In writing this essay I am much in debt to the work of Ralph Cohen. See *The Art of Discrimination* (London: Routledge & Kegan Paul, 1964); "Literary Theory as a Genre," *Centrum,* 3 (1975), 45–64; and "Innovation and Variation: Literary Change and Georgic Poetry" in *Literature and History: Papers Read at a Clark Library Seminar,* March 3, 1973 (Los Angeles: William Andrews Clark Memorial Library, 1974), pp. 3–42. I have viewed the essays belonging to this controversy as critical "discourses" which are, for the most part, "persuasive." (On this point see Siegfried Schmidt, "Literary Science of Argument," *NLH,* 7 [1976], 467–82.) In identifying the "parts" of critical discourses and their "arrangement" or "layout," I have relied heavily on Steven Toulmin's theory of argumentation in his *The Uses of Argument* (Cambridge: At the University Press, 1958).

3. I have placed Scholes in category "B" because of the kind of warrant he uses in this particular argument, which, I believe, is close to the "intentionalist" conception of the text that

Wellek and Warren describe and reject in *Theory of Literature,* namely, that "the genuine poem is in the total experience, conscious and unconscious, during the time of the creation" (149). His "work," especially his recent work in semiotics, is different.

4. "The Pedagogue as Critic," in *The New Criticism and After,* ed. Thomas Daniel Young (Charlottesville: University of Virginia Press, 1976), p. 45.

5. "The Critic as Pedagogue," pp. 44–45.

6. See *Structuralist Poetics* (London: Routledge & Kegan Paul, 1975), esp. pp. 3–31 and 113–238; "Literary History, Allegory, and Semiology," *NLH,* 2 (1976), 259–70; and "Beyond Interpretation: The Prospects of Contemporary Criticism," *CL,* 28 (1976), 244–56. For an excellent account of the similarities and differences between Culler's theory of criticism and other reader-oriented theories of criticism, see Steven Mailloux's "Reader-Response Criticism?," *Genre,* 10 (1977), 413–31.

7. I have argued elsewhere that it would be useful to distinguish between the text as an indeterminate system of signs from the determinate "willed-text" of the author and the separable but equally determined "read-text" of the critic. See "The Use of the Word 'Text' in Critical Discourse," *CE,* 39 (Oct., 1977), 121–36.

8. *Structuralist Poetics,* pp. 137–38.

9. *Ibid,* pp. 156 ff.

{Works Cited, Selected from Sosnoski Bibliography}

1941   Levin, Harry. *James Joyce.* New York: New Directions, 1941. Pp. 41–43.

1948   Kenner, Hugh. "The *Portrait* in Perspective." *James Joyce: Two Decades of Criticism.* Ed. S. Givens. New York: Vanguard Press, 1948, augmented edit., 1963. [For revision of this essay see Kenner, 1995.]

Schorer, Mark. "Technique as Discovery." *The World We Imagine.* New York: Farrar, Straus and Giroux, 1948. Pp. 3–23.

1955   Kenner, Hugh. "The *Portrait* in Perspective." *Dublin's Joyce.* London: Chatto and Windus, 1955; Bloomington: Indiana University Press, 1956. Pp. 119–33. Reprinted in *A Portrait of the Artist as a Young Man,* ed. Chester G. Anderson (New York: Viking Press, 1968), pp. 416–39.

1959   Beebe, Maurice. "Joyce and Stephen Dedalus: The Problem of Autobiography." *A James Joyce Miscellany.* Second Series. Ed. M. Magalaner. Carbondale: Southern Illinois University Press, 1959.

1961   Booth, Wayne. "The Problem of Distance in *A Portrait of the Artist.*" *The Rhetoric of Fiction.* Chicago: University of Chicago Press, 1961. Pp. 324–36. Reprinted in *Portrait,* ed. Anderson, Viking Press, 1968, pp. 455–67.

Scholes, Robert. "Stephen Dedalus: *Eiron* and *Alazon.*" *Texas Studies in Language and Literature,* 3 (1961), 8–15.

1964   Beebe, Maurice. "The Tradition and the New Novel." *Ivory Towers and Sacred Founts.* New York: New York University Press, 1964. Reprinted in *Portrait,* ed. Anderson, Viking Press, 1968, pp. 340–57.

Beebe, Maurice, "Comment." *The Cross: Studies in Irish Culture and Literature.* Ed. R. Browne, W.J. Roscelli and R. Loftus. Purdue University Studies, 1964. [See Brandabur, 1964.]

Brandabur, Edward. "Stephen's Aesthetic in *A Portrait of the Artist.*" *The Cross: Studies in Irish Culture and Literature.* Ed. R. Browne, W.J. Roscelli and R. Loftus. Purdue University Studies, 1964.

Ryf, Robert S. *A New Approach to Joyce: The Portrait of the Artist as a Guidebook.* Berkeley: University of California Press, 1964.

Scholes, Robert. "Stephen Dedalus, Poet or Esthete?" *PMLA,* 89 (1964), 484–89. Reprinted in *Portrait,* ed. Anderson, Viking Press, 1968, pp. 468–80.

1965   Kenner, Hugh. "Joyce's *Portrait*—A Reconsideration." *University of Windsor Review,* 1 (1965), 1–15. [For revision of this essay see Kenner, 1976.]

Sprinchorn, Evert. "A Portrait of the Artist as Achilles." *Approaches to the Twentieth Century Novel.* Ed. John Unterecker. New York: Thomas Crowell Co., 1965. Pp. 9–50.

1966   Goldman, Arnold. *The Joyce Paradox: Form and Freedom in His Fiction.* London: Routledge & Kegan Paul, 1966. Pp. 22–73.

1967   Grayson, Thomas W. "James Joyce and Stephen Dedalus: The Theory of Aesthetics." *JJQ,* 4 (1967), 310–19.

Lemon, Lee T. "*A Portrait of the Artist as a Young Man:* Motif as Motivation and Structure." *Modern Fiction Studies,* 12 (1967), 439–50.

Naremore, James. "Style as Meaning in *A Portrait of the Artist.*" *JJQ,* 4 (1967), 331–42.

Rubin, Louis D. *The Teller in the Tale.* Seattle: University of Washington Press, 1967. Pp. 3–23, 141–77.

Sharpless, F. Parvin. "Irony in Joyce's *Portrait:* The Stasis of Pity." *JJQ,* 4 (1967), 320–30.

1968   Anderson, Chester G. "Controversy: The Question of Esthetic Distance; Editor's Introduction." *A Portrait of the Artist as a Young Man: Text, Criticism and Notes.* Ed. Chester G. Anderson. New York: Viking Press, 1968. Pp. 446–54.

Murillo, L.A. *The Cyclical Night: Irony in James Joyce and Jorge Luis Borges.* Cambridge: Harvard University Press, 1968. Pp. 3–32.

Schutte, William M. "Introduction." *Twentieth Century Interpretations of A Portrait of the Artist as a Young Man.* Ed. W.M. Schutte. Englewood Cliffs: Prentice Hall, 1968. P. 14.

1971   Brandabur, Edward. *A Scrupulous Meanness: A Study of Joyce's Early Work.* Urbana: University of Illinois Press, 1971.

Robinson, K.E. "The Stream of Consciousness Technique and the Structure of Joyce's Portrait." *JJQ,* 9 (1971), 63–84.

1973   Tobin, Patricia. "A Portrait of the Artist as Autobiographer: Joyce's Stephen Hero." *Genre,* 6 (1973), 189–203.

1975   Rossman, Charles. "Stephen Dedalus' Villanelle." *JJQ,* 12 (1975), 281–93.

1976   Benstock, Bernard. "The Temptation of St. Stephen: A View of the Villanelle." *JJQ,* 14 (1976), 31–38.

Kenner, Hugh. "The Cubist *Portrait.*" See Staley [1976], 171–84.

Klein, James. "Out of Mere Words: Self-Composition and *A Portrait of the Artist.*" *JJQ,* 13 (1976), 293–305.

Staley, Thomas F. "Strings in the Labyrinth: Sixty Years with Joyce's *Portrait.*" *Approaches to Joyce's Portrait: Ten Essays.* Ed. Thomas F. Staley and Bernard Benstock. Pittsburgh: University of Pittsburgh Press, 1976. Pp. 3–24.

Wallace, Ronald. " 'Laughing in Your Sleeve': James Joyce's Comic Portrait." *Essays in Literature,* 3 (1976), 61–72.

1977   Lanham, Jon. "The Genre of *A Portrait of the Artist as a Young Man* and 'the rhythm of its structure.' " *Genre,* 10 (1977), 77–102.

The Artist as Text:
Dialogism and Incremental
Repetition in *Portrait*

R. B. KERSHNER

Il se promène, lisant au livre de lui-même
—Mallarmé, quoted to Stephen in *Ulysses*

For several generations of readers, Stephen Dedalus has embodied the young but maturing artist especially in his relationship with language. Despite the authority of Kenner's ironic reading of *Portrait,* we are still inclined to see Stephen as the model of a creative, generative consciousness, increasingly a master of language from his first song about the green rose to his final impassioned invocation of an absent father. Yet we have also become increasingly aware of the extent of Joyce's use of borrowed materials in his work; as a postmodernist portrait of Joyce the mosaic-worker emerges more clearly in the critical consensus we are inclined to take more seriously his own disclaimers of originality as it is conventionally construed. After all, it was thirty years ago that Kenner, echoing Eliot, suggested that Joyce had many voices but no "style"; twenty years ago, Scholes and Kain noted that "it becomes increasingly apparent that Joyce had either an actual or a literary source in mind for almost every passage in *A Portrait.*"[1]

In the wake of Barthes and Derrida, it is more acceptable to see Joyce as the enormously inventive and resourceful arranger, parodist, *pasticheur* of the texts of the world, simultaneously master of and mastered by language, rather than the creator whose authenticity, selfhood, and patriarchal status as origin is reflected in a privileged *logos.* Perhaps Bakhtin offers the most accurate metaphor for the mind of Joyce in his concept of the "dialogic imagination," the locus of fertile interplay among the world's heterogeneous lan-

Reprinted from *English Literary History* 53, no. 4 (Winter 1986): 881–94. © The Johns Hopkins University Press.

guages—of *heteroglossia,* to invoke a term Joyce realizes in the *Wake.* And surely no author illustrates more elegantly than Joyce Bakhtin's image of the novel as a consciously structured hybrid of languages.[2] The implications of this view for Joyce's portrait of an artist are manifold, and may help to illuminate several aspects of the text: the meaning of Joyce's foregrounding of language in *Portrait,* and its relationship to the development of Stephen's consciousness; the question of Stephen's originality; the status of the narrator; and the most strikingly unusual but seldom-remarked characteristic of the text, its frequent use of incremental repetition.

I

LANGUAGE AND THE SELF

Bakhtin has remarked that "language, for the individual consciousness, lies on the border between oneself and the other. The word . . . becomes 'one's own' only when the speaker populates it with his own intention, his own accent, when he appropriates the word, adapting it to his own semantic and expressive intention" (293). Much of *Portrait* reflects—or embodies—Stephen's possession by the languages that surround him, and his attempts to appropriate them in turn. First, in remarkably explicit terms, each of the phases of Stephen's life appears—to him and to the reader—as a language. Near the end of his stay at Belvedere, he feels "regret and pity as though he were slowly passing out of an accustomed world and were hearing its language for the last time."[3] His harrowing experience at the Christmas dinner is at root a battle between two highly developed rhetorics, the nationalist and the Irish Roman Catholic, in each of which he has some investment. Dante proclaims that she will remember when he grows up "the language he heard against God and religion and priests in his own home," while Mr. Casey cries, "Let him remember . . . the language with which the priests and the priests' pawns broke Parnell's heart . . ." (33–34). Stephen, like the modern novel itself, is a product of heteroglossia. There is no language in which he is at home. English, the language of the dean of studies and of Stephen himself, is alien; Stephen thinks, "His language, so familiar and so foreign, will always be for me an acquired speech. I have not made or accepted its words" (189).

Yet the novel is permeated with the nostalgic sense of a lost linguistic innocence, a time when language was "natural," without its burden of alterity. The opening of *Portrait,* the voice of the father, is also the opening of narrative possibility: "Once upon a time and a very good time it was . . ." (7). The time is what Bakhtin terms the "absolute past" (34), the infinitely distant time of earliest narrative. There is no separation between this narrative event and Stephen himself: "he was baby tuckoo." Yet, as soon as the relationship is posited, it collapses; the "wild rose blossoms" song is deformed through Stephen's lisping and transposition to emerge as a new song that is "his song." From this point on there can be no unmediated, purely received language for the boy; indeed, the narrative patterns which had been so easily committed to memory in the child's infancy—his perfect past—take on a life of their own. The "Pull out his eyes, / Apologise" rhyme which, eerily, seems to be narrated by no one at all, serves as metonym for alien language. Hiding under the table is no protection; as Kenner has pointed out, the chiasmic structure of the rhyme will be echoed throughout the remainder of the book, and becomes one of the most easily identifiable patterns of Stephen's thought.[4]

At each significant stage in the development of Stephen's consciousness, he undergoes a period of painful sensitivity to "raw" language, language that seems in some respects to lack denotation. In structuralist terms, he is confronted by the signifier in the absence of the signified. In the first chapter, he dwells upon his own name and God's name (which seem to mean nothing) (16), the self-describing word "suck" (11), the ambiguous word "belt" (9), the deceptive word "heartburn" (11), and even the sounds that are almost-words, like the "little song of the gas" (14). On the trip to Cork, the word "foetus" triggers a series of vague realizations that seem to have no rational connection with the word's reference, and he is given to mindless narration:

> I am Stephen Dedalus. I am walking beside my father whose name is Simon Dedalus. We are in Cork, in Ireland. Cork is a city. Our room is in the Victoria Hotel. Victoria and Stephen and Simon. Simon and Stephen and Victoria. Names. (92)

Names, with their purely ostensive quality rush in to fill the empty spaces in his thought. When he attempts to write a poem for Parnell, the names of his Clongowes classmates appear beneath his pen (70). During the retreat, Stephen begins to fear that he is a mere beast, and " a faint glimmer of fear began to pierce the fog of his mind. . . . The letters of the name of Dublin lay heavily upon his mind, pushing one another surlily hither and thither with slow boorish insistence" (111). Yet there is a reassurance in the very alienness of these words over which he has no power, a reassurance like that offered by the embrace of patriarchal language which is simply there, given and unmediated. After his performance in the Whitsuntide play, in a state of agitation and unable to face E.C. and his family, he can calm his heart only by staring at "the word *Lotts* on the wall of the lane" (86). And words which are not names can be made to relinquish their denotations, to become empty and thus no longer a threat. Stephen awakens from sleep on the train to Cork filled with vague fear:

> His prayer . . . ended in a trail of foolish words which he made to fit the insistent rhythm of the train; and silently . . . the telegraphpoles held the galloping notes of the music between punctual bars. This furious music allayed his dread and, leaning against the windowledge, he let his eyelids close again. (87)

During his self-consciously esthetic phase, Stephen begins to learn to allow a dialogue between the alien language that surrounds him and his own generative power, so that the menacing quality of words is first converted to a reassuring empty neutrality, and then to creative possibility in the form of a literal heteroglossia, and an abandonment to language:

> [He] found himself glancing from one casual word to another on his right or left in stolid wonder that they had been so silently emptied of instantaneous sense until every mean shop legend bound his mind like the words of a spell . . . as he walked on in a lane among heaps of dead language. His own consciousness of language was ebbing from his brain and trickling into the very words themselves which set to band and disband themselves in wayward rhythms. . . . The word now shone in his brain, clearer and brighter than any ivory sawn from the mottled tusks of elephants. *Ivory, ivoire, avorio, ebur.* (178–79)

II
INTONATIONAL QUOTATION AND INCREMENTAL REPETITION

Stephen is at least partially aware of his relationship with disembodied forms of language, language without context, *parole* magically divorced form *langue.* He is much less conscious of his assimilation of embodied forms, languages that approach the sequentiality of narrative. Yet these are clearly signalled in the text of the novel, first by the multitude of sentences and phrases that should be enclosed in Bakhtin's "intonational quotation marks" (76), then by Joyce's striking use of incremental repetition in the narration of *Portrait*.[5] Both of these effects are most prevalent in the first chapter, during the critical period when Stephen is exposed to the varieties of public language used by his school fellows and masters, and both are embedded in the *style indirecte libre,* the pseudo-stream-of-consciousness narration through which we experience much of Stephen's life.[6]

The intonational quotation marks make their appearance almost immediately in the second section of the first chapter; Stephen is brooding over new and strange expressions—those that are not "nice," those that have the odd authority of schoolboy jargon, those that have the ring of the adult language-world of moral imperatives, or those that unmistakably smack of mysterious taboos:

> Rody Kickham was not like that: *he would be captain of the third line* all the fellows said.

> Rody Kickham was *a decent fellow* but Nasty Roche was *a stink.*

> And his father had told him if he wanted anything to write home to him and, whatever he did, *never to peach on a fellow.* (8–9)

Was it true about the black dog that walked there at night *with eyes as big as carriagelamps?* (19)

What did that mean about *the smugging in the square?* (42)

The boy tries the strange phrases in his mind, repeating them over and over, replacing them within changing contexts, conjugating them as he would his Latin verbs:

Was that a sin for Father Arnall *to be in a wax* or was he allowed *to get into a wax* when the boys were idle because that made them study better or was he only letting on *to be in a wax?* (48)

For long stretches during this phase of his development Stephen's thoughts simply are not his own. His mind buzzes with borrowed expressions, languages which he tries on like suits of clothing; but unlike his grey belted suit he cannot discard them at will. Just as with the words emptied of meaning, there is a certain reassurance in repeating word sequences he has learned; ironically, in his illness he enjoys repeating "Canker is a disease of plants / Cancer one of animals" (10, 21). But even when the words are ostensibly his own, Stephen characteristically *recites* them, rehearsing these miniature narratives in a form which he later repeats, with minor variations. While pretending to play football, he thinks,

That was mean of Wells to shoulder him into the square ditch because he would not swop his little snuffbox for Wells's seasoned hacking chestnut, the conqueror of forty. How cold and slimy the water had been! A fellow had once seen a big rat jump into the scum. (10)

Soon after, in the playroom, he is taunted by Wells, and thinks:

It was Wells who had shouldered him into the square ditch the day before because he would not swop his little snuffbox for Wells's seasoned hacking chestnut, the conqueror of forty. It was a mean thing to do; all the fellows said it was. And how cold and slimy the water had been! And a fellow had once seen a big rat jump plop into the scum. (14)

Here not only can we hear the echo of the schoolboy phrases describing the items to be exchanged—almost kennings in their ritual, formulaic quality—but we can also witness the development of a narrative Stephen prepares *as if* to tell his classmates. The second, somewhat more sophisticated version, has the advantages of an appeal to consensus and a literary touch ("plop").

Caryl Emerson has pointed out that in Bakhtin's model the individual "forms lateral ('horizontal') relationships with other individuals in specific speech acts, and he simultaneously forms internal ('vertical') relationships" between the outer world and his own psyche. These double activities are constant, and their interactions in fact *constitute* the psyche."[7] As Joyce's narrative presents the process of Stephen's consciousness, the formation of "vertical" relationships is suggested by the boy's mulling upon the universe of given words and phrases. The formation of "horizontal" or interpersonal relationships is mirrored not simply in the passages of dialogue—where, in fact, Stephen does his best to perform uninterrupted monologues—but in repeated meditations such as the passage on Wells. The potentially public context of this narrative fragment should not mislead us; Stephen's mind works in much the same way when he has no intention of presenting his thoughts to an audience. For instance, his Christmas dinner meditation on Eileen recurs, hardly altered, on his return to Clongowes, triggered by the thought of Tusker Boyle's fingernails:

> Eileen had long white hands. One evening when playing tig she had put her hands over his eyes: long and white and thin and cold and soft. That was ivory: a cold white thing. That was the meaning of *Tower of Ivory*. (36)

> Eileen had long thin cool white hands too because she was a girl. They were like ivory; only soft. That was the meaning of *Tower of Ivory* but protestants could not understand it and made fun of it. (42)

Repetition lulls Stephen, as it does any child; he identifies the smell of the peasants in the back of the chapel as "air and rain and turf and corduroy," and then immediately afterwards imagines himself in their cottage breathing "the smell of peasants, air and rain and turf and corduroy" (18). Sometimes, indeed, the thought of repetition itself evinces a formal repetition. In the refectory:

> He leaned his elbows on the table and shut and opened the flaps of his ears. Then he heard the noise of the refectory every time he opened the flaps of his ears. It made a roar like a train at night. And when he closed the flaps the roar was shut off like a train going into a tunnel. . . . He closed his eyes and the train went on, roaring and then stopping; roaring again, stopping. (13)

Shortly afterward, in the study hall, he thinks of the alternation of term and vacation:

> It was like a train going in and out of tunnels and that was like the noise of the boys eating in the refectory when you opened and closed the flaps of the ears. Term, vacation; tunnel, out; noise, stop. (17)

Several things are going on simultaneously in such passages. Certainly we are being shown the young verbal artist, forming and treasuring his phrases before he is aware he is doing so, just as later, in a moment of stress or exaltation, he will draw forth "a phrase from his treasure" (166). We are also being played upon by Joyce's most characteristic rhetorical turn, lyrical repetition.[8] But most importantly we are being shown a mind whose mode of conscious perception is narrative. Stephen not only thinks but perceives in phrases and sentences. We might say his consciousness is "narratized."

But the most arresting examples of incremental repetition are not, strictly speaking, repetitions for which Stephen is directly responsible at all: they are embedded in sections of the narrative that only obliquely represent his train of thought. The relationship between narrator and protagonist has been a crux of Joyce criticism for years; for the present argument it is probably most important to realize that although the narration eschews overt retrospection, moving through time with Stephen and altering its language as his consciousness grows more sophisticated—most obviously in the movement from paratactic to hypotactic structures between the first and second chapters—nonetheless, at least until the final section of the book, where Stephen himself narrates through his diary the narration is always in advance of Stephen.[9] Perhaps this enveloping narration can best be imagined as a more articulate, more sophisticated version of the narrative he is constantly creating about himself. Yet despite its relative sophistication, it is more closely linked with the verbal structures of Stephen's mind than is the case in any earlier *Bildungsroman*. For Joyce, as for Bakhtin, consciousness itself is all but identified with language, and both consciousness and language develop through interactive processes. "Consciousness becomes consciousness only once it has been filled with ideological (semiotic) content, consequently only in the process of social interaction," and language is "the semiotic material of inner life—of consciousness (inner speech)."[10]

Yet it is the very literal way Joyce shows language to be the material of Stephen's inner life that is responsible for the difficulty in ascertaining the epistemological status of the book's narration, a problem that is most acute in the early sections of the novel. The opening paragraph of the Clongowes section, which moves from a description of the playground to Stephen's thoughts about himself and Rody Kickham, is a case in point: the sentences become smoothly and increasingly "internal." Midway through the paragraph, we read, "after every charge and thud of the footballers the greasy leather orb flew like a heavy bird through the grey light" (8). Later, ill in bed, Stephen remembers himself "a long time ago then out on the playgrounds in the evening light, creeping from point to point on the fringe of his line, a heavy bird flying low through the grey light" (22). The language that had been ambiguously attached to the narration has now become more intimately associated with Stephen; in the second passage we are being given something close to the hallucinatory stream-of-consciousness. But is the bird image Stephen's? And if so, are we to assume he is conscious of this? It has undergone a transformation during the intervening time, so that now it seems to refer to the boy himself, the fledgling poet-albatross, rather than simply to the football.

This effect is still more evident in another repeated passage describing the sound of the cricketbats "through the soft grey air. They said: pick, pack, pock, puck: like drops of water in a fountain slowly falling in the brimming bowl" (41). At the chapter's close, Stephen listens in the "soft grey silence," and hears "through the quiet air the sound of the cricket bats: pick, pack, pock, puck: like drops of water in a fountain falling softly in the brimming bowl" (59). Unlike the passages of schoolboy language, we are given no implied source for the words; they simply come to Stephen, as if they had been given by the narrator. Yet what can this mean? The passage, in both versions, is in a sort of "Edwardian novelese" (to use Kenner's term) with echoes of Pater, Meredith and, particularly, Swinburne;[11] on the level of symbolism, the referents are only slightly more mysterious than those of the "heavy bird" passage. At least since Joseph Frank's "Spatial Form in Modern Literature" we have learned to accept such language and imagery as part of the mosaic pattern of the book, as formal markers of Joyce's presiding esthetic consciousness.[12] Yet to read the passages thus is a betrayal of the very language before us and of the phenomenological acuity of the novel. The words are Stephen's, only slightly less so than if he had spoken them aloud. If we must specify a source, they are the language of his own future consciousness, which is to be formed in part by the "subversive authors" (78) from whom his verbal style will derive.

The text of *Portrait,* with all its stylized incremental repetition and all its virtuoso verbal effects, is nonetheless fundamentally bound to the narrative of Stephen's consciousness; it should be read more mimetically than we are accustomed to reading it. The boy is learning a language, and the incremental repetition witnesses to that process. Within the context of the chapter, perhaps, we are tempted to regard it as Stephen's own language, but in the context of the book as a whole we may well doubt that such a characterization has much meaning. Neither Stephen nor Joyce (as "implied author") possesses a language purely his own here; as Bakhtin has noted with respect to *Eugene Onegin,* there is a mutual interpenetration of author's and protagonist's speech. "The hero is located in a zone of potential conversation with the author, in a zone of *dialogical contact*"; the author "dialogizes [the protagonist's language] from without" (45, 46).

III

DIALOGISM

Stephen is a product of his listening and reading, an irrational sum of the texts, written and spoken, to which he has been exposed. He is aware that his reading emerges, in distorted and syncretic form, in his writings, as when he admits that "all the leisure which his school life left him was passed in the company of subversive writers whose gibes and violence of speech set up a ferment in his brain before they passed out of it into his crude writings" (78). He is much less aware that the very structure of his consciousness is dependent upon these texts, but it is significant that when he inadvertently alters a text he reacts with inordinate self-disgust. Misquoting a line of Nash's can convince him that "his mind bred vermin" and "His thoughts were lice born of the sweat of sloth" (234).

To a surprising extent, his relationship with the Church is a linguistic affair; during the retreat sermon, the distinctions among the text of the sermon proper, Stephen's retrospective paraphrase of it, and his inner reflections become hopelessly blurred. His religious crisis thus appears a clear case of possession by liturgical language, which will require exorcism by the prostitutes. Even his temptation to join the priesthood seems, almost ludicrously, largely a matter of curiosity about definitions: "He would know then what was the sin of Simon Magus and what the sin against the Holy Ghost . . ." (159). We are reminded of the young boy's painful curiosity about the words around him, and his attempts to assume the languages he hears, just as "he had assumed the voices and gestures which he had noted with various priests" (158). In a similar manner, but silently, he had narrated his imaginary reconciliation with Emma in the voice of the Blessed Virgin, a voice drawn from the religious texts of his childhood: "Take hands, Stephen and Emma. It is a beautiful evening now in heaven. You have erred but you are always my children . . ." (116). At the opposite extreme of experience, Stephen is appalled to discover that his most heartfelt cry of bestial anguish is "but the echo of an obscene scrawl which he had read on the oozing wall of a urinal" (100).

For Stephen, as for Bakhtin, the distinction between text and voice is minimal, not only because he is hypersensitive to intonation and style in written language but also because public discourse in Ireland was then, as it is now, a highly written phenomenon; *logos* and *graphesis* interpenetrate. The speech he hears is unusually literary, not in its context and content, but in its discrete stylization, its consciously idiosyncratic formulation, and its rich and precise allusiveness. Dismissing the Irish public leaders of today, in contrast to the great men of the past, Simon Dedalus says, "No, Stephen, old chap, I'm sorry to say that they are only as I roved out one fine May morning in the merry month of sweet July" (97). Simon's use of language itself as metonym here is a characteristically sophisticated colloquial turn.

Throughout the book, Stephen studies accents, vocabularies, intonation and delivery much like an actor unsure which of an infinity of possible parts he will be called upon to play. Having heard his father imitate the "mincing nasal tone of the provincial," Father Conmee (72), Stephen establishes a schoolboy reputation as mimic, assuming "the rector's pendantic bass. . . . *He that will not hear the churcha let him be to theea as the heathena and the publicana*" (75–76). He imagines the "sleek lives of the patricians of Ireland" in Maple's Hotel who "gave orders to jarvies in high-pitched provincial voices which pierced through their skintight accents" (238). The "genteel accent, low and moist, marred by errors" of the old captain in the National Library suggests to him a noble lineage which has been diluted by incest (228). He notes the "sharp Ulster voice" of MacAlister (193) and the "hard jingling tone" of the dean of studies (187), while his attitude toward his friends seems determined by their speech habits. He is "won over to sympathy" by Davin's "simple accent" (182). Lynch is favored for his habit of swearing in "yellow" and his detection of Cranly's pretentious solecism "let us eke go" (204), while Cranly's usage of "sugar" as a vulgarism to denote dead friendships strikes Stephen as a "heavy lumpish phrase" and brings on a gloomy meditation on his companion's speech:

> Cranly's speech, unlike that of Davin, had neither rare phrases of Elizabethan English nor quaintly turned versions of Irish idioms. Its drawl was an echo of the quays of Dublin given back by a bleak decaying seaport, its energy an echo of the sacred eloquence of Dublin given back flatly by a Wicklow pulpit. (195)

Stephen finds a certain derivative shoddiness in Cranly's voice before he becomes aware of his friend's limitations; he anticipates betrayal in Cranly's language before he detects a hint of it in his friend's actions and manner.

In an essay that lays stress upon the social dimension of Stephen's consciousness of language, James Naremore points out that "Stephen's own rather prissy, formal way of speaking is, as he himself tells us, a carefully acquired habit, an attempt to disentangle himself from his environment and the 'nets' which have been flung at him."[13] But of course this attempt is foredoomed; Stephen has no choice but to select among the languages surrounding him, languages that speak through and within him regardless of his wishes. Bakhtin emphasizes the stratification of literary languages, both written and spoken.:

> Certain features of language (lexicological, semantic, syntactic) will knit together with the intentional aim, and with the overall accentual system inherent in one or another genre: oratorical, publicistic, newspaper and journalistic genres, the genres of low literature (penny dreadfuls, for instance) or, finally, the various genres of high literature. . . . In addition, there is interwoven with this generic stratification of language a *professional* stratification of language . . . : the language of the lawyer, the doctor, the businessman, the politician, the public education teacher and so forth. (288–89)

For all of his objectifying analysis of the social and literary languages surrounding him, all of his attempts to eschew the language of the marketplace, Stephen eventually must become aware that his own language is a hybrid, that he is *spoken through* even in his private thoughts, in a sort of mental ventriloquy. He could hardly ignore this, since his entire formal education has been based upon the inculcation of "key passages" from a variety of sources; his accomplishment has been evaluated with an eye to his ready and graceful appropriation of such tags and passages in his own essays. As Don Gifford notes,

> Stephen's knowledge is based on a study of selected passages, key points or moments, presented in textbooks which advertised themselves as *Synopsis of the Philosophy of.* . . . As Stephen puts it to himself, he has "only a garner of slender sentences." The educational practice of focusing study on memorable key quotations provided the student with a package of quotable phrases and tended to suggest that thought was aphorism.[14]

That Stephen has a reputation for originality is not a reflection of any putative originality of discourse; rather, it is due to his ability to harness traditional authority to unusual contexts—as when he quotes Aquinas and the physiologist Luigi Galvani in support of a Pateresque esthetic—and to call upon unusual or obscure sources such as Giordano Bruno. And this is true not only of Stephen's public performances within the book, but of the current of his thoughts as well. There it also becomes clear that Stephen's internal discourse is composed of a spectrum of popular languages as well as literary ones. In the two concluding chapters, Stephen assumes a variety of voices, and is sometimes disturbed to discover himself doing so. Annoyed by a fellow student's dully pragmatic question at a lecture, Stephen thinks that "the student's father would have done better had he sent his son to Belfast to study and have saved something on the train fare by so doing"; and then immediately he corrects himself. "That thought is not mine, he said to himself quickly. It came from the comic Irishman in the bench behind" (193). As we immediately recognize, it cames from Simon Dedalus, whose language Stephen so reluctantly shares.

A complete acknowledgment of the extent to which his mind is an amalgam of preexisting texts would be difficult and painful for the young artist. He has a personal investment in the romantic concept of self, an authentic and vital soul that, like God, creates *ab nihilo.* In his esthetic, the artist's personality, purely expressed in the lyric, passes into narration in the epic, and is finally refined out of existence in the dramatic form. But in *Portrait* the reverse is more nearly the case: an originally undifferentiated ego slowly takes on form and selfhood, expressed as inner narrative, by way of a continuous series of dialogic encounters with and among the languages surrounding it, from which the artist has always already vanished.

Notes

1.   Hugh Kenner, *Dublin's Joyce* (Bloomington: Indiana Univ. Press, 1956), 12. Robert Scholes and Richard M. Kain, *The Workshop of Daedalus* (Evanston, Ill.: Northwestern Univ. Press, 1965), xiii. Cf. *The Dialogic Imagination: Four Essays by M. M. Bakhtin,* ed. Michael

Holquist (Austin: Univ. of Texas Press, 1981), 47, on *Eugene Onegin:* "The author participates in the novel (he is omnipresent in it) with *almost no direct language of his own.*"

2.   *Dialogic Imagination,* xxix. Joyce would seem to be the perfect illustration of nearly all of Bakhtin's major concepts, and was certainly known to Bakhtin's circle in the 1930's. Katerina Clark and Michael Holquist in *Mikhail Bakhtin* (Cambridge: Harvard Univ. Press, 1984), 317, point out that between 1934 and 1965 Joyce could not be praised in print in the Soviet Union, which left Bakhtin the choice of condemning him or remaining silent on the subject. All further citations of this work will be included parenthetically in the text.

3.   *A Portrait of the Artist as a Young Man,* ed. Chester Anderson (New York: Viking Press, 1968), 156. All further citations of this work will be included parenthetically in the text.

4.   On chiasmic structure (essentially repetition with formal rearrangement), see Hugh Kenner, *Ulysses* (London: George Allen & Unwin, 1980), 7–8 and passim. See also Elliott B. Gose, Jr., "Destruction and Creation in *A Portrait of the Artist as a Young Man," James Joyce Quarterly* 22 (Spring 1985): 259–70.

5.   On the significance of repetition in a somewhat different context, see J. Hillis Miller, *Fiction and Repetition* (Cambridge, Mass.: Harvard Univ. Press, 1982). Discussing Bakhtin's own repetitiousness; Caryl Emerson observes that, strictly speaking, Bakhtin does not admit the idea of simple repetition: "Nothing 'recurs'; the same word over again might accumulate, reinforce, perhaps parody what came before it, but it cannot be the same word if it is in a different place." Preface to Bakhtin, *Problems of Dostoevsky's Poetics* (Minneapolis: Univ. of Minnesota Press, 1984), xxv. My essay explores a special instance of this idea.

6.   Although I am restricting my discussion to the rather special case of the dialogizing of Stephen's own language, as embodied in indirect inner monologue, it should be noted that the more "objective" narrative sections of *Portrait* elegantly demonstrate the heteroglossia of Joyce's voice in what Bakhtin designates as "character zones," "the field of action of a character's voice, encroaching in one way or another upon the author's voice" (316). This of course corresponds closely to what Kenner has termed the "Uncle Charles Principle" in *Joyce's Voices* (Berkeley: University of California Press, 1978), 15–38.

7.   Caryl Emerson, "The Outer Word and Inner Speech: Bakhtin, Vygotsky, and the Internalization of Language," *Critical Inquiry* 10 (December 1983): 248, 249. Reprinted in Gary Saul Morson, ed., *Bakhtin: Essays and Dialogues on His Work* (Chicago: Univ. of Chicago Press, 1986), 21–40.

8.   Frank O'Connor first pointed out—rather scornfully—the crucial role of repetition in Joyce's lyrical mode in a passage reprinted in Anderson, ed., *Portrait,* 371–77. It seems clear that repetition and rearrangement, from the level of the phoneme through that of entire passages, is a major determinant of Joyce's prose, though far less obviously than in the work of his rival Gertrude Stein.

9.   See R. B. Kershner, Jr., "Time and Language in Joyce's *Portrait," ELH* 43 (1976): 604–19.

10.   V. N. Volosinov, *Marxism and the Philosophy of Language,* trans. Ladislav Matejka and I. R. Titunik (New York: Seminar Press, 1973), 11, 14. Caryl Emerson suggests that Bakhtin either wrote this work or was a dominant collaborator with Volosinov (*Critical Inquiry* 10: 261 n. 2).

11.   *Joyce's Voices,* 68.

12.   Joseph Frank, "Spatial Form in Modern Literature," *Sewanee Review* 8: 2–4 (Spring–Autumn 1945), adapted in *The Widening Gyre: Crisis and Mastery in Modern Literature* (New Brunswick, N.J.: Rutgers Univ. Press, 1963).

13.   James Naremore, "Consciousness and Society in *A Portrait of the Artist,*" in Thomas F. Staley and Bernard Benstock, eds., *Approaches to Joyce's "Portrait": Ten Essays* (Pittsburgh: Univ. of Pittsburgh Press, 1976), 128–29.

14.   Don Gifford, *Joyce Annotated,* 2nd ed. (Berkeley: Univ. of California Press, 1982), 10. Sidney Feshbach in "Writ Our Bit as Intermidgets: Classical Rhetoric in the Early Writing of James Joyce" argues that Joyce's early style, like Stephen's, is "based directly on some of the most traditional European conventions." *James Joyce Quarterly* 17 (Summer 1980): 379.

Riddles, Silence, and Wonder: Joyce and Wittgenstein Encountering the Limits of Language

Thomas C. Singer

I

Words and Worlds

From August of 1914 through the end of 1916 a Viennese serving as a soldier in the Austro-Hungarian army kept a notebook in which he recorded his reflections on language, thought, and the world. An entry for May 23, 1915 reads, "*Die Grenzen meiner Sprache* bedeuten die Grenzen meiner Welt": *The limits of my language* means the limits of my world.[1] During these same years an Irish expatriate living in the Austro-Hungarian port city of Trieste was reworking a novel for serialization in the English literary journal *The Egoist*. In the issue for May 1, 1914 the young hero of the novel listens to his elders speaking of politics, their native land, and the stories of their families: "Words which he did not understand he said over and over to himself till he had learned them by heart: and through them he had glimpses of the real world about him."[2] In the December 15, 1914 issue of *The Egoist* this young man becomes aware that he is breaking with the religious traditions of his family and country, and he "feel[s] a regret and pity as though he were slowly passing out of an accustomed world and were hearing its language for the last time" (*P*, 156). James Joyce and Ludwig Wittgenstein were hearing the language of prewar Europe for the last time. But in *A Portrait of the Artist as a Young Man* and the *Tractatus Logico-Philosophicus* we can hear something quite different: for the first time we can hear the language of our age and our world.

It is one of history's unexpected gestures that the Austro-Hungarian Empire should have provided the scene for the early writings of an Irishman and a Viennese who would become, respectively, the most acclaimed and influential prose writer and philosopher of the English-speaking world for the middle and late twentieth century. Ludwig Wittgenstein would finish out the

Reprinted from *English Literary History* 57, no. 2 (Summer 1990): 459–84. © The Johns Hopkins University Press.

war as a prisoner in Italy before his eventual move to England. In order to avoid imprisonment as an unfriendly alien—as happened to his brother Stanislaus—James Joyce would flee Trieste for neutral Zurich in July of 1915, only two months before the appearance of the final installment of *A Portrait of the Artist as a Young Man*. Although Joyce briefly returned to Trieste after the war, he finished *Ulysses* in Paris in 1921, the same year in which Wittgenstein finally found a publisher for the work he had begun in his notebooks, the *Tractatus Logico-Philosophicus*.

In elaborating his theory of art the hero of the *Portrait,* Stephen Dedalus, announces: "For my purpose I can work on at present by the light of one or two ideas of Aristotle and Aquinas" (*P,* 187). In this essay I propose to work by a somewhat analogous method and will bring forth some of Wittgenstein's ideas on the assumption that they may serve as a lamp to throw light on Joyce's *Portrait.* As my brief historical introduction suggests, Joyce and Wittgenstein were both contemporaries in time and citizens, for a while, of the declining Austro-Hungarian Empire. But it is the intellectual affinities, rather than historical, political, or sociological ones, that I wish to explore here. Common to both of these writers is a fascination with the relationship between our language and our world, with the way in which the one both creates and is created by the other.

So interrelated are word and world that the one can be easily confused for the other. The editorial history of *Ulysses* proves just how. When thinking of "hell," Martha Clifford writes in her letter to Leopold Bloom, "I called you naughty boy because I do not like that other world" (*U,* 63). The old Modern Library edition of 1934 changed "world" to "word," and the new Modern Library edition of 1961 changed it back again. This is just the kind of confusion upon which Joyce built the towers of his major works. Moreover, as *Portrait* shows, this very confusion can be the beginning of clarity if it poses to us the riddle of our existence. This is not a riddle that is resolved by our possession of any answer. Rather, the riddle is itself its own answer insofar as it is a sign that points silently to the miraculousness of existence, of wonder before the world that calls forth from us an affirmation of the spirit of life.

Wittgenstein and Joyce are strikingly similar in the methods they employ to reawaken in us this feeling of wonder before the world. In the first place, they are united in thinking of themselves as both poets and philosophers. Joyce's literary hero was Dante, "the first poet of the Europeans" (*SH,* 41) and the great synthesizer of medieval thought in verse. Indeed, at times Joyce conceived of himself as doing for the early twentieth century what Dante had done for the early fourteenth. Stephen Dedalus is redolent with "the true scholastic stink" (*P,* 214), disliking only the premises of medieval philosophy, and he freely admits that his aesthetic is "applied Aquinas" (*P,* 209), as is obvious in the final chapter of *Portrait.* His creator Joyce wrote poetic prose with a feeling for design and symmetry that recalls a medieval builder constructing a cathedral in stone or a *Summa philosophica* in words.

Wittgenstein, for his part, has affinities with the ascetic Catholicism of the seventeenth-century master of French prose style, Blaise Pascal. But more directly, he conceived of his philosophy as being a kind of poetry: "I think I summed up my attitude to philosophy when I said: philosophy ought really to be written only as a *poetic composition*" (*CV,* 24). The conclusion of the *Tractatus,* as well as the many parts of his other writings where he relies on metaphor to convey his meaning, do approach poetry, much to the dismay of more traditional academic philosophers. Wittgenstein believed that philosophy ought to be written as a poetic composition if only that, as for Pascal, the style of presentation was of supreme importance. Two years before his death Wittgenstein wrote, " 'Le style c'est l'homme même.' . . . [A] man's style is a *picture* of him" (*CV,* 78).

Joyce's and Wittgenstein's philosophical poetics begin by exposing a state of paralysis. For Wittgenstein this paralysis comes from our bewilderment by notions of the ideal in language and in thought: "The ideal, as we think of it, is unshakable. . . . It is like a pair of glasses on our nose through which we see whatever we look at. It never occurs to us to take them off" (*PI,* #103). The problem with the ideal is that one can do nothing with it—it is a wheel that turns but does no work, that does not connect with anything else. "We have got on to slippery ice where there is no friction and so in a certain sense the conditions are ideal, but also, just because of that, we are unable to walk. We want to walk: so we need *friction.* Back to the rough ground!" (*PI,* #107). Wittgenstein wants to unmask the ideal, to point the way back to the rough ground. When Stephen's mother says to him that she "would like to read some great writer, to see what ideal of life he has," Stephen replies in exasperation, "But that is wrong: that is the great mistake everyone makes. Art is not an escape from life! . . . [It] is the central expression of life" (*SH,* 85–86). Here, Stephen is only repeating what his young creator already had made clear to the mystical poet A.E. (George Russell) when he went calling on him in the middle of the night in 1902 and proclaimed to him that he "abhorred the Absolute above everything else."[3] However it is that art illuminates our lives, it is not by the light of the ideal, it is not "a light from another world" (*P,* 212). Explaining his intention in writing the early collection of stories *Dubliners,* Joyce wrote to his friend C. P. Curran that he wished "to betray the soul of that . . . paralysis which many consider a city" (*LT,* 1:55). Like "the late lamented Patrick Morkan" and his "never-to-be-forgotten Johnny" in "The Dead" (*D,* 207), his characters circle around and around the center of an empty ideal, persuaded only that they are not paralyzed because they move about in place.

What ties these two writers together above all else is their belief that the ordinary is the extraordinary, that the wonder of this world is not hidden behind any veils but is open to our view, and that language is both a revelation of this wonder and its riddle. Wittgenstein writes: "And I will now describe the experience of wondering at the existence of the world by saying:

it is the experience of seeing the world as a miracle. Now I am tempted to say that the right expression in language for the miracle of the existence of the world, though it is not any proposition in language, is the existence of language itself" (*LE,* 11). Wittgenstein adds that "we cannot express what we want to express": which is to say that we cannot say the wonder, the miracle—but we can show it. Indeed, "the existence of language itself" is one way in which "the world as a miracle" shows itself.

II
DUBLIN'S BALLAST OFFICE CLOCK AND WITTGENSTEIN'S STOVE

Stephen tells his friend Cranly during one of their peripatetic walks through the city of Dublin "that the clock of the Ballast Office was capable of an epiphany," by which he means "a sudden spiritual manifestation" (*SH,* 211). Stephen intends to shock Cranly by locating the wonderful in the trivial, in an object that they pass by daily on their walks so that through constant familiarity it has become almost invisible to them. In the section of *Portrait* that appeared in the June 1, 1915 issue of *The Egoist,* Stephen identifies the three "necessary phases of artistic apprehension." Following his reading of Aquinas, they are *integritas, consonantia,* and *claritas.* "When you have apprehended that [thing] as one thing and have then analysed it according to its form and apprehended it as a thing you make the only synthesis which is logically and esthetically permissible. You see that it is that thing which it is and no other thing. The radiance of which he [Aquinas] speaks is the scholastic *quidditas,* the *whatness* of a thing" (*P,* 211–13). That is, first you separate the object from the world, *integritas,* then you see it as a world in and of itself, *consonantia,* and then its radiance, its *claritas,* its *whatness* will shine forth.

In a notebook entry for October 8, 1916, Wittgenstein presents a similar "epiphany": "If I have been contemplating the stove, and then am told: but now all you know is the stove, my result does indeed seem trivial. For this represents the matter as if I had studied the stove as one among the many things in the world. But if I was contemplating the stove it was then my world, and everything else colourless by contrast with it" (*NB,* 83). Like Joyce with the Ballast Office clock, Wittgenstein first isolates his stove from the world that surrounds it, then sees it as a world in itself, and finally apprehends it in its radiant color, in its miraculous existence. This seeing of the stove as a world is the miracle of aesthetic perception. Twelve days later he writes in his notebook: "Aesthetically, the miracle is that the world exists. That what exists does exist" (*NB,* 86).

This insistence on the aesthetic properties of common, mass-produced objects like stoves and clocks, on the apprehension of their existence as pure objects, is one of the most characteristic gestures of the new sensibility of early twentieth-century culture. It appears during these years not just in literature and philosophy but in the visual arts as well. In 1914 Marcel Duchamp purchased his first readymade, the "Bottlerack," and he remarked that its "functionalism was . . . obliterated by that fact that I took it out of the earth and onto the planet of aesthetics."[4] The placing of the object by the mind and its perception as pure object become the fundamental elements of aesthetic vision.

Stephen uses the language of Catholic sacramental ritual for his aesthetic, showing, as Cranly tells him in *Portrait,* "how your mind is supersaturated with the religion in which you say you disbelieve" (*P,* 240). Cranly is observant, though it perhaps would be more correct to say it is not so much religion itself that fascinates Stephen as it is its language. Nevertheless, apart from terminology, Stephen has as much, if not more, in common with the aesthetic of Wittgenstein and the art of Duchamp as he shares with the theology of the Fathers of the Church. Duchamp, Joyce, and Wittgenstein all insist upon the extraordinary nature of the ordinary, and they do so in a way characteristic of early twentieth-century thought. The world is miraculous not because it is a reflection of some ideal or transcendental realm but simply because it *is.* And this holds equally for everything in the world. As Wittgenstein writes in his notebook on October 8, 1916, "As a thing among things, each thing is equally insignificant; as a world each one is equally significant" (*NB, 83*).

Wittgenstein's aesthetic is perhaps less well known than his critique of linguistic meaning in logic and in ordinary language. However, the two are very much related, so much so that I believe the one cannot be fully appreciated without some consideration of the other. Moreover, this play between the theory of aesthetics and the theory of linguistic meaning is as important in understanding Stephen Dedalus in Joyce's *Portrait* as it is in comprehending Wittgenstein's writings. Stephen's constant questioning of the meaning of words both leads to and influences his attempt to propound a theory of the nature of the beautiful and of the place of art in our lives. I first want briefly to show the place of Wittgenstein's aesthetics in the context of his better known logical and philosophical investigations, examining his collapsing of aesthetics and ethics, his distinction between showing and saying, and his conception of the place of silence and nonsense in philosophical thought. In the sections to follow, I will use these ideas to throw light on Joyce's *Portrait.*

In a letter to Ludwig von Ficker, a friend and prospective publisher of the *Tractatus Logico-Philosophicus,* Wittgenstein emphasized that the point of his book was "an ethical one." He tells von Ficker that he meant to include an additional sentence in his preface that would "perhaps be a key to the work." The sentence would have read: "My work consists of two parts: the one presented here plus all that I have not written." Given that the title of the book announces it to be a treatise on philosophical logic, Wittgenstein's statement of his purpose and his missing sentence are extremely enigmatic. The next sentence of his letter to von Ficker is equally puzzling: "[I]t is precisely this second part that is the important one" (*LF*, 56–57). The second part of the *Tractatus,* the unwritten part, is the important part. How are we to understand him?

The rest of this paragraph in Wittgenstein's letter offers only a partial clue as to what he might mean: "My book draws limits to the sphere of the ethical from the inside as it were, and I am convinced that this is the ONLY *rigorous* way of drawing those limits. In short, I believe that where *many* others today are just *gassing,* I have managed in my book to put everything firmly into place by being silent about it." Wittgenstein's concern is to "draw limits to the sphere of the ethical," and this must be done "from the inside." The "everything" that he has put "firmly into place" is the ethical rather than the logical; moreover, he has put it into place "by being silent about it." First in need of explanation here is what Wittgenstein understands by "the ethical."

On July 24, 1916, Wittgenstein writes in his notebook: "Ethics and aesthetics are one" (*NB,* 77). If ethics and aesthetics are one, then Wittgenstein is surely not using the word as philosophers traditionally do. On October 7 of that same year he explains how he understands the connection between what is more often considered to be two separate realms of thought and experience: "The work of art is the object seen *sub specie aeternitatis;* and the good life is the world seen *sub specie aeternitatis.* This is the connexion between art and ethics" (*NB,* 83). He adds: "The usual way of looking at things sees objects as it were from the midst of them, the view *sub specie aeternitatis* from outside. In such a way that they have the whole world as background." Wittgenstein's cryptic comments about the *Tractatus* in the letter to von Ficker become clearer if one remembers the reflections in the notebooks about his aesthetic contemplation of his stove. The stove has "the whole world as background" when it is isolated as a world. This is what it would mean to see the stove *sub specie aeternitatis.* And this makes his contemplation of the ordinary object an aesthetic experience.

During a conversation among the Vienna Circle in 1929 about Heidegger's *Being and Time,* Wittgenstein comments on the ethical, the limits of language, and nonsense: "This running-up against the limits of language is Ethics. . . . Yet the tendency represented by the running-up against *points to something.* St. Augustine already knew this when he said: What you wretch, so you want to avoid talking nonsense? Talk some nonsense, it makes no difference!" (*HD,* 80–81). When confronted with the ethical, the alternatives are silence or nonsense. Both have their place. In his published philosophical writings Wittgenstein leaned toward silence. In his writings Joyce preferred nonsense. But Wittgenstein never disparaged the nonsense of others—so long as they recognized it as such. As late as 1947 he reminded himself: "Don't *for heaven's sake,* be afraid of talking nonsense! But you must pay attention to your nonsense" (*CV,* 56).

Wittgenstein was only disturbed by those who wrote nonsense but did not recognize it as such—they are the ones, in the letter to von Ficker, who "are just *gassing*." In the "Lecture on Ethics" prepared for a society at Cambridge the year after his remarks on Heidegger, Wittgenstein again collapses the ethical and the aesthetic: "I am going to use the term Ethics," he announces, "in a sense which includes what I believe to be the most essential part of what is generally called Aesthetics" (*LE*, 4). This opens a discussion on the limits of language: "I see now that these nonsensical expressions [e.g., those about "the miracle of the existence of the world"] were not nonsensical because I had not yet found the correct expressions, but that their nonsensicality was their very essence. For all I wanted to do with them was just *to go beyond* the world and that is to say beyond significant language. My whole tendency and I believe the tendency of all men who ever tried to write or talk about Ethics or Religion was to run against the boundaries of language. This running against the walls of our cage is perfectly, absolutely hopeless" (*LE*, 11–12). "Absolutely hopeless" it may be, but the tendency is still significant; it still points to something; and that something is "the most important part."

When in the *Tractatus* Wittgenstein refers to the limits of his world he means the limits of the world of facts that can be represented by significant language. When in the "Lecture on Ethics" he refers to "running against the boundaries of language," he means the boundaries of significant language. Significant language forms "the walls of our cage," and it is absolutely hopeless to try to say something significant about the ethical, which lies outside. Outside is the world of art, of religious experience, of the mystical. About the outside we can only speak nonsense or be silent.

Wittgenstein writes in the *Philosophical Investigations,* "My aim is: to teach you to pass from a piece of disguised nonsense to something that is patent nonsense" (*PI,* #464). "Disguised nonsense" is only bad philosophy or bad criticism, while "patent nonsense" can be the stuff of art. He makes this paradox clearer by a later remark: "Don't take it as a matter of course, but as a remarkable fact, that pictures and fictitious narratives give us pleasure, occupy our mind.... ([F]ind it surprising, as something that disturbs you....)" And then, in a doubly parenthetical addition: "((The transition from patent nonsense to something which is disguised nonsense))" (*PI,* #524). Here, Wittgenstein considers the nature of bad art or bad philosophy, and so he reverses the terms of his earlier statement. But art ought to be surprising and wonderful: "One might say: art *shows* us the miracles of nature. It is based on the *concept* of the miracles of nature. (The blossom, just opening out. What is *marvellous* about it?) We say: 'Just look at it opening out!' " (*CV,* 56). But how do we distinguish art, "patent nonsense," from "disguised nonsense"?

The important difference is that art says: "just look!" Patent nonsense—*offenkundigen Unsinn*—is open to our view. It hides behind no veils. It lies right before us. It does not try to say, to explain, what is miraculous and marvelous about the blossom. On November 29, 1914, Wittgenstein writes in his notebook: "What *can* be shown cannot be said" (*NB,* 34). And toward the end of the *Tractatus* he writes: "There are, indeed, things that cannot be put into words. They *make themselves manifest.* They are what is mystical" (*TL,* #6.522).

What Wittgenstein is silent about—"All that I have not written"—is the ethical, the aesthetic, or the mystical. This is the important part because therein the existence of the world appears as a wonder. In the *Tractatus* Wittgenstein attempts to show the limits of philosophical thought and logical language: "It [philosophy] must set limits to what can be thought; and, in doing so, to what cannot be thought. It must set limits to what cannot be thought by working outwards through what can be thought" (*TL,* #4.114). Setting limits to logical thought from the inside is a double gesture, for thereby Wittgenstein also shows what is outside. About the outside he remains silent. By attempting to draw the limits of language from the inside, he avoids writing nonsense, at least until the conclusion of his treatise when "patent nonsense" does appear. Joyce's method, which is the method of the artificer, is different. He is not afraid of writing nonsense. But he is a great artist precisely because he pays attention to it.

Before moving to the *Portrait,* I should say a word on my method here. I am using Wittgenstein as a lamp to elucidate Joyce. This method is justified, I believe, precisely because the direction of illumination could easily be reversed: that is, it also would be possible to use Joyce as a lamp to elucidate Wittgenstein. In this essay there simply is not the space to do both. However, two brief examples, one on pain sensation, the other on language acquisition during infancy, will serve to point the direction in which such an analysis might proceed. I have chosen these specific examples because I think they touch on essential parts of Wittgenstein's arguments in the *Philosophical Investigations* and because they will be useful later in my analysis of *Portrait of the Artist.*

Wittgenstein asks in the *Philosophical Investigations:* "How do words *refer* to sensations? . . . [H]ow is the connexion between the name and the thing named set up? This question is the same as: how does a human being learn the meaning of the names of sensations?—of the word 'pain' for example" (*PI,* #244). Wittgenstein's argument on pain sensation is as controversial as it is central to his critique of the presuppositions of modern philosophy. The argument is meant to support his ideas about the impossibility of a private language, which in turn is the cornerstone of his attack on the notion that has ruled philosophy since Descartes, that what we can be most sure of and, hence, what we can ground our epistemology on, is the clearness and certainty of our own subjective ideas and sensations. But notice how Stephen learns the meaning of "heartburn" during his infancy: "When Dante made that noise after dinner and then put up her hand to her mouth: that was heartburn" (P, 11). Stephen thus shows that he has learned the meaning of "heartburn," and by extension of the rest of his vocabulary of pain sensation, not by the appearance of an inner sensation to which he afterward applies a name by a kind of private ostensive gesture but in the public realm where it is subject to publicly verifiable criteria. That is, Stephen already has learned the grammar of pain before he has given names to individual occurrences of it. As Wittgenstein insists: "When one says 'He [an inventor of a private language] gave a name to his sensation' one forgets that a great deal of stagesetting in the language is presupposed if the mere act of naming is to make sense. And when we speak of someone's having given a name to pain, what is presupposed is the existence of the grammar of the word 'pain'; it shews the post where this new word is stationed" (PI, #257).

Related to the problem of pain sensation is the larger question of how infants learn language. The *Philosophical Investigations* opens with Wittgenstein's discussion of—and eventual rejection of—the model of language acquisition presented in Augustine's *Confessions*. Augustine argues that language is built up out of separate instances of ostensive meaning. That is, first we learn the meaning of words by having someone point out individual objects to us. For example, "*this* is a chair," "*this* is a house." Then we learn how to piece these atomic units of meaning into sentences: "The chair is in the house." Wittgenstein concludes his discussion of Augustine: "And now, I think, we can say: Augustine describes the learning of human language as if the child came into a strange country and did not understand the language of the country; that is, as if it already had a language, only not this one. Or again, as if the child could already *think*, only not yet speak. And 'think' would here mean something like 'talk to itself' " (PI, #32). Wittgenstein's point is that the child must learn the grammar or language of ostensive definition before any learning by ostensive definition can take place. But what language can teach this grammar? Surely not the language of ostensive definition itself. Rather, Wittgenstein argues, in what is perhaps the central thesis of the *Philosophical Investigations,* that the child learns language as a form of life.

Compare how Stephen Dedalus learns language:

> Once upon a time a very good time it was there was a moocow coming down along the road and this moocow that was coming down along the road met a nicens little boy named baby tuckoo. . . .
> His father told him that story: his father looked at him through a glass: he had a hairy face.
> He was baby tuckoo. (P, 7)

Stephen's words come into the world not paired up with things, as in Augustine's model, but "in a fiction, in a dream of passion." His words first come in the language of fables. And language does not enter alone into the child's consciousness: it brings the child's sense of his own identity with it—"He was baby tuckoo." Joyce changes the Cartesian motto from *Cogito, ergo sum* to *Fabulo, ergo sum*. When Stephen first finds himself, he finds himself inscribed in a story, named by the language of his father's story. In *Portrait* Stephen will try to transform, through thought and art, the language and the identity that the world imposed on him during childhood. The creature will strive to become creator; the child to become a father.

III
THE GREEN WOTHE BOTHETH

Perhaps the most remarkable difference between the representation of Stephen Dedalus in *A Portrait of the Artist as a Young Man* and in what remains of *Stephen Hero* is the introduction into *Portrait* of numerous passages that show Stephen grappling with the meanings of particular words and with the nature of language in general. So insistent is Joyce, that the story of Stephen growing up is transformed into the story of his struggle with language—on the one hand with the language into which he was born, the language that identifies him as a turn-of-the-century Irish Catholic, *and* on the other hand with the language that he must create if he is to become an artist. The limits of Stephen's language mean the limits of his world. In rewriting *Stephen Hero*, Joyce designed his novel so that Stephen's language changes in pace with his world; in so doing Joyce made *Portrait* into the first characteristically twentieth-century story of a young man's education.

The story of Stephen's changing words and worlds, as an infant and a schoolchild, can be seen in miniature through his changing thoughts about a "green rose." This motif appears first in the opening section of the novel following the "baby tuckoo" tale:

> He was baby tuckoo. The moocow came down the road where Betty Byrne lived: she sold lemon platt.
> *O, the wild rose blossoms*
> *On the little green place.*
> He sang that song. That was his song.
> *O, the green wothe botheth.* (P, 7)

"He was baby tuckoo": language has formed Stephen. The tale of baby tuckoo presents him with a mirror in which he can see himself placed in a world. But immediately thereafter Stephen forms language, and by that act he creates a song that is his own: "That was his song." He makes the song his by putting his mark upon it, and through that metaformation comes creation: "the wild rose" becomes "the green wothe."

To the child first coming into language, there is no problem with a green rose. It is not that a green rose is more or less likely than any other kind of rose; rather, the question of its likeliness just does not arise as a problem. To the infant, the real and the unreal, words and things, are all equally new and therefore equally strange and wonderful and frightening. Nor is there any distinct problem with the meaning of words. Words have not yet collided with the world, so that nonsense and significant language are not recognizably antagonistic opposites.

However, linguistic meaning is a problem for the young schoolboy subject to the often brutal society of early education. When Stephen's schoolmate Wells asks him, "Tell us Dedalus, do you kiss your mother before you go to bed," Stephen does not know what to reply. When he answers "yes," his schoolmates mock him; when he answers "no," they mock him even more. Stephen is sure that there must be a right answer to the question, and he suspects that the answer can be located in the meaning of "to kiss": "What did that mean, to kiss? You put your face up like that to say goodnight and then his mother put her face down. That was to kiss" (*P*, 14–15). It is also at Clongowes that Stephen thinks again of "the green wothe": "White roses and red roses: those were beautiful colours to think of. . . . Perhaps a wild rose might be like those colours and he remembered the song about the wild rose blossoms on the little green place. But you could not have a green rose. But perhaps somewhere in the world you could" (*P*, 12). Stephen has discovered what Alice already knows when she meets Humpty Dumpty in *Through the Looking Glass:* you cannot do just anything with language—not unless you want to be subject to the ridicule of your classmates or to the polite disapproval of young girls. For the schoolboy a green rose is just nonsense. Stephen no longer knows what the words might mean. But because he remembers that once the words did make sense to him, he is left wondering whether "somewhere in the world you could have" one, whether there might be a world for those words after all.

More troubling, I believe, for our understanding of Stephen in both *Portrait* and in *Ulysses* is the meaning of "love." As was the case with the green rose, it is a word that made sense to Stephen at one time. Love was something that anyone could see: it was when, for example, his mother leaned over to kiss him, just as heartburn was "when Dante made that noise after dinner and then put up her hand to her mouth." But in the course of *Portrait* Stephen loses his sense of the obvious, the patent, meaning of love. At the conclusion of his walk with Cranly in the last chapter, his friend inquires:

—. . . Let me ask you a question. Do you love your mother? Stephen shook his head slowly.
—I don't know what your words mean, he said simply. (*P*, 240)

Is love then nonsense? And what kind? Furthermore, is love, as Hans Gabler asserts in his controversial addition to the "Scylla and Charybdis" chapter of *Ulysses: The Corrected Text,* the "word known to all men" (*U*, 161)?

IV
RIDDLE ME, RIDDLE ME, RANDY RO

The last proposition of the *Tractatus* reads: "What we cannot speak about we must pass over in silence" (*TL,* #7). This is not merely some kind of negative injunction. For Wittgenstein silence is a way of speaking, or, rather, a way of showing what cannot be said. As Wittgenstein insists in his letter to von Ficker, "I have managed in my book to put everything firmly into place by being silent about it." The second part of the *Tractatus,* all that Wittgenstein has not written, is the important part. This sounds like a riddle, like nonsense, and that is precisely what it is; but Wittgenstein, like Joyce, pays attention to his nonsense.

Joyce, too, is a master of silence. He was impatient with those modern artists who were merely obscure, and he claimed that he could justify every word in *Ulysses.* I believe that he might have made a similar assertion for *Portrait.* Of course, this rejection of obscurity does not make Joyce easy reading in the sense that the common reader might find Dickens or Thackery easy. Like Wittgenstein, Joyce chose a technique of elliptical exposition that allowed him to show what he cannot say. And because of this Joyce's readers are themselves left to make connections that other novelists would have made for them. The readers must fill the spaces of silence with words that are their own.

Two instances from *Portrait* of Joyce's elliptical construction, both of which bear on the subject of love, will serve as examples. During Stephen's short-lived translation into terrestrial sainthood, he thinks about the theological mysteries of the church: "The imagery through which the nature and kinship of the Three Persons of the Trinity were darkly shadowed forth in the books of devotion which he read—the Father contemplating from all eternity as in a mirror His Divine Perfections and thereby eternally begetting the Eternal Son . . . —were easier of mental acceptance by reason of their august incomprehensibility than was the simple fact that God had loved his soul from all eternity" (*P,* 149). Stephen, "the Eternal Son," is very serious about the "august incomprehensibility" of "the Father contemplating from all eternity as in a mirror His Divine Perfections." Joyce's method is not to tell us explicitly what he wants us to think. Instead, he gives us the earthly correlate to this theological mystery.

Stephen's father first appears in the novel at the beginning of the Christmas dinner scene at Bray: "Mr. Dedalus looked at himself in the pierglass above the mantelpiece, waxed out his moustache-ends and then, parting his coattails, stood with his back to the glowing fire: and still, from time to time, he withdrew a hand from his coattail to wax out one of his moustache-ends" (*P,* 27). Staring into the pierglass, the father admires his earthly perfections, his moustache-ends. The reader either makes the connection between these two passages or does not and is left to draw his or her own conclusions from it. Stephen *says* what he feels about the theological mystery of Catholicism at this point in his life; Joyce *shows* us what he thinks. And as he shows us throughout his writings, it is the mystery of human love rather than the "simple fact" of God's eternal love that fascinates him.

After his family has moved into the city of Dublin in chapter 2, Stephen tries to capture a moment of young romantic love in poetry, the goodnight farewell to Emma on the tram after he rides home with her following a party. Joyce had used a similar incident for one of his early epiphanies. However, Stephen is not so fortunate as his creator. His Byronic poem to "E——C——" never takes form in the novel, and while struggling with it he remembers another moment of poetic impasse: "He saw himself sitting at his table in Bray the morning after the discussion at the Christmas dinnertable, trying to write a poem about Parnell on the back of one of his father's second moiety notices" (*P,* 70). Stephen's attempt to write this poem about Parnell would have occurred, then, after the third section of chapter 1, the Christmas dinner scene, and before the fourth section, when Stephen seeks justice from the rector for his unfair pandying by Father Dolan. In the fourth section, Stephen and his classmates find historical models for themselves in their search for justice in "the senate and the Roman people" (*P,* 53). Joyce is a master of transitions, even when they come many pages later, but what has Parnell to do with Roman history?

The reader does not know if Stephen Dedalus ever completes the poem about Parnell after this initial impasse. But Joyce did: the poem was "Et tu, Healy," and John Joyce was so pleased with it he paid for its printing so that it could be circulated through Dublin and later claimed that he had even sent a copy to the Pope.[5] As the poem's title suggests, the betrayal of Parnell by his lieutenant, Healy, is likened to the betrayal of Julius Caesar by Brutus. Healy was a member of the so-called Bantry gang (*P,* 228), and Stephen will recall his father's hatred of them years later when he is jealous of Emma and fears that his friends are betraying him. Why does Joyce not signal this transition to us in *Portrait* itself? Surely no reader can make the connection between Stephen, Parnell, and Caesar with only the novel before him. Is it because Stephen himself cannot make the connection, cannot know why, at the pinnacle of his triumph among his cheering schoolmates, "he was alone" (*P,* 59), yet another Irish hero awaiting his betrayal by the very people for whom he has risked himself?

However, this explanation is not entirely convincing, for Joyce often signals information or themes to the reader that lie beyond the immediate knowledge of his characters. Was it because Joyce had already used a poem about the death of Parnell to end the *Dubliners* story "Ivy Day in the Committee Room"? Was the poem one of the many episodes contained in the lost parts of *Stephen Hero* that did not find an appropriate place in *Portrait*? Both of these suggestions might help explain why Joyce left "Et tu, Healy" out of *Portrait,* but they do not explain why he then left in the motif of "the senate and the Roman people," which is precisely the phrase that "Et tu, Healy" places in context. In any case, the key to the Roman motif lies outside *Portrait* itself. In his later works Joyce often asks those readers who seek to unravel minor riddles, and sometimes even major ones, to look for their solution outside of the text in question. What is the exception in *Portrait* becomes the rule in *Finnegans Wake*.

In a letter written to Harriet Weaver, the editor of *The Egoist,* on November 8, 1916, Joyce included an "account of my books" that was to be forwarded to B. W. Huebsch, the American publisher of *Portrait.* Among his early publications he includes: " 'Parnell' a pamphlet written when I was nine years old (in 1891) on Parnell's death. It was printed and circulated in Dublin. I do not know if any copy is to be found today" (*LT,* 1:99). In fact, no copy has been located. A solution to the riddle of "the senate and the Roman people" that appeals to me would have Joyce leave the title of his poem out of *Portrait* precisely because it had been lost among his early works. The hole in *Portrait* mirrors the hole in the corpus of his published works. An accidental loss is thereby incorporated into the novel much as Duchamp incorporated into his art work the accidental cracks that appeared in his *The Large Glass* following its transportation from an exhibition in 1926.

Duchamp's art provides another analogue to Joyce's writings. He began work on *The Large Glass* in 1915, and by 1923 he felt that he had brought it to a suitable state of incompleteness. In 1934 Duchamp issued *The Green Box,* an edition of cardboard boxes in which he assembled facsimiles of drawings, manuscript notes, and photographs meant to guide the viewer through the labyrinth of *The Large Glass. The Green Box* stands to *The Large Glass* as Joyce's manuscript notes, his preliminary drafts, and even his missing early pieces stand to his published works. Following *Portrait,* Joyce was scrupulous in saving all of these materials that are now appearing in *The James Joyce Archives.*

Both *The Large Glass* and *The Green Box* are descriptive titles for objects that have the same official title precisely because they are parts of the same work: *The Bride Stripped Bare by Her Bachelors, Even.* The work of art is neither *The Large Glass* nor *The Green Box* but the relationship between the two, the thinking that produced them both, a thinking that spectators or readers recreate as they move back and forth between them. Duchamp's art shines in the space between his objects. Similarly, Wittgenstein stated that the point of the *Tractatus* was not that someone would read his book and understand what he had to say, but that someone already would have had the same thoughts and would discover in the book a mirror of his own mind.

V
WHAT KIND OF A NAME IS THAT?

A name, a proper name, is no mere word among words, least of all to its bearer. From his early school days at Clongowes, Stephen "frets in the shadow" (*P,* 189) of his surname, "Dedalus":

And one day he [Nasty Roche] had asked:
—What is your name?
Stephen had answered:
—Stephen Dedalus.
Then Nasty Roche had said:
—What kind of a name is that?
And when Stephen had not been able to answer Nasty Roche had asked:
—What is your father?
Stephen had answered:
—A gentleman.
Then Nasty Roche had asked:
—Is he a magistrate? (*P,* 8–9)

Stephen's self-consciousness of his surname is a burden and a challenge to him, from this exchange with Nasty Roche at the beginning of *Portrait* to Davin's reproach at the end—"What with your name and your ideas . . . Are you Irish at all?" (*P,* 202).

The upper-class schoolboys at Clongowes have inherited their fathers' proud consciousness of their privileged social rank. Nasty suspects that the strangeness of Stephen's name has something to do with the equivocal position of his father. The conversation breaks off when Nasty asks, "Is he a magistrate?" Joyce does not tell us what Stephen replies or if he has any response to make. Nevertheless, according to Nasty's schoolboy logic the implied answer to this question is certainly "no." Stephen does not have a name like Nasty's surname; therefore, Stephen's father cannot have a job like Nasty's father. The name is a signpost that places the bearer in the social hierarchy. Or, as Stephen later will want to believe with respect to his own name, it reveals that the bearer does not belong anywhere in the social hierarchy—he is alone and aloof from others, "a being apart in every order" (*P,* 161).

In spite of his strange name, or perhaps even because of it, Stephen is drawn into Nasty's kind of snobbery both at Clongowes and afterward. He does not understand why Father Dolan has to ask him twice for his name before he pandies him and suspects that the prefect is making fun of him: "The great men in the history had names like that and nobody made fun of them. It was his own name that he could have made fun of if he wanted to make fun. Dolan: it was like the name of a woman that washed clothes" (*P,* 55). Stephen has heard from Athy, the riddler he meets in the infirmary, that Dedalus is "like Latin" (*P,* 25). Surely "a woman that washed clothes" would not be numbered among the august body of "the senate and the Roman people," and it is upon this historical stage that Stephen and his schoolmates imagine that the drama of their search for justice—Stephen's visit to the rector—is being played. Stephen shows pride in his name precisely because in going to see the rector he will make a name for himself among his schoolmates; he will show that "Dedalus" is a heroic appellation and that he is like one of those "great men in the history."

As a student at the university Stephen is made painfully aware of the heights from which his family's fortunes have fallen when he sees pawn tickets on the kitchen table bearing the common, nondescript names "Daly and MacEvoy" (*P,* 174), base aliases to disguise his family's shameful poverty. And passing a troop of Christian Brothers as he crosses over the Tolka Bridge on his way to North Bull Island he is sure that "their piety would be like their names" (*P,* 166). Stephen is well aware of the mean snobbishness of this thought, but he cannot help himself. Joyce is careful to let us know from whom Stephen inherited his scorn for these commoners working among the lower classes: "Christian brothers be damned! said Mr Dedalus. Is it with Paddy Stink and Mickey Mud? No, let him stick to the jesuits in God's name since he began with them" (*P,* 71). Christian Brothers with names like Brother Hickey and Brother Quaid and Brother MacArdle and Brother Keogh would be just the class of men to teach Paddy Stink and Mickey Mud.

The riddle of Stephen's last name is remarked upon by Athy, the boy he meets in the infirmary at Clongowes in chapter 1: "You have a queer name, Dedalus, and I have a queer name too, Athy. My name is the name of a town." Athy then proposes a riddle: "Why is the county Kildare like the leg of a fellow's breeches?" Stephen, who admits that he is not very good at riddles, has no answer. Athy tells him: "Because there is a thigh in it. Do you see the joke? Athy is the town in the county Kildare and a thigh is the other thigh." Athy then says that the riddle can be asked another way, and when Stephen cannot figure out what that other way might be, he ends the conversation: "There is another way but I won't tell you what it is" (*P,* 25–26).

There are other riddles in *Portrait,* some explicitly posed to Stephen as such, like Cranly's riddle of the crocodile and the child (*P,* 250), others more subtly presented, like the nature of the "champagne"—the explosives—that Mr. Casey's friend manufactures (*P,* 28). However, Athy's riddle is the first explicitly posed as such, and it therefore becomes a model both for Stephen's understanding of the nature and the place of riddles in life and for the reader's understanding of their place in Joyce's art. At times, Joyce's riddles can be infuriating to those readers who want to know everything, for they are not always open to view in the sense of having an answer that makes sense. Rather, the riddle is itself its own answer.

Athy is a fascinating minor character who seems strangely out of place in *Portrait* in much the same way that the mysterious man in the macintosh is out of place in *Ulysses.* Both characters are enigmas who serve to pose insoluble riddles. In the *Tractatus,* Wittgenstein writes: "When the answer cannot be put into words, neither can the question be put into words. The *riddle* does not exist" (*TL,* #6.5). Once again, Wittgenstein is returning to the limits of significant language in representing the facts of the world. The riddle does not exist as it can be posed in significant language. In the *Philosophical Investigations,* Wittgenstein would say that the meaning of a riddle is not necessarily found in its answer any more than the meaning of a name is necessarily found by pointing to its bearer. Naturally enough, there are instances when the meaning of a riddle is found in the answer or the meaning of a name in its bearer, but more generally the meaning of both riddles and names are found in the uses we make of them.

The meaning of Athy's unposed riddle is precisely the use to which it is put in helping us to understand Stephen's character. Stephen is frustrated that Athy will not tell him the other way of asking the riddle, and he imagines that Athy's father, unlike his own, must be a magistrate. In withholding the riddle, Athy demonstrates a power over language that makes Stephen feel inadequate and jealous. Unlike Stephen, Athy seems to recognize that he can master his strange name by weaving a riddle around it. The mystery of his name thereby becomes *his* mystery in the same way that Stephen's deformation of the song about roses blossoming makes it into his song. In this sense, the meaning of Athy's riddle is to show us that Stephen is himself the riddle.

VI

THE WORD KNOWN TO ALL MEN

"I fear those big words . . . which make us so unhappy," Stephen says to Mr. Deasy in *Ulysses* (*U,* 26). While Stephen probably would not be any happier if all the "big words" were to disappear from the face of the earth, they do serve as centers of gravity around which his unhappiness clusters and through which it is revealed to the reader. "Love" is one such big word. In *Stephen Hero* Stephen tells Emma that "there is no such thing as love in the world" (*SH,* 198). In *Portrait* Stephen tells Cranly that he does not know what the word means (*P,* 240). In Ulysses, Stephen stands over the slow learner, Cyril Sargent, and ponders a mother's love for her child, "*amor matris:* subjective and objective genitive. . . . Was that then real? The only true thing in life?" (*U,* 23).

When meditating on the mysteries of the Trinity, Stephen supposes that God's eternal love is a "simple fact." But love is only a simple fact in the same way that heartburn is a simple fact. On the one hand, love is as patently open to our view as is any other human emotion or sensation—we can see it on people's faces and in their actions. On the other hand, love is sometimes used as a name for the wonder we feel in the presence of other human beings, and as such it is an unanswerable riddle precisely because it reaches down to touch the bottomless miracle of human existence. And so love may be "the only true thing in life." But its truth, then, will be the truth of nonsense rather than the truth of fact, though it is no less central to our lives for that.

Stephen is wary of the ideal, of "those big words" like God and his eternal love. In *Ulysses,* Stephen seems to have discovered an open or patent meaning for God that does not make him an ideal or absolute concept of philosophy or theology. He listens to the cries of the boys in the playfield and tells Mr. Deasy that God is a shout in the street (P, 28). It is more problematic whether Stephen is ever able to disentangle love from the realm of the ideal—where it is by turns either a great mystery or a great hoax. In the course of *Portrait* Stephen seems to unmask the ideal in religion, nationalism, and the family not to banish it from the world but only to relocate it in his own self.

The twentieth-century man tends to be skeptical of everything but himself: the holy fane of skepticism. In *Ulysses* Haines gives perfect expression to his inflated sense of his own person when he pompously announces, "Personally I couldn't stomach that idea of a personal God" (U, 17). For Stephen in *Portrait,* as one would expect, the problem of the self finds expression in his ideas about language and style. Contemplating "a phrase from his treasure"—"a day of dappled seaborne clouds"—Stephen ponders its appeal and concludes that "he drew less pleasure from the reflection of the glowing sensible world through the prism of a language manycoloured and richly storied than from the contemplation of an inner world of individual emotions mirrored perfectly in a lucid supple periodic prose" (P, 166–67). Stephen's ideal of "an inner world of individual emotions" suggests that there is a discrepancy between his impersonal aesthetic theory and his very personal poetic taste.

On the one hand, Stephen tells Lynch that he now understands that Aquinas's conception of *claritas* has nothing to do with "symbolism or idealism, the supreme quality of beauty being a light from some other world, the idea of which the matter is but the shadow, the reality of which it is but the symbol" (P, 213). On the other hand, he defines art as the "image of the beauty we have come to understand" after having tried "slowly and humbly and constantly to express [ourselves], to press out again, from the gross earth or what it brings forth, from sound and shape and colour which are the prison gates of our soul" (P, 207). About the first passage, Joyce remarked to his Spanish translator, "Plato's theory of ideas, or more strictly . . . Neo-Platonism, [are] two philosophical tendencies with which the speaker at that moment is not in sympathy" (LT, 3:130). Stephen's dismissal of beauty as a "light from another world," and of the dichotomies of idea and matter, reality and symbol, show his lack of sympathy for Plato. But in the second passage this rejection is not so clear cut, for what is the reference to "the prison gates of our soul" but a variation on a Platonic commonplace? It is as though the ideal has been shown out the front door only to reappear through the cellar.

Platonic idealism has come back through Stephen's idealization of himself, of his "inner world of individual emotions"—which is, of course, a notion that Plato would have found abhorrent. In a sense, Stephen is for himself his own ideal. His emotions are the reality; the world is the mere data of sense perception, of sound, shape, and color. By locating beauty in himself, Stephen makes himself both the subject and object of aesthetic wonder, and that is a recipe for catastrophic personal disappointment. Cranly will ask him: "Alone, quite alone. You have no fear of that. And you know what that word means?" (P, 247). Stephen's answer ought to be "no," but he seems to think that his idea of himself is more of a "simple fact" than is either the faith in God's eternal love for him or the certainty of his mother's love. But the certainty of his mother's love is found in the "sound and shape and colour" that he can sense when she kisses him. These sensations are not "the prison gates of our soul" that separate us from the ideal; rather, they are, as Wittgenstein would say, the "rough ground" that we need if we are to walk, or, to use Stephen's preferred image, the air that our wings must push off of if we are to fly.

In idealizing his own inner emotions, Stephen is committing a *felix culpa* rather than merely making an error in philosophical judgment. In *Ulysses,* when Eglinton suggests in the National Library that Shakespeare's marriage to Anne Hathaway was a mistake and that he "got out of it as quickly and as best he could," Stephen rudely replies, "A man of genius makes no mistakes. His errors are volitional and are the portals of discovery" (*U,* 156). Joyce is presenting us with the portrait of a youthful mind as it develops in time, and Stephen's "errors" show us the path of his wanderings, for they are, or can be, "the portals of discovery." His mistakes are necessary ones both in the sense of being appropriate to his youth and to the intellectual culture that formed him. Stephen's own poetic taste in *Portrait* shows that he is not yet the kind of artist that "like the God of the creation, remains within or behind or beyond or above his handiwork, invisible, refined out of existence, indifferent, paring his fingernails" (*P,* 215). And it is precisely Stephen's intuition that art and the artist are anything but "indifferent" that keeps him away from the Scylla of artistic effacement, though in his lyric phase he does run aground against the Charybdis of emotional idealism. If the artist were really to refine himself "out of existence," he would be incapable of expressing the wonder that is human love, for that wonder is found only in existence and is expressed only in our human handiwork.

In the songs and poems that Stephen hears or thinks of, Joyce keeps the mention of love just beyond his hero's horizon. For example, when Stephen returns home to find the Dedalus children singing Thomas Moore's *Oft in the Stilly Night* (*P,* 163), we do not hear the lyrics of the song that Stephen himself must hear, "the words of love then spoken." And when, at the conclusion of the novel, Stephen recalls William Blake's poem "William Bond," we hear of Bond's illness (*P,* 249), but not the final lines:

> Seek Love in the Pity of others Woe
> In the gentle relief of anothers care
> In the darkness of night & the winters snow
> In the naked & outcast Seek Love there.

Love, I would like to say, is the important part of *Portrait* and of *Ulysses,* and it is the part that Joyce leaves largely unspoken. He mentions it only enough so that the reader will sense that it is a riddle at once clearly open to our view and strangely wonderful. Similarly, I think that the ethical, "in a sense which includes . . . the most essential part of what is generally called aesthetics" (*LE,* 4), is the important part of Wittgenstein's *Tractatus.* Although Wittgenstein has much to say about aesthetics in his notebooks, he decided not to include in the *Tractatus* itself any of those passages like the one about his stove; in fact, he leaves as a clue to guide the reader only a single mention of aesthetics, in which he equates the ethical with it (*TL,* #6.421). The rest of the thinking about aesthetics must be done by the reader.

In *Portrait* Stephen is mostly silent above love. He only says that he does not know what it means. Joyce meant it to be that way and I think that he makes clear to the reader his reasons why. When Cranly and Stephen walk through Dublin they hear a woman singing:

> Behind a hedge of laurel a light glimmered in the window of a kitchen and the voice of a servant was heard singing as she sharpened knives. She sang, in short broken bars, *Rosie O'Grady.*
>   Cranly stopped to listen, saying:
>   —*Mulier cantat.*
>   The soft beauty of the Latin word touched with an enchanting touch the dark of the evening, with a touch fainter and more persuading than the touch of music or of a woman's hand. The strife of their minds was quelled. (*P,* 244)

In the wonder of this epiphany, as strife gives way to harmony with the world, to love, Stephen's mind finds a moment of peace. But this peace lasts only until Cranly destroys the moment by trying to *say* it. Cranly sings the end of the song's refrain: "There's real poetry for you, he said. There's real love." Cranly's remark is only partly in jest. He thinks that he knows love's real name.

Is love the "word known to all men"? I think it is a connection that a reader might make and might be able to defend. But I am sure that Joyce realized that he could not *say* so in *Portrait* or in *Ulysses.* However, he could *show* it. Joyce left the connection between "love" and the "word known to all men" to be made in the mind of the reader and not on the pages of the text. As I have tried to show, this is a characteristic gesture in early twentieth-century aesthetics and is shared by Wittgenstein in philosophy and by Duchamp in the visual arts. And that is why I think it unfortunate that Hans Gabler, in *Ulysses: The Corrected Text,* chose to include the passage in the "Scylla and Charybdis" chapter identifying love as the "word known to all men" (*U,* 161). Joyce realized that to *say* that love was the word known to all men was to say nothing. Like Wittgenstein, he chose to say everything by remaining silent. Joyce was sharing in his poetry the same feeling that Wittgenstein experienced in his work when he wrote, "So in the end when one is doing philosophy one gets to the point where one would like just to emit an inarticulate sound" (*PI,* 261). Just the kind of inarticulate affirmation of life that Molly Bloom emits when she says, "and yes I said yes I will yes" (*U,* 644).

Gabler's addition to *Ulysses* is the equivalent of an editor adding passages from the notebooks or from the *Proto-Tractatus* to Wittgenstein's published text because they help the reader by making his thought about aesthetics clearer in the sense of being more explicit. But that is not the kind of clarity that either Wittgenstein or Joyce was seeking. Even if Joyce originally left the passage on love out of "Scylla and Charybdis" by an accidental oversight—and how can we know that?—he saw that the oversight made sense and decided to make use of that accident much as Duchamp made use of the cracks in *The Large Glass*. In any case, had he wanted to say rather than to show that love was the word known to all men, it is inconceivable that he would not have caught and corrected so important a mistake. Being human, Joyce was capable of oversights, but he was never sloppy. Joyce makes love the "word known to all men" not by identifying it as love's "real name" but by constructing his novels in such a way that the word is left on his readers' lips rather than on the page.

Reflecting on the family resemblances between art and philosophy, Wittgenstein writes that "it seems to me too that there is a way of capturing the world sub specie aeterni other than through the work of the artist. Thought has such a way—so I believe—it is as though it flies above the world and leaves it as it is—observing it from above, in flight" (*CV,* 5). It is as "thought . . . flies above the world and leaves it as it is" that Wittgenstein the philosopher meets Joyce the poet. Joyce's hero, Stephen Dedalus, stands on the porch of Dublin's National Library seeking an augury in the sky above him: "What birds were they? . . . He watched their flight; bird after bird: a dark flash, a swerve, a flash again, a dart aside, a flutter of wings. . . . A sense of fear of the unknown moved in the heart of his weariness, a fear of symbols and portents, of the hawklike man whose name he bore soaring out of his captivity on osierwoven wings . . ." (*P,* 224–25). The rest is silence.

Notes

1.   Ludwig Wittgenstein, *Notebooks, 1914–1916,* ed and trans., G. E. M. Anscombe (New York: Harper Torchbooks, 1969), 49; hereafter cited in the text as *NB*. Other works by Wittgenstein are cited in the text and abbreviated as follows: *CV: Culture and Value,* trans. Peter Winch, ed. G. H. Von Wright (Chicago: University of Chicago Press, 1984); *HD:* "On Heidegger on Being and Dread," in *Heidegger and Modern Philosophy,* ed. Michael Murray (New Haven: Yale University Press, 1978); *LE:* "Lecture on Ethics," *Philosophical Review* 74 (1965): 3–26; *LF:* "Letter to Ludwig von Ficker," trans. in William Bartley, *Wittgenstein* (Philadelphia: Lippincott, 1973); *PI: Philosophical Investigations,* 3rd ed., trans. G. E. M. Anscombe (New York: Macmillian, 1958); *TL: Tractatus Logico-Philosophicus,* trans. D. F. Pears and B. F. McGuinness (London: Routledge and Kegan Paul, 1961). For an excellent study of Wittgenstein's concept of the mystical see Peter C. John, "Wittgenstein's 'Wonderful Life,' " *Journal of the History of Ideas* 49 (1988): 495–510.

2.   James Joyce, *A Portrait of the Artist as a Young Man* (New York: Viking, 1964), 62; hereafter cited in the text as *P.* Other works by Joyce are cited in the text and abbreviated as

follows: *D: Dubliners* (New York: Modern Library, 1969); *LT: The Letters of James Joyce,* ed. Stuart Gilbert and Richard Ellmann, 3 vols. (New York: Viking, 1966); *SH: Stephen Hero* (New York: New Directions, 1963); *U: Ulysses,* ed. Hans Walter Gabler (New York: Vintage, 1986).

    3.   From Cornelius Weygandt, *Irish Plays and Playwrights* (Boston, 1913); reprinted in *The Workshop of Daedalus,* ed. Robert Scholes and Richard M. Kain (Evanston, Ill.: Northwestern University Press, 1965), 165.

    4.   *Marcel Duchamp,* ed. Anne d'Harnoncourt and Kynaston McShine (n.p.: Museum of Modern Art and the Philadelphia Museum of Art, 1973), 275–76.

    5.   Richard Ellmann, *James Joyce,* 2nd ed. (New York: Oxford University Press, 1982), 33–34.

[The Strength and Sorrow of Young Stephen: The Dialectic of Harmony and Dissonance]

MICHAEL BRUCE MCDONALD

A certain anecdote concerning James Joyce's eccentric music-making appears several times, with only minor variations, in the course of Richard Ellmann's biography of the most famous of Irish exiles. The substance of the story is that those who heard Joyce sing at his various residences on the Continent were typically quite impressed by his "fine, pleasant voice," but were just as often, like his friend Ottocaro Weiss, "scandalized . . . by a totally unacceptable accompaniment," played on a guitar, or on "an old upright piano badly out of tune" (Ellmann, *James Joyce* 393). Although Ellmann himself treats this story as one more anecdote among the hundreds he presents in the course of what is, after all, a monumental study, my argument depends upon the notion that this paradox of a fine voice, somehow pleasantly singing despite the singer's scandalously discordant self-accompaniment, captures the precise aesthetic effect of Joyce's mature art. This is to say that Joyce's prose persistently manages, improbably enough, virtually to sing in the very midst of its own jangling discords; even when the most outrageous dissonances, the harshest sounds and ideas, are brought into opposition with the harmoniousness of his work, as in *Ulysses* and *Finnegans Wake,* a certain euphony still obtains there. The question informing this study is, therefore, Why *should* harmony prove to be so persistent in the work of such a master of the art of dissonance?

Ellmann's seemingly incidental anecdote, intimating as it does the precise nature of the crucial tension and interplay between harmony and dissonance throughout Joyce's work, sketches an interrelationship which is of the utmost significance for my argument. Again and again, Joyce finds ways to foreground the fact that consonance and dissonance can never be constituted apart from one another, thus subverting any notion that harmony can somehow do without dissonance, or that dissonance might ever finally overwhelm the interests of harmony. Rather, one of the great lessons of Joyce's art is that harmony lacks grandeur—becomes, indeed, *merely* banal—when it suppresses dissonance, and that dissonance deteriorates into mere noise in the absence of

Reprinted by permission of *Twentieth Century Literature* Vol. 37, No. 4 (Winter 1991): pp. 361–89.

harmony. I shall argue for the necessity of understanding precisely how Joyce foregrounds this profoundly close-knit interrelationship between harmony and dissonance in his work, on the grounds that knowledge of this dynamic is indispensable for an adequate understanding of the overall concerns of his aesthetics. In addition, it seems to me very appropriate that an initial study of this crucial dynamic should focus on *A Portrait,* since the interrelationship which constitutes this dynamic is emphatically staged in the depiction of Stephen's resolute dream of attaining some sort of harmony, and by the subsequent disruption of that dream by the dissonances Joyce so powerfully opposes to it. From a more general perspective, moreover, conceiving Joyce's aesthetics in terms of a profoundly close-knit interrelationship between harmony and dissonance offers a useful corrective to the dualism all too frequently evident in scholarly approaches to the question of harmony—and of order itself—in Joyce.

The aforementioned dualism is specifically marked, on one hand, by a tendency among certain critics to celebrate Joyce as quite nearly the closest thing to an apostle of harmony that European modernism—given the overwhelming anomie characterizing its historical moment for this view—could ever reasonably hope to produce. Here, harmony is typically understood either structurally[1]—especially in terms of the supposed realization throughout the Joyce canon of the aesthetic theory articulated by Stephen Dedalus in the final chapter of *A Portrait*[2]—or more thematically, with Leopold and Molly Bloom as exemplary figures of the spirit of reconciliation thought to grace even the most obdurately arcane moments in Joyce's work.[3] Not surprisingly, critics who understand the role of harmony in Joyce in this way tend to ignore the monumental dissonances of *Finnegans Wake* altogether, or tend to give the aesthetic problem such dissonances represent but scant mention in the course of their studies.[4]

The other aspect of the dualism evident in many approaches to the question of harmony and dissonance in Joyce is most typically revealed in the work of those critics who read Joyce backward from the *Wake.* This approach tacitly celebrates the seemingly unrelieved dissonances of the *Wake* as the culmination of an aesthetics toward which Joyce's earlier productions, however tenuously, are everywhere thought to point.[5] The latest manifestation of this tendency is the post-structuralist valorization of dissonance as the crucial aesthetic element deemed to have been emancipated, finally—at least, and especially, in the works of revolutionary writers like Joyce—from the logocentric tyranny of binary opposites considered endemic to Western metaphysics. In this view, dissonance attains the stature of an entity whose field of play can no longer merely be delimited according to the imperatives of harmony, and whose playfully disruptive orientation no longer betrays concern for the telos of its own resolution in harmony.[6]

My argument departs from the tacit dualism of such approaches in its insistence that the unrelentingly *dialectical* understanding of harmony and dissonance as mutually informing, rather than antagonistic, categories is necessarily central to any productive discussion of the modalities of Joyce's aesthetics. My conviction that these concerns should be understood dialectically is given special impetus by Theodor W. Adorno's insights concerning the role played by the dialectic of harmony and dissonance in Western philosophy and art, insights most fully articulated in his *Aesthetic Theory,* that grand and thorny work which Fredric Jameson has rightly described as "the aesthetics one writes when it is impossible to write aesthetics" (Stephanson 29).[7] What follows stems largely, then, from my sense that the implications of Adorno's insights concerning the nature and overall significance of the dialectic of harmony and dissonance have yet to be satisfactorily considered in respect to literary studies in general, much less to the specific aesthetic concerns we have come to associate with the name of James Joyce.

In opposition to aesthetic formulations that posit the artistic process as an attempt to harmonize art with transcendent absolutes—the very tack taken, at first, by Stephen in *A Portrait*—Adorno refuses to admit the viability of any aesthetics which ignores the ways in which works of art are inevitably grounded upon the dissonances which, in his view, no principle of harmony, no matter how sophisticated, can *ever* fully resolve. Moreover, in Adorno's view it is precisely the individual artist's repudiation of the notion that consonance or euphony can exist *apart* from this principle of irresolvable dissonance that enables the production of aesthetically advanced works of art. Indeed, for this view the aesthetic sensibility only becomes truly equal to the challenge of art when it is firmly grounded upon the realization that

Aesthetic harmony is never fully attained; it is either superficial polish or temporary balance. Inside everything that can justly be called harmonious in art there are vestiges of despair and antagonism. (Adorno 160)

Pointing out that those who advocate "an aesthetic notion of [a fully realizable] harmony and cognate ideas" typically ignore the inescapable "vestiges of despair and antagonism" which always rest *within* harmony, Adorno proceeds to argue that it is the recognition of harmony's *own* inherent unattainability that informs the mature style of rightfully eminent artists (161). In other words, artists gain genuine aesthetic maturity only inasmuch as they are, first, able to recognize the inherent unattainability of harmony and then proceed to recapitulate, aesthetically, the *inevitability* of this recognition:

The more deeply works of art become engrossed by the idea of harmony, of appearing essence, the less they can feel content with it . . . *Dissonance is the truth about harmony.* Harmony is unattainable, given the strict criteria of what harmony is supposed to be. These criteria are met only when the aspect of unattainability is incorporated into the essence of art. . . . (161—emphasis added)

In effect, this incorporation of harmony's "aspect of unattainability" into the work of art brushes aesthetic taste "against the grain," thereby exposing the discords which, though they inevitably *inform* taste, taste tends to deny.[8] For Adorno, it is important to see that this revelation of harmony's *own* informing discords need not be an occasion for despair, but rather betokens the useful insight that harmony can never escape the dissonance that is its own *truth,* the dissonance that is the fundamental informing principle that makes harmony possible in the first place. In this view, therefore, it is wiser simply to recognize the inevitable operation of dissonance *within* harmony than to work futilely to create a harmony that would spuriously seek to banish dissonance altogether, or that would pretend that the problem of dissonance can somehow be wished away under the fleeting, intoxicating sway of harmonic cadences.

My argument follows, therefore, from the notion that Joyce's ability to incorporate precisely this "aspect of unattainability" into the structure and thematics of his work marks his achievement of what Adorno would term a mature art. Moreover, even as his work reveals the ways that dissonance actually *becomes* "the truth about harmony," Joyce also shows us how dissonance itself is threatened with a loss of cogency when the principle of harmony is severely compromised by an excessive proliferation of unrelieved discord. In order to get at the particular nature of this dialectic in Joyce, it is necessary that we understand the nature of his response to the literary milieu which, more than any other, convinced him that his aesthetic practice could not be content merely to acknowledge, but must rather actively portray, the inherent unattainability of harmony. This aesthetic pursuit gained its initial, and indeed lasting, impetus from Joyce's highly charged response to the facile harmonies he thought typical of the Irish Literary Revival.

The complexity of Joyce's ambivalence toward the writers affiliated with the Revival, and toward their literary productions, is compellingly set forth in Ellmann's biography (*James Joyce* 98–104). At first, Joyce was simultaneously drawn to, and repelled by, the Revival's overwhelming drive to ensure a strong, indeed constitutive role for literature in modern Irish politics. For the writers affiliated with the Revival, literature was to have the important didactic function of teaching the modern Irish about their supposedly glorious Celtic past, and to play an even larger political role by urging the Irish to shake off British rule in order to reassume their illustrious Celtic birthright. The productions of the Revival were driven by the assumption that the essence of Celtic culture remains available to the modern Irish in the plenitude of its vitality, and that this culture has proven itself to be essentially impervious to the ravages of history, even to the long and brutal period of colonial occupation by the British.

In "The Necessity for De-Anglicising Ireland," a document which in many ways marks the moment of the Revival's full-blown emergence in 1892, Douglas Hyde exhibits a striking insistence on the harmony of the modern Irish, degraded as their present state may be, with their ancient fore-bears. Threatened though this harmony may sometimes *seem* to be, its power is such that it is endlessly vital, endlessly renewable. The sheer vigor of the harmony of the modern Irish with the genius of their ancestors is conveyed by Hyde's insistent reference to the enduring unity of the primordial Irish "race," a collectivity unified not only "racially," but also through participation in the very language, Gaelic, now almost lost to the modern Irish:

> The bulk of the Irish race really lived in the closest contact with the traditions of the past and the national life of nearly eighteen hundred years, until after the beginning of this century . . . it may be said, roughly speaking, that the ancient Gaelic civilization died with . . . [the] neglect of . . . racial customs, language, and traditions . . . (Hyde 142)

Even the apparent "death" of this ancient civilization cannot, in Hyde's view, preclude its rebirth and renewal, so powerful remain its lingering harmonies.

Hyde believed that the restoration of an idiomatically Irish civilization must be predicated upon the reclamation of the vitality of Irish Gaelic, a proj-ect ultimately aimed at Gaelic's reinstitution as the predominant language of the land:

> I have no hesitation at all in saying that every Irish-feeling Irishman, who hates the reproach of West-Britonism, should set himself to encourage the efforts which are being made to keep alive our once great national tongue. The losing of it is our greatest blow, and the sorest stroke that the rapid Anglicisation of Ireland has inflicted upon us. In order to de-Anglicise ourselves we must at once arrest the decay of the language. (145)

Apparently, the complex issues attending the degradation of Irish history and folkways are to be resolved through the reclamation of a linguistic harmony deemed powerful enough to unite the Irish people in the present, and also to bring the modern Irish into fruitful harmony with the genius of their leg-endary past. Moreover, the notion that the reinstitution of Gaelic represents a virtual reclamation of *racial* potency evidently puts to rest, for Hyde and his ilk, the disquieting issues attending the various internal differences—and indeed bitter conflicts—within Irish culture and daily life. Arguably, how-ever, these informing, and indeed *constitutive* differences were well entrenched in Ireland long before the beginning of the nineteenth century.[9] Hyde could not have known of the diversity of his country's ancestral life—a diversity whose extent contemporary sociological and historical studies continue to dis-cover[10]—but he would not have *wished* to know of that diversity, either; the revelation of such durable diversity and difference necessarily upsets the notion that the Irish people were historically united, in almost every way, by the harmony tacitly imparted to their "racial" legacy through the primary force of a shared ancestral language.

While it may be justly argued that Hyde's emphasis on racialism is expressive of a tendency pandemic to late nineteenth-century thought, we must also remember that this particular essay still holds considerable weight for *contemporary* Irish thought; Hyde's manifesto has continued to exert an unprecedented influence on Irish politics and culture well into the late twentieth century. Indeed, Joyce seems almost prophetic in his understanding that, in struggling with the ideas of thinkers like Hyde, he was struggling to shape the profoundest sensibilities of an emerging nation. Even so, Ellmann shows that Joyce benefited immensely from the creative energy the Revival imparted to Irish literature in general—and to the formation of an atmosphere highly conducive to the production and reception of new literary works in Ireland—despite the scorn Joyce always held for the naive racialism evinced by Hyde and many other writers associated with the Revival (*James Joyce* 98). Indeed, it must be insisted that, despite the widespread tendency to regard Joyce's aesthetic sensibility as maturing in splendid isolation from the vagaries of Irish culture, his work simultaneously resists, and succumbs to, the aesthetics of the Revival.[11]

Joyce's ambivalent sense of the Revival—and of his own position in respect to it—is encapsulated in "The Holy Office," that bit of bilious doggerel noteworthy for its parody of the literary modes of the Revival, for its expression of Joyce's scorn for many of its most celebrated writers, and for the fun he pokes at his own relationship with the movement:

> But all these men of whom I speak
> Make me the sewer of their clique.
> That they may dream their dreamy dreams
> I carry off their filthy streams
> For I can do those things for them
> Through which I lost my diadem,
> Those things for which Grandmother Church
> Left me severely in the lurch.
>
> (*CW* 151)[12]

In the inversion of everyday Irish values accomplished here, Joyce's very *sins*—acts which *he* views, however, not so much as sins as creatively iconoclastic dissonances, dissonances insusceptible to the Church's harmonious vision of repentance and forgiveness—somehow enable him to *serve* the Revival, a movement in many ways predicated upon the assumption of a sort of purity indigenous to the Irish character. Ironically, Joyce's willingness simply to accept his own impurity enables him to serve—in the very midst of personal degradation—the very movement which bespeaks, at every turn, the utter ascendancy of an unimpeachably moral spirit among the Irish from their most primordial beginnings.

Precisely because the Revival refuses to acknowledge the abiding dissonances that ineluctably oppose themselves to its vision of an unsullied Ireland, it *requires* someone who not only can acknowledge these dissonances, but is virtually able to "carry them off," away from the "pure" vision whose harmony they might otherwise disturb. By relentlessly focusing on such dissonances in his own work, Joyce tacitly permits himself to be perceived as aberrant rather than simply honest, even as he thereby enables the Revival to present its own productions as embodiments of Irish purity. Strangely, Joyce thus finds empowerment in serving as a sort of literary drudge to the dreamy dreamers he scorns but must also acknowledge—not entirely without envy— as a more or less harmonious *company:*

> So distantly I turn to view
> The shamblings of that motley crew . . .
> Where they have crouched and crawled and prayed
> I stand the self-doomed, unafraid . . .
> And though they spurn me from their door
> My soul shall spurn them evermore.
>
> (*CW* 152)

Forever removed from the company of the Revival's "motley crew," and yet always turning back to view the impact of their "shamblings" upon an Irish polity he would himself influence, Joyce distantly serves a movement that takes no notice of his service even as it implicitly derives benefit from his artistic drudgery. "The Holy Office" thus indicates the manner whereby, even as Joyce could jokingly parody the predilections of the Revival, his ambivalent attitude toward its polemical literary program—and toward the "motley crew" whose status as a sort of community he could not entirely gainsay— came to be one of the most fundamental elements informing the makeup of his aesthetic sensibility.

Joyce's early skepticism toward the Revival was fueled, additionally, by his sense that the plenitude of Gaelic had been forever lost to the modern Irish, that the site of its presence was now occupied by another language whose own presence could never be wholly dislodged from that site, the more or less imminent prospect of an end to centuries of British occupation notwithstanding. Thus, the idea of a "de-Anglicisation of Ireland" eventually became a virtual oxymoron for Joyce; for him, the infusion of the Irish sensibility with the attitudes and perceptions inscribed in English had gone so far as to preclude the very possibility that Ireland could ever *be* "de-Anglicised." Even so, he writes tellingly of the chafing of an Irish sensibility under the imposition of the English language:

The language in which we are speaking is his before it is mine. How different are the words *home, Christ, ale, master,* on his lips and on mine! I cannot speak or write these words without unrest of spirit. His language, so familiar and so foreign, will always be for me an acquired speech. I have not made or accepted its words. My voice holds them at bay. My soul frets in the shadow of his language. (P 189)[13]

For Stephen, as for Joyce himself, the problem of forever having to inhabit the shadowy realm between an imposed colonial language and a moribund native one becomes, in turn, the problem of inhabiting a realm characterized by unrelenting dissonance. This is a realm that can never be brought under the auspices of verbal harmony, precisely because the most eloquent verbalization in one language only serves as a remainder of the dislocation necessarily entailed in the use, or *nonuse,* of the other.

A remarkable contemporary statement of the pernicious consequences resulting from this form of linguistic discord is offered us by the Kenyan writer Ngũgĩwa Thiong'o, who explicitly concerns himself with the neocolonialist appropriation of those works of indigenous writers which happen to be composed in the language of the colonizer:

> If . . . I criticise the Afro-European (or Euroafrican) choice of our linguistic praxis, it is not to take away from the talent and the genius of those who have written in English, French or Portuguese. On the contrary I am lamenting a neo-colonial situation which has meant the European bourgeoisie once again stealing our talents and geniuses as they have stolen our economies. In the eighteenth and nineteenth centuries Europe stole art treasures from Africa to decorate their houses and museums; in the twentieth century Europe is stealing the treasures of the mind to enrich their languages and cultures. (xii)

This conviction has prompted Ngũgĩwa to go so far as to declare that he will henceforward write exclusively in two of the indigenous languages of Kenya rather than in English, precisely so as to prevent the European bourgeoisie from "stealing" his work.[14] In strikingly similar fashion, Hyde was concerned, above all, with finding ways to accomplish the political and literary "de-Anglicisation" of Ireland, a project aimed at precluding, at the very least, the ongoing appropriation of Irish arts by British connoisseurs.

A significant difference obtains, however, between Hyde's situation and Ngũgĩwa's, insomuch as Hyde's popular translations of *The Lovesongs of Connacht* were partially aimed at making their *own* ancestral literary tradition available to the large segment of the Irish population for whom Gaelic had already become incomprehensible by the late nineteenth century. Thus, where Ngũgĩwa is able to presume the ongoing vitality of indigenous linguistic and literary traditions, Hyde's translations are offered in a spirit already bent on the recovery, even exhumation, of the Gaelic verbal arts indigenous to Ireland, but now languishing there. In offering these translations from their own Gaelic tradition to his fellow Irish, Hyde inevitably—if inadvertently—*also* makes them available to the likes of Haines, the emblematic figure of benevolent colonial appropriation in *Ulysses,* who is thus enabled by Hyde himself to arrogate the Gaelic tradition to his own purposes, an act Stephen likens to that of a "penitent thief."

Jacques Derrida, of course, offers a view that counters the notion that this literary and linguistic problem can ever be properly described as *essentially* an effect of the intransigence of colonialism. For Derrida, even the most blatant displacement effected by way of the incommensurability of competing modes of discourse should never be deemed *merely* an effect of the disruptiveness of colonialism, for in his view our embeddedness in language itself is characterized by a perpetual deferral of the closure of meaning—a deferral of the harmonic resolution, as it were, of linguistic acts—and by an enduring play of irresolvable differences. This is the case for the simple yet monumentally disturbing reason that the "transcendental signified" which alone could guarantee discursivity's self-replete presence to itself can never be inscribed *in* language. That is, a "transcendental signified" could only guarantee the plenitude of discourse if discursivity itself were an effective *substitute* for that signified's own replete self-presence, yet Derrida is adamant in his assertion that language does not, cannot, serve *as* such a substitute: "The substitute does not substitute itself for anything which has somehow exited before it" (280).

This notion takes on special poignancy when applied to Stephen's condition as an Irish speaker of English. In this respect, we must recognize that the language Haines bears, rather than Haines himself, is the usurper Stephen fears and scorns. For Stephen, as for Hyde himself, the gap between Gaelic and English is unbridgeable through translation. English does not simply substitute itself for Gaelic, but rather is used in an attempt to usurp the place of Gaelic altogether, as the colonizers seek to erase the very possibility that Gaelic might one day somehow *resubstitute* itself for English. While English successfully comes to occupy the position formerly held by Gaelic as the everyday spoken language of Ireland, however, it fails to occupy the mythic dimension of Gaelic as well, a dimension in which Gaelic still persists, paradoxically embodied as a presence *felt* as an achingly real absence. English, that is, far from substituting itself for Gaelic, imperfectly situates itself in the site Gaelic had formerly occupied, a site where the very fact of linguistic presence now signifies rupture, rendering the indigenous language of Ireland practically "a central presence which has never been itself, has always already been exiled from itself into its own substitute" (Derrida 280) from the standpoint of the modern, Anglophone Irish.

While Derrida's remarks are broadly directed at a general description of a rupture "in the history of the concept of structure" (278), his characterization of the general effects of this rupture is especially germane to the politicized linguistic concerns Stephen articulates in the passage from *A Portrait* quoted above. These are precisely the concerns, moreover, that eventually come to fruition in the "Scylla and Charybdis" episode of *Ulysses.* Here, Stephen attempts to oppose George (A.E.) Russell's blithe assertion that art has to do with "formless spiritual essences" (*U* 9.49)[15] by advancing counter, "dagger definitions" of art's inevitable embeddedness in the material existence of the artist:

> Unsheathe your dagger definitions. Horseness is the whatness of allhorse. Streams of tendency and eons they worship. . . . they creepycrawl after Blake's buttocks into eternity of which this vegetable world is but a shadow. Hold to the now, the here, through which all future plunges to the past. (*U* 9.84–89)

Even as he savors his impending triumph over Russell, a triumph to be accomplished by adamantly holding "to the now," Stephen—in curious anticipation of Ngũgĩwa—suddenly finds to his chagrin that he can no longer confidently propound his definitions *in* English, the only language, paradoxically, which is available to him.

The paradox here is that even Stephen's obvious mastery of English *unsettles* his bid for mastery in his argument with Russell; Stephen is unmastered in this context by his inability to accept English as a proper substitute for the indigenous language it has displaced, even though he *has* no language other than English. Lacking any confidence in the vitality of the relationship between the indigenous language he does not know and the alien one he has mastered—the very relationship that the idea of an effective substitution must rely upon—Stephen finds that he cannot confidently pursue the argument he has initiated with Russell. Momentously, Stephen's resolve to wield dagger definitions against Russell is subverted precisely at the instant wherein Haines's intention to procure a copy of Hyde's *Lovesongs* is brought to light. The revelation of this act of appropriation, an act whose seeming innocuousness is belied by Hines's indelible embeddedness within a pernicious colonialism, elicits an odd string of internal associations from the now significantly silent Stephen:

> We feel in England. Penitent thief. Gone. I smoked his baccy. Green twinkling stone. An emerald set in the ring of the sea. (*U* 9.101–02)

Suddenly, Stephen's very ability to wield dagger definitions seems to have evaporated; the references made to Hyde and Haines have undermined his confidence in the language, English, which he must wield in order to *create* such definitions, a language which informs *and* imperils his very identity even as it elicits his profound resentment.

As the passage quoted above illustrates, the increasing play—or rather deliberate oscillation—of significance in the text itself closely parallels Stephen's growing sense that the place of the center or origin which would anchor his discourse has become a site irremediably marked, for him, by a keen sense of rupture and absence. Indeed, the entire episode is animated by Stephen's increasingly disturbing realization that the very language in which he must articulate and understand his predicament holds—and has forever held—no center for him at all. In this respect, Joyce's portrayal of Stephen in *Ulysses* sketches the universal linguistic predicament that for Derrida attends our embeddedness in language itself, but does so in a way that retains the sense that this predicament is heightened—becoming more poignant and existentially painful—when the factor of colonial linguistic usurpation is added to it. While it is therefore true that the complexity of Stephen's linguistic predicament more and more comes to foreshadow that identified so powerfully by Derrida, the careful reader of *Ulysses* is never permitted to lose the sense that Stephen's predicament is especially poignant because of its foundation in an ongoing act of colonial usurpation. Joyce's portrayal of this predicament thus has little, necessarily, of the sense of luxurious elevation characterizing Derrida's.[16]

The foregrounding of a sort of proto-Derridean linguistic predicament in "Scylla and Charybdis" is powerfully foreshadowed at the close of *A Portrait*. Here it is precisely Stephen's nascent realization of his linguistic predicament that acts as the catalyst for his abandonment of the quest for an aesthetics based on art's supposed ability to harmonize itself with a transcendental signified, with that which is implicitly transcendent and yet, paradoxically, already *known:*

> . . . Michael Robartes remembers forgotten beauty and, when his arms wrap her round, he presses in his arms the loveliness which has long faded from the world. Not this. Not at all. I desire to press in my arms the loveliness which has not yet come into the world. (*P* 251)

This passage clearly intimates the dynamic of Stephen's growing realization that the Revival's emphasis on art as a kind of Platonic anamnesis inevitably glosses over the unique linguistic dilemma faced by the modern Irish; moreover, it also intimates how this realization will, eventually, strongly influence his decision to exile himself from his native land. Clearly, he will carry Ireland's linguistic dilemma with him into exile, but his act of repudiation, his protest—like Hyde's, like Ngũgĩwa's, like that of Joyce himself—will carry a lasting resonance; this is the peculiar resonance that is established, as we shall see, through the foregrounding of dissonances that resolutely oppose themselves to the harmony that would deny the force *of* such dissonances, especially their power to block the facile resolution that a harmony so conceived all too readily tends to settle for.

It is precisely this resonance of an irresolvable dissonance that comes to fruition in "Scylla and Charybdis," where Stephen's intimation of the speciousness of the sort of harmonic resolution he had earlier dreamed of asserts itself, ironically enough, even as his factitious hope of opposing the likes of Russell by propounding dagger definitions is decisively overthrown. While Stephen will despair at the shattering of this hope, he will gain much from his eventual recognition of the ways in which dissonance intractably precludes the harmonic resolution of such hope; Russell, on the other hand, will implicitly remain mired in the "dreamy dream" of harmonic resolution, failing to see how harmony's own discords necessarily render such resolution forever beyond his reach.

Stephen's tenacious desire to embrace a beauty "not yet come into the world" is closely related to his burgeoning excitement, and discomfort, over the ways in which language fundamentally delimits his—and by extension our own—sense of beauty, and delimits the very perception of what *is* beautiful, of what beauty can be. Indeed, inasmuch as *Ulysses* may be considered the book that Stephen will one day write, or at least aspire to write, it represents very particularly the manner whereby a new sort of beauty comes into the world by way of a new approach to language, an approach which makes something significant out of the linguistic dilemma, the seeming void, into whose vortex Stephen is so nearly swept as he passes through the perilous psychic landscape of "Scylla and Charybdis." This dilemma is precisely that incurred by the harmoniousness that seeks to insinuate itself at every turn in human discourse, only to have its aims cut off as its "dagger definitions"—the clarity, that is, upon which discursive harmony's hope of attaining the "quietus" of resolution necessarily rests—are inevitably undermined by their own inward-turning, self-blunting, unharmonious discordances. These are the discordances which simply follow from the fact that no transcendental signified exists in language to guarantee the closure of the oscillating meanings that every definition, no matter how pointed, sets up through an inevitable reliance upon figurative language, language that by its very nature can never be controlled or brought to resolution through recourse to the "rules" of grammar or syntax.[17]

Given the oppositional force of such obstacles to his psychological and aesthetic development, how is it, then, that the timid, fragile schoolboy depicted at the opening of *A Portrait* comes to find the strength to choose the austere isolation of exile rather than capitulate to the illusory harmonies held out to him by Irish culture, the very harmonies parodied in the depiction of Russell in *Ulysses*? We can begin to address this key question by examining the manner in which the formation of Stephen's subjectivity is portrayed, from the first, in terms of his confrontation with the discursive aporias of the Dedalus household, with a contextual disjointedness powerfully conveyed, initially, through the disarming simplicity of a nursery rhyme:

> Pull out his eyes,
> Apologise,
> Apologise,
> Pull out his eyes.
> (*P* 8)[18]

With this rhyme, *A Portrait* opens on the haunting image of a child agitated by the confounding discursive disruptiveness with which his world is imbued. The poignancy of Stephen's condition is conveyed by the sheer abruptness with which his enchantment with seemingly harmless images of "moocows" and a "nicens" little boy named "baby tuckoo" is banished by the rhymes which, in the relentlessness of their very harmonies, strike terror into his childish heart.

It is no accident that Joyce's economical account of Stephen's very early subject formation should culminate in the appalling image of a child terrorized by seemingly innocuous nursery rhymes. In Stephen's world, as in our own, the nice banalities of moocows—the gentle banalities of a child's vision of harmony—*must* be overwhelmed by the rapacious "eagles" of a collective ideology whose threats are precisely those of an enforced harmony, one that everywhere insists on itself as a protection against dissonance. Paradoxically, this culturally enforced harmony insists on its prophylactic quality against dissonance, even as it feeds upon the dissonance embodied in the demand that the child apologize for an unstated crime, the dissonance figured in the implication that Stephen, anyway, must apologize simply in order to *be*. Thus, this rhyme embodies the stark social demand that the dissonant, unstructured economy of childhood give way before the rigors of civilization's too-often-repressive order, an order everywhere pursued, ironically enough, in the name of harmonious adult relations. The music of childish rhymes, often proffered to the child in the very name of imaginary delight can, with terrifying speed, be transformed into the means by which adults threaten the child who fails to conform to the dictates of the acculturation which is the prerogative, and relentless demand, of language itself.[19]

Crucially, Stephen's childish rhyme, expressive of a sort of music always so volatile in the mouths of children precisely because it simultaneously evokes and subverts the staid harmonies of adult music, is given utterance in a way that evinces both the spirit of play and the tones of cramped repression. Indeed, this rhyme is necessarily repressive, for the violent and unrelenting demand for an apology is aimed at nothing less than exacting the child's utter submission before the dictates of a restrictive social order. This quality of repression which—as Freud has shown in *Civilization and Its Discontents*—is endemic to the symbolic economy of adulthood, is treated as the necessary outcome of that economy's own logic by Jacques Lacan. For Lacan, the child necessarily forfeits the undifferentiated harmony which marks the imaginary milieu of infancy as she or he is assimilated to the "symbolic order" constitutive of adulthood; in other words, once the child attains a subject position within this symbolic order, a return to the plenitude figured in the infant's undifferentiated, even harmonious, experience of the imaginary is unthinkable.[20] To state the problem somewhat differently, even the simplistic rhyming which might *seem* to be the natural prerogative of children is wielded by adults as a means to subdue the implicit antagonism figured, from the adult's perspective, in the infant's relentless noise-making. Thus, the heavily accented rhythms and rhymes of the kind of discursivity offered children in the very name of childish delight can betray, as they surely do here, the adult's attempt to enforce the child's submission to the repressive order implicit in musical harmony, rather than merely serving as the vehicle through which the child is to be introduced to the delights of ordered sound.

In his landmark study *Noise: The Political Economy of Music,* Jacques Attali asserts that "noise is a weapon and music, primordially, is the formation, domestication, and ritualization of that weapon as a simulacrum of ritual murder" (24). Thus, as alluring as the novel's opening images of "moocows" and "baby tuckoo" certainly are, from this perspective the rounded vowels in which these images are articulated can be regarded as actually constituting a sort of music aimed at domesticating the weapon that Stephen's childish noise-making surely represents for the adults he lives with. As such, these images herald the process whereby Stephen's diffuse energy begins to be domesticated according to the dictates of the symbolic order, a process whose humorless nature is confirmed with the stark demand that he apologize for an unstated offense. This process of enforced domestication to the restrictive economies of adulthood is represented here as a noticeably horrendous simulacrum of the ritual murder of the threatening aspect which uncurbed childish behavior, and especially the child's relentless noise-making, inevitably poses from an adult perspective.

The problem here is not so much that childish noise-making should be curbed, for indeed it must be; crucially, however, the simulacrum of its murder tends actually to quash, rather than simply curb, its potentially creative dissonances right along with its noisiness, a conflation whose destructive quality Stephen will eventually come to experience with particular poignancy. Moreover, while Stephen is obviously far too young to recognize the implications this moment holds for his subsequent development, it nevertheless prefigures the harsh action of the cultural forces that will prompt his ultimate rejection of the facile harmonies of Irish culture. These harmonies, recapitulating the psychological dynamic of the Dedalus household, also tend to quash the creative potential of dissonance in their attempt to root out the childish noisiness from Irish daily life. These are the harmonies that Stephen will come to perceive as everywhere demanding apology for the sheer existence of the dissonances which, in tending to confuse dissonance with noise, such harmonies cannot tolerate; Stephen, however, will come to regard such dissonances as simply inescapable in the sheer force of their irresolvability, and thus necessary to confront in life and art alike.

For Stephen, as indeed for Joyce himself, Irish culture will loom as the figure of that which has merely domesticated, rather than aesthetically confronted, its own noise. This domestication is frightful to the extent that it represents a convincing, though artfully occluded, simulacrum of the ritual murder of the very element of Irish culture which—if it *were* creatively confronted—might, through the force of its transformed aspect as aesthetically charged dissonance, reinvigorate that culture. For Joyce the noise of Irish culture is too often merely speciously tamed or deliberately ignored, as in the literary productions he deemed most typical of the Revival. Of course, it must be remembered that, since the ritualized murder of noise *is* only a simulacrum of murder, no individual sacrifice is literally exacted in the novel's opening pages; if Stephen's childish vitality *is* sacrificed, the act is accomplished as it essentially is for all children. More significantly, it is not merely the potential weapon of Stephen's childish noise-making that is "sacrificed" through a process of domestication; it is rather the vital dissonances which might reinvigorate Stephen's Ireland, but which therefore also threaten to subvert the tenuous hegemonies of its power structure, that are symbolically sacrificed in the name of social harmony as the novel opens.

Despite the implications of its title, *A Portrait* is arguably more concerned with tracing the formation of Stephen's overall subjectivity than in following the narrow development of his artistic sensibility. From this perspective there is a certain strange, subjective logic to the manner in which the text simply jumps from portraying his confrontation with the terrifying music of childhood to the less ordered but no less threatening sounds of his schoolmates at play at Clongowes:

> The wide playgrounds were swarming with boys. All were shouting and the prefects urged them on with strong cries. . . . He kept on the fringe of his line, out of sight of his prefect, out of the reach of the rude feet, feigning to run now and then. (*P* 8)

Paradoxically, these swarming boys enjoy a certain harmony in the very unanimity of their sheer noisiness, while it is the silent Stephen whose position is dissonant, emblematic of an element which is not readily accounted for within a pedagogical economy that can tolerate the noise of boys at play precisely because it successfully circumscribes their potential disruptiveness in almost all other ways. That is, as noisy as the boys and prefects are, their response to a single imperative cry is immediate, and significant as a characteristic expression of their submissiveness before the dictates of order at Clongowes:

> A voice cried far out on the playground:
> —All in!
> Then other voices cried from the lower and third lines:
> —All in! All in! (*P* 11)

It becomes clear in these early pages that noise and, to a lesser extent, ordered sound mediate Stephen's growing perception of his own distinctiveness amid the strong drive toward homogeneity at Clongowes. At one point, he opens and shuts the flaps of his ears in order to control the impact of the noise of the refectory upon him, an effect he likens to the sudden cessation of the roar of a train as it enters a tunnel (*P* 13); in another instance, he sits in the crowded playroom, pretending to watch a game of dominos, but actually intent upon the small personal triumph of being "able to hear for an instant the little song of the gas" once or twice amidst the room's constant roar (*P* 14). Stephen's sense of his position at Clongowes as a somewhat marginal one is thus clearly tied to his awareness of the ubiquitous noise of the school as an overwhelming threat to his very individuality; moreover, his sense of his own uniqueness is just as clearly tied to the incremental gains he makes in his efforts to control the ability of noise to impinge upon his consciousness. Noise typically attends—along with his persistent attempt to control its impact upon him—the narrative of Stephen's perception of himself as fundamentally different from the other boys, while it is in juxtaposition with noise that the silence and ordered sounds of the Clongowes environment gain their considerable expressive power for him.

While Stephen will ultimately despair of resolving the discursive conflicts which attend his coming-to-subjectivity by means of aligning himself with the promise of a larger harmony—the very promise held out to him by Irish politics and religion alike—he nevertheless comes to believe that the discordances adhering to the daily life of his family, to life at Clongowes, and to the general life of Ireland itself may at least be transformed aesthetically, through the agency of art. Such an aesthetics necessarily involves the recognition of the positive aspects of dissonance, for dissonance, unlike noise, inheres in the very manner whereby harmony manifests itself, even as the coexistence of dissonance with harmony is always marked by an uneasy, volatile tension. In this respect, the narrative of the formation of Stephen's subjectivity illustrates the manner whereby the presence of irresolvable dissonance *within* harmony undoes the presumption that harmonic resolution can be readily achieved "according to its own criteria" (Adorno 161), even as the abiding drive toward such resolution prevents dissonance from falling back into the condition of intractable noise, into the aporetic state of confusion endemic, in Stephen's view, to the deceptively ordered world of Clongowes.

Even as Stephen's subjectivity begins to take clear shape over against the noisy homogeneity of the environment at Clongowes, his early sense of Irish politics is also shaped by the experience of unrelenting noise. In an unconscious bid for the family unity that his experience will soon show him to be, in fact, practically nonexistent, Stephen wonders if his family, though physically far removed from him, is arguing whether "Parnell was a bad man" at the very moment in which he debates this question with himself. In his simple assertion that noisy arguments are "called politics," Stephen uncannily hits on the way that—in Joyce's Ireland at least—the noise of argument forever supersedes the possibility of adjudicating political discussions to some productive end. In Joyce's Ireland, the dissonance of intractably opposed political ideas is shown to be insusceptible to the sort of healing national harmony that Hyde writes so passionately of in "The Necessity for De-Anglicising Ireland." Stephen's nascent sense that political argument reduces itself to sheer noise is, in fact, borne out during the dreadful discussion of Irish politics that ruins one memorable Christmas dinner in the Dedalus home. In the absence of a viable dialogue between the theology of the Church, which offers the Irish a harmony of transcendence, and the secular harmony that Parnell's shattered career had once seemed to promise them, this particular discussion of politics is fated to deteriorate into merely counterproductive noise, noise which overpowers the transformative potential of the dissonance always present—albeit in much more manageable form—in productive discussion.[21]

The incommensurability of the position of Dante Riordan—who despite her love for Parnell must stand against him with the Church—with that of Simon Dedalus and John Casey—who are compelled to stand with Parnell against the Church they nonetheless love—is illustrated in the following exchange, which turns on the adults' sense of the impact of the evening's argument upon young Stephen:

> —O, he'll remember all this when he grows up, said Dante hotly—the language he heard against God and religion and priests in his own home.
> —Let him remember too, cried Mr. Casey to her from across the table, the language with which the priests and the priests' pawns broke Parnell's heart and hounded him into his grave. . . . (*P* 34)

In the absence of an ability to engage in a productive dialogue about the issues which most concern them, these antagonists will remain unable to adjudicate, much less resolve, this intolerable situation to their mutual satisfaction. The harmonizing project embodied in political *discussion* thus necessarily breaks down into the intolerably harsh discord of a nasty political argument, and indeed breaks down into sheer noise, as the dinner progresses.

Ironically enough, the memory of the sheer noise of embattled argument clearly comes to have a greater impact upon Stephen than any of the specific arguments advanced upon this occasion. Moreover, the notion that noise is the predominant *effect* of this argument may help to explain the significance of Casey's odd digression on "a very famous spit." In recounting the manner whereby he had "replied" to an old woman who had reviled Parnell by spitting in her eye, Casey unwittingly provides Stephen with a crucial image of Irish politics as unrelenting noise:

> She stuck he ugly old face up at me . . . and I had my mouth full of tobacco juice. I bent down to her and *Phth!* says I to her like that. (*P* 36)

While the way that Casey likens the sound of his "famous spit" to an utterance could be read as simply emblematic of his lack of education and refinement, his crude action actually does "say" quite as much about the state of

Irish politics as any other utterance made here; where the dialogics of political discussion gives way to the unrelieved dissonance of noisy argument, *all* utterances devolve to the abject level of order as ordure, and thus this passage anticipates, in its own small way, the thematics of *Finnegans Wake*.[22] Indeed, by the end of this profane Christmas dinner the general level of discourse has been reduced to a state which, while not precisely excremental, is clearly debased: Dante has reduced herself to the level of execration ("Devil out of hell! We won! We won! We crushed him to death! Fiend!"), while Casey has stopped to that of maudlin bathos:

> —Poor Parnell! He cried loudly. My dead king!
> He sobbed loudly and bitterly.
> Stephen, raising his terrorstricken face, saw that his father's eyes were full of tears. (*P* 39)

This passage admirably illustrates Joyce's keen sense of the delicate interrelationship between harmony, dissonance, and noise. Where a conception of harmony which attempts to spurn dissonance altogether is likely to result in the bland productions of the Irish Literary Revival, dissonance without harmony leads to the unrelieved noise which heralds the total breakdown of communication captured so powerfully in this episode. In Stephen, Joyce has created a protagonist sensitive enough simply to *register* the full effect of such noise, a character sensitive enough to *be* properly terror-stricken in the face of an unrelenting assault which, like the thunder that terrorized Joyce all his life (Ellmann, *James Joyce* 25), embodies a kind of noise unrelieved by the ameliorating force of harmony. Stephen's retention of the strong impression of his terror in the face of this revelation of a politics from which any vestige of harmony has been stripped away is of the utmost significance. This recollection will serve as a lasting challenge, and persistent foil, to his attempt to create for himself a position from which to confront the noise of Irish politics in some productive fashion.

The inability of Irish society to confront, effectively, the noise of its own politics—thus missing, perhaps, the chance to transform that noise into something productively meaningful—becomes one of the key sources of Stephen's resolve to forge the "uncreated conscience of his race" (*P* 253). For Stephen, as indeed for Joyce himself, art and not politics becomes the realm wherein the seemingly overwhelming confusion of Irish public life—a state of confusion closely allied to a sense that the dissonances of that public life tend to proliferate beyond the scope of anyone's ability to control them—can be creatively confronted. This creative confrontation can occur only by way of an aesthetic process wherein the endlessly proliferating—and thus merely noise—dissonances of Irish life are subjected to aesthetic control by the deliberate juxtaposition of carefully selected dissonances—dissonances, crucially, which are thus given unprecedented value—with the cadences of a suddenly chastened, though strangely reinvigorated, sense of harmony.

Stephen's apprenticeship in this aesthetics of selective dissonance necessarily involves the subversion of his allegiance to all sorts of facile harmonies. Thus we can see, for instance, why it is so necessary that the harmonies of the aesthetics he expounds in the company of Lynch should be effectively overturned in a brief but nonetheless crucial passage in the final chapter of *A Portrait*. Here a clangorous dray momentarily disrupts the serene obliviousness to external phenomena characteristic of Stephen's expository mode, and very consciousness, throughout this episode:

> —This hypothesis, Stephen began.
> A long dray laden with old iron came round the corner, covering the end of Stephen's speech with the harsh roar of jangled and rattling metal. Lynch closed his ears and gave out oath after oath till the dray had passed. Then he turned on his heel rudely. Stephen turned also and waited for a few moments till his companion's ill humour had had its vent.
> —This hypothesis, Stephen repeated . . . (P 209)

As silly as Lynch's repeated oaths certainly seem, his rude manner curiously acknowledges the sheer existential power embodied in the dray's noise, the power to disrupt the grandeur of all philosophy, the power to bring discourse itself to a full stop. Stephen, on the other hand, attempts to continue his pedantic exposition of aesthetic principles as if nothing has happened, but his stubborn insistence on elaborating his theory of abstract beauty in the face of the demands placed on his attention by this avatar of stark materiality marks the tenacity of his allegiance to a rigorously harmonious aesthetic conception, one which simply cannot account for the problem posed by the dray's intractable noisiness. The irony in Stephen's position in this respect follows from the fact that noise can only be excluded, never accounted for, by an aesthetics which has no place for noise *as* dissonance, even though noise ceases to be *merely* noisy once the importance of its dissonant role in respect to harmony is duly recognized. Despite his considerable aesthetic sophistication, Stephen is unable to recognize the importance of this distinction for his aesthetics, and therefore unknowingly helps to set up the sequence of events that will subsequently lay his aesthetics low.

Here Joyce has selectively set the representation of the dray's intractable dissonance over against that of Stephen's position as a privileged thinker, and has done so in such a way that the wisdom of Stephen's aesthetic thought is effectively called into question for the reader attentive to the problematic I have described here. Moreover, Joyce has decisively begun to advance an aesthetic mode which stands in stark opposition to the facile certainties about the *independence* of harmony from dissonance characteristic of movements such as the Irish Literary Revival. Despite T. S. Eliot's view of Joyce's modernism as a noble attempt to do the best one can with the depraved materials of modern life, organizing those materials, however parodically, in order to bring them into harmony with the transcendence Eliot implicitly ascribes to the traditions of Western art (26), Joyce's narrative betrays no longing for the lost plentitude of those traditions. Rather, the revelation of the inadequacy of Stephen's oblivious solipsism, of the very condition which justly makes him a figure of fun, signals a crucial transition in Joyce's aesthetics to a mode which everywhere challenges its own representations. Thus, the subversion of the protagonist becomes a kind of ironic ritual sacrifice, a sacrifice which expends Stephen's integrity in order to negate his own spurious negation of the material contingencies and intractable dissonances of Irish life, to negate, that is, the tendency he shares with the exponents of the Revival.

The aesthetics of *selective* dissonance which Joyce practices here may never quite serve as a fully successful corrective to the problematic aspects of Irish politics and daily life—much less actually transform those problematic qualities into something recognizable as harmony—but it does at least perpetuate the memory of the fundamental inability to confront noise that too frequently devolves from certain facile tendencies in Irish thought. In this perpetual re-presentation of the memory of what has become its own terrifying noise to the Irish conscience, Joyce's art keeps alive the hope that such terror, such noise, may one day actually be successfully confronted in the political realm. In the face of an Irish polity that suppresses the awareness of its own noisy discords in the name of a bland conception of social harmony, Stephen's would-be art—like Joyce's achieved aesthetics—aspires simply to *retain* the terror associated with the noise of Irish life so that the forces which underlie that terror might themselves one day appear as the creatively iconoclastic dissonances which only art can make of them. As dissonances, these elements can finally be perceived for what they are, rather than repudiated as the unthinkable terrors which the act of mere repudiation in fact always *makes* of them.

Through the mediation of art, noise is transformed into dissonance, into a quality which harmony can at least address, even if such dissonance must remain unresolved. Thus the sheer terror of noise is transformed into a phenomenon that begins to be understandable, a phenomenon that can be usefully juxtaposed with the facile expectation of resolution forever held out, and snatched away, by the promise of harmony. Whereas Joyce himself cowered at the sound of thunder, his art enables his readers to begin to confront the terrifying rumblings of their own embroiled socio-political lives, to begin to hear those rumblings as simply the dissonances which inevitably attend all dreams of harmony, rather than as noises that can only be cowered from, or repudiated at our peril. In this respect, his art fulfills the promise of a singer singing beautifully in the very midst of an accompaniment that is never quite right, and which thus highlights the enduring fragility of the singer's melody, and the self-awareness of his harmony's ultimate unattainability, all the more.

Notes

1. This tradition begins with T. S. Eliot's famous remark that *Ulysses* marks a crucial "step toward making the modern world possible for art" (Eliot 27). Eliot celebrates Joyce's supposed attempt to shore up the vestiges of harmony in Western culture against the forces of what Yeats would come to call the "filthy modern tide." This view enables Eliot to praise the structural harmony of *Ulysses*—a harmony evidenced for him by the novel's unifying mythic theme—even in the face of the unprecedented proliferation of linguistic dissonance which so often seems to undermine such harmony in Joyce. This view holds a certain resonance for the reader-response critics who have built on the work of Wolfgang Iser (especially his "Patterns of Communication in Joyce's *Ulysses*"). Iser's theory of indeterminacy of meaning renders Joyce's dissonances as hermeneutic gaps which, even as they disrupt the reader's expectations, force the reader to search for, and indeed create, the narrative "world" that more traditional narrative models represent much less problematically (Iser 232). Arguably, Iser's method ultimately places the reader where Eliot had situated Joyce himself, at the heart of a dilemma where one must do one's best "with the materials at hand" to control the unruly stuff of modern life. This elevation of the reader to the status which previous criticism had accorded Joyce himself is variously evidenced in the work of a number of critics who have extended, and modified, Iser's insight into the dynamic whereby a unified reading is fashioned by the reader in the face of the sheer indeterminacy in Joyce. See Michael Patrick Gillespie, Karen Lawrence, John Paul Riquelme, and Brook Thomas.

2. S. L. Goldberg's work is most noteworthy in this regard. Much of the vigor of Goldberg's study stems from his dissatisfaction with precisely the dualistic tendency in Joyce criticism whose persistence I have reasserted here. However, Goldberg's discussion of *Ulysses* is so carefully tied to his presentation of Stephen's aesthetic concerns in *A Portrait* that he comes to present the dissonances of *Ulysses* as structurally organized by a *mere* further elaboration of Stephen's aesthetics. His strong predilection for this view prevents Goldberg from adequately acknowledging the ways in which the dissonances of *Ulysses* never fully harmonize with the work's structural order, however the *nature* of that order may happen to be understood.

3. Richard Ellmann's sense of the reconciliatory drive embodied in *Ulysses* enables him to assert that Molly's monologue is less "an addition" to the dialogue between Bloom and Stephen than a sort of happy "correction" for what that dialogue simply omits. In this view, "Penelope" becomes the site of a surprisingly complete resolution of the thematic concerns of *Ulysses*: "None of the principal figures is complete in himself, but together they sum up what is affirmable. At the end we are brought back to the earth, to spring, to vegetation, and to sexual love" (*Ulysses on the Liffey* 167).

4. Few critics have gone so far as Robert S. Ryf in asserting that *A Portrait* is the key which gives us mastery over the entire Joyce canon. Significantly, however, Ryf largely ignores the various problems that the *Wake* poses for such an argument. With the "Joyce industry" typically producing several studies of *Ulysses* each year which make only passing mention of the problematic status the *Wake* holds for the study of *any* work in the Joyce canon, the extent to which the *Wake* is crucial for any new study remains a difficult one for the future direction of Joyce criticism.

5. In this regard, see especially Attridge and Ferrer, eds., *Post-structuralist Joyce*. My assertion that post-structuralist critics tend to read Joyce backward from the *Wake* is evidenced by every essay in this collection. In contradistinction to such an approach, I would argue for

the persistence of harmony in the *Wake,* even if such harmony must be understood as sub-servient to the work's monumental dissonances. Indeed, the dialectical relationship between harmony and dissonance is retained within the syntactical strategies of the work's convention-ally structured sentences, which continually evoke the harmonizing force such structure signi-fies, even as a relentless proliferation of neologisms and portmanteau words in substitution for recognizable nouns and adjectives ensures the reader's perpetual confrontation with the text's confounding dissonances.

6.   I do not mean to suggest that post-structuralist readings invariably elide the telos of harmony arguably so persistent in Joyce's work *despite* the presence of dissonances so over-whelming as to render, at least seemingly, that telos inoperative. Patrick McGee, for instance, builds on the insights of post-structuralism without discounting the vestiges of harmony in Joyce's work, accounting of the obdurate polysemy of Joyce's dissonances without eliding the ideological pointedness of his parodic drive. In this regard, McGee is especially incisive in his reading of the parody, in "Cyclops," of the harmony offered up by the purveyors of the sort of myopic nationalism Joyce could never endure (see especially 78–85).

7.   Clearly, Jameson's sense of the impossibility of formulating a totalizing aesthetics, an impossibility especially evident in our historical moment, mirrors Adorno's own conviction that the absolutes which once served as the putative guarantors of aesthetic formulations are no longer thinkable in the wake of the decisive split between the subject and object that is the legacy of the Enlightenment. In this view, the Enlightenment pursued instrumental reason in the name of ending human subservience to nature, only to create a new subservience to the "second nature" which evolved as the means of production, arrogated in an attempt to subdue nature, failed to serve humanity's liberation from natural necessity, serving instead to ensure the eventual domination of the industrialized state. For Adorno, the legacy of the Enlighten-ment therefore logically culminates not *in* enlightenment but in the horrors of Auschwitz. See Horkheimer and Adorno, *Dialectic of Enlightenment,* especially the chapters entitled "The Con-cept of Enlightenment" (3–42), and "Elements of Anti-Semitism: Limits of Enlightenment" (168–208).

8.   Adorno is particularly interested in the manner whereby "artists of extremely sensi-tive taste . . . have used taste to brush taste against the grain, suffusing the concept of taste with a dialectic that pushes it beyond itself towards truth" (161). This "determinate negation" of the tendency to prefer mere taste to truth proceeds from anything but a spirit of gratuitous iconoclasm. Indeed, the quality of determinate negation—of negating the specious negations which *taste* itself makes as it pursues its facile affirmations—is historically inscribed, in Adorno's view, in modernism's very expectations of what the work of art should *be:* "The demand that present-day art be reflective means, among other things, that it must become conscious of, and articulate, its aversions. There is a sense, then, in which art is an allergic reac-tion against art. . . ." (52–53).

9.   See R. F. Foster's study of the milieu of the Revival and its backgrounds (431–60). Foster's account of the forces informing the rise of the Revival demonstrates just how various, and obdurate, the internal differences firmly in place among the Irish by the late nineteenth century, and earlier, actually were. See also Seamus Deane in this regard. My work is indebted to Deane's careful contextualization of Joyce in the milieu of the Revival, a movement for which Deane evinces considerable sympathy even as he refuses to minimize the complexities attending the material and cultural conditions in which it emerged, the very conditions which the Revival itself too often tended to slight. Deane's chapters on "Joyce and Stephen: The Provincial Intellectual" (75–91), and "Joyce on Nationalism" (92–107), are particularly perti-nent to the concerns of my discussion.

10.   See Foster's excellent bibliographic essay, especially 648–52, for a copious sampling of works relevant in this regard.

11.   The view that the development of Joyce's art depended upon his liberation from Irish mores has been both affirmed and extended under the influence of Bernard Benstock's

James Joyce: The Undiscover'd Country. Amplifying the argument already strongly suggested in Ellmann's biography and throughout Hugh Kenner's work, Benstock asserts that Joyce ultimately rejected Ireland in favor of the large—and in this view aesthetically less problematic—European literary tradition. The importance of Seamus Deane's work on Joyce and the Revival as the first serious response of informed scholarship to Benstock's influential study cannot be minimized.

12.   References are to the text in James Joyce, *The Critical Writings of James Joyce,* hereafter cited as *CW.*

13.   References are to James Joyce, *A Portrait of the Artist as a Young Man,* hereafter cited as *P.*

14.   Curiously, Ngũgĩwa gives his blessing to those who will translate his subsequent work into English (xiv). One may well wonder what the consequences of this blessing are for his expressed desire to forestall the Euro-American appropriation of his work. It could be argued, perhaps, that to the extent in which translation can be posited as an inherently secondary activity, only a *representation* of Ngũgĩwa's work can be stolen once it is translated, not the work itself.

15.   References are to James Joyce, *Ulysses,* The Corrected Text, hereafter cited as *U.* Citations are by chapter and line number(s), following the practice established for this edition.

16.   It is not my intention to engage in the banalities of deconstruction-bashing here. I would simply point out that the sheer delight Derrida so evidently takes in exposing our linguistic predicament, while certainly present in Joyce, is strongly tempered, especially in his portrayal of Stephen, with a great deal of sadness. This sadness takes much of its particular shape from an inability to *enjoy* the mastery of English in any sustained fashion, a condition stemming, at least in part, from the uniquely problematic status attending the Irish mastery of the tongue of the usurper in the milieu of Stephen's Dublin. In this regard at least, Stephen truly *is* the son of Simon Dedalus, who experiences a keen sense of this dilemma as well.

17.   Derrida has spoken to this dilemma in many places, but for an especially cogent and compelling articulation of this problem, see Paul de Man, "The Resistance to Theory." For instance:

> The resistance to theory is a resistance to the rhetorical or tropological dimension of language, a dimension which . . . can be revealed in any verbal event when it is read textually. Since grammar as well as figuration is an integral part of reading, it follows that reading will be a negative process in which the grammatical cognition is undone, at all times, by its rhetorical displacement. (17)

18.   Chester G. Anderson argues that Stephen himself composes this rhyme as a way to reduce the trauma inflicted upon him by Dante Riordan's threatening remark that, if he does not apologize, "the eagles will come and pull out his eyes" (*P* 8). While I do not agree that the question of the rhyme's authorship can be so easily settled, its inscription of boundless terror, along with its simultaneous domestication of that very terror through the agency of ordered sound, seems to me to be irreducible. Anderson's reading, while approaching the arcane in a number of places, remains one of the finest sustained Freudian studies of *A Portrait.*

19.   For Jacques Lacan the subject hardly has a choice whether to acquiesce before the dictates of symbolic language: unless we are mad enough to be institutionalized, we know ourselves, indeed are who we are as recognizable subjects, *in* symbolic language. See especially "On a Question Preliminary to Any Possible Treatment of Psychosis" in this regard. Given the relative absence of any suggestion of the possibility for active resistance to the tyrannies of the symbolic order in Lacan's thought, Julia Kristeva's notion of the semiotic becomes especially significant for my reading of Joyce's art as one informed by resistance to those tyrannies. For Kristeva, the concept of the semiotic represents the process by which imaginary discourse, linked to the biological drives which can never be subsumed by the symbolic order, breaks

through the barriers established by "official," unitary discourse at the points of slippage which inevitably attend the conflicts, and mutual incommensurabilities, of its discursive practices. See Kristeva, *Desire in Language,* especially the chapter entitled "Word, Dialogue, and Novel" (64–91).

20.   See Lacan, "On a Question Preliminary to Any Possible Treatment of Psychosis." In extending—and to some extent resisting—Lacan's views in this regard, Kristeva's idea of "the semiotic" underscores the notion that the imaginary persists despite the best efforts of symbolic language to suppress it, since it is tied to those creaturely drives (Trieben) which symbolic language can neither fully control nor account for. See Kristeva (162–63).

21.   Jürgen Habermas develops the distinction between productive argument and mere conflict in *Communication and the Evolution of Society.* See especially 88–90. Also see Paul B. Armstrong's discussion of the distinction between productive and unproductive conflict in *Conflicting Readings: Variety and Validity in Interpretation* (147–50).

22.   "And he clopped his rude hand to his eacy hitch and he ordurd and his thick spch spck for her to shut up shop, dappy. And the duppy shot the shutter clup. . . ." (*FW* 23). Thus Joyce articulates the early note of supremely dissonant confusion in the *Wake.* Here the attempt to order the phenomenal world by means of language has been hopelessly mixed up with the sheer grossness of ordure, emblematic of the intractability of stark materiality to any project which would euphemize its sheer thingness away. This dynamic is staged, in this instance, through the egregious bullying of "Jarl von Hoother Boanerges himself, the old terror of the dames" (*FW* 22). Jarl's gross self-emptying exacts another's "shutting up," devolving, in turn, into a self-indulgent rant expressed as a stream of nonsense syllables. But the sense in Jarl's lack of it is precisely the degeneration of the spoken word's harmony, garbled as it comes to reflect an action so gross as to be insusceptible to even the most eloquent efforts of amelioration. Indeed, such moments of nearly total linguistic degeneration, and they are legion in the *Wake,* may signify Joyce's tacit assertion of the inability of ordered language ultimately to get at certain experiences, a disordering of language being the very condition upon which some experiences are based.

Works Cited

Adorno, Theodor W. *Aesthetic Theory.* Trans. C. Lenhardt. New York: Routledge, 1984.

Anderson, Chester G. "Baby Tuckoo: Joyce's 'Features of Infancy.' " *Approaches to Joyce's Portrait: Ten Essays.* Ed. Thomas F. Staley and Bernard Benstock. Pittsburgh: U of Pittsburgh P, 1976. 135–69.

Armstrong, Paul B. *Conflicting Readings: Variety and Validity in Interpretation.* Chapel Hill: U of North Carolina P, 1990.

Attali, Jacques. *Noise: The Political Economy of Music.* Trans. Brian Massumi. Minneapolis: U of Minnesota P, 1985.

Attridge, Derek, and Daniel Ferrer, eds. *Post-structuralist Joyce: Essays from the French.* Cambridge: Cambridge UP, 1984.

Benstock, Bernard. *James Joyce: The Undiscover'd Country.* New York: Barnes, 1977.

Deane, Seamus. *Celtic Revivals.* London: Faber, 1985.

de Man, Paul. "The Resistance to Theory." *The Resistance to Theory.* Foreword Wlad Godzich. Minneapolis: U of Minnesota P, 1986. 3–20.

Derrida, Jacques. "Structure, Sign and Play in the Discourse of the Human Sciences." *Writing and Difference.* Trans., Intro., and Notes Alan Bass. Chicago: U of Chicago P, 1978. 278–93.

Eliot, T. S. "Ulysses, Order and Myth." *Critical Essays on James Joyce.* Ed. Bernard Benstock. Boston: Hall, 1985. 25–27.

Ellmann, Richard. *Ulysses on the Liffey.* New York: Oxford UP, 1972.

————. *James Joyce*. New and Revised Edition. New York: Oxford UP, 1983.

Foster, R. F. *Modern Ireland: 1600–1972*. Harmondsworth: Penguin, 1988.

Freud, Sigmund. *Civilization and Its Discontents*. Trans. James Strachey. New York and London: Norton, 1961.

Gillespie, Michael Patrick. *Reading the Book of Himself: Narrative Strategies in the Works of James Joyce*. Columbus: Ohio State UP, 1989.

Goldberg, S. L. *The Classical Temper: A Study of James Joyce's Ulysses*. New York: Barnes, 1961.

Habermas, Jürgen. *Communication and the Evolution of Society*. Trans. Thomas McCarthy. Boston: Beacon, 1979.

Horkheimer, Max, and Theodor W. Adorno. *Dialectic of Enlightenment*. Trans. John Cumming. New York: Continuum, 1987.

Hyde, Douglas. "The Necessity for De-Anglicising Ireland." *Irish Literature: A Reader*. Ed. Maureen O'Rourke Murphy and James Mackillop. Syracuse: Syracuse UP, 1987. 137–47.

Iser, Wolfgang. "Patterns of Communication in Joyce's *Ulysses*." *The Implied Reader: Patterns of Communication in Prose Fiction from Bunyan to Beckett*. Baltimore: Johns Hopkins UP, 1974. 196–233.

Joyce, James. *Finnegans Wake*. New York: Viking, 1959.

————. "The Holy Office." *The Critical Writings of James Joyce*. Ed. Ellsworth Mason and Richard Ellmann. New York: Viking, 1959. 149–52.

————. *A Portrait of the Artist as a Young Man*. Text, Criticism, and Notes. Ed. Chester G. Anderson. New York: Viking, 1975.

————. *Ulysses*. The Corrected Text. Ed. Hans Walter Gabler. New York: Vintage, 1986.

Kristeva, Julia. *Desire in Language: A Semiotic Approach to Literature and Art*. Ed. Leon S. Roudiez. Trans. Thomas Gora et al. New York: Columbia UP, 1980.

Lacan, Jacques. "On a Question Preliminary to Any Possible Treatment of Psychosis." *Écrits: A Selection*. Trans. Alan Sheridan. New York and London: Norton, 1977.

Lawrence, Karen. *The Odyssey of Style in* Ulysses. Princeton: Princeton UP, 1981.

McGee, Patrick. *Paperspace: Style as Ideology in Joyce's* Ulysses. Lincoln: U of Nebraska P, 1988.

Ngũgĩwa wa Thiong'o. *Decolonising the Mind: The Politics of Language in African Literature*. London: Currey, 1987.

Riquelme, John Paul. *Teller and Tale in Joyce's Fiction: Oscillating Perspectives*. Baltimore: Johns Hopkins UP, 1983.

Ryf, Robert S. *A New Approach to Joyce:* The Portrait of the Artist *as a Guide Book*. Berkeley and Los Angeles: U of California P, 1962.

Stephanson, Anders. "Regarding Postmodernism—A Convention with Fredric Jameson." *Universal Abandon? The Politics of Postmodernism*. Ed. Andrew Ross. Minneapolis: U of Minnesota P, 1988. 3–30.

Thomas, Brook. *Joyce's* Ulysses: A Book Of Many Happy Returns. Baton Rouge: Louisiana State UP, 1982.

Framing, Being Framed, and the Janus Faces of Authority

VICKI MAHAFFEY

In *A Portrait of the Artist as a Young Man,* Stephen Dedalus is represented as a sensitive reader of cultural signs, trying to forge an identity for himself consistent with his patrimony. What he shows through his erratic behavior is that his fathers have bequeathed him not one but two mutually incompatible models of responding to righteous authority, and as the book progresses, we watch Stephen alternating helplessly between an obedient and a scornfully defiant response to the imperative to sacrifice himself for a communal cause. The reason that Stephen is powerless to detach himself from the pendulum swing of these two responses is that he never questions the major premise of authority: its idealization of ultimate transcendence.[1] Stephen's aim is to establish for himself an authority comparable to the authority he admires and resists, to see himself raised above his peers, and to resist any awareness of the universality—the commonness—of his feelings. Stephen fails to realize not only that his own reaction to authority is ambivalent, but also that the authority he would appropriate is itself split: its "head" or consciousness is divided from its body or sensual apprehensions. Christian morality has denominated these two bases of authority as "good" and "evil," respectively, thereby delegitimating sensory perception as an important part of what it means to be human. It is difficult for Stephen to see that, when he periodically defies the injunction to become a martyred hero, he is not rejecting Christian morality so much as responding to another authority, that of the senses, which awakens him poetically to the color and music of language. Stephen remains bound to his confusion not only because he accepts the view that mental and sensual impulses are antithetical but also because he upholds a view of authority as something that transcends its human and social context. His salvation and temptation are mapped onto the "higher" and "lower" regions of an individual being; by focusing on the singularity of that being, he is able to disregard the social and linguistic traditions and conventions that

An abridged and redacted version of "*A Portrait of the Artist as a Young Man*" from *Reauthorizing Joyce* (Cambridge University Press, 1988; paperback University Press of Florida, 1995), by permission of the author.

to some extent frame every individual. *A Portrait of the Artist* urges readers to recognize the kind of contextual frames that Stephen himself disregards, while remembering the real if not unlimited capacity of a narrator to frame personal experience, in turn.

Portrait, like *Ulysses, Finnegans Wake,* and even *Dubliners,* explores the similarity and the tension between mental and sensory authorities. The authority Stephen initially prefers is the authority of deliberate intention, which produces cultural and religious heroes. Such authority, in its conscious-ness and rationality, works better in theory (and in crises) than in everyday practice, when it is easily undermined by less conscious desires. Stephen's lan-guage repeatedly reveals the conflict between will and hidden desire, between his intended meaning and the meaning that his metaphors imply. Joyce prompts us to hear, in the underlying figures that shape language less obtru-sively than do conventionally determined meanings and logic, the clusters of puns that trace what James Merrill once called "the hidden wish of words."[2]

In *Portrait*, Stephen's model for sovereign authority —the authority of heroic self-sacrifice—is the head, which he associates with Christ. His metaphor for sensory authority and for rebellious uprising is his penis, which serves as an intimate embodiment of Lucifer and of the romantic poets. In the end Stephen tries to reconcile mind and body by becoming an author, by appealing to words as authorities that combine meaning and sensuality, but, although Stephen is finally able to balance the rival claims of mind and body through language, he is not a self-conscious enough reader to understand the complex dialogical relation between words or texts, on the one hand, and the human, social contexts that both define and are explained by them, on the other.

Stephen's subconscious sensitivity to the "unauthorized," figurative or poetic dimension of language is the source of the book's subtle humor. When, for example, the priest at the end of the third chapter tells him, "As long as you commit that sin, my poor child, you will never be worth one farthing to God" (*P,* 145), Stephen's conscious interpretation of the sentence acknowl-edges the priest's benevolent intention: he knows that the priest is urging him to reform so that his soul may regain its value in God's eyes. Uncon-sciously, however, he registers the economic nature of the metaphor very sharply, as we can see three pages later, when he pictures his devotion as a heavenly "sale": "[H]e seemed to feel his soul in devotion pressing like fingers the keyboard of a great cash register and to see the amount of his purchase start forth immediately in heaven, not as a number but as a frail column of incense or as a slender flower" (*P,* 148). Stephen has intuited the underlying materialism of what he believes to be a purely spiritual order, and he expresses his unauthorized knowledge through figures, illustrating his deter-mination to ensure that he will be worth much more than one farthing to God. Like Issy in *Finnegans Wake,* who will "confess it by her figure and . . . deny it to your face,"[3] Stephen "knows" two faces of verbal meaning at any one time, one conventional and intentional, the other sensual and figurative. Stephen's approach to language is as concrete as his approach to materiality is abstract, but he lacks conscious awareness of the doubleness of his response. As a result, his two kinds of knowledge are frequently in conflict in a way that makes him unable to sustain either.

It is the conflict between the authorities Stephen consciously embraces and those that he unconsciously, but demonstrably, hears and responds to that makes the first four chapters of *Portrait* difficult to read.[4] Stephen's receptivity to conflicting authorities causes the reader to react to him with ambivalence: his acute sensitivity to the latent metaphoricity of language evokes sympathy from similarly "artistic" readers, but his willful insensitivity to the discrepancy between his intuitive knowledge and his rational determinations prompts sharply analytical readers to regard him ironically. Stephen's growing power to articulate and encompass his experience is similarly double-edged. As *Portrait* progresses, Stephen learns to double and redouble his story, which is itself a doubling of "history," producing a gradual enrichment of text and context. At first we may be tempted to see Stephen as an ever-widening frame who manages to recapitulate, in his mind and verse, the stylistic evolution of the nineteenth century from Byron through Pater. By the last chapter, however, it has become apparent that Stephen's very ability to appropriate various styles constitutes an artistic failure: his poetic productions are doubly derivative of his reading and of his adolescent emotions. It is at this point, when we see that Stephen himself has been "framed," that we are in a position to appreciate the way Joyce's language has succeeded in overspilling the boundaries of Stephen's consciousness. The power of Joyce's language to frame Stephen illuminates the power of Stephen's own language to surpass as well as contain his thought. Stephen's discoveries can never be more than recoveries as long as he refuses to see that authority has not one but two faces, and that those faces are always partially framed by the changing forces of history and language.

AUTHORITY AS DOUBLE-BIND

Joyce poses the problem of the double-bind in both the first and last chapters of *Portrait,* bracketing the book with the dilemma it is meant to reproduce and leave behind. The first major event to leave its mark on Stephen's consciousness is the experience of being bullied—first by Wells, then by Father Dolan. When Wells shoulders him into the square ditch, Stephen retaliates physiologically, by getting sick, and imaginatively, by intertwining his story with history, envisioning himself as Little and Parnell, dead: "And Wells would be sorry then for what he had done" (*P,* 24). Stephen actively implements the same strategy when he is later bullied by Father Dolan: in his effort to become a hero, he models himself after a head—"some great person whose head was in the books of history"—and in particular the great men mentioned in Peter Parley's tales about Greece and Rome whose names resembled his own (P, 53, 55). He places his trust in heads or leaders and in names, a trust that ultimately seems justified when the rector fulfills the promise of his name and position by rectifying Stephen's wrong.

The glory of Stephen's double triumph, imaginative and active—a triumph that transforms him in his own eyes into "Stephen Hero"—tends to overshadow the fact that Wells bullies him twice, verbally as well as physically, and that Stephen fails to understand the more subtle taunting that mocks his own habits of mind. When Wells asks Stephen whether or not he kisses his mother before he goes to bed, he implicitly limits the range of responses to two mutually exclusive possibilities, so that, whether Stephen answers yes or no, he is still bound by the configuration of the question. The questioner retains his authority and reaffirms his superiority as long as the respondent accepts the terms of the question, a situation that bewilders Stephen when Wells and his friends laugh at him: "Stephen tried to laugh with them. He felt his whole body hot and confused in a moment. What was the right answer to the question? He had given two and still Wells laughed. But Wells must know the right answer for he was in the third of grammar" (P, 14). What Stephen fails to see is that Wells's question encapsulates the dilemma of distance that has baffled not only Stephen but many of his readers as well. The only way to escape ridicule is to reject not the gesture of kissing and the love that gesture represents but the simplistic model of relationship as something that is either neurotically close or unnaturally distant. Stephen never succeeds in escaping the domination of that question: his responses to his mother at the beginning and end of the book—naive identification and insensitive independence—are his two answers to Wells writ large.

When Cranly asks Stephen a version of Wells's question near the end of the book—"Do you love your mother?"—Stephen answers, "I don't know what your words mean" (P, 240). By that point Stephen has learned to escape laughter but not the rhetorical tines of a two-pronged question. Ten days later, Cranly, who alone among Stephen's friends seems sympathetically interested in the dilemma, propounds the problem in an altered form to Dixon and to Emma's brother, as Stephen records in his diary: "A mother let her child fall into the Nile. Still harping on the mother. A crocodile seized the child. Mother asked it back. Crocodile said all right if she told him what he was going to do with the child, eat it or not eat it" (P, 250). The tone of easy familiarity that Stephen assumes in retelling the story is misleading in one sense but absolutely appropriate in another: the story of the mother and the crocodile exemplifies in an almost scholastic form the comic hopelessness of unnaturally limited alternatives, a trap that Stephen, despite his knowledgeable air, has never been able to elude. Like the mother who cannot save her child by giving the crocodile either of the answers he suggests, Stephen stands to lose no matter how he responds to the riddle of relationship as traditionally formulated. He has tried both answers (with Wells) and no answer (with Cranly), but neither his eagerness to give the appropriate answer nor his refusal to respond at all constitutes an effective challenge to the question.

Readers of *Portrait* who accept the model of relationship imposed by the questions of Wells, Cranly, and the crocodile are themselves caught in a cognitive trap that resembles Stephen's. The reader who chooses to sympathize with Stephen without balancing such sympathy with a more detached analysis of Stephen's shortcomings may see a reflection of his or her propensity to identify with a superior figure when Stephen chooses to identify himself with a literary or historical "hero" such as Parnell, Byron, or Daedalus. As Stephen shows, such proclivities, while evidencing imagination and feeling, leave those who indulge them vulnerable to ridicule. If, on the other hand, the reader goes to the other extreme and reads everything ironically, the Stephen of Chapter V again reflects the reader's own hauteur. An ironic reading must inevitably condemn Stephen for not knowing "what the heart is and what it feels" (*P,* 252) as he jauntily escapes to Paris, but a reader who eschews sympathy altogether becomes guilty of the same dismissiveness he or she is criticizing.

Stephen continues to regard his attachment and vulnerability to others as a problem that must be categorically affirmed or denied, but elsewhere in the first chapter Joyce presents him with an alternative approach to the dilemma of relationship: he could restructure the question. When Stephen is in the infirmary suffering the consequences of Wells's bullying, Athy gives him a breezy reading lesson that takes his own name as its text. Having told Stephen that Athy is the name of a town, he asks him a riddle: "Why is the county Kildare like the leg of a fellow's breeches?" When Stephen gives up, Athy answers the riddle—"Because there is a thigh in it" (*P,* 25). He then challenges Stephen to ask the riddle another way, but when Stephen declares himself unable to re-riddle the question, Athy refuses to help him. The reader, like Stephen, is being asked to reformulate old riddles ("That's an old riddle, he said" [*P,* 25]), to structure them in new ways. In the infirmary Athy presents to Stephen a way to get well (and to get Wells), but Stephen is still entranced with the old riddle of heroism and betrayal, as his subsequent vision of Parnell's death shows. When readers in the 1960s debated the question of our aesthetic distance from Stephen, they reenacted Stephen's own dilemma about authority. Whether defending or attacking Stephen's character, the reader is trapped by a single question and for that reason vulnerable to the laughter of more experienced schoolfellows. As we now know, both responses and neither response are appropriate. The "old" riddle of mutually exclusive possibilities must be analyzed and reformulated.

Athy's riddle has a significant structural feature; it does not explicitly recognize either the speaker's or the listener's investment in the riddle of naming. Although the riddle forges a relation between a town and a part of the leg, it fails to indicate that it is Athy's own name that makes such a pattern of relationship significant. The structure of the question makes it possible for the listener to separate the riddle from the context that makes it personally meaningful—its relation to the person recounting it, as well as its relevance to the person listening to it ("You have a queer name, Dedalus, and I have a queer name too, Athy" [P, 25]). The riddle allows us to bypass teller and auditor as named entities importantly implicated in the network of language and to focus instead on more coincidental and remote symmetries of sound. Finally, the riddle challenges us to link two different contexts that enclose a common sound—trousers containing a thigh, and a county that includes the town of Athy—and thus celebrates the power of auditory correspondence by presenting perceived incongruities as a problem that language solves. We are reminded of the power of names not only to represent but to integrate objective experience.

The only way to reformulate Athy's riddle is by challenging habitual assumptions about what it means to read. Our automatic reading practices allow us to abstract the author from the puzzle, honoring him or her as the operator of language and not as someone upon whom language operates, an exemption that we can then extend to ourselves as readers. The curtaining off of authors and readers from the textual performance facilitates a denial of the ways that the text reflects not only the observer but also the author and the sociohistorical context. Instead of splitting ourselves off from the text, on the one hand, and the author, on the other, *Portrait* urges us recognize the many possible doubles that language offers us. "Doubling" is not only a process of recognizing our own potential reactions within a text—seeing our own features in different aspects of Joyce's portrait—but it also, like "Athy," echoes the name of an Irish town that geographically situates and silently authorizes the author's riddles.

In order to ask Athy's riddle "the other way," Stephen would have to revise his assumptions about language, seeing it as something that overflows the boundaries of any one of its formulations, its authority more capacious and capricious than that of the person or structure that gives it a momentary shape, but meaningless without a shape to exceed.[5] Moreover, he would have to be more consciously aware of the way that a text must interact with a variable context to produce meaning. He would have to recognize language as the sham double that makes reflection possible. *Ulysses* forces its readers toward such realizations: its willful opacity compels the reader to look *at* language, as well as trying to peer through it, and its disorienting panoply of changing styles forces us, finally, to regard and use language as the ever-varying constant that allows us to plot and evaluate temporal and spatial change. In *Portrait,* however, language plays its uncanny role more subtly: it acts as a complex frame of reference for the perceptions of author, character, and reader without compelling any recognition that it *is* the dominant system of reference.

If language is the dominant *frame* of reference, Stephen acts as a *point* of reference within that frame that enables us to plot the variable relationship between the author and the reader, the living and the dead, with greater precision. Our challenge is to position, somewhere between Joyce's and our own, Stephen's growing ability to balance imaginative engagement and critical detachment, and his increasing facility in interweaving and disentangling his story and history. Stephen's value is precisely that he, unlike Joyce, is not a "finished artist," despite his drunken assertion to the contrary in "Circe."[6] He represents not the artist but the dialogical process of verbal recreation that we tend to split into reading and writing.[7]

When writer and reader are exposed as imaginatively intermingled in a shared text that has the power to reflect both, the illusion of authorial privilege is shattered. Language emerges as the shared domain of reader, author, and character, the place where all "multiplicity is focused."[8] It becomes more difficult for the author and reader to disguise the relationship between their own identities and the answers to the riddles they contemplate, as Athy did by memorably emphasizing the link between a town and a part of the body, rather than the link between the names of both and his own. Language, so conceived, acts as an interface that, like a portrait, gives back a compound image that both resembles and fails to resemble the perceiver. Joyce's *Portrait* has this capacity: it changes as the artist changes, but it also changes as its reader changes, acting as a stylistic equivalent to what Oscar Wilde used as subject rather than medium, the picture of Dorian Gray.[9]

In *Portrait,* then, the opposite positions of artist and reader often run together in relation to the fiction they share. Reading and writing mirror each other as contradictory and interdependent processes. For years, readers have argued over whether Stephen actually becomes an artist in *Portrait,* focusing attention on the two instances wherein his verbal productions are presented directly to us so that we may evaluate them: the aesthetic theories that he propounds to Lynch in the last chapter and the villanelle that he composes in the section that follows (*P,* 204–16, 217–24). Ironically, however, the determination of whether or not Stephen has a right to the title of artist tends to be made independently of an equally important determination that is intimately related to the first: what kind of a *reader* do Stephen's productions reveal him to be?

Stephen's theory of reading should be measured against his reading practice, and his theory and practice compared to that of the book's author and readers. Such an approach produces a more complex practical awareness of the book's reflexivity, its emphasis on the parallels between Stephen's attempts to read his world, and our attempts to read Stephen. To the extent that our activity reproduces Stephen's, the text contextualizes us; if we accurately identify a representation of our mode of reading within the novel, we can then supplement that methodology with alternatives that are also represented within the fiction. By applying strategies represented in the novel to our own way of reading the novel, we allow the text to teach us more sophisticated ways of framing it and in that way regain momentary interpretive control over the "portrait" that had framed us, and will do so again—in different ways—on subsequent readings. If we then repeat the process, it is with the awareness that we are using the interplay between text and context to multiply the number of available interpretive frames. Event and context, reader and character, story and history repeatedly exchange positions as a condition of their mutual development. The condition that makes development possible but never finite is the imbalance between the employment of a word and the multiple possibilities for meaning that such employment excludes between an individual story and the panoply of history.

The tension between a realized network of meaning and potential networks of meaning, between the precision of definition and its ultimate inadequacy, is the central conflict in *Portrait,* a conflict that is dramatized in both social and linguistic terms. In the first chapter Stephen's attempt to realize a relation to his name, to his schoolfellows, to his country, and to history itself is intermingled with his desire to define the meanings of words and phrases that puzzle him: God, politics, "tower of ivory." Comparably, his growing isolation in the second chapter presents itself as an evaporation of the meanings he has succeeded in attaching to language, and he watches words and names lapse back into a meaningless sensuality that reflects his own: when he tries to recall some of the vivid moments of his childhood, he remembers only names, dissociated from the images and events that gave them significance—Dante, Parnell, Clane, Clongowes (*P,* 93). The ability to read, to attach significance—quite literally—to signs, deserts him: "He could scarcely interpret the letters of the signboards of the shops" (*P,* 92). When language loses meaning, the speaking subject also dissolves, and the capability of speech is assumed by the sensual organs that convey it, the tongue and the lips.[10] When Stephen encounters the prostitute at the end of the second chapter, "his lips parted though they would not speak," and when Stephen surrenders to her, "body and mind," he is "conscious of nothing in the world but the dark pressure of her softly parting lips. They pressed upon his brain as upon his lips as though they were the vehicle of a vague speech," but what issues from between them is not speech but the sensual reality of her tongue, its pressure "softer than sound" (*P,* 101).

The theory of reading that Stephen outlines in the last chapter, although complicated, is surprisingly illuminating when applied to the reading of *Portrait* itself. According to Stephen, the apparent capriciousness of language as it gathers up and then empties itself of meaning produces a "rhythm of beauty" that he attempts to describe to Lynch (*P,* 206). Stephen argues that such a rhythm has the power to prolong and finally dissolve a state of mind that he describes as "esthetic stasis." "Stasis" is a moment of integration that temporarily satisfies the intellect and/or the imagination, an achieved construct that must repeatedly be dissolved and reconstituted as the relationship between individual events and their narrative contexts change.

What Stephen experiences as the achievement and dissolution of relation, and what he describes more analytically as the rhythms of beauty and truth, is a structural rhythm that individuals may participate in but not initiate or control. What individuals can control are the stages of apprehension, an understanding of which allows us to initiate and accelerate the rhythms of imaginative and intellectual comprehension. Three words from Aquinas provide the text for Stephen's commentary—*integritas, consonantia,* and *claritas*—but the arrangement of these prerequisites for beauty into a dialectic of apprehension that can be learned and applied is Stephen's. Stephen's formula for apprehending the uniqueness of any perceived object is simply to separate it from its immediate context and then to analyze its structure and significance. The synthesis of this process of separation and integration is the "enchantment" or stasis that is born of the momentary balance of two forces—forces such as illumination and darkness, which reach equilibrium in the image of a "fading coal" that Shelley used to describe the mind in creation (*P,* 213).

Stephen uses the term *apprehension* to designate the appreciation of the structural relationships that comprise any whole. Stephen's theory is therefore a theory of reading, and if we consciously apply it to our reading of *Portrait,* it allows us to evaluate Stephen's own reading in a more balanced way. If, for example, we detach ourselves from Stephen when he is puzzling out the meaning of a word or phrase and perform the same activity independently as well as vicariously, we can arrest and contemplate the point where Stephen's strengths meet his limitations, generating a "balanced" view that should in turn produce an ambivalent response. In the first chapter Stephen is repeatedly troubled by a phrase from the Litany of the Virgin Mary, "Tower of Ivory." He connects it in his mind with Eileen because she is a Protestant and "protestants used to make fun of the litany of the Blessed Virgin. *Tower of Ivory,* they used to say, *House of Gold*! How could a woman be a tower of ivory or a house of gold? Who was right then?" (*P,* 35). Stephen solves the problem by linking Eileen with the Virgin: he calls up an image of Eileen's hands, "long and white and thin and cold and soft" and thinks, "That was ivory: a cold white thing. That was the meaning of *Tower of Ivory*" (*P,* 36).

Stephen's "definition" of *Tower of Ivory* is ingeniously economical: he furnishes the Holy Virgin with attributes of the virgin who lives on his street. However, if we take the phrase out of its immediate context (appreciating its *integritas*), "apprehend it as complex, multiple, divisible, separable, made up of its parts, the results of its parts and their sum, harmonious" (Stephen identifies the structural complexity of an individual unit as its *consonantia*), and then "make the only synthesis which is logically and esthetically permissible" (*P,* 212, 213), we can see that "Tower of Ivory" is also "ivory tower," an encoded commentary on Stephen's habits of mind. For all of his ingeniousness, Stephen lives in a many-storied ivory tower. He has written himself into a fairy tale that begins, "Once upon a time and a very good time it was," a tale that takes place in Clongowes castle, site of heroic deeds that he hopes to imitate, a tale passed down to him by his father, a gentleman who, he fondly believes, may one day be a magistrate.

Our experience of Stephen's aesthetic theory allows us to redefine and recontextualize Stephen's experience at Clongowes as his storied rendition of a lived experience that is itself an unconscious response to the stories of childhood, in particular, to the fairy tale. That this story antedates Stephen himself is clear from the opening of the novel: the book begins with a story, but not until the third sentence do we learn that "he" is the subject of that story. The story is told before its subject is identified, before the life-story of the subject has even begun. Like a reader whose knowledge of language precedes specific knowledge of an individual text, Stephen's experience of language and narrative anticipates and shapes his experience of the world; but knowledge of the world and the text forces both the reader and Stephen to redefine the meaning of language as it was first conceived.

Chapter I traces the impress of the fairy tale on Stephen's mind, a narrative that Joyce prompts us to connect with that of the gospels. The gospels, like the fairy tale, present a fable of identity motivated and shaped by a desire for self-definition that is partly realized through the definition of human doubles—words. The last of the four New Testament gospels (the nonsynoptic gospel) explicitly affirms the primacy of the word over world: St. John proclaims, "In the beginning was the Word," a word that precedes its own definition: "and the Word was God." The movement from word to reality to a more complex understanding of the word is the movement of the Christian Bible from Word to Incarnation ("And the Word was made flesh") to the crucifixion that makes ultimate Revelation possible.

As an account of the crucifixion and resurrection of the Word, the gospel can be read as one of the most powerful narrative illustrations of the rhythm of truth that Stephen analyzes more abstractly in the last chapter: the human referent must be lost in the flesh in order to be regained through the word, a process that must be periodically repeated if our dual consciousness of word and flesh, and their reciprocity, is to be kept alive. In the first chapter Stephen establishes, almost unconsciously, a meaning for both his Christian name and his patronym by identifying himself with Christ and Christ's doubles in the twin realms of Church and State: St. Stephen, on the one hand, and Parnell together with the Greek and Roman national heroes recalled by Stephen's classical surname, on the other. However, the principle of connection that binds the various narratives is not allegorical, which would place history in the service of this story, but verbal, which equalizes the relationships among narratives and allows them to illuminate each other.[11]

If we apply Stephen's formula to "Tower of Ivory," its reconstitution as "ivory tower," when supported by the fairy-tale structure of the chapter, presents us with an instantaneous double image of the beauty and limitation of a sensitive child's vision. When, in the midst of the discussion of the mysterious sin committed by Simon Moonan, Tusker Boyle, and the others, Stephen comforts himself by remembering his triumph of definition, reflecting with satisfaction, "By thinking of things you could understand them" (*P,* 43), his connection should prompt the reader to rethink and reevaluate the possible relation between his attempt to imagine the Virgin Mary and his desire to realize the meaning of punishment by proxy. This relation is apparent through verbal links that show how concretely Stephen makes the transition from an image of the Virgin to the story of Christ's martyrdom; in this case, it is hands that draw Mary, Christ, and Stephen together when Stephen is pandied in retaliation for the sexual misconduct of his schoolfellows.

Stephen's memory of Eileen's ivory hands is sparked by his recollection of "Lady" Boyle paring his nails. Unconsciously, Stephen sees these two pairs of hands as linking the puzzle of virginity with the enigma of sexual transgression and punishment. If we apply Stephen's formula for insightful apprehension to his description of the hands of Mr. Gleeson and Lady Boyle, the inner narrative that motivates Stephen, turning him into his schoolfellows' savior, becomes clear. The word *nails,* detached from the referent that its immediate context dictates, attaches itself to different hands and to an older narrative that serves not as an allegorical equivalent to but as a critical commentary on this one. The focus of Stephen's concern has shifted from the Virgin to the Son, from the puzzle of purity to that of sin and symbolic atonement. Sharp nails can excruciate as well as extend and beautify a hand, and Stephen's unconscious understanding of this is reflected in his concentration on Mr. Gleeson's hands as an image of the paradox of gentleness and pain, implicated in the sin as well as in its punishment:

> He had rolled up his sleeves to show how Mr Gleeson would roll up his sleeves. But Mr Gleeson had round shiny cuffs and clean white wrists and fattish white hands and the nails of them were long and pointed. Perhaps he pared them too like Lady Boyle. But they were terribly long and pointed nails. So long and cruel they were though the white fattish hands were not cruel but gentle. And though he trembled with cold and fright to think of the cruel long nails and of the high whistling sound of the cane and of the chill you felt at the end of your shirt when you undressed yourself yet he felt a feeling of queer quiet pleasure inside him to think of the white fattish hands, clean and strong and gentle. (*P,* 45)

When Stephen is cast in the role of scapegoat, "punished," as Fleming anticipated, "for what other fellows did" (*P,* 43), when his own hands are made to burn, tremble, and crumple "like a leaf in the fire" (*P,* 50) for the sin of Tusker Boyle's long white hands and Mr. Gleeson's fattish ones, he takes it upon himself to complete the narrative by interceding with the Father, the "rector" whose name promises rectification of wrongs, on behalf of himself and his schoolfellows. In the process he constructs a glorious and recognizable meaning for his own name, translating it, in his own mind, into "Stephen Hero." As Stephen Hero, he realizes the meaning of his "Christian" name, which is that of the first Christian martyr, St. Stephen, at the same time that he extends his earlier identification with Parnell, the national martyr.

In the first chapter of *Portrait,* the reader, like Stephen, is confronted with problems of definition: specifically, she or he is asked to define Stephen's relationship to a world of words by contrasting the fantasies that he uses to define mysterious words, phrases, and songs with the more complex meanings and associations that Stephen does not yet understand. Such definitions show not only what Stephen has read—the Bible and fairy tales—but *how* he reads them, vicariously and not critically. He positions himself within them, and never outside them, a strategy that makes heroes but not authors or critical readers. What he does manage to do is to assimilate, in his own life story, heroic figures that history has set in opposition to one another: Christ and the Romans, Christ and Parnell. He has constructed "the most satisfying relations of the intelligible"—what is intelligible to him as a hopeful, obedient, and naive child—and in the process has defined for himself a cluster of puzzlingly attractive words. To the extent that we can appreciate those definitions, our reading is sympathetic, whereas more ironic possibilities emerge when we focus on the larger contexts of Stephen's definitions, the contexts that he ignores. As Stephen will later understand in theory, the only balanced reading is a double one that can appreciate, in rhythmic alternation, both the triumph and the inadequacy of definition.

NIGHT WORSHIP: HEAVENLY BODIES

In Chapter I Stephen gradually defines a heroic identity for himself by constantly interrogating individual words and by unconsciously exploring his relationship to the Word. By juxtaposing Stephen's unconscious identification with Christ with an account of Stephen's repeated attempts to understand the meaning of language, Joyce emphasizes the extent to which the New Testament presents itself as an allegory of communication, as a history of a creative Word moving toward a Revelation expressed as a final sentence, or judgment. The larger contours of the New Testament are, according to such a view, reproduced in miniature in the life of one man, conceived as a divine word penetrating the tympanum of a woman's ear, his corpus/corpse a literal embodiment of human communication, represented by the eucharistic bread and wine. Such an allegory represents and promulgates an idealistic view of reading as a transcendent communion made possible through communication, which is always, by definition, a sacramental act. The story of Christ suggests that the sensual incarnation of the abstract Word is significant primarily because it makes ultimate transcendence possible, a transcendence effected through atonement and symbolic communication. Christian scripture celebrates the power of language to abstract itself—eventually—from its sensual referents, its mesh of defining circumstances, and to reunite itself with the will of its creator. A Christian ideology, as its constitutive language suggests, celebrates oneness: atonement is literally a compound of the words "at one"; atonement, by implication, is a way of being "at one" with the will of another, an experience that, in Christian scripture, defines communication.[12]

Stephen's initial response to the problems posed by language and identity is primed by a literal, if unconscious, reading of the gospels as a parable of how communication works. Identity must be defined through language, and language incarnated in experience so that it may be abstracted and reassimilated. Stephen's struggle to equate language and sensual experience—to understand "tower of ivory" as Eileen's hands, "suck" as the sound of draining water (P, 11), Leicester Abbey as the lights of Clongowes castle (P, 10)—is an effort to give flesh to words, to effect their incarnation. These words have life but no meaning for Stephen, like the vivid words that pass between Dante and Mr. Casey over Christmas dinner. Stephen responds physically, even mimetically, to the passionate words—the glow of anger on Mr. Casey's face rises in his own as "the spoken words thrilled him" (P, 38)—but he knows no larger context to play the words against, so he can neither assimilate perspectives nor produce a meaning that can help him bridge the distance between himself and the scene he is witnessing. It is not until Stephen inadvertently atones for the sins of Tusker Boyle and Simon Moonan that he discovers a way of being "at one" with the worlds from which he had been alienated through his relative youth and ignorance: with the community at Clongowes, and with his divided family. His punishment allows him to seal the rift separating him from his immediate environment, as well as the rift that divided his family, by playing the role of savior, a role that reconciles the narratives of Parnell and Christ, allowing him to live out and join the meanings of two abstract words that had puzzled him—God and politics.

Christian scripture, when considered as a commentary upon language, takes as its ideal the transcendent power of imaginative integration. But, as Joyce suggests in the second and fourth chapters, the language of scripture can be interpreted imagistically as well as literally, as an exploration not of the word but of the body. This more romantic interpretation reads Christ and Lucifer as representations of heavenly bodies, Lucifer as falling star and Christ as rising sun, as well as rising Son (see "Was Jesus a Sun Myth?" in "Circe," U, 15.1579). Stephen's formula for apprehension, when applied to key words in Christian scripture, shows how coherently its language supports such an interpretation, unveiling "East-er" as the time (place) where the Son (sun) rises in order to compensate for the fall of Eve (eve)—the coming of evil. So interpreted, Christian narratives, like pagan ones, are anthropomorphic accounts of heavenly bodies that differ from their Greek counterparts in focusing not on constellations and their genesis but on the dramatic opposition between day and night, the perpetual revolution in the heavens.

If, as a parable of reading, scripture idealizes the value of communion through a transcendence of meaning, it reverses that emphasis when read poetically, in terms of the images that the sounds of its words imply. Whereas the philosophical idealist represents the ideal as a heavenly abstraction, the sensual idealist pays romantic homage to heavenly bodies, the moon or the stars, thereby idealizing *distance* rather than "at-one-ment." If Christ sheds his mortal body to live eternally as an abstract and transcendent Word, Lucifer takes two forms, both of which are physical. In his prelapsarian state he takes the form of a heavenly body, the morning star, a traditional symbol of pride of the intellect, having the power to enlighten ("Lucifer" means "light-bringer") but doomed to fall. In his fallen state he takes the form of a snake, a representation of the sexual part of a male body that, like the intellect, is marked by rise and fall. Lucifer, in his duality and in the relative weakness of the light he brings, is inferior to a greater heavenly body, the Son (sun), who must fall in order to re-arise into heaven in the morning/during mourning. The counterpart of Lucifer-Satan in his opposition to the Son is woman, who also takes two forms—Mary and Eve, virgin and temptress. Mary, like the unfallen Lucifer, is represented by the morning star, harbinger of the sun; not only does she take the form of the same heavenly body as Lucifer but her mortal body is made heavenly as well: she is impregnated when God's Word passes the membrane of her ear, not by the rupturing of a "lower" membrane. The fallen Eve, Satan's lure and victim, sins by listening not to God's word but to the blandishments of the body and promises of divine knowledge offered suggestively to her by a snake. The stories of Lucifer-Satan and his female counterparts facilitate not an imaginative transcendence of the body but a particularization of the symmetry of mental and sexual processes, fraught with a directive to privilege thought and communication over sexuality.

In *Portrait,* Stephen learns to see the transcendent desires of childhood as unrealistic and escapist by replaying his story, in Chapter II, in the "anatomical" theater of troubled adolescence. The readings that frame Stephen shift accordingly: the classical heroes of Peter Parley's Tales (*P,* 53) are replaced by romantic poets, particularly Byron and Shelley; the fairy tale yields to tales of adventure; Christ as portrayed in the gospel is displaced by a Miltonic Satan, romantically interpreted. Stephen's heroes are no longer saviors but heretics; his drive is not toward atonement but toward separation and exile—what, from an orthodox point of view, is called "sin." Exiled from the fairy tale, he discovers adventure, a narrative different in mood and in the *nature* of its resolution, but identical in its movement from isolation to reconciliation. Stephen exiles himself from the spiritual world he had built in Chapter I through the painstaking accretion of sensual definitions and gravitates instead toward a physical one, where communion is private and sensual rather than public and symbolic, and the desire to consume the body is subsumed by the desire to experience its sensual particulars. Whereas the first chapter celebrated a triumph of social and historical at-one-ment, the second represents the pleasures of critical deconstruction, the process by which human and written characters shed their more symbolic significations and display their hidden sensuality.

In Chapter II Stephen's growing sense of alienation is most frequently expressed in his own mind as a process of fading. What is fading away in the second chapter is the network of self-defining associations that Stephen had constructed in the first. His removal from Clongowes and the physical dislocation of his family from Blackrock to Dublin has the effect of eroding all of the heroic fantasies that he had shored around himself in childhood. As in the first chapter, Stephen longs to shed "weakness and timidity and inexperience" (P, 65), but, initially, in his proud and rebellious phase, what he actually shuns is the consciousness of his own body, an awareness that his idealistic yearnings are shadowed by sexual drives. Stephen's fantasies are repeatedly interrupted by reminders of the ineluctable physicality of existence, reminders from which he recoils in horror. When he is watching the firelight, listening to an old woman's pathetic reports about "Ellen," he focuses his attention on "the words," "following the ways of adventure that lay open in the coals," until Ellen herself actually appears in the doorway (P, 68). Stephen sees Ellen as a grotesque reminder of the feeble animality of the body; he describes her as a "skull," a feeble, whining, monkey-like creature whose silly laughter exposes the silliness of his own idealizations. Similarly, the word *foetus* that Stephen discovers carved into a desk in the anatomy theatre in Cork mocks him with its semantic specificity, its horrifying power to bring the dead and the unborn to life and to challenge, with uncompromising realism, the attenuated sensuality of romantic desire.

Stephen's desire to fade out of existence manifests itself verbally as the desire to divest word and narrative of any personal or worldly meaning. When he writes his Byronic poem to E—— C—— he strips the account of their shared tram ride of all of its noncelestial characteristics: all the "elements which he deemed common and insignificant fell out of the scene. There remained no trace of the tram itself nor of the trammen nor of the horses: nor did he and she appear vividly. The verses told only of the night and the balmy breeze and the maiden lustre of the moon" (P, 70). As Stephen's carefully constructed myth of himself lapses, his definitions of words and names undergo a similar divestment. The first chapter illustrated ways in which words accrued meaning; and, as Stephen learned to define words and phrases sensually, the reader was prodded to resituate those phrases in other well-known narrative contexts. In the second chapter, Stephen concentrates on the art of dissociating words from contexts to create a soothing, rhythmic music, as he does when he "prays" on the night mail to Cork: "His prayer, addressed neither to God nor saint, . . . ended in a trail of foolish words which he made to fit the insistent rhythm of the train" (*P*, 87). The sensual sounds of words also console him when gathered into the less furious music of poetry or song: Shelley's fragment on the moon, or the "come-all-you" that his father sings about exile and the fading of love (*P*, 96, 88).

Stephen's physiological changes have exiled him from the theatre of his mind, forcing him to look for a new part to play in a different theatre, an anatomical one that will allow him first to displace and eventually to act out his physical desires. Stephen's weary sense of fading and being stripped, along with the language that mimics his state of mind, prepares him for the experience of physical contact, anticipating his observation of the prostitute as "she undid her gown" (*P*, 100). The desire for familial reconciliation that drew him to the "family romance" of Christian scripture and fairy tale has been ousted by the desire for sexual union that draws him from family romance to romanticism, from the general and mythic to the particular and physical, from a respect for the power of symbolic communication and revelation to an appreciation of the sibilant and sensual activity of the tongue. Memories of his family and his childhood fade in preparation for his initiation into "another world" (*P*, 100), a "fallen," "evening" world of darkness and abandonment, in which other, softer ties replace familial ones, and other lips press their story upon his brain.

Stephen's yearnings for a higher existence, his lyrical preoccupation with "the maiden lustre of the moon" (*P*, 71), "wandering companionless" (*P*, 96), are bound to his fierce physical desires, which he identifies as "the tides within him" (*P*, 98). The moon governs these tides, as it governs those of the sea; his identification with a heavenly body both masks and represents a new awareness of his physical body: both bodies induct him, subtly, into the rituals of night worship, although he fails to appreciate their interdependence. Not until the opening of the third chapter does he begin to betray an unconscious awareness that heavenly and earthly bodies may be equated, and that the prototype for such an equation is Christ's counterpart, Lucifer.

Lucifer, as the sermon will remind Stephen, is a star turned snake, a "son of the morning" who "took the shape of a serpent" (*P*, 118). In these two forms he represents intellectual and physical assertiveness, the double pride that sharply contrasts with Christ's humility. In the third chapter Stephen is most aware of himself as a snake, whose mind winds itself in and out of curious questions of "spiritual and bodily sloth" (*P*, 106), whose soul sickens "at the thought of a torpid snaky life feeding itself out of the tender marrow of his life and fattening upon the slime of lust" (*P*, 140); his archetype is his penis, "the most subtle beast of the field" that "feels and understands and desires" (*P*, 139). If Stephen sees his body as serpentine, he sees his soul as Luciferian, "stars being born and being quenched" (*P*, 103). At the beginning of the chapter, the stars begin to crumble "and a cloud of fine stardust" falls through space (*P*, 103), a simultaneous idealization and literalization of a Luciferian fall.

Viewed in one way, Stephen's experiences in the first and second chapters are as different as day and night; viewed in another way, they illustrate complementary phases of the same experience. In the first chapter he is alienated from family and peers through youth and ignorance; in the second chapter he wills such a separation, finally objectifying his sense of difference through sin. In both cases he is punished for his detachment: in the first chapter, he is pandied for breaking his glasses, for his helpless inability to see what is nearest him; in the second chapter he is twice chastised for a more calculated and critical detachment—for his written affirmation of the soul's inalterable distance from the Creator, which Mr. Tate condemns as "heresy" (P, 79), and for the detachment from conventional morality reflected in his preference for Byron over Tennyson. As in the first chapter, he is again cast in the role of a scapegoat: he is whipped with Heron's cane, pummelled with a knotty cabbage stump, and pushed into barbed wire for his defense of Byron's "heresies." Both at Clongowes and at Belvedere, in both his Christian and his Luciferian incarnations, Stephen is brought to book for differing from his fellows. At Clongowes, Stephen used his chastisement to bridge that difference, whereas at Belvedere his treatment at the hands of his friends confirms the apprehension of difference that Stephen has learned to savor: "He chronicled with patience what he saw, detaching himself from it and testing its mortifying flavour in secret" (P, 67). However, even his critical detachment leads him back to the world he had scorned, not through social communion or verbal communication but through the private pleasures of physical contact.

Sexual sin brings its own sense of at-one-ment, a physical oneness that Christianity defines as the opposite of spiritual atonement. Joyce defined sin as a separation that is paradoxically inseparable from atonement, arguing, in his essay on Oscar Wilde, that "the truth inherent in the soul of Catholicism" is the understanding "that man cannot reach the divine heart except through that sense of separation and loss called sin."[13] The "sin" of sexuality and the "virtue" of atonement are evaluative interpretations of the same paradox, the coincidence of identity and difference. Christ's atonement is portrayed as a reconciliation with the heavens, but it is also an excruciating separation from the earth; comparably, sexual sin may sunder an individual from the community, but it also constitutes the most intimate form of contact. Lucifer's "fall" from the heavens is also a "rise"—a rising against God that takes as its alternative form a rising of the flesh.

If a fall interpreted one way constitutes a rise when interpreted another, then the very separability of opposites when divorced from the contexts that authorize them must be called into question. Joyce's methodologies not only emphasize the importance of contexts, they also generate new interpretations for the narrative contexts they recall. Both Lucifer and Christ participate, in complementary ways, in a single rhythm, the rhythm of separation and integration that multiplies and individuates language and experience. Scripture—and language—can only be understood as a double experience, as allegory and poetry, meaning and sense, just as human life is equally dependent upon the vitality of mind and body. The last half of *Portrait* illustrates Stephen's unusual sensitivity to both kinds of experience, and his comic blindness to their interrelationship. If we read not only with Stephen but against him, reading imagistically when he reads literally, and literally when he reads imagistically, playing his story off against the history that informs and shapes it, then the humorous possibilities of that interdependence become apparent.

RETREAT

The atonement that climaxes the third chapter of *Portrait* is also, as the event that prompts it suggests, a retreat. The Church uses the strategy of "retreat" to simulate the "withdrawal," or separation, that can inspire a desire for its counterpart, atonement. This is how the rector, another righter of wrongs, defines it (*P,* 109). But Stephen's formula for apprehension, which is basically a strategy for gaining a more distanced perspective on language and narrative, allows us to appreciate the relevance of its other meanings—a retreat is also a recession, a retrogression, a place of safety or refuge (*OED*). This is the effect of the retreat on Stephen: he regresses to a childlike piety and simplicity, reestablishing his imaginative association with obedient goodness and purity. Stephen's retreat to the world of childhood innocence is precipitated by the unexpected resurgence of the past: he notices his old master, Father Arnall, seated at the left of the altar, and the narrator explains, "The figure of his old master, so strangely rearisen, brought back to Stephen's mind his life at Clongowes." His soul, as these memories came back to him, became again a child's soul" (*P,* 108–9). He reenacts, in response to the words of the sermon, the highlights of his experience at Clongowes: instead of a burning hand, he is given a "burning ear," a fire that spreads through his body and brain (*P,* 115, 125). As at Clongowes, he longs to "be at one with others and with God," a longing that leads him toward the renewed experience of communication and communion that the eucharist represents for him (*P,* 143, 146).

Christ's separation from authority through incarnation mirrors Lucifer's separation from authority through insurrection, as His refusal to plead with his Roman captors mirrors and reverses Lucifer's successful persuasion of Adam and Eve. Joyce's treatment of Stephen in the contexts of both narratives suggests that the conflicts of "scripture" are representations of different attitudes toward language, attitudes that have also defined the alternating tendencies of literary history—the classical and the romantic tempers, which Joyce associates with Christ and Lucifer, respectively. Joyce presents these tendencies as structurally identical, their apparent differences merely differences of accent. In *Portrait* Joyce portrays classicism, usually characterized as a predominantly rational attitude, as a triumph of imaginative integration, and romanticism, frequently portrayed as irrational, as a triumph of critical deconstruction.[14] The emphasis of classicism is upon truth, but the road to its apprehension is imaginative, not critical, and the emphasis of romanticism is upon beauty, apprehended through uncompromising criticism. Both individually and together, classicism and romanticism reproduce the rhythms of beauty and truth.

When Stephen tries to model himself on an ideal, his language reasserts his—and its—ineluctable materiality; when he revels in his own sensuality, the structure of his experiences and his accounts of them betray his indebtedness to ideas. When, in the fourth chapter, Stephen is attempting to transform himself into a hero of the early Church, beginning each day "with an heroic offering of its every moment," imagining himself "kneeling at mass in the catacombs," and believing that he can mortify his senses (*P,* 147, 150–51), the sensuality of his own response to language betrays him. Sensitive to the hidden rose in "rosary," he relates without conscious irony that "The rosaries too which he said constantly—for he carried his beads loose in his trousers' pockets that he might tell them as he walked the streets—transformed themselves into coronals of flowers of such vague unearthly texture that they seemed to him as hueless and odourless as they were nameless" (*P,* 148). Stephen thinks of the flowers as "nameless" because their names—roses—would prompt him to realize that a sensual referent is coloring his response to a sacred practice.

When Stephen attempts to turn words, and himself, into abstract outlines of an ideal meaning, the sensuality of the body and of the word reasserts itself, exposing the comic naïveté of Stephen's project. In counterpoint, it is when Stephen would affect an appreciation of purely carnal or sensual knowledge that his expressions become most chaste and chastened. His account of the prostitute's caresses is as transparently reverent as his ecstasy in the presence of the bird-girl. Stephen's desire for flight—realized in his imagination, reflected in his high-flown prose, and projected onto the vision of a wading girl—is an attempt to deny the limitations of the body that the "pitiable nakedness" of his adolescent friends so clearly exposes. Stephen, "remembering in what dread he stood of the mystery of his own body," casts himself as a triumphant Daedalus, with the result that "the body he knew was purified in a breath and delivered of incertitude and made radiant and commingled with the element of the spirit" (*P,* 168, 169). Listening to "a voice from beyond the world," he shuts out the voices from the world that call him a garlanded ox: "Bous Stephanoumenous! Bous Stephaneforos!" (*P,* 168). Dreaming of Daedalus, the "hawklike man flying sunward above the sea," Stephen ignores the voices from the sea that remind us of Icarus's fall: "O cripes, I'm drownded! . . . Stephaneforos!" (*P,* 169). He fancies himself a classical hero and a risen Christ, whose "soul had arisen from the grave of boyhood, spurning her graveclothes" (*P,* 170), when in reality he has only separated himself once more from the "dull gross voice of the world of duties and despair" (*P,* 169).

In his epiphany of the bird-girl, Stephen has found another deity ("Heavenly God!" [*P,* 171]), has "felt the strange light of some new world" (*P,* 172), and has surrendered himself to the embrace of yet another breast, that of the earth. He thinks that he has discovered a new vocation, when he has simply combined the calls of the older ones. His "discovery" is an imaginative retreat into religious ecstasy, but it is also a sensual surrender to the romantic blandishments of language. He sees himself as Daedalus, but with "his cheeks aflame and his throat throbbing with song" (*P,* 170) he is also, without realizing it, Shelley's skylark. Stephen's song, like that of the lark, derives its beauty from "ignorance of pain"; like the unseen bird, his is the "shrill delight" of a "scorner of the ground." Stephen's aim is still to transcend his human limits. By the end of the fourth chapter, Stephen has drawn together his classical and his romantic yearnings, but only in the world of his own mind. What is most palpably lacking is an understanding of the social context that partially frames him—an awareness of Dublin.

DUBLIN AS FRAME: TEXT AND CONTEXT

The delusion that inspires Stephen more often than any other is the conviction that he can transcend the meanness of his environment. The euphoria that accompanies his anticipations of transcendence is expressed in many ways—in the literal uplift that raises him above his fellows at the end of the first chapter, as he is carried along in "a cradle of their locked hands" (*P,* 58); in his expectation that he will be transfigured when he encounters his Mercedes, that "weakness and timidity and inexperience would fall from him in that magic moment" (*P,* 65); in the ascent of prayers from his purified heart (*P,* 145); in the idealized flights that conclude both the fourth and the fifth chapters. The most celebrated passage in *A Portrait of the Artist* is one in which Stephen directly expresses his determination to elude the claims of his environment: "When the soul of man is born in this country there are nets flung at it to hold it back from flight. You talk to me of nationality, language, religion. I shall try to fly by those nets" (*P,* 203). It is Stephen's commitment to transcendence that makes him heroic in *both* a classical and a romantic sense, yet the continuity of life and narrative impedes any real transcendence, which would be possible only through death. Any reader of *Portrait* whose reading is impelled by a transcendent ideal, by a desire to escape the "nets" of language, religion, and nationality will experience the resistance the book offers to such flightiness. The only lecture Stephen attends in the last chapter is on the subject of electrical resistance, which should alert us to the importance not only of sympathizing with Stephen's desire-driven narratives but of resisting their illusions of ultimate triumph or escape, as well.

In *Portrait,* as in *Dubliners, Ulysses,* and *Finnegans Wake,* the last chapter recomplicates the context in which the book has been read up to that point. Chapter V makes it clear that Stephen's struggle is the struggle between an individual and his context, a struggle that also shapes the process of reading. The end of the chapter, in particular, is not only a diary of a young man preparing for flight, his entries alternately callow and full of hope—dismissive of the past, contemptuous of the present, and in love with the "wild spring" of the future—but also a compressed casebook of the problems posed by language, nationality, and religion, bringing them into shared focus as representative problems of context: the pressure of a collective, past-laden present on the future-oriented individual. Stephen's "nets" are the nets of context (from *contextus,* woven together), nets that can and must be unwoven and rewoven but can never be left behind, as the comic ironies of the first four chapters demonstrate.

Stephen's vision of Ireland actually is what Yeats's *The Countess Cathleen* was loudly accused of being: a view of Ireland as a country that would sell her soul. Stephen famously spurns Ireland as a devouring mother—"the old sow that eats her farrow" (*P,* 203)—a judgment that he uses (along with condescension toward his real mother) to justify his desire for flight. However, the jaunty optimism with which the book ends exposes itself as uncharacteristically poor reading, which in turn highlights the sharpness of the theory of reading presented earlier in the chapter. Stephen shows himself in this last chapter to be both a theoretically precise reader and an emotionally limited one, but both his strengths and his limitations map out avenues through which the reader can enter Joyce's *Portrait* and his Dublin. Unlike the undisciplined Temple—the Rousseau of University College—Stephen trains himself to hear "the unspoken speech behind . . . words" (*P,* 242), which is how he comes to realize a crucial difference between himself and Cranly. Whereas Stephen must idealize or crassly dismiss the feelings of women, Cranly is capable of empathy for them. Stephen thinks that Cranly "felt then the sufferings of women, the weaknesses of their bodies and souls: and would shield them with a strong and resolute arm and bow his mind to them" (*P,* 245). Stephen, in sharp contrast, is almost immune to the pity and terror aroused by a sympathetic contemplation of the other; he only feels the moral power of empathy briefly, when he is "thrilled by [Cranly's] touch" and touched by the revelation of Cranly's "cold sadness" (*P,* 247).

Immediately after the account of Stephen's momentary intimacy with Cranly, the narrative is interrupted by Stephen's diary. The diary is significant partly because it is a record of Stephen's "final" interpretations, a record that he himself makes. It shows that Stephen's reading, like his experience, is not extensive; as he notes, "Have read little and understood less" (*P,* 248). However, the diary can also be seen as a compendium of various interpretive possibilities that the rest of the book enables us to evaluate. Read against the context of the first four chapters, Stephen's "readings" all emerge as different techniques for framing his perceptions, and these techniques are as relevant to our way of reading Stephen as they are to his way of reading his peers.[15]

Stephen's diary begins with a grossly reductive reading of Cranly that is all the more repulsive in contrast to the eloquent scene that precedes and inspires it. For a moment Stephen understands Cranly's sympathy for women as a product of his loneliness and fear, but in his diary entry for that day he distances himself from his feeling for Cranly by using a particular exegetical strategy: he isolates a single fact to "explain" Cranly's difference in perspective—the age of his mother. Stephen frames Cranly through his imaginative reconstruction of the circumstances of Cranly's life, dismissing his "despair of soul" as that of a "child of exhausted loins" (P, 248). Stephen's first "reading" is almost a parody of the biographical fallacy, an expose of the distortion caused by oversimplifying the contexts of interpretation.

The next morning Stephen elaborates on his reading of Cranly by identifying him with a figure from the Bible—John the Baptist. Not only is his reading allegorically reductive but it is clearly self-serving as well: he subordinates Cranly to himself by casting Cranly as his precursor, which makes Stephen Christ. Again, Stephen's ploy exposes, through caricature, the distortion caused by reading through only one frame of reference, a distortion often motivated by the desire to see in someone else's situation a prophecy of one's own. The one-sidedness of Stephen's interpretation of Cranly acts as a warning against methodologies that link a character with a single precursor, whether that precursor be Christ, Satan, Daedalus, or Icarus. By implication, the contexts of interpretation must be as complex and variable as Dublin itself.

When Stephen quotes a portion of Blake's "William Bond" as an expression of his fear that Emma might die, his error is again to ignore the context of the excerpt. Stephen makes fun of the pathos of the poem—"Alas, poor William"—and in so doing violates the spirit of the poem as a whole, which implores its readers to "Seek Love in the Pity of other's Woe." Insensitivity to context does not increase sensitivity to the individual; on the contrary, it stifles it. It is only when Stephen glimpses the inadequacy of his prior readings, the reductiveness of his interpretive tendencies, that he begins to appreciate and even to enjoy his experience of others. When he records his meeting with Emma in Grafton Street, he caricatures his own posturings, and for a moment he approaches genuine liking for her and a consciousness of his own limitations: "Yes, I liked her today. A little or much? Don't know. I liked her and it seems a new feeling to me. Then, in that case, all the rest, all that I thought I thought and all that I felt I felt, all the rest before now, in fact . . . O, give it up, old chap! Sleep it off!" (P, 252).

What Stephen lacks is not an awareness of his own contradictory nature but an acceptance of it. This is apparent throughout the last chapter, where Stephen's omissions help to create the very context by which he can be evaluated. What he omits in his theoretical discussion with Lynch is consistent with what is lacking in each of the other climactic scenes of the last chapter: he tells Lynch, "When we come to the phenomena of artistic conception, artistic gestation and artistic reproduction I require a new terminology and a new personal experience," and Lynch replies, "But you will tell me about the new personal experience and new terminology some other day" (P, 209–10). Similarly, in the scene with Cranly, Stephen is unable to answer when Cranly asks him if he has ever loved anyone (P, 240); during his composition of the villanelle, Stephen's onanism suggests that his artistic creations are as pleasurable and fruitless as his solitary, physical ejaculation. Artistic conception, gestation, and reproduction result from a union of opposites in the act of love, a doubling that, together with Dublin, Stephen elects to escape. What he fails to understand is not only the double construction of authority, an awareness that would make him an "artist" as well as a portrayed subject, but also the social, geographical, and historical contexts that both define authority and allow it to change. What Stephen does not yet see, in the words of Jeremy Lane, is that there is "no final authorisation, no simple authority, no single author; but a relative authorisation, the sanction of relation whose dual principle seeds plurality, admitting and containing its contrary."[16]

To paraphrase Wordsworth's famous statement, an author differs from other characters in degree, but not in kind. What differentiates authors—and readers—of a fiction from the characters within a fiction is, potentially, a more disturbing awareness of the nets that no individual can elude, and that all must attempt to elude, a sensitivity to the complex interdependence of all human and verbal contexts, and an acceptance of the multiplicity and sameness of all characters participating in an interactive system. With such an awareness, an "author" can recreate and interpret such systems through imaginative doubling, whereas without such an awareness the "character" will reenact prior narratives in unintentional and unproductive—repetitive—ways. However, this distinction between "author" and "character" is itself, like all oppositions, a heuristic one, since it is impossible to be permanently inside or outside a system so long as that system and our awareness of it are subject to change. Every author is necessarily a character, or subject, and every character an author—and authority—in a dialogical process that produces no final synthesis: Joyce is, alternately, both within and outside the book, as are other authors, such as Shelley and Byron, and all of its readers, including ourselves. In this respect, as in several others, the language of the book defines a community not unlike the community Stephen is attempting to escape at the end, as he goes "to encounter for the millionth time the reality of experience" (P, 252–53). Ironically, the book ends with Stephen asking his father, and author, to direct him by his precedent: "Old father, old artificer, stand me now and ever in good stead" (*P,* 253). Stephen is recording his hope that his father will continue to do what he was doing for Stephen when the book opened, authoring and authorizing the story of Stephen's youth. What Stephen needs, however, is not the continued authorization of men but more of the emotional responsiveness he associates with women.

The Stephen that Joyce portrays is unfinished; his lack of completeness is a consequence of his identification with a Janus-faced authority whose faces are both male. In *Portrait* Stephen has no understanding of female experience whatsoever, as Joyce shows by highlighting Stephen's insensitivity to his mother, his alternation of "brutal anger" and unworldly homage for E.C. (*P,* 220), and his surprise mixed with contempt when he realizes that Cranly "[h]ad felt then the sufferings of women . . . and would . . . bow his mind to them" (*P,* 245). Stephen smiles when Moynihan scorns MacCann's agenda to win "votes for the bitches" (*P,* 195); women engender in him an admixture of terror and incomprehension. He sees them as seductively blood-sucking and faithless, as he sees the peasant woman whom he describes as "a batlike soul waking to the consciousness of itself in darkness and secrecy and loneliness and, through the eyes and voice and gesture of a woman without guile, calling the stranger to her bed" (*P,* 183). Women are not quite human: instead, they are marsupials (as Stephen suggests in *Stephen Hero*), birds (such as the bird-girl at the end of Chapter IV), bats, or progeny-devouring pigs, like Ireland, "the old sow that eats her farrow" (*P,* 203).

Stephen's thoughtless misogyny is still apparent in *Ulysses,* but in the later book Joyce introduces Molly as the carnal counterpart of Stephen, whose ramifying language and flesh expose and fulfill the emptiness of his ideal abstractions. Through its three-part structure, in which Stephen and Molly oppose and complete each other on either side of Bloom, *Ulysses* silently suggests that Stephen's concern with the two male faces of moral authority calls up as a necessary supplement the burgeoning of a weblike textuality associated with women. Stephen's attention to male rationality contributes only the plot of the human story; its poetry and music, unexpectedly enough, emerge from subconscious memory, in the rhythmic interconnectedness and discontinuity of images that in *Ulysses* is orchestrated by women. In *Portrait* Cranly is the John the Baptist who prophesies what *Ulysses* will later show, even if Stephen never consciously understands it: "Your mother brings you into the world, carries you first in her body. What do we know about what she feels? But whatever she feels, it, at least, must be real. It must be. What are our ideas or ambitions? Play. Ideas! Why, that bloody bleating goat Temple has ideas. MacCann has ideas too. Every jackass going the road thinks he has ideas" (*P,* 242). *Ulysses* is not, like *Portrait,* a discovery of ideas but an exploration of the unknown experience of the other; a quest not only for a spiritual father but for the buried reality of the mother.

Notes

1. One of the most concrete examples of the claim that authority promises transcendence is provided by an analysis of the relation of God, Christ, and Lucifer to transcendence. God—at least after the last Old Testament revelations—is detached by virtue of not being apprehensible to the senses (and Stephen sees His detachment as being extreme; He "remains within or behind or beyond or above his handiwork, invisible, refined out of existence, indifferent, paring his fingernails"; James Joyce, *Portrait of the Artist as a Young Man* [New York: Viking Press, 1968], 215; hereafter cited in the text as *P*). Christ is promised transcendence in return for forgoing it on earth; if He submits Himself totally to the will of God, he will achieve an at-one-ment that atones for the sins of others, and His reward will be that he will be restored to Heaven as part of the Godhead. Lucifer wants to achieve detachment (or independence) by a less circuitous and painful route; he would claim his equality with God at the outset, and he is punished through the hopeless transcendence of banishment and exile. See "Night Worship: Heavenly Bodies," below.

2. James Merrill, "Object Lessons," review, *New York Review of Books* 19 (November 30, 1972), 31–34. Cited by Judith Moffett, *James Merrill: An Introduction to His Poetry* (New York: Columbia University Press, 1984), 118.

3. James Joyce, *Finnegans Wake,* 271.14–15; hereafter cited in the text as *FW.*

4. The first spurt of sustained critical interest in *Portrait* was a belated one: not until the 1950s and early 1960s did the critical dialectic grow to its polemical crescendo, taking Stephen as its issue. Those who read Stephen as "Stephen Hero" faced off against Hugh Kenner, Stephen's wittiest detractor. Constituting, as it did, a critical Scylla and Charybdis, *Portrait* attracted an impressive array of minds to map its dangers, including Wayne Booth, Caroline Gordon, Robert Scholes, Maurice Beebe, and S. L. Goldberg. Then, in 1966, Arnold Goldman articulated an acute synthesis in his often neglected study *The Joyce Paradox.* His solution is, essentially, not a solution at all but a sharp definition of the problem that gives it both a name (paradox) and a philosophical legitimacy (via Sartre, Ibsen, and Kierkegaard). The doubleness of the concept of doubling locked the readers of *Portrait* in a classical double-bind, until the name *paradox* gave us a means of distancing ourselves from a reading experience that, in its wild fluctuations between appreciation and contempt, reproduced Stephen's own experience.

5. The other way to ask Athy's riddle is buried in the darkness of *Finnegans Wake:* it is Shem's "first riddle of the universe." Shem asks, "when is a man not a man?" "All were wrong, so Shem himself, the dictator, took the cake, the correct solution being—all give it up?—; when he is a—yours till the rending of the rocks,—Sham" (*FW,* 170.5; 170.21–24). Athy might have answered, "when he is a thigh"; or a more general respondent, "when he is a name" ("Shem" means "name" in Hebrew). A name is a sham, and "sham" is here a variation of the teller's name, a teller inevitably implicated in the riddle of naming he or she contemplates.

6. James Joyce, *Ulysses,* 15.2508; hereafter cited in the text as *U.*

7. Derrida's attack on the desire to freeze and thereby contain meaning in "The End of the Book and the Beginning of Writing," *Of Grammatology,* 2–26, is relevant here.

8. Barthes argues that the reader is where all multiplicity is focused (*Image-Music-Text,* 148).

9. In *The Picture of Dorian Gray,* Basil Hallward tells Harry that "every portrait that is painted with feeling is a portrait of the artist, not that of the sitter." Basil knows that the beauty and corruption in his picture of Dorian is his own—that in painting it, he has exposed himself. What Basil had no way of knowing is that his portrait is also a portrait of the man observing it, Lord Henry; that it is their dual participation in Dorian's life that the portrait will monstrously come to reflect. The first five words of Joyce's title, when considered in relation to their context in *The Picture of Dorian Gray,* suggest that Joyce's portrait, like Basil's, is a composite portrait of artist, character, and observer with an uncanny power to adapt its features to reflect our own. The distinction between writing and reading is, for someone engaged in either,

a misleading one, since artists are always readers, and readers are always artists with the power to paint verbal portraits anew through the inevitable selectivity of observation and memory.

10. See Derek Attridge's excellent account of this phenomenon in the "Sirens" episode of *Ulysses:* "Joyce's Lipspeech: Syntax and the Subject in 'Sirens,' " in *James Joyce: The Centennial Symposium,* ed. Beja et al., 59–66.

11. The assumption that Joyce's allusions have an allegorical significance is responsible for many of the more rigid and less credible interpretations of both *Portrait* and *Ulysses.* Some of the allegorical grids have been classical, but most have been Christian.

12. At the end of *Portrait,* Stephen can understand love and communication only in these terms, as a humiliating at-one-ment. When Cranly asks him if he has ever loved anyone or anything, Stephen replies that he has tried to love God, which he defines as uniting his will "with the will of God instant by instant" (*P,* 240).

13. *CW* 205; see Yeats's "Tables of the Law," in *Mythologies,* which, according to Ellmann and Mason, Joyce knew by heart.

14. Joyce's distinction between the classical and romantic tempers is first presented in his 1902 essay on "James Clarence Mangan" (*CW,* 73–83) and is presented again in *Stephen Hero,* 78–79.

15. Although not concerned primarily with the reading process, Michael Levenson's essay on Stephen's diary is an excellent, full treatment: "Stephen's Diary in Joyce's *Portrait*— The Shape of Life," *English Literary History* 52 (1985): 1017–35.

16. Jeremy Lane, "His Master's Voice? The Questioning of Authority in Literature," in *The Modern English Novel: The Reader, the Writer and the Work,* ed. Gabriel Josipovici (New York: Harper and Row, 1976), 126.

Index

◆

Page numbers followed by n. refer to endnotes (nn. to multiple endnotes) on that page. When the subject of an endnote is not directly cited in the text, the page number of its context is in parentheses.

The Volume Editors

Philip Brady received his B.A. from Bucknell University, M.A.s from the University of Delaware and San Francisco State University, and a Ph.D. from SUNY Binghamton. His poems, stories, and critical essays have appeared in dozens of American and Irish journals, including *Poetry Northwest, The Honest Ulsterman,* and *The Massachusetts Review.* He has been awarded a Thayer Fellowship from New York State, an Ohio Arts Council Fellowship, an Academy of American Poets Prize, and residencies at Yaddo, The Headlands Center, The Millay Colony, Hawthornden Castle in Scotland, Fundacion Valparaiso in Spain, and The Tyrone Guthrie Center in Ireland. His collection of poetry, *Forged Correspondences* (1996), was named *Editor's Choice* by Maxine Kumin of *Ploughshares.* Brady has taught at the University of Lubumbashi in Zaire and University College Cork, Ireland. Currently he is an Associate Professor of English at Youngstown State University, where he directs the YSU Poetry Center.

James F. Carens, Professor Emeritus of Bucknell University, received an A.B. from Harvard College, an M.A. from Yale University, and a Ph.D. from Columbia University. He is the author of *The Satiric Art of Evelyn Waugh* and editor of *Critical Essays on Evelyn Waugh.* James Carens edited and wrote the commentary for *Many Lines to Thee,* letters Oliver St. John Gogarty wrote an Oxford friend, containing early portraits of Yeats, James Joyce, and George Moore, and he is the author of *Surpassing Wit: Oliver St. John Gogarty, His Poetry and His Prose.* Editor of a series of monographs on modern Anglo-Irish writers, he has contributed essays or chapters to a number of works dealing with Irish literature of the twentieth century, among them a study of Joyce's *Dubliners* in relation to George Moore's Irish stories and essays on Yeats and Gogarty and Joyce and Gogarty. With Zack Bowen he edited *A Companion to Joyce Studies* for which he wrote the chapter on *A Portrait of the Artist as a Young Man.*

The General Editor

Zack Bowen is professor of English at the University of Miami. He holds degrees from the University of Pennsylvania (B.A.), Temple University (M.A.), and the State University of New York at Buffalo (Ph.D.). In addition to being general editor of this G. K. Hall series, he is editor of the James Joyce series for the University of Florida Press and the *James Joyce Literary Supplement*. He is the author and editor of numerous books on modern British, Irish, and American literature. He has also published more than one hundred monographs, essays, scholarly reviews, and recordings related to literature. He is past president of the James Joyce Society (1977–1986), former chair of the Modern Language Association Lowell Prize Committee, and current president of the International James Joyce Foundation.